ARTIFICIAL PSYCHOLOGY

The Quest for What It Means to Be Human

JAY FRIEDENBERG

Psychology Press
Taylor & Francis Group

New York   Hove

Psychology Press
Taylor & Francis Group
711 Third Avenue
New York, NY 10017

Psychology Press
Taylor & Francis Group
27 Church Road
Hove, East Sussex BN3 2FA

© 2008 by Taylor & Francis Group, LLC

International Standard Book Number-13: 978-0-8058-5885-3 (Softcover)

Visit the Taylor & Francis Web site at
http://www.taylorandfrancis.com

and the Psychology Press Web site at
http://www.psypress.com

CONTENTS

FIGURES

TABLES

PREFACE

THE THEME OF THIS BOOK

One thing that can be surely said about humanity is that we are fascinated with ourselves. Who are we? How do we do the things we do? Is there anything that makes us special or unique? How did we come into existence? These questions have been addressed historically from many different perspectives and have been answered in various ways by mythology, religion, the arts and the humanities.

Of course, science and engineering have also had much to say on these questions. However, it is only within the past half-century or so that developments in these fields have enabled a more refined notion of what it means to be human. These advances have come two-fold. First, scientific discoveries now tell us in great detail how the brain and body operate. Second, advances in engineering allow us to construct devices that replicate many human capabilities. To illustrate, researchers in the field of artificial intelligence have created computer programs that perform the same type of mental operations we do. Robots also exist that perform many human-like physical actions.

The engineering perspective is a particularly interesting one. When one is forced to build something, one learns quite a bit about it. In fact, it is probably the case that we can never truly understand something until we are forced to construct it. The focus of this book is not on designing a bridge or skyscraper, but on designing the most complex thing we know: us. The attempt to build a person or at the very least a construct that cannot be distinguished from a bona fide person may be impossible. But the pursuit of this goal will certainly tell us a lot about ourselves.

This book therefore examines whether an artificial person could be constructed and the important questions that arise from such an endeavor. The study and attempt to engineer human capabilities can be thought of as the field of **artificial psychology**, although it has also been called **cognitive engineering** (Bringsjord, 1992). Although this field does not yet exist as a formal discipline, it may be considered an adjunct of the broader field of

cognitive science, which is the scientific interdisciplinary study of mind. Like cognitive science, artificial psychology is interdisciplinary in nature, and draws on material from many different fields, including philosophy, cognitive psychology, neuroscience, linguistics, evolution, artificial intelligence, and robotics.

OVERVIEW OF CONTENT

The organization of this book follows that of a textbook in introductory psychology. The order and content of each chapter is similar to most books on this topic. Many of the chapters deal with specific human capacities that would need to be reproduced in an artificial person. These capacities include perception, learning, memory, thought, language, intelligence, consciousness, motivation, and emotion. The book concludes with an anticipation of what the future may hold for man-machine interaction and a comment on the nature of humanity.

Due to its interdisciplinary nature and scope, there is no attempt to review all information on each topic. Instead, the focus is on research describing how a particular ability functions in people and how it might be realized in a machine. The similarities and differences between the two will be noted. This is a compare and contrast approach, with a naturalistic perspective based on biology and psychology on one hand and a technological perspective based on artificial intelligence and robotics on the other.

DISTINCTIVE FEATURES

Many standard textbooks in psychology and the cognitive sciences are organized by broad areas of human ability such as perception, memory and language. Experiments outlining human capacities and limitations are then described within each of these arenas. However, little concern is given to motivating this organization. In this work we provide a theme that links these different topics together. This theme is the construction of an artificial person. If we are to build an artificial human, then it must be able to do everything a person can do, such as recognize patterns, solve problems, reason, and even experience emotions.

This work examines these abilities in a new light. It poses each of these skills as an operating requirement that our artificial person must have. It defines what they are and why they are important. The biology underlying some of these capacities in people is then sketched out. An up-to-date summary of recent technological innovations comes next showing how close we are to reproducing these functions. For example, we detail the latest in artificial noses, speech systems, affective architectures, and social robots. We conclude with a discussion of the philosophical implications of trying to replicate these particular aspects of humanity.

There are a number of distinctive features in this text that are not found in one package elsewhere. First, the work is intended to be systematic and comprehensive in its scope. All the standard chapter headings found in a cognitive psychology textbook are here. In addition, however, we provide coverage of topics that are given short thrift in other comparable works. For instance, there are sections on computer creativity, free will, life, and ethics. An entire chapter is devoted to the issue of social behavior, covering what a society of artificial people might be like and what a hybrid human-machine society could hold in store.

INTENDED AUDIENCE

The book may be used as a primary or ancillary text for undergraduate or introductory graduate level courses in cognitive psychology, cognitive science, artificial intelligence, robotics, or philosophy of mind. The text also makes a nice reference source for graduate students, faculty, researchers and professionals in these various fields.

Although there are some technical topics, they are described at an introductory level. An undergraduate student with no prior knowledge of the material should have few difficulties in comprehending the content. There are no required prerequisite courses. Relevant background information is given before discussion of more advanced ideas. The material is designed to be accessible and engaging to both students and lay readers alike.

ACKNOWLEDGMENTS

I would like to thank Michael Alfieri for his work on the references, glossary, and indexes. Juan Flores and Patrick Walsh were also helpful in reading the manuscript and in providing feedback from a student perspective. Many thanks also to Gabriele Schies of Sichtwerk, Inc. who created and assisted with the figures. Finally, I extend gratitude to my editors, Lori Handelman, Steve Rutter, and Paul Dukes, who provided invaluable guidance.

ABOUT THE AUTHOR

Jay Friedenberg is Associate Professor and Chairperson of the Psychology Department at Manhattan College where he also directs the Cognitive Science Program. He teaches courses in cognition, perception, biological psychology and research methods. His research interests are in the areas of visual perception and philosophy of mind. He is a member of Phi Beta Kappa and the Psychonomic Society.

1

INTRODUCTION

What a piece of work is man! How noble in reason! how infinite in faculties! in form and moving, how express and admirable! in action how like an angel! in apprehension, how like a god! the beauty of the world! the paragon of animals!

—**William Shakespeare, from *Hamlet* (II, ii, 115–117)**

THE AMAZING HUMAN

The preceding quote from Shakespeare eloquently describes the incredible capabilities of human beings. If you stop and think about it for moment, we really are amazing creatures. Our physical feats are quite varied. We can run, swim, and climb. But beyond this, we have the ability to perceive the world through senses like vision and audition, to think and solve problems, and to experience emotions such as joy and sadness. The list of such abilities goes on and on. How is it that we do all these things?

One gets a sense of how difficult even simple human abilities are when we try to recreate them using technology. Take the example of reaching out to pick up a pen. This seemingly simple action requires a tremendous amount of skill. You first have to look out at the world and identify the pen from a complex visual scene containing numerous other objects. You then need to guide your arm toward the pen's location and grasp it. The grasping action alone involves a complex sensorimotor process in which tactile feedback from the fingers is used to maintain a grip and prevent the pen from slipping. Now imagine designing a machine that can do all of this. Researchers in artificial intelligence (AI) and robotics are only just now developing machines capable of such actions.

If grabbing a pen seems so hard, then you might think we are centuries away from getting machines to perform some of our other supposedly more advanced capacities. Can we ever create a machine that is creative and able to write poems or paint pictures? What about a machine that can understand what we say and talk back to us? Or a machine that is aware of itself and the world around it? The purpose of this book is to show that many of the abilities we consider to be human, even uniquely human, may be difficult but at least not in principle impossible for us to construct.

WHAT DOES IT MEAN TO BE HUMAN?

What does it mean to be human? Various philosophers throughout the ages have addressed the definition of **personhood**. In the 17th century, John Locke said to be human one must have the capacity for (1) reason or rationality; (2) mental states like beliefs, intentions, desires, and emotions; (3) language; (4) entering into social relationships with other persons; and (5) being considered a responsible moral agent. Do you think this list is too brief? Would you add other capacities like awareness and free will? Do you think that the essence of humanity can even be reduced to a list at all? Is it something that can't be defined? We address each of these capacities and many others in greater detail at various points later in the book.

Dennett (1978) presents a more modern take on this issue. He identifies six necessary conditions of personhood. Some of these overlap with those proposed by Locke.

1. Persons are rational beings. We are capable of thinking rationally and logically.
2. Persons are beings to which states of consciousness are attributed, or to which psychological or mental states are ascribed.
3. A person is a being to which an attitude or stance of personhood is taken, i.e., a person is someone who is treated as a person by others.
4. The object to which the stance ascribed in number three above must be capable of reciprocating in some way. In other words, to be a person is to treat others as persons, perhaps in a moral way.
5. Persons must be capable of verbal communication or language. This excludes all nonhuman animals.
6. Persons are conscious in some special way that other species are not.

Notice that conditions 2–5 are not intrinsic properties of an individual. They require a social level of description. For number 2, mental states, because of their subjective and psychological character, cannot be proven objectively. Partly for this reason, Dennett proposes they be ascribed by others. This theme is echoed in condition 3 where we see that a person is again extrinsic, a property attributed to one by others. Condition 4 simply makes this a two-way street, that a person is someone who is not only considered by others as human but in turn treats them as if they too were people. Condition 5 is also social as the purpose of language is to exchange information between individuals.

The idea of a person being a person because someone else thinks they are is unsatisfying from a scientific perspective. Science is an objective endeavor and would like to be able to find some crucial human physical property that can be measured and detected. Imagine a "person-meter" that we could point at someone. If it detected this critical property, a green light would come on indicating personhood. If this property were absent and not detected, a red light would appear indicating the absence of personhood. Unfortunately, no such device exists and we are stuck with the subjectivity problem of mental states. This issue is

Table 1.1 Different definitions of personhood according to Foerst (2004).

Homo Type	Definition	Description
Homo sapiens	The thinker	Having the ability to think and be intelligent.
Homo faber	The builder	Capable of constructing things and shaping the world with the help of tools and technology.
Homo ludens	The player	Being playful but also taking on a role in a society such as father.
Homo economicus	The economist	Engaging in economic activity. Trading goods and services. But also being self-centered and pleasure seeking.
Homo religiosus	The spiritualist	Practicing religion. Praying, worshiping and exhibiting spiritual beliefs.
Homo narrans	The storyteller	The construction of narratives or stories.
Homo objectivus et rationalis	The objective rationalist	Being objective and rational. Capable of using reason and logic.

dealt with in more depth in the chapter on consciousness. For more on stances, intentionality and attribution, we refer the reader to the chapter on thinking. For additional conceptions of personhood, see Table 1.1.

An important issue concerning what it means to be a person centers on the body. Is a body necessary in order to be human? Nowhere in any of the definitions given above do we see that having arms, legs, internal organs, or for that matter, even a brain, as necessary. There is no mention of what exact physical form a person needs to take. Instead, it is the capacity to have mental states that is emphasized. If this were the case, then a being with the right sorts of mental states would be human regardless of their underlying physical structure. People could be made of bricks, toothpicks, or any other component parts as long as the system as a whole was capable of supporting the appropriate mental states.

VARIETIES OF MAN-MACHINE

Before continuing, it is worth defining several important terms that we will be using repeatedly throughout this text. We start with the most general and farthest removed from what might be considered human and work our way toward the concept of an artificial person.

A **machine** is any mechanical or organic device that transmits or modifies energy to perform or assist in the execution of tasks. Machines typically require some energy as input and accomplish some sort of work. People have designed and used mechanisms and machines throughout much of recent human history to facilitate the performance of jobs. Note that work in this sense can be physical, as is the case with an elevator that can lift loads, or purely computational, as is the case with a calculator that is used to add a list of numbers. Note also that according to this definition, a machine can be mechanical, made of fabricated or synthetic parts like gears or circuits, or biological, consisting of organic molecules.

A **computer** in the most general sense is a device designed to represent and compute information. The hallmark of a computer is that it is incapable of interacting with the physical world. A computer can pass information back and forth through space with other computers via a network, but unless connected to some sort of actuator, like an artificial limb, is incapable of acting on objects in the world. A computer can therefore manipulate information but not material objects.

A **robot** on the other hand is a construct that is capable of moving around and/or interacting with the physical world. Some robots are in a fixed position but can move objects using arms or other effectors. Others are capable of moving about under their own power and are called mobile robots. Likewise human operators control some robots while others have autonomous control over their own actions. Robots can but need not look like people.

A **cyborg** or cybernetic organism is a creature that is a mix of organic and mechanical parts. By the stricter definition of the term, a human cyborg is someone who has had some basic physiological function replaced by an embedded machine part. A person with a pacemaker thus qualifies but someone wearing contact lenses or using a mobile phone does not. Cyborgs bring up many interesting questions. Imagine a cybernetic person named John who is continually augmented with technology. At some point, does John stop becoming a person? If more than half of John were mechanical would you say he is no longer human? What if all of John's body but not his brain were mechanical? If we gradually replaced more and more of John's brain with functionally equivalent computer parts, would he at some point cease to be human?

An **android** is an artificially created being that resembles a human being (see Figure 1.1). In literature and other media an android is loosely defined in the sense that it can

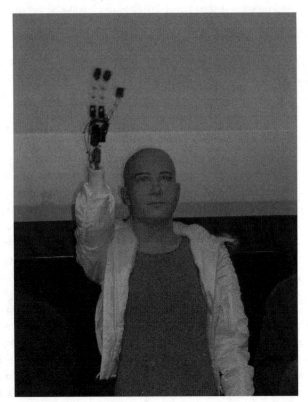

Figure 1.1 The android "Jules" by Hanson Robotics shows off at NextFest 2006. Androids look and act like people but are not considered human.

be entirely mechanical, entirely organic, or some combination thereof. Thus, a robot or a cyborg that looks human can be considered an android. Androids as they are customarily treated in the literature, although resembling people, need not act or be exactly like people.

In this book, we will be discussing the creation of an artificial person. An **artificial person** is an artificially created being that is by its nature and actions indistinguishable from a human, but need not look exactly like one. An artificial person is functionally no different from a real person. Their behavior in any given situation or test could not be reliably differentiated from that of an actual person. Although an artificial person may look different on the inside or the outside, from a behavioral standpoint they are identical in every respect to people. Like an android, an artificial person may be mechanical, organic, or some combination of the two.

THE ARTIFICIAL PERSON IN MYTHOLOGY AND LITERATURE

The history of storytelling is replete with human attempts to construct an artificial person. Perhaps the earliest of these comes from ancient Greece. Hephaestus was a god born as the son of the goddess Hera, wife of Zeus. He became the god's "handyman," creating various contraptions for them with his forge. These included Achilles' shield and Apollo's chariot. His most complex creation was Talos, a bronze robot that guarded the island of Crete. Talos roamed the island and could throw large rocks at passing ships.

During the Middle Ages, the alchemist Paracelsus is attributed with first using the term **homunculus**, which literally translated from the Latin means "little man." He reports having made a one-foot tall homunculus using bones, sperm, pieces of skin and animal hair. This was then laid in the ground and surrounded by horse manure. After 40 days, an embryonic version would form. Another equally ludicrous recipe involves poking a hole in the shell of an egg laid by a black hen, inserting human sperm and sealing the opening with parchment. Thirty days after burial in the ground, a small person would emerge who would serve their creator in exchange for being fed lavender seeds and earthworms!

Later in Europe we find the **golem**, an animated being crafted from inanimate material. The story of the golem originates from Jewish folklore. According to these tales, golems are crafted from mud. They are unintelligent, usually lacking the ability to speak and used primarily for menial labor, where they are assigned to perform some simple task repetitively. Only a holy person such as a rabbi is capable of creating a golem. Because rabbis were close to God, they gained some of God's power and were able to create limited versions of people. One of the better-known golem stories is of rabbi Judah Low ben Bezalel, who, in the 16th century, produced a golem to defend the Prague ghetto against Anti-Semitic assaults (Bloch, 1972).

Frankenstein is a novel written by Mary Wollstonecraft Shelley and was first published in 1818. It is the story of Victor Frankenstein, a proto-scientist who creates a manlike creature from corpses. Horrified at its appearance, he runs away, whereupon the creature itself also disappears. Later events find the creature asking Frankenstein to build him a female partner. After Frankenstein destroys the partially made female in disgust, the creature seeks revenge and kills Frankenstein's wife. Frankenstein himself now hunts the creature down, pursuing him through the artic wastes and ultimately perishing in the attempt. A prominent theme in this classic is the loneliness and isolation of the creature that wants companionship from humanity and from a kindred creature like itself.

The first use of the word robot comes from a play by the Czech Karel Capek called *Rossum's Universal Robots*, first performed in 1921. Capek tells the story of beings who are manufactured for the sole purpose of work. These creatures are created in a large factory out of organic materials. They both look and act like people but have no feelings. The wife of the factory owner takes pity on them and asks the factory manager to instill feelings in them so that they will be happier and can get along better with their human counterparts. He agrees, but the robots, now realizing their superiority, revolt and massacre almost everyone. The play ends with a truce between the robots and humankind and a hope for a better future.

Modern science fiction of course offers us many instances of artificial persons along with morality tales warning us of the consequences. In Arthur C. Clarke's *2001: A Space Odyssey*, the computer HAL suffers a breakdown and murders the crew of a spaceship because of an inability to resolve conflicting mission instructions. In *The Terminator* movies, intelligent machines designed for national defense fulfill their duty too well by deciding to wipe out the human race. A similar theme is echoed in *The Matrix* films where computers win a war against people by imprisoning them in an artificial virtual reality.

The apocalyptic visions portrayed in these stories reflect our fear that in constructing an artificial person we will also bring about our own demise. In other words, our mechanical reproductions will not only possess what makes us great, but contain our flaws as well. There is also the lurking anxiety that they may become smarter or better than we are, deciding to ignore or do away with us entirely. The quest to create an artificial person thus has a light and dark side. By creating an artificial person we are able to figure ourselves out and thus transcend ourselves. But in so doing, we run the risk of becoming obsolete and insignificant. These themes are explored further in the conclusion chapter.

THEOLOGY AND ARTIFICIAL PEOPLE

Anne Foerst, in her 2004 book *God in the Machine* discusses the theological implications of constructing an artificial person. The first question she addresses is why we should even want to engage in such an endeavor. Most people have mixed feelings about humanlike robots. Many are scared of them and perceive them as a threat. They trigger in some of us a sense of insecurity because of the possibility that they might equal or exceed our own abilities. Artificial people thus jeopardize our sense of uniqueness, the idea that humans are special or privileged in some way.

However, we are also attracted to the notion of interacting with beings similar to ourselves. It seems we humans are lonely. We have a strong desire to share experiences and to interact not only with one another, but with others like us. This is evident in the quest to communicate with other animal species like chimpanzees and dolphins and in the search for extraterrestrial intelligence. Curiosity about our nature seems to be another underlying factor. The process will undoubtedly teach us more about who we are and how we work.

Perhaps another reason for desiring to recreate ourselves is that in so doing we seem to transcend our own limitations and become like gods. Most religions have a God figure that creates humankind. These acts of creation are related in the form of stories depicting how the gods or a God created humans. If we ever become capable of such a feat, it seems to imply that we too have achieved a God-like status. Some may interpret this notion as heretical because by acquiring some of God's powers we usurp God.

Foerst (2004) provides a contrary theological interpretation in which recreating our own likeness is not a transgression against God but a celebration of him. She argues that the construction of an artificial person such as a golem is an act of prayer. By engaging in golem building, we learn more about God's creation of people and about our special abilities. Because God created us in his image, participating in this particular version of God's creativity allows us to celebrate God and to better appreciate his wonder. In this view, creativity becomes an act of prayer. The more complex the creative act, the stronger the prayer becomes and the more we praise God. Because humans are the most complex things we know about, constructing them is the ultimate creative act and therefore the highest form of worship.

In this view, rather than make us arrogant, golem building instead makes us humble. By understanding the incredible complexity and intricacy that make us up, we gain a new found appreciation of ourselves and of God's ability. The result is not a sense of superiority but of modesty and humility. This same sentiment has been expressed by a number of scientists. The astronomer Carl Sagan describes the sense of awe he and others have felt when appreciating the amazing workings of the universe. The physicist Albert Einstein, when crossing the Atlantic on a ship, realized how small he and the ship were in comparison to the vast surrounding ocean. He relates the feeling as humbling and awe-inspiring.

EARLY ATTEMPTS AT CONSTRUCTING AN ARTIFICIAL PERSON

Although there were a number of attempts at constructing artificial people prior to the 18th century, they were somewhat crude. The level of sophistication increased dramatically with the automatons of the French engineer and inventor Jacques de Vaucanson (1709–1782). An **automaton** is a self-operating mechanical moving machine designed to resemble human or animal actions. In a more general sense, an automaton is a device or system that acts in a completely well-understood manner. Vaucanson created a flute player who by accounts could play 12 different tunes by moving his fingers, lips, and tongue. Vaucanson's most memorable creation was an artificial duck. Made of copper and rubber tubing, it could drink, quack, and flap its wings. Flying was apparently not part of its behavioral repertoire.

The most sophisticated automaton of this period is attributed to the Swiss clockmaker Henri Maillardet, born in 1745. Spring-driven cams power this "Draughtsman-Writer." The automaton is in the form of a girl that sits in front of a desk with her right hand grasping a pen. When wound up, it looks down and writes poems in French and English and draws several elaborate pictures including a sailing ship and a pagoda. The automaton was first presented to the Franklin Institute in Philadelphia in 1928; it exists there to this day.

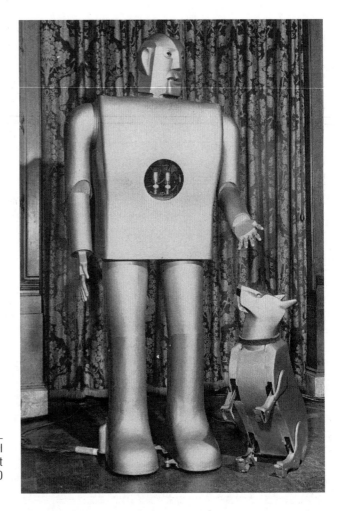

Figure 1.2 Elektro and Sparko, mechanical man and dog, get together before going out to the Westinghouse Exhibit at the 1939–40 World's Fair. © Bettmann/CORBIS

The 1939–40 World's Fair in New York was the showcase for one of eight robots built by Westinghouse Corporation. It was 7 feet tall and weighed 300 pounds but appeared humanlike. Elektro could walk forwards and backwards, dance, and even smoke a cigarette. With the aid of a record player, it could count to 10 and say 77 words. Elektro even had a companion, Sparko the robot dog, who could bark, sit and beg (Figure 1.2).

Several themes run through these early creations. We can see that as new technology develops, it gets incorporated into artificial people. Eighteenth century automatons operated using springs, gears, and cams. Their internal workings resembled that of a complex clock. Later, when electricity became available, it served as a power source. Robots like Elektro were controlled by electric relays and vacuum tubes. Notice also that all of these artificial people were created for the purpose of entertainment. It wasn't until later in the 20th century that robots would be designed for labor or as investigative research tools. We present a brief history of modern computers in the next chapter and discuss modern robots later on.

THE NATURAL AND THE ARTIFICIAL

Most of us tend to think of the natural and the artificial as being two very different sorts of things. However, from a scientific perspective, they are best characterized as being the same. The scientific world view is that the universe is entirely physical or material in nature, being made up of matter and energy (although, at a fundamental level, matter and energy are identical). Everything in the universe can be understood through physical laws. These laws describe the way any physical system, no matter how complex, should operate.

If this assumption is correct, we can use the laws of computer science and electrical engineering to explain what a computer is doing at any given moment. Our knowledge of the architecture and operating characteristics of the electronic circuits and other parts would allow us to give a very good account of the computer's behavior. The human brain, like a computer, is a physical system governed by known laws. Given a sufficient understanding of the laws that govern it, among them neuroscience and molecular biology, we could also explain what a person is doing at any given moment.

There are two philosophical views that reflect these ideas. According to **universal mechanism**, everything in the universe can be understood as a completely mechanical system—a system made up entirely of matter in motion, governed by natural laws. All phenomena can be explained by the collision of matter, where one particle or object moves and induces some effect in another. This view has sometimes been described by the phrase "clockwork universe" in which the universe is viewed as a giant clock, filled with springs and gears, each moving in an orderly, understandable way. The French mathematician Pierre-Simon Laplace (1749–1827) was a proponent of this view.

There is another version of this perspective called **anthropic mechanism**. Anthropic mechanists believe that although everything in the universe may not be explained as a mechanism, everything about human beings can. In this view everything about the brain and body, including consciousness and free will, can be reduced to the operation of mechanistic forces. The French philosopher Julien Offray de La Mettrie (1709–1751) was an anthropic mechanist. He advocates the position in his book *Man and Machine* written in 1748. Both forms of mechanism imply **determinism**: if everything about either the universe or people can be explained, then everything about that particular system must also be determined. Determinism poses a problem for freedom and free will. It is discussed at greater length in the chapter on decision making.

The basic premise of this book is that there is no reason, in principle, why people should be treated any differently in terms of the way they are understood than should a computer or robot. Technological devices, which are mechanistic, have been shown to be very good models for how the body and the brain operate. Recent years have seen the development of more sophisticated prosthetic limbs and artificial organs. These devices demonstrate that the function of body parts can be effectively carried out in a mechanistic fashion. The same also appears true for the brain. The field of **cognitive psychology** views the mind as a mechanistic information-processor and was influenced by the rise of the computer. It has been very successful in explaining mental functions like perception, memory, and reasoning using models where information is represented and processed in a formal mechanistic way.

UNDERSTANDING: WHAT ITS LIKE
TO REALLY KNOW SOMETHING

Understanding how something operates is prerequisite to being able to construct something like it. Someone who has no concept of the wheel or of internal combustion could never build a car that requires these features. So prior to our discussing how an artificial person might be constructed, we need to know if it is possible to understand people. Our discussion here will thus center on what it means to understand and the application of understanding to human beings.

Science gives us an idea of what it means to understand. Three basic functions of science are description, explanation and prediction (Elmes, Kantowitz, & Roediger, 1999). Science strives to achieve these goals in the study of any phenomena or system. For example, a meteorologist would not be content with merely describing rain, he or she would also want to explain why it rains and predict when it will rain. We can also think of this trio as constituting the three pillars of understanding. We don't truly understand something unless we can describe, explain, and predict it.

Description is like asking the question: What is this thing like? It involves a listing of the parts and the characteristics of the parts that make up the system under question. A comprehensive description of a person would be quite detailed. It would include anatomical data of brain and body structures at a gross but also microscopic level. In other words we would need to describe not only organs and organ parts, but the individual cellular structure underlying them. A full understanding requires a description beyond even this, one involving the atomic level. A problem with description is that it becomes more difficult to do, the finer the level of spatial scale. At a sufficiently small level of analysis, the quantum level, perfectly accurate descriptions may not even be possible. The quantum objection is discussed later on.

The next piece of understanding is based on description. An **explanation** is like asking the question: How does this thing work? It involves a functional or causal explication of how a system operates. An explanation of a person's behavior must resort to the parts and the nature of the parts obtained previously during description. An explanation for a behavior such as solving a crossword puzzle would resort to the brain structures involved in performing the behavior. It would also specify what actions they perform and in what order. Explanations typically take place within a temporal-spatial and causal framework. They involve different structures that act on one another with one structure's action triggering or causing another's action. These actions unfold in space and time following known physical laws.

The third component of understanding is prediction and it, in turn, follows from explanation. **Prediction** is like asking the question: When will this thing do such and such? It involves anticipating or knowing in advance what the behavior of a system will be like. If we can describe and explain a person in sufficient detail, then we can also predict their behavior under a given set of circumstances. To use our current example, if Mary likes crossword puzzles and finds herself with a pencil, a copy of the Sunday newspaper and time to kill, then we could predict with reasonable certainty that she will sit down and start solving the puzzle in the paper.

The better we can describe and explain a system, the better we can predict it. In theory, with enough knowledge of Mary's brain, we could even predict which words she would solve first, which one's she would have trouble with and which ones she might not be able to get at all. It is important to note that complete prediction requires knowledge of the context in which a behavior occurs. It must specify the environmental conditions that precede and co-occur with the action. In this example, these would include the conditions Mary finds herself in, such having time on her hands, possession of the pencil, and the characteristics of the crossword puzzle itself. Complete prediction may also require knowledge of much more antecedent conditions such as her prior training and experiences.

REPRODUCTION: MAYBE MORE THAN JUST A COPY

A consequence of truly understanding a system is also another cornerstone of the scientific method. If we understand something well enough, then we can recreate it and expect it to act the same way it did before. This principle is known as **replication**. To illustrate the way this works in science, imagine a researcher who designs an experiment and obtains a certain result. Uncertain of the result, the researcher then does the experiment over again in exactly the same way. If the effect is valid, the result should be the same. If the effect occurred simply by chance, the result will be different.

The concept of replication can in principle be extended to the reproduction of any system, no matter how complex. If we understand the system well enough, i.e., if we can describe, explain, and predict it, then we should also be able to reproduce the system and expect our reproduction to act in the same way as the original. Now let's apply this to the case of an artificial person. Assume first that we can sufficiently understand Mary. Next assume we are capable of creating an artificially engineered version of Mary based on this understanding. The reproduction can then be expected to act in a way that is nearly indistinguishable from the original.

There are two ways to create an artificial Mary that acts like the original. First, we can create an identical copy or duplication. That is, we can reproduce, exactly as possible, all aspects of the original Mary. Identical twins are nature's way of accomplishing this. An artificial means of producing it is through cloning. Now you might be thinking that a mother can distinguish the behavior of her two identical twin offspring. This is true and, in fact, identical twins do act differently. However, these differences are due to the fact that the twins were not subject to identical environments. Small changes in environmental conditions, both pre- and post-natal, can produce alterations in development and consequent behavioral outcomes. When these environments are held constant, the behavioral discrepancies should vanish.

We could also reproduce Mary by creating a nonidentical copy. In this case, the artificial Mary would be constructed differently from the original, but based on the same underlying principles of operation. Rather than replicate Mary exactly, we could construct an artificial version of her that would operate in the same way. If the artificial Mary had the same vocabulary, problem-solving skills, and other cognitive functions as the first, then the two versions would solve a crossword puzzle the same way. Two systems with differing architectures but same processes possess **functional equivalence**. They differ in their hardware or internal organization, but produce the same behavior when exposed to the same environments.

There are two fundamental approaches to designing an intelligent system. In the human approach, one looks at how people do things and then attempts to get a computer or robot to perform them the same way. In what has been deemed the "alien" approach researchers use whatever means they have at their disposal to create an ability regardless of the way it might be executed in people. It may be that human attempts are always doomed to failure because of engineering limitations, while the alien approach, which is free to pursue other options, can succeed. An example of this comes from flying (Figure 1.3). Early attempts at flying involved recreating as closely as possible the actions of birds. These devices had flapping wings. Eventually, the airplane was invented that could fly successfully, but its operation only loosely resembled that of a bird. The same outcome may be the case with an artificial person. We may find that there are many alternative engineering solutions to creating human functions.

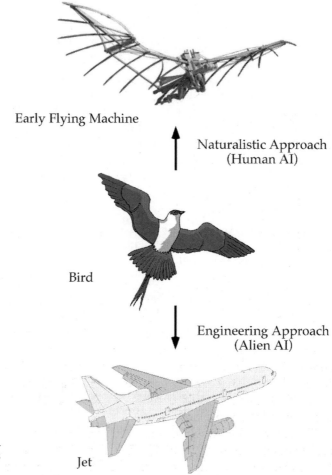

Early Flying Machine

Naturalistic Approach
(Human AI)

Bird

Engineering Approach
(Alien AI)

Figure 1.3 Natural and artificial approaches to engineering a capacity like flying.

Jet

OBJECTIONS AND COUNTER-ARGUMENTS

So, let's pause and recapitulate our central argument that comes in three parts. (1) There is no difference between what we call natural and artificial systems because all systems are made up of matter and energy and are governed by universal physical laws. (2) Sufficient understanding of a system in the form of description, explanation, and prediction allows us to replicate or reproduce it. (3) Exact or functionally equivalent reproductions of original systems that are subject to the same environments will exhibit indistinguishable behavior. As you might imagine, these are very general and controversial statements and there are quite a few objections to them. In this section, we introduce some of these objections and counter them.

The Incompleteness Objection

This objection states that science has yet to provide a complete description of any system, even relatively simple ones. In 2002, Sydney Brenner, H. Robert Horvitz, and John E. Sulston won the Nobel Prize in physiology for specifying how all 959 neurons of the *Caenorhabditis elegans* worm develop from a single cell. The location and function of these neurons is well recorded. But this information, as detailed as it is, is still not enough to entirely describe the worm's actions or to create an artificial worm with the same behavioral repertoire.

The response to this is that increased degrees of understanding enable increased degrees of reproducibility. As we learn more about the human brain, we should be correspondingly better able to replicate various aspects of its function. Whether or not a complete understanding ever comes to pass, increases in partial understanding should at least result in better reproductions, ones that more closely approximate the behavior of the original.

Just as it may not be possible to know everything about a given system or entity, it may not be possible to know everything about its environment or history. In order to perfectly predict what a person might do, we may need access to all of that person's experiences and what impact those experiences had on the person. Since every person's experiences are unique and last over many years, being able to understand and reproduce them is problematic.

Although it may not be possible to accurately reproduce a person's entire history, this may not be necessary. Certain key events in a person's life might be more important than others and these could then be reproducible in an artificial person through training or simulation. If an event were strong enough to influence a person's behavior, then it should leave a measurable imprint on them. This imprint could take the form of a neural circuit or some other physiological alteration. This alteration could then be reproduced. So, in a sense, people carry their history around with them. This physical record shows what they have experienced, learned, or remembered. Reproducing the imprint of an experience in an artificial person would cause it to behave in the same way as an original person who actually had the experience.

There is another incompleteness problem posed by formal descriptive systems like logic and mathematics (Gödel, 1930). The simplified version of this problem is called Gödel's Incompleteness Theorem and is named after its progenitor, the mathematician Kurt Gödel.

It goes as follows: In any consistent formal system within which a certain amount of elementary arithmetic can be carried out, it can be shown that there is a statement that can be proved neither true or false. In a nutshell, this theorem states that formal descriptive systems are limited in the sense that there will always be some fact they cannot account for. In terms of our argument, there may always be some aspect of the brain or body that a logical or mathematical analysis cannot explain. We discuss the incompleteness theorem more in the Brain and Mind chapter.

The Complexity Objection

The brain and other phenomena, like the stock market and the weather, are examples of complex systems. A **complex system** is one whose properties are not fully explained by an understanding of its component parts. There are several features of such systems (Goldenfeld & Kadanoff, 1999). To begin, they are very sensitive to changes in initial conditions. Alterations in starting conditions propagate through the system, producing unanticipated outcomes. An oft-cited example of this is that if a butterfly flaps its wings in Brazil, the result is a tornado in China or some other far-flung location. In a complex system, there are multiple interactions between the many different components. The parts affect one another in an intricate causal dance that is hard to track. These features make complex systems very difficult to predict, understand or control. If the human brain and body are complex systems, then, some say, we may never be able to figure them out.

One response to this is that just because a system is complex, doesn't mean that it can't be simplified or understood. We can think of a complex system as a tangled plate of spaghetti. Each strand represents a causal influence. At each point where one strand contacts another it exerts an effect. When we step back and look at the plate of spaghetti, it appears as a tangled unexplainable mess. But if we start to pick apart the strands, or can measure them in some way to determine where they start and end or touch each other, the situation starts to become clear. It may be the case that future methods of measurement or mathematical modeling can simplify and demystify all or some aspects of complex systems. We will discuss complex systems in greater depth later in the book.

The Quantum Indeterminancy Objection

Quantum theory or quantum mechanics as it is sometimes called, is a theory of physics used to describe small-scale phenomena, those at the atomic and subatomic level (Griffiths, 2004). According to quantum theory, certain attributes of particles, such as their position or momentum, cannot be known with certainty. Instead, they are best understood using probabilities that describe the chance that, for example, a particle is located in a certain region of space. What is interesting about this theory is that it implies some events don't actually exist or fail to exist. They are in a state of indeterminancy or probability until being observed, at which point they are made certain. A complete explication of quantum theory and its implications is beyond the scope of this text and we will mention it only to the extent that it affects our discussion of certain points.

Quantum theory poses problems for hopes of our ever being able to fully understand things such as the human brain, whose operation might rely on quantum scale phenomena. If we can never accurately say exactly where a particle is or what it is doing at any given moment in time, then our understanding of people and our capacity to produce an artificial person may be limited.

One counter to the quantum theory interpretation has been that probabilities are simply an expression of what we don't know. They reflect an absence of knowledge rather than a state of reality. Albert Einstein himself doubted that the world was at heart probabilistic when he said, "God doesn't play dice" (Calaprice & Dyson, 2005). Even if quantum theory turns out to be true, it is possible that it may not affect our understanding of certain larger phenomenon. It could be the case that human thought is not influenced by tiny quantum level events, that such events are simply too far removed in scale to have any sort of impact on what we are thinking.

Alternatively, a further understanding of quantum theory may tell us more about the brain. The physicist Roger Penrose and his colleague Stuart Hameroff have formulated a quantum theory of consciousness (Hameroff & Penrose, 1996). They suggest that conscious awareness is the result of quantum fluctuations taking place inside neurons. If consciousness should ultimately depend on such phenomena, there is the possibility that we could then use quantum-based engineering techniques to create consciousness. Quantum computers have already been constructed that use the quantum properties of particles to represent and perform operations on data (Nielsen & Chuang, 2000).

The Engineering Limitation Objection

Whereas the preceding three objections have been primarily aimed at understanding, this objection is instead aimed at reproduction. The engineering limitation objection states that we might lack the ability to ever produce an artificial person. It may require a technological sophistication forever beyond our reach. An examination of our brains and bodies reveals a multitude of intricate small moving parts. A single cell considered in isolation is a marvel to behold, filled with organelles and molecules that among other things serve to store information, transport materials, and catalyze chemical reactions. If we can't replicate a single cell like a neuron, what hope do we have of replicating a brain and body, which is made up of billions of such elements?

The answer is that we may not have to. Just because we are made up of organic material organized a certain way does not mean that an artificial person need be. As mentioned earlier, there are two ways to construct an artificial person, by replicating or reproducing the design of an actual person or by creating one that is functionally but not architecturally equivalent. If human traits depended on organic material, we could engineer one using such materials. Biologists are already becoming more adept at using organic compounds. An example of this comes from the field of DNA computing, in which molecules can be used as information processors to solve certain types of problems more quickly than traditional computing methods (Amos, 2005).

A major distinction that is sometimes made between natural and artificial systems is that the former are products of evolution while the latter are products of design (Dennett, 1994). Biological organisms are the consequence of evolutionary processes. They are adaptations to environmental conditions that change unexpectedly over time. As a result, from a scientific viewpoint, there is no plan or purpose behind them. Artificial systems, on the other hand, are artifacts. They are the intentional product of a thinking mind or minds and result from deliberate planning and preconception. Only the complex and intricate process of biological evolution playing out over billions of years, some claim, can ever give rise to humanity and wonderful things like conscious awareness. It could never result from engineering, because we are simply too limited in our thinking.

There are two responses to this. First, intent or its absence may be of little import in creation. According to evolutionary theory, the selection processes that drive species change are random events and not planned ahead of time. What seems to matter more is the creative process itself. It is the right process that will produce the right end results. In the case of biological organisms, that process is evolution. Second, nature does not have an exclusive patent on the use of evolution. These processes can be harnessed and used by humans as well. In fact, researchers in the cognitive sciences have been using evolution to create for quite some time now. We see this in the fields of robotic assembly, evolutionary algorithms, and artificial life, all of which will be discussed later. We must also consider the possibility that evolution may not be crucial to the construction of an artificial person in which case some other process, either currently available or yet to be discovered, can be employed.

2

BRAIN AND MIND

My mind to me a kingdom is.
Such perfect joy therein I find
That it excels all other bliss
That world affords or grows by kind.

—**Sir Edward Dyer, 1588**

THE BRAIN: WHERE IT ALL STARTS

The **brain** is truly magnificent. It is this structure that underlies our conscious experience. It regulates homeostatic body functions like heartbeat, movement, and most all the other abilities we will discus, including emotion and thinking. The fact that it can do this and only be the size of a melon is even more amazing. A brain in any vertebrate animal is the coordinative center of the nervous system, which consists also of nerves that feed sensory information to it from the body and world and motor and other commands away from it to muscles and glands.

Nervous systems are made up of cells called **neurons**. The job of a neuron is to receive and transmit electrical signals from and to other neurons. It is this action that forms the basis of mental functioning. The human brain has been estimated to contain one hundred billion (10^{14}) individual neurons, each of which can be connected to as many as ten thousand others. Neurons communicate by releasing a chemical called a neurotransmitter across a small gap called the synapse that separates one cell from others.

Figure 2.1 shows the basic parts of a neuron. A neuron is essentially an individual "decision maker." It receives multiple incoming signals. Some of these signals from other cells are excitatory, tending to increase the likelihood that the neuron will send off a signal of its own. Others are inhibitory, tending to decrease this likelihood. The neuron then summates the strength of these inputs. If they exceed a certain threshold, an electrical impulse is generated and passed down the cell's axon, where it can then output its message to other

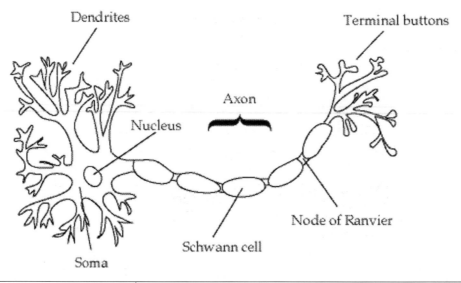

Figure 2.1 The anatomy of a neuron.

neurons. It does this through neurotransmitter release at the synapse. The neurotransmitter molecules, after traveling across the gap, attach to receptors on the postsynaptic surface. This, in turn, may trigger another signal in the receiving cell.

At a microscopic level, the brain is composed of neurons, but when one steps back and examines it at a larger spatial scale many different structures become present. Figure 2.2 shows a mid-sagittal section of the human brain. This is a cut through the midline taken from the front to the back. Many of the brain's major parts are listed. Table 2.1 lists each of these part's functions. We do not provide a detailed account of the entire brain here. We do, however, elaborate on the functional significance of some of these areas in later chapters.

THE MIND: WHAT THE BRAIN DOES

It is the brain that underlies the mind. **Mind** is a term that refers to our subjective, conscious experience of brain function. While the brain is physical and can be studied objectively, there has been and continues to be much debate about the exact nature of mind (Figure 2.3). **Monism** is the belief that there is only one kind of "stuff" in the universe and that brain and mind are the same thing. There are essentially two schools of monism. Those subscribing to **physicalism** or materialism hold that only the physical is real and that the mental can be reduced to the physical. In **idealism**, only the mental world is real and the physical can be reduced to the mental. **Dualism,** instead, states that there are two sorts of "stuff" in the universe, the physical and the mental. There are various schools of dualism that differ mainly in which of these two controls or causally influences the other.

The modern scientific study of mind exemplified by the cognitive sciences has essentially abandoned dualism and idealism. Although still defended by some theologians and phi-

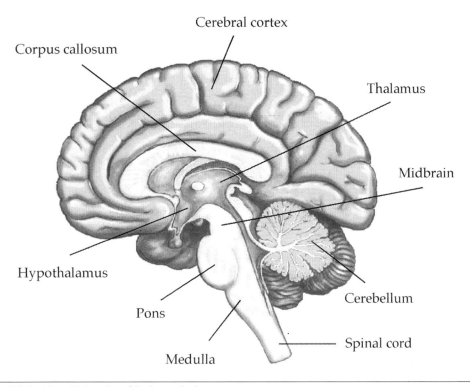

Figure 2.2 A mid-sagittal section of the human brain.

losophers, they are untenable scientific positions because they require defense of a mental or supernatural world for which there is no empirical evidence. A monist physicalist stance is adopted in this text. As outlined in the introductory chapter, the assumption of a single material universe that is understandable and governed by known or discoverable laws is the only proper philosophical foundation for the construction of an artificial person.

Table 2.1 Major parts of the human brain and their function.

Anatomical Region	Function
Medulla	Controls vital reflexes including respiration, heart rate, vomiting, salivation, coughing, and sneezing.
Pons	Place where axons in one half of the brain cross over to the opposite side of the spinal cord.
Cerebellum	Control of balance, coordination, movement.
Midbrain	Contains a number of structures including visual and auditory relay centers.
Hypothalamus	Contains many nuclei that regulate motivated behavior like drinking, feeding, temperature regulation, sexual behavior, fighting, and activity level.
Thalamus	Relays sensory information to the cortex.
Corpus callosum	Pathways that transfer information between the two hemispheres.
Cerebral cortex	Lobes mediate higher order perceptual and cognitive function including planning, attention, reasoning and problem solving.

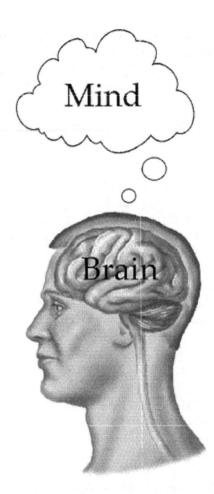

Figure 2.3 Is the mind the same as the brain?

For our purposes, mind is a way of describing a certain type of process. When you are hungry, there is a particular pattern of neural activity in your brain. This is true for the normal experience of any mental phenomenon, whether it be feeling sad or thinking about your summer vacation. Conversely, we can induce a given mental state by stimulating appropriate neurons. Activation of neurons in the occipital lobe produces flashes of light because this area governs visual perception. This direct correspondence between neural activity and mental experience suggests that the mind is "what the brain does."

But are brains the only things capable of giving rise to mental experience? This has direct bearing on the creation of an artificial person. If minds were synonymous with brains, then we would have to literally construct a brain to give an artificial person a mind. This would correspond to a duplication or copying process, where we would need to reproduce the actual anatomy and physiology of known brains to create an artificial mind. But, as mentioned in the first chapter, this may not be the case. It could be that the process or function is what's critical and not the physical substrate on which it happens to be running. In other words, the experience of thinking about a rose, let's say, may depend on the execution of a specific process. As long as that process is running, it should give rise to the thought of a rose. If this were the case, we could get an artificial person to think about a rose by executing the process using nonorganic materials or organic materials organized differently than they are in brains. This idea is known as **functionalism**. Functionalists believe that mind can be instantiated in many different possible substrates, so that a person, a computer, or an alien may all have minds, even though they differ in their underlying hardware.

WHAT ARE MINDS FOR?

Not all creatures have brains and the minds that go with them. Why then are minds important? What purpose do minds serve? Knowing the answer to this question should clarify our designs to construct one. Rodolfo Llinas, in his 2001 book *I of the Vortex. From Neurons to Self*, argues that minds evolved to allow animals to move around and interact successfully with their environments. He points out that many organisms that don't move also don't have nervous systems, while almost all mobile creatures do. A mind allows an organism to predict what it should do next, based on incoming sensory data. This is perhaps the earliest and simplest form of decision making and we need to do it constantly, when determining how to reach out and grasp an object or how to best walk around an obstacle.

Others have echoed this basic idea. Franklin (1995) states that the purpose of mind is to produce the next action. He defines action in a very broad sense, meaning all actions, not just those tied to manipulation or locomotion. Most of our cognitive faculties ultimately serve the goal of what to do next. For instance, recognition, and memory are processes that both generate information that can be used in planning or problem solving. Imagine that Bob has been dating Sarah for 2 years. Should he ask her to marry him? The outcome of this decision and all decisions determine a future course of action. In fact, most aspects of mind, not just perception and cognition, are tied to actions. Motivations like hunger and sex impel our behavior, driving us to find food or a mating partner. Emotions like fear cause us to avoid potential harmful situations. Mind, it seems, is there to tell us what to do next.

If this is why we have minds, then a mind cannot be considered in isolation. It must be considered as part of a world with which it interacts. Brooks (2002) proposes two notions that capture what this means. An **embodied** creature has a physical body and experiences the world at least partially through the influence of the world on that body. People like you or me and mobile robots with sensors and effectors are embodied. We have bodies and can perceive and move around through them. A **situated** creature is embedded in the world and experiences it immediately through sensors that directly influence its behavior. An airline reservation system is situated because it receives information directly from the world that affects what it does. However, because it lacks a body, it cannot move about or physically influence its surroundings.

It is an interesting question then, to ask whether either one or both of these are necessary to produce a mind. Could a computer that is disembodied but situated develop a mind? If the computer could sense and effect within a complex virtual or electronic environment it might. Most computers now participate in a virtual network world. They are connected to the Internet and both download and upload information to and from it dynamically. It is conceivable that a computer system or software program existing within a complex network environment may develop a mind (Blackmore, 2004). Alternatively, it may be that having a body is necessary, in which case computers inside robots inside a world could become mindful.

A HISTORY OF EARLY COMPUTERS

A **computer** is a device or machine used for making calculations or controlling operations expressible in numerical or logical terms. Computers have components that perform simple well-defined functions. Throughout history the way in which computers compute has changed as technology changed. Wilhelm Schickard (1592–1635) built the first automatic calculator in 1623. His machine could add and subtract six digit numbers and indicated overflow by ringing a bell. Blaise Pascal (1623–1662), a French philosopher, physicist, and mathematician built the second, starting in 1642. His machines, of which some 50 were built, became known as Pascalines. They were designed to help calculate taxes and operated by the turning of metal dials. Because the gears that performed the calculations could not go backwards, subtraction could only be determined indirectly. The first mechanical calculator capable of multiplication and division is attributed to the German philosopher, scientist, and mathematician Gottfried Leibniz (1646–1716), who, among other achievements, developed, along with Isaac Newton, modern calculus.

None of these machines was programmable. They could only perform built-in functions. It wouldn't be until some 200 years later that a programmable computer was developed that could be given specific instructions to follow. The English mathematician Charles Babbage (1791–1871) was the first to design such a machine, which he called the Analytical Engine. Babbage's Analytical Engine was meant to be a general purpose computer, meaning it could have computed a wide range of mathematical problems. It was to be powered by a steam engine and would have been over 90 feet long and over 30 feet wide. Data and programs were input to the machine in the form of punch cards. After performing its calculations, it produced output using a printer and curve plotter. The machine had a memory store capable of holding some 1,000 50 digit numbers. It even supported looping and conditional branching, two key features of modern day computers. A portion of the Analytical Engine was under construction at the time of Babbage's death.

The next major conceptual breakthrough in the development of computers came from George Boole (1815–1864). He devised a Boolean algebra in which decimal numbers could be broken down into a binary number system, consisting of just zeros and ones. This proved crucial for the later development of computers based on electricity. Electrical computers can use relays or switches that have two states, either on or off. These states can then be used to represent and compute numbers using Boolean algebra. Vacuum tubes were eventually used in place of relays starting in the 1940s because they are faster and more reliable.

Perhaps the greatest figure in the history of computer science was Alan Turing (1912–1954). He was a brilliant mathematician who assisted in cracking the German Enigma code during the Second World War. This was done with the aid of "Colossus," a vacuum tube computer built in Britain in 1943. Turing hypothesized that one could construct what has since become known as a **Turing machine**, a device capable of performing any computational process that can be performed. In other words, it can solve any problem capable of formal description, i.e., of being solved using an algorithm. Modern day serial computers are essentially Turing machines using a different architecture.

The first all electronic vacuum tube computer was the Electronic Numerical Integrator And Computer (ENIAC). The U.S. Army built it to calculate artillery trajectories. It was used more or less continuously for military and scientific computation from 1946 to 1955. The machine was a giant, requiring 17, 468 vacuum tubes and a large room to house it. The machine weighed 27 tons and consumed an enormous amount of electricity. This was followed with the first commercial computer made in the United States, the UNIVersal Automatic Computer (UNIVAC). Built in 1951, it is notable because it was the first computer designed specifically for business and administrative purposes.

The invention of the transistor in 1947 would revolutionize the computer industry once more. Transistors are capable of performing Boolean switching operations faster and more reliably than a vacuum tube. They are also much smaller, meaning computers could now be built that were the size of current desktop models. Further advances in electronics and circuit design brought the cost of computers down even further. This made them accessible to a general consumer audience and started their widespread use in society.

COMPUTERS AND INFORMATION PROCESSING

What makes a computer special is its ability to represent and process information. Computers can be programmed or given a set of well-defined instructions to follow. These instructions are known as an **algorithm**. When given the appropriate data as input, the computer can apply an algorithm to them to produce a recognizable output. In this way, computers can be used to perform tasks or solve problems. A very simple algorithm may take two numbers as input, sum them, and see if they are greater than 10. If they are, it will return the number 1 as output. If they aren't it will produce the number 0 as output.

Computers are at heart information processors. They represent and compute information. In representation, a piece of information is used to stand for some object or aspect of the external world. Representations can take many forms. They can be symbols like letters or numbers, or they can be images, like a picture of a sailboat. In computation, some process or transformation is applied to a representation. Two numbers could be multiplied together or the image of the sailboat could be moved from left to right. In these two cases, the computational processes would be arithmetic addition and spatial translation respectively.

There are two primary types of representation. In digital representations, information is coded in a discrete way with set values. Symbols are digital representations. The advantage of using symbols is that they specify values exactly. A number, for instance, can be accurate to as many decimal places as needed. Analog representations in contrast, represent information continuously. A mercury thermometer is an analog representation of temperature because changes in the height of the mercury bar correspond directly to changes in temperature. Analog representations can provide simple direct solutions to certain problems, like those involving spatial comparison.

BRAINS AND COMPUTERS: ARE THEY THE SAME?

In this section, we will compare and contrast brains and computers, highlighting their similarities and differences. After all, if want to build an artificial brain, we need to model it on the way we know human brains operate. Even if artificial brains ultimately end up radically different in design, an understanding of these two types of computing devices can provide us with some useful insights. We next evaluate brains and computers along several criteria.

Representation and Computation

To start, both brains and computers are information processors. There has been heated debate though over exactly what and how they perform computations. Some artificial intelligence researchers advocate the classic view that brains process symbols algorithmically as computers do. Others, especially those in the field of connectionism who study neural networks, argue that there are no symbols in the brain, only patterns of connection strengths between neuron-like elements. Processing is not the application of a formally specifiable algorithm, but the spreading of activity through the network.

One reason for believing in the symbol processing view comes from the amazing things that these systems can do. According to the **Symbol System Hypothesis**, any universal symbol system such as a computer can, with sufficient memory and internal reorganization, exhibit intelligence. It can sense and act effectively in a changing environment. Behaviorally, this is just what people do. The strong version of this hypothesis goes further and states that thoughts themselves are the result of symbol crunching and that any sophisticated computational device, human or otherwise, can give rise to thought. This is a reconceptualization of the functionalist idea presented earlier.

A way to reconcile these two views is to adopt a broader view of representation and computation. By stepping up one level of abstraction we can allow a symbol to mean any form of representation and computation to mean any type of processing. The strong symbol system hypothesis is a step in this direction. It makes no claim on architecture. As such it defines "symbol" broadly to include distributed representations like the pattern of weights in a neural network as well as the more local representations in computers.

Processing Style

The human brain employs a **parallel processing** or distributed computing style, where a task is performed by the simultaneous execution of multiple processors. For example, in human vision, unique aspects of the visual scene are broken down and processed separately by distinct brain regions. One area processes color, another form, and yet another motion. The results of all these computations can then be integrated or evaluated at some later stage. This makes sense when we think of the brain's architecture, which is a network of billions of neurons. Each neuron or collection of neurons can act as a processing element performing some specific task. Separate aspects of a computationally intensive problem like object identification can thus be broken up and assigned to multiple specialized processors. This distributes the workload and accelerates the time it takes to perform the task.

Most contemporary computers are **serial processors**. They process information one step at a time. In this type of architecture, one instruction gets carried out before another can begin. Information is fed to one processor, which performs its computation. The result of this computation then serves as the input to the next processor and so on in a linear fashion. In performing a mathematical operation, a desktop computer would need to execute each step in the process one at a time. Having stated this, it is possible to build parallel processing computers that mimic brain function. These are discussed below. Figure 2.4 depicts examples of both parallel and serial processing architectures.

Speed and Accuracy

You might think that a parallel processing style would always solve a problem more rapidly. But this isn't always true. For one thing, it depends upon the actual speed of processing. A fast serial processor could solve a problem more quickly than a slow parallel processor. It

Parallel processing architecture

Processing Unit

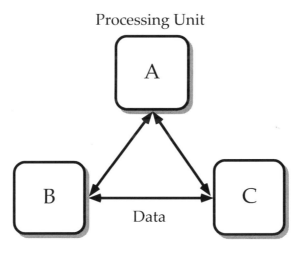

Serial processing architecture

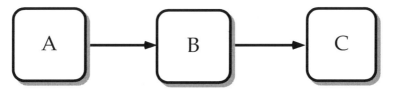

Figure 2.4 Parallel and serial information-processing architectures. Boxes indicate modules or places where computations take place. Arrows indicate the flow of information as inputs and outputs between modules.

really depends on the speed with which those steps can get executed. Human neurons are limited to firing or sending off an electrical signal at about one thousand times a second. Modern computer chips are much faster, capable of 10^9 operations within the same time frame. However, if one takes into account the total number of neurons and multiplies them by their firing rate, the brain has the edge, with 10^{16} computations per second.

Computers differ from brains in their accuracy as well as speed. In his classical 1958 paper *The Computer and the Brain*, John von Neumann compares the two. He finds that computers, even those in use nearly half a century ago, can represent and use variables with up to twelve decimal places of accuracy. The neuron is limited to about only two decimal places of accuracy. This is especially troubling for extended computations, because small errors made early on can become magnified in later steps. Perhaps the reason the brain performs its wonders without this kind of accuracy is that it relies primarily on analog representations or on nonnumerical symbolic representations.

Tasks and Strategy

Brains and computers also vary in terms of the kinds of task they are good at. In **ill-defined tasks,** there is no single best solution. The problem scenario is ambiguous and doesn't lend itself well to a precise formal description. In these situations, there may be several alternate solutions, some of equal effectiveness. Driving a taxi cab is an instance of an ill-defined task, since there is usually more than one way to get to a destination or to avoid traffic jams. On the other hand, a **well-defined task** is one that can be described formally. Here, a precise set of instructions can be given which if followed provides a solution. Mathematical problems are well defined. Computers excel at these sorts of tasks and are, typically, faster and more accurate at them than people. In the intelligence chapter, we more fully specify the types of environments that AI systems are good at handling.

These two sorts of tasks lend themselves well to different strategies. An ill-defined task is often best solved by the use of a **heuristic**, which is a simple rule of thumb that doesn't always guarantee a correct solution, but works well under most circumstances. In contrast, well-defined tasks are best solved using algorithms. The correct execution of an appropriate algorithm will always result in a correct solution. Humans typically use heuristics while computers typically use algorithms. To illustrate, imagine that you have misplaced your sunglasses. You know that they are in your house, but you aren't sure exactly where. You would probably employ the heuristic of looking first in places that you think you may have left them, such as on your desk or near the door. A computer could instead employ a search algorithm by systematically scanning every possible location in every room until they were located. It should be noted that a heuristic is a kind of algorithm and, as such, can be specified so that it can be run on a computer. Heuristics are thus computable. We talk more about how computers may employ heuristics in the section on search in the intelligence chapter.

World Knowledge

The above example illustrates another difference between brains and computers. People have over their lifetimes acquired extensive world knowledge. We know, based on experience, where we may have placed our sunglasses. We also know something about sunglasses and about the world that additionally specifies likely places to look. For instance, it is unlikely that we would have placed them in the toilet or the kitchen cupboard. This is because we know that other things go into these sorts of containers. In order for a computer to reason this way, it must have an extensive **knowledge base** that includes general information about the world. In this case that would include an understanding of common household objects and their function.

The advantage of a knowledge base is that it can provide its user with commonsense knowledge. **Commonsense knowledge** is information about the world that seems obvious when explicitly stated. Examples include knowing that chairs have four legs and are used for sitting or that bicycles are used for getting people from one place to another. An artificial person would need to draw on commonsense in order to move around and use objects. Dreyfus (1992) doubts whether computers can ever effectively use commonsense. He argues that commonsense knowledge is so great that it cannot be adequately encoded into a knowledge base. He also points out that in a database of sufficient size, it is difficult to efficiently search and access information. However, knowledge bases have already been built into some computer systems that are able to use them successfully. We extend our discussion of them in the chapter on learning and memory.

In summary, many of the supposed differences between brains and computers are really not such big differences after all. Both are information processors, capable of maintaining representations and performing computations on them. Both can employ a parallel processing style. Computers are faster and more mathematically accurate than brains. Currently, this speed difference is compensated for in brains by their greater parallel processing ability, while the accuracy difference may be due to the brain's reliance on nonnumerical forms of representation. Traditionally, computers have lagged behind brains in dealing with ill-defined tasks, but the use of heuristics shows that they can also cope with these scenarios. Computers can additionally be given world knowledge in the form of a knowledge base, which enables them to deal more effectively with complex real-world situations.

BUILDING AN ARTIFICIAL BRAIN

The Serial Digital Computer

Contemporary digital computers have architecture that bears some similarity to certain brain functions (Figure 2.5). The **Central Processing Unit**, or CPU, is the part of a computer that carries out instructions and controls the order in which they get executed. The CPU might divide two numbers or test the truth or falsity of a statement. It operates in a serial fashion, executing one instruction after another. There is no precise equivalent of the CPU in the human brain. We have no centralized area where all decisions get made. The frontal lobes of the cerebral cortex might come the closest, since damage to these areas results in disorders where patients have trouble initiating, terminating, or planning actions. But the brain can better be characterized as decentralized, with multiple decision making centers spread throughout different regions. The interplay between these areas also accounts for our behavior.

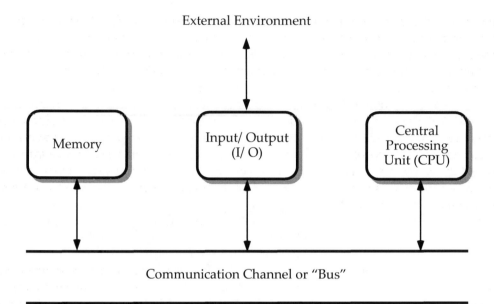

Figure 2.5 The basic functional hardware of most modern computers consists of memory, input-output devices, and a central processing unit that share a common communication bus. This is also known as a Von Neumann architecture.

Memory is the second major component of the modern computer. It is here that instructions, partial and final results are stored. Computers have both a short-term or main memory containing information that needs to be accessed and used immediately. This data is stored on a rewritable chip. They also have a long-term memory for storage of information not necessary for immediate use. This data is typically stored on a "hard drive" or disk. People also have the equivalent of short- and long term-memory. Short-term or working memory in humans serves essentially the same function as in computers. It is the place where information concerning our current thoughts reside. There are multiple brain areas underlying different aspects of working memory, including the prefrontal cortex and posterior parietal cortex. The human brain additionally has a long-term memory, also used for more permanent storage. Some of the areas involved in long-term memory processing in the human brain are the hippocampus, limbic cortex, and basal ganglia.

The **input/output (I/O) devices** refer to the hardware and software that enables the computer to interact with the external world. Input devices that get information into the computer include a keyboard and mouse. Output devices that present information out from it include a monitor or printer. The human equivalent of the I/O devices would be the perceptual and motor systems. The eye and optic nerves supply the brain with visual information. The pyramidal tract carries voluntary motor output from the cerebral cortex.

The final major element of the modern computer is the **communication bus**. This pathway allows information to be transmitted between the three previously mentioned items. Instructions that don't need to be executed right away may pass along the bus from the CPU to memory and, at some point later in time, back again. Data from the keyboard or mouse passes through the bus, as does information that needs to be displayed to the monitor. In humans the nearest equivalent to the bus would be nerve tracts. These are bundles of individual nerve fibers that carry information from one brain area to another. The corpus callosum is an example of a nerve tract that shuttles information back and forth between the left and right hemispheres.

It is important to note that similarities between this basic computer architecture and the brain are at a fairly abstract level of description. A computer memory bears little actual physical resemblance either in structure or operation to the brain structures underlying human memory. But the presence of such a device in both natural and artificial information processors bears testimony to its importance. The same is true for all of these components. Apparently, any information processor that must interact with an environment must use some incarnation of these devices.

PARALLEL DISTRIBUTED PROCESSING

Our discussion so far has been about the organization of the typical modern computer. But what if we wanted to design a computer that deliberately mimicked human brain function? Parallel processing is such an important aspect of the way human brains work that any artificial person would need to operate on this principle. There are several ways that one can build a computer to approximate the distributed computing of human brains. First, we can simulate parallel processing on a serial computer. This is the approach taken with artificial neural networks. Second, we can build a machine with a truly parallel architecture. Third, we could link many serial computers together in a network configuration. Researchers in the field of distributed AI use these last two options. Let's examine each possibility.

Artificial Neural Networks

Artificial neural networks are a software implementation of parallel processing (Gurney, 1997). They rely on instructions that simulate this processing style, but the software itself is running on the hardware of a serial computer of the sort described above. Nodes and links characterize these networks. A node is a basic computing unit modeled after neurons, while links are the connections between them. Nodes follow decision rules and will "fire" if the activation they receive from other nodes exceeds a preset threshold. Links between nodes have weights that specify the strength of the connection. Generally, weights run between zero and one, with larger values signifying a stronger connection. If a node is activated, the strength of its signal is multiplied by the weight of the links it travels across. These new values now serve as inputs to other nodes.

A **perceptron** network was one of the earliest artificial networks and usually consisted of a single layer of nodes. It was designed to recognize patterns. Later networks were organized into more layers. For instance, they might have an input layer, hidden layer, and output layer (Figure 2.6). Links connect nodes within and between layers. In a typical network of this sort, a stimulus would activate nodes in the input layer that would then activate nodes in the hidden layer. These nodes, in turn, would stimulate output layer nodes. The output activation pattern corresponds to the network's response to a stimulus.

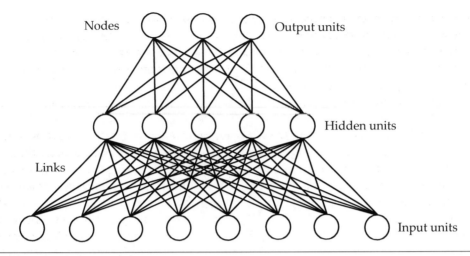

Figure 2.6 An example of a three-layer artificial neural network.

The beauty of artificial neural networks is that they can learn. They are capable of altering their behavior over time to respond in a desired way. Please see the chapter on learning and memory to discover more about how artificial neural networks learn.

Another interesting feature of these networks is in the way they represent and compute information. Serial computers use localized symbols and apply operators to those symbols to compute. Networks use distributed representations. Information is coded in a pattern of weights on links spread throughout the net. Computations correspond to the activation and alteration of these weights. This more closely resembles the way brains work.

So, the advantage of artificial neural networks is that they are biologically plausible. In terms of their structure and function, they are more similar to human brains than the serial computer architecture. However, they have failed in some ways to live up to the initial hype that surrounded them. Currently, we can only construct artificial neural networks with a limited number of nodes and links, not even close to what we see in biological brains. Also, the activity in these networks dies down over time as the network settles on a stable configuration. Biological networks show oscillatory and chaotic action; their behavior fails to settle down over time.

Parallel Computing

Parallel computing is the simultaneous execution of the same task on multiple processors in order to obtain faster results. Each individual processor in a computer of this type is a CPU of the sort introduced earlier. Systems with large numbers of such processors, the human brain included, are called massively parallel. The majority of recent supercomputers, those that are the fastest in the world at the time of their introduction, use parallel computing architectures. Many home computers now employ multicore microprocessors that significantly speed up computation.

Japan's Ministry of International Trade and Industry began work in 1982 on what it called the Fifth Generation Computer System. Five individual machines were built that ran concurrently through a parallel interface. They utilized a specialized parallel hardware and operating system. Several applications ran on the system, including database management, legal reasoning, and theorem-prover programs. Developments in CPU and software performance made the project obsolete, but it demonstrated the possibility of constructing a hardware version of a highly parallel computing system.

A few words are in order on processing speed. Doubling the number of processors does not necessarily double the speed with which a task gets executed. It depends on the nature of the task. To illustrate, digging a ditch is a task that can benefit tremendously from multiple processors, 100 men digging a ditch can complete the task 100 times faster than one man alone. But automobile assembly may only reap a partial benefit because the execution of one task is often dependent upon the results of another. The worker who attaches the wheels to the axle must wait for the axel to be completed. Prior to this, the worker who completed the axle might have had to wait for the completion of the chassis, and so on. Parallel processors thus benefit parallel tasks, those with few processing interdependencies, the most. Ways around this problem include rewriting algorithms to make them less sequential and load balancing, where processors are kept busy by moving tasks from those that are heavily loaded to those that are less so.

Multi-Computer Systems

In parallel computing, multiple processors or CPUs within a single computer distribute the workload and reduce execution time. In **multi-computer systems** or grid computing this principle is employed on a larger scale. Here, computers that are physically separated from each other are connected together in a network configuration and exchange information. The World Wide Web is an example of a multi-computer system made up of widely separated heterogeneous computers that access and share data. Although the individual computers connected to the Web may differ in their hardware, they can each display and send content to one another using a common protocol. Researchers have also used clusters of computers wired together to solve problems.

Distributed Artificial Intelligence

Distributed artificial intelligence (DAI) is a subfield of AI that develops solutions to complex problems not easily solved using the traditional algorithmic approach. A full definition and discussion of this area is given in the chapter on social behavior. DAI researchers employ both parallel computing and multi-computer system techniques. One of the hallmarks of this approach is the use of multiple interacting agents. An **agent** is defined as an autonomous entity that can receive information about its environment, process and then act on it. In DAI systems, agents exchange information with each other in much the same way people do in a society. In cooperative systems agents all have the same goals but may do different things in order to fulfill them. In noncooperative systems agents can have different goals. They may cooperate but only when its serves their own "self-interest."

Multi-agent systems like these make decisions and solve problems in a decentralized way. The overall behavior of the system, and not the action of any single constituent, agent produces the solution. Notice this is in stark contrast to the centralized decision making of the serial computer, where the CPU has the ultimate say. Multi-agent systems don't follow a set algorithm. In some cases it may be difficult to even understand how they have arrived at a solution. The behavior of some DAI systems can be **emergent**. An emergent property is a global characteristic of a system not shared by any of the local entities or agents making it up. It cannot be easily explained or predicted by their behavior. In contrast, according to **reductionism**, one can explain the overall behavior of a system simply by explaining the actions of its parts. Many important properties of mind, like consciousness, seem to be an emergent property of the brain where neurons or neural systems are the agents. We talk more about emergence in the chapter on consciousness.

CAN WE BUILD IT?

The Brain Perspective

Is it possible to build an artificial human brain? At the current level of technology, the answer would have to be no. It is just not possible now to reproduce the functional equivalent of one hundred billion (10^{14}) neurons with their 10,000 or so connections. Even reproducing the decision-making capability of a single neuron is difficult because of the many complex molecular actions that occur. The sheer number of cells and their interconnections in a complete brain is just too complex to reproduce completely at this time. Keep in mind that this idea is reductionistic. By reproducing exactly the way the brain's parts work, it is hoped that we can reproduce the behavior of the brain itself.

A barrier to creating a brain in totality is that we don't yet have the equivalent of a wiring diagram for it. This diagram would specify every neuron and each of its connections. Having this knowledge would yield key insights into function because we could see the anatomical structure underlying various circuits. In the future, researchers could use a microscopic scanner to produce a comprehensive three-dimensional brain map. This kind of undertaking may take many years to complete, and be akin to the human genome project (Kurzweil, 1999). This is a reverse engineering approach, where engineers figure out how something works by taking it apart and then reconstructing it.

Anatomy and physiology go together like hand and glove. Knowing neural structure at a microscopic level must be supplemented by the study of physiology at the same level. This would require a device that could measure individual neuronal activity. Investigators are now using a technique called **magnetoencephalography** (MEG) to measure the small changes in magnetic fields that occur when neurons fire (Schwartz, 1999). MEG has both fine spatial and temporal resolution, being able to measure the activity of neurons in a region as small as a millimeter and over times as fast as several milliseconds. The technique is noninvasive. The patient wears a helmet filled with an array of super-cooled magnetic detectors. Data are then converted to a three-dimensional static or moving image showing the precise location of activity. Although MEG is not yet capable of individual neuron resolution, the technology to achieve this looks promising.

Even if we could artificially reproduce all brain activity, the possibility exists that this would still not be enough to give rise to mind. Although we might be able to replicate all the information processing capabilities of the brain, we still might be left with a "zombie" or artificial person who might have cognitive function, but no consciousness. Let's consider several objections then. First, mind may require a brain that is embedded, one that is in a body and experiences a world. If this were the case, the artificial brain would need to be inside an artificial body and develop over time with the world, just as we do.

Second, it could be that reproducing neuron level functioning is not sufficient for mind, it might require engineering on an even smaller scale. In this scenario, we would have to reproduce not just the functioning of neurons but of synapses and other events inside neurons. Whether there is a limit to this reduction is unclear. Recent advances in nanotechnology and molecular computing show we are becoming more and more adept at small-scale construction.

The third objection comes from the philosopher John Searle. He says that mind cannot be reduced to the mechanistic operation of small elements like neurons. Instead, the mind is an emergent feature of the brain, caused by the complex interaction and relationships among its parts (Searle, 1992). Just as the function of a stomach is to digest, Searle remarks that the function of a brain is to be conscious. By implication, this suggests that artificial attempts at creating a brain will fail because there is something special about the way biological brains operate that gives rise to mindfulness. This view is called **biological naturalism**. A functionalist would counter that there is, in fact, nothing special or privileged about biological brains. Reproducing the way they operate at a sufficient level of complexity is enough to create their higher-order properties.

The Computer Perspective

Recall from chapter 1 Gödel's Incompleteness Theorem that says that any formal system like logic or mathematics will always be unable to prove a particular proposition true or false. Take the following proposition: "This sentence is false." If it is true, then it must be false. However, if it is false, then it must also be true since a proposition can either be only true or false and nothing else. A computer following the laws of logic can't handle this statement. However, people don't seem to have much of a problem accepting indeterminant states of this sort. This suggests that computers that use formal systems to generate and evaluate expressions are fundamentally limited and incapable of human comprehension.

Marvin Minsky, co-founder of the AI laboratory at M.I.T., has a response to this. He says that we can program computers any way we want. They need not follow the rules of formal systems and thus be subject to the incompleteness paradox. We could model computers using some of the other less specifiable ways people think, adding heuristics, guessing, and creative processes to the list of what computers can do. These processes can be modeled with the help of random number generators that introduce an element of uncertainty into the computation. Minsky believes the noncomputability argument is false in its assumption that thinking has to be computable in the formal sense. Some aspects of human thought may be described formally, others may not, but this doesn't preclude them from being implemented in a machine.

Futurists usually underestimate the time it takes for things to happen. Early AI researchers were no exception. They were excessively enthusiastic about the potential of the field. They made bold claims, often in front of reporters, about computer programs that could fluidly comprehend and produce language, drive cars, and solve complex problems in law, commerce, and medicine. All of these abilities, it seemed were "right around the corner" and would be built in just a few years time. Although many of these claims may come to fruition in the years ahead, it will apparently take longer than initially realized. The failure of AI to live up to such proclamations led a number of critics to point out that computers are fundamentally limited and will never be able to do some of the things we can. One such critic is Hubert Dreyfus. In his 1972 book *What Computers Can't Do*, he points out four human cognitive abilities that he says computers will never be able to emulate. Let's take a moment to examine and evaluate each of them.

Fringe Consciousness

Computers are only able to focus on a limited aspect of a situation. Unlike people, they cannot take into account the context or background in which events occur. This fringe consciousness is useful because it helps us determine the best way to solve a problem. In chess, expert players don't consider the position of each position in isolation (Newell & Simon 1972). Based on past experience they instead see the entire configuration of the board as a **gestalt**. The concept of a gestalt is similar to that of an emergent property. It is a holistic perception or thought where the whole is greater than the sum of its parts. The recognition of gestalt patterns guides experts into selecting the right move from among the vast number of potential moves. For example, they may recognize in their peripheral attention a cluster of pieces surrounding the Queen that reminds them of a move they used in a previous game. Computers, instead, treat each board position as completely new and then attempt to search heuristically through the space of possible moves. The use of heuristics reduces the total number of potential solutions a computer must look through, but is still less effective than relying on experience.

The solution to this is to introduce peripheral or situational awareness in a computer so it too can recognize and learn from its past experiences. This would require the computer to form gestalts. Gestalt programming means the computer must capitalize on the relationships between parts and be able to group them into wholes. It also requires that it associate gestalts with their successes, i.e., know which ones worked and which ones did not so that it could draw on these in the future when needed. This programming can be implemented in a machine based on existing rules of perception and learning.

Ambiguity Tolerance

Another supposed computer deficiency is the inability to deal with ambiguous situations. Computers need to be told exactly and precisely what to do. Humans though, can tolerate ambiguity. We can use context to make sense of information that is not fully specified. Take for instance the sentence "Do you know what time it is?" A computer would respond to this by responding "yes" if it knew or "no" if it did not. A person would evaluate the sentence according to the situation. If at a bus stop, they would respond by stating the actual time, since they would correctly interpret this as an inquiry about the bus schedule. If they were very late for an important meeting, they might say nothing, since this would be a rebuke for their delayed arrival.

The ability to cope effectively with ambiguity requires situational awareness or knowledge of the context in which an event occurs. The presence of a knowledge database provides this because it contains information about the world and how one should act in it. This means a computer must through experience or programming, acquire general information about the world. They can then apply this experience to disambiguate uncertain situations. The use of pragmatics along with context can facilitate language comprehension. **Pragmatics** are the social rules underlying language use. They include the strategies speakers use to make themselves clear. For example, a person stating, "It is cold in here" is using an assertive by stating their belief, while someone saying, "Turn on the heat" is issuing a directive which requires action. There are several different types of speech, each implying a different response from the listener (Searle, 1979). A computer with knowledge of these types and of what is going on around it could make the appropriate response.

Essential/Inessential Discrimination

Problem-solving algorithms typically begin with a start state that is the problem itself and terminate with an end or goal state, which is the solution. To obtain a solution requires the formation of subgoals that are intermediary states that lead to the goal and the application of operators to achieve them. This form of problem solving is called **means-end analysis**. But how does one select these subgoals and operators? In other words, how does one know where to even begin? In well-structured problems there are a fairly limited number of operators. Under these conditions, a program can use a trial and error procedure where it keeps applying different operators until it finds one that succeeds. For example, if the ultimate goal is to stack three colored blocks on top of one another in a certain order, a computer program can try all the various combinations that places block B on top of block A and then all the remaining combinations that places block C on top of B.

The difficulty with this is that in some well-defined situations and especially in ill-defined situations, one does not know what the subgoals are. In these situations, people make crucial discriminations that allow them to pursue a proper solution path and to ignore others. In logic problems, we may realize that we can ignore certain differences between logical connectives or the order of symbols. This insight or intuition simplifies the problem and makes it tractable. Our ability to make these kinds of discriminations again comes from previous experience. Once more, this means getting computers to learn from and apply their past like people do. One way is to have computers notice the similarities between a current problem and a previous one like it. They can then apply the old strategy to see if it works. This is what happens when people reason using metaphors or analogies, which can be useful in problem solving (Gick and Holyoak, 1980).

Perspicuous Grouping

Dreyfus concludes by noting that the computers of his day have difficulty in recognizing patterns because they define objects as a feature list, i.e., a banana is yellow, curved, a certain size, etc. Identifying a banana or discriminating it from other fruit then requires an exhaustive search through a feature list and a comparison against other such lists. People, though, seem to recognize objects by grasping invariant features, things that don't change under different viewing conditions. The size, shape, and color of a banana could all differ depending on changes in distance, perspective, and lighting. Rather, we seem to ignore these differences, treating them as noise. Human perception, Dreyfus notes, is a combination of the previous three principles. It involves fringe awareness, ambiguity tolerance, and discrimination. He calls this combination perspicuous grouping.

Tremendous progress has been made in the area of visual pattern recognition since the 1970s. We now have at our disposal a number of algorithms that allow computers to do a much better job at recognizing objects. These include computational, feature integration, and recognition-by-components models (Goldstein, 2002). Calculating an object-centered description defined by invariant features such as elongation and symmetry axes can help with the invariance problem. Processing and using regions of the visual field that surround an individual object can also clarify the identity of an ambiguous object.

3

PERCEPTION AND ACTION

I like things to happen; and if they don't happen, I like to make them happen.

—**Winston Churchill, 1959**

This chapter is on perceiving and acting in the world. First, we will see that it is possible to construct artificial versions for each of the human senses. We will also see technological equivalents for the major structures involved in any action, including muscles and specific limbs like arms, hands, and legs. For both the perceptual mechanisms and the motor structures, there are purely robotic creations and prosthetics that can be attached to a person. Following this, we will examine the basic categories of human action including navigation, reaching, grasping, and locomotion. When we decompose and formalize these actions we will see that they are really quite complex. But research on them has helped us to understand how they are executed in a person and how they may be reproduced.

A common theme running through many of these topics is that the dividing line between the natural and the artificial is blurring. It is no longer quite clear where one ends and the other begins. Sensors and effectors can be biological or technological. Electronics can control physiological functioning and vice versa. From an operational and control perspective, there is little difference between them. If technology can someday produce a perfect artificial working version of a hand that you could feel and control in every way like the one you were born with, would you conclude that it is in any way different from the one you possess now? Would you come to regard this hand as a natural part of you? The future may hold the answer to these questions.

PERCEPTUAL MECHANISMS

Perception is the process by which we take in and process information about an environment. Obviously, perception is a crucial function for any animal. Humans possess a number of different senses. We can see, hear, touch, smell, and taste. In addition, we have sensory systems that monitor the internal state of our bodies. Proprioception is an instance of internal perception. It is an awareness of our body's position in space and is provided by sensory neurons in the inner ear and in the joints and muscles. Machines such as robots can have the equivalent of these human senses. For instance, they can be provided with two video cameras for binocular vision or auditory sensors that pick up and process sound information. In addition, machines can be given sensors that humans lack, such as lasers, infrared, and sonar.

In this section, we examine selected aspects of the five human senses and summarize recent attempts to construct artificial versions of each. We begin with a discussion of computer vision because more research has been done on human vision and on computer modeling of human vision than on any of the other senses.

HUMAN AND COMPUTER VISION

Sight is the sense we humans rely upon the most. There has been extensive research done on the science of human vision. There has also been a great deal of work in the field of machine and artificial vision systems. We could devote several books to these topics, so in this section we merely scratch the surface, summarizing some of the major aspects of vision along with recent technological products.

Human vision can be considered as a set of different abilities. Our visual systems allow us to process various aspects of the world we see. First and foremost, what we see when we open our eyes are objects. We can make out things like our friend's face, buildings, and trees. Each is defined by differences in brightness that we resolve as edges or contours. The ability to do this and to meaningfully interpret what we see is known as **object recognition**. A number of computer programs exist that can recognize objects and that have overcome the invariance problem discussed in the previous chapter.

One type of object important to us is the human face. The ability to locate and recognize faces is fundamental to social interaction. Machines are also now getting quite good at visual face processing. Researchers at Carnegie Mellon University have developed an artificial neural network system that can detect faces in a cluttered background like a crowd. The program was trained by having it scan thousands of still images. At optimal performance, the network could locate faces with 90% accuracy (Rowley, Baluja, & Kanade, 1998). Other systems can recognize faces by matching a single stimulus image of a full frontal view to one of many thousands or more possible face images stored in a database. A recent test of these systems by U.S. Government agencies found they were reliable over 80% of the time and could even, in many cases, identify a face when it was seen from a profile or angled perspective.

Other aspects of human vision include color, depth, and motion perception. Color is important when making fine level discriminations between objects, like telling the difference between two types of apple. Color sensing can be added to the grayscale capacity of many robotic vision systems. Because we live in a 3-D world we need to know how far away objects are. Depth perception is key to obstacle avoidance and navigation as discussed elsewhere in this chapter. Depth sensing can be provided by stereoscopic vision, where the image disparity between two cameras spaced apart indicates object distance.

It can also be provided by range sensing devices that bounce a laser or sonar signal off an object and record reflection time. Motion perception is another important visual ability. Moving objects tell us how quickly and in what direction we are heading and assist us in maintaining balance. Movement sensors and motion processing algorithms have also been incorporated into machine vision systems.

ARTIFICIAL EYES

Vision in a healthy adult is the product of light reflecting from surfaces in the environment. This image is focused by the eye onto the retina, a layer of photoreceptors located on the inside of the back of each eye. The pattern of retinal stimulation indicates the distribution of light intensities in the image, in essence capturing a "snapshot" of the visual scene. This information is then passed along the optic nerve to brain areas like the visual cortex in the occipital lobe that process it further allowing sight. However, in some patients, the retina degenerates, resulting in visual impairments and blindness.

There is exciting new work in creating prosthetic vision systems that can now aid those with these types of visual problems. Mark Humayun at the University of Southern California has developed such a system (Weiland & Humayun, 2005). It consists of a small lightweight video camera mounted on a pair of glasses. The images picked up by the camera are transmitted wirelessly to a receiver hidden behind the patient's ear. From there, they are sent to an electrode array implanted in the retina. The electrodes stimulate the retina in much the same way as a pattern of light from a real image would. These messages are then sent back to the brain by the intact optic nerve recreating some aspects of normal vision. Clinical trials show that patients who were severely blind could now tell the difference between shapes like a cup, plate, or knife, and could detect large moving objects in their visual field.

Alternative approaches involve implanting light sensitive chips directly into the eye, obviating the need for cameras. The Optobionics Corporation has created an Artificial Silicon Retina (ASR) that directly stimulates retinal neurons. Their ASR is 2 mm in diameter and thinner than a strand of hair. It is powered entirely by light and requires no batteries or external power source. It has already been implanted in several patients who reported improvements in perception of brightness, contrast, color, motion, and size (Chow et al., 2004).

Rather than supplement an existing retina by electrode stimulation, investigators at the University of Pennsylvania have gone one step further and created an artificial retina that may one day completely replace their natural cousins (Zaghloul & Boahen, 2004). It is made of transistors on a silicon chip that reproduce the way the retinal cell layers operate.

In some patients, retinal implants or artificial retinas are not possible. They have damage to the "front end" of their visual system. Injury to the eye, retina, or optic nerve in these cases precludes retinal stimulation as a way of restoring vision. This means the visual cortex itself needs to be stimulated and the researcher William Dobelle has in fact already done this (Kotler, 2002). His apparatus consists of cameras attached to eyeglasses that feed to a belt-mounted signal processor. The processor converts the image into messages the brain can understand. These are transmitted through cables directly to a cortical implant that stimulates neurons in the brain's primary visual center. One patient who had been blind in both eyes for many years could perceive the world accurately enough with this prosthetic to drive a car around a parking lot. This approach has great potential for those with normal vision, as any type of visual input such as Internet or cable television content could be fed to and interpreted by the brain.

ARTIFICIAL EARS

Prosthetic ears in the form of cochlear implants have been around for quite some time now (Clark, 2003). These devices work on much the same principle as retinal implants. They use sound information to stimulate neurons representing different kinds of sounds. The cochlea is a curled, fluid-filled structure located in the inner ear. Different areas of the cochlea contain neurons that code for distinct frequencies. Sound vibrations in the air induce a wave to travel through the cochlear fluid. This wave will maximally stimulate the cochlear region corresponding to its largest frequency component. High frequency sounds produce a peak wave and greatest neural stimulation close to where the cochlea starts. The waves from low frequency sounds peak later, closer to where it ends. The cochlea is thus somewhat like a piano keyboard, where sounds "play" the keyboard to produce our perception.

Cochlear implants are used in patients who have suffered damage to the hair cells that stimulate cochlear neurons. The device consists of a number of parts. A microphone behind the ear picks up sounds and transmits this information to an external processor. The processor amplifies, filters out noise, and converts the sound into an electronic signal. This signal is then broadcast as radio waves to an internal receiver located under the skin. The receiver transmits the signal along wires to a tube inside the cochlea. The tube stimulates the different cochlear regions corresponding to the frequency characteristics of the sound. In this way, the implant mimics the way the ear would normally process sound.

Cochlear implants have restored hearing to those with full or partial deafness. However, the success of the procedure depends on a number of factors such as the duration and age of deafness onset in the patient, how long the implant is used, and the extent of initial damage. The quality of hearing from these devices is also less than optimal. Some patients report speech as sounding disconnected and artificial. Future models may eliminate this by increasing the number of stimulated regions and adding more sophisticated processing algorithms.

Another aspect of hearing is sound localization, the ability to determine where in space a sound originates. We do this by comparing the arrival time of sounds to either ear. If a sound hits our left ear before our right, then it is on our left side. If a sound arrives at both ears at roughly the same time, then it is located directly in front or behind us. This is why our two ears are separated and located on either side of our head. Localization is important because it allows us to orient toward and deal with objects in the environment that have survival significance such as other people.

Binaural machine hearing operates on this same principle. Here, two transducers located a minimum distance apart on a robotic head determine the direction from which acoustic waves are coming. They do this by comparing the relative lag times and/or loudness of the incoming sound. If the system is confused, the robot can move its head to obtain a meaningful bearing. Some robotic toy dogs on the market have this capability, allowing them to orient to the voice of their owners.

ARTIFICIAL NOSES AND TONGUES

We will consider olfaction and gustation, the perception of smell and taste, together. There are several reasons for this (Goldstein, 2002). Both are molecule detectors. Olfaction involves the detection of gaseous molecules in the air, while gustation involves the detection of liquid molecules in food. Smell and taste serve a "gatekeeper" function. They inform us about compounds we are about to take into our bodies and can warn us of potentially dangerous agents like smoke or poisonous food. The two also work together to determine our sense of flavor. This is why the nose is located above our mouth. The nose can immediately pick up gaseous molecules wafting off of food or released by chewing. If you ever doubt the role of smell in flavor, try eating something with your nose pinched shut.

Olfactory and gustatory mechanisms bear some similarities. Our ability to smell the wonderful scent of a grilling steak or a rose is the consequence of odorant molecules activating a sensory surface called the olfactory mucosa located on the ceiling of our nasal cavity. Ultimately, any given odor stimulates a pattern of activity among a number of olfactory receptor neurons in the mucosa. These neurons project to the olfactory bulb and then to other brain areas for further processing resulting in our perception of smell.

Taste occurs when liquid molecules activate taste cells located in taste buds on the tongue. There are four basic types of receptor on taste cells, corresponding to the basic taste sensations of bitter, sweet, sour, and salt. Molecules from substances with these tastes activate each of the individual receptor types. The consequent messages sent upstream to brain areas for processing produce our perception of taste.

An electronic, or "E-nose" is built on the same general principles as a biological nose. Pumps suck an odorant-containing vapor over a sensor array that reacts differently to different odors, in effect producing a unique "signature" response to each smell. This activation pattern is then fed to a computer that performs the recognition. Funded by the California Institute of Technology, Cyrano Sciences, Inc. has commercialized the Cyrano 320, a portable handheld odor detector. It has an array with 32 receptors made up of a polymer. When odorant molecules come into contact with the polymer, they expand, altering its electrical resistance. Different odors cause the polymer to expand by differing amounts. This alters the overall conductivity pattern of the chip, producing a unique pattern for any given odor.

There are many other examples of electronic noses (Aylett, 2002). Researchers from the University of Pisa in Italy have developed an artificial olfactory system for detecting olive oil aromas and for monitoring lab environments "Smelly," a small mobile robot from the University of Portsmouth in England draws in odors through two tubes connected to small pumps, effectively "sniffing" the air around it. Joseph Ayer has created a "RoboLobster" with sensors on its top. It is designed to study how biological lobsters locate their prey by following chemical plumes along the sea bottom.

Most E-noses serve the same general gatekeeper function as real noses. Security personnel use them to identify explosives in luggage. The food industry employs them to detect spoilage, for example, whether mayonnaise or wine has become rancid. E-noses can be more sensitive than the human nose to certain compounds, although current models suffer from certain drawbacks. They are sensitive to moisture and when sensors burn out and are replaced, they lose their memory of previously learned odors (Ouellette, 1999).

University of Texas investigators are developing an electronic tongue that should be able to taste the differences in a variety of liquids. Their device is modeled almost exactly on the way human tongues work. It consists of an array of taste buds housed in pits on the surface of a silicon chip. Flavor molecules corresponding to tastes like bitter, sweet, sour, and salty attach to different buds and cause them to change color, again resulting in a coded signature pattern. The "E-tongue" is planned for beverage quality control but can be extended beyond human taste to analyze substances in blood or urine, or to test for the presence of poisons in water (Kellan, 1999).

ARTIFICIAL SKIN

Perhaps the sense most people think the least about is **somatosensation**. These are senses related to the body. Somatosensation includes information about the world conveyed to us by our skin as well as information about the position and movement of our limbs. These last two are referred to as proprioception and kinesthesis. The skin provides us with a wealth of data about the environment. We have pressure receptors there that enable us to tell us about an object's weight or roughness and so aid in our ability to manipulate. There are also sensory neurons for temperature and pain. These are crucial for survival, as we need to maintain a proper body temperature and avoid pain if we are to function properly. The proprioceptive and kinesthetic senses originate from receptors inside the body and are necessary for maintaining balance and moving around. Impulses from all these sensory neurons, whether from the skin or inside the body, pass to the spinal cord and brain, where they undergo further processing.

One approach to the creation of an artificial pressure sensor is to embed a polarized crystal between two membranes. When force is applied to the surface, the crystal inside bends and its electrical properties change. This is known as the piezoelectric effect. The greater the force applied the greater the change in electrical charge. This change is measured and indicative of the amount of applied pressure. Identification of an object can then proceed through a 2-D map of the conductive differences and how they change over time.

Researchers at the University of Tokyo have used a related technique (Sekitani, Iba, Kato, Kawaguci, & Sakurai, 2004). They created a flexible film or sensor skin with a half-millimeter-thick layer of rubber embedded with electrically conductive graphite particles. When the layer bends, its conductive properties alter and are processed by an array of cheap and easy to manufacture organic transistors. The film can be rolled around a narrow cylinder and serve as a robotic finger covering. It can also be placed in floors to identify people or sense when a hospital patient collapses.

Skin serves a number of purposes other than perception. It provides a protective covering that prevents damage to internal parts, regulates temperature, and keeps out bacteria. But to be effective at these tasks, a skin has to be able to repair itself. A team at the University of Illinois has produced a material that, like human skin, can repair itself when scraped or torn. The material is filled with small capsules of polymer building blocks and catalysts. When the material is damaged, the capsules rupture and release their contents that then bind the fractured areas together.

MOTOR MECHANISMS

Action, specifically **motor action**, refers to how an agent such as a person or robot interacts with or influences the world. In motor action, a command is given to move a limb such as an arm or leg. Sensory feedback produced by limb motion is then usually monitored continuously to provide the basis for further commands and adjustments. Robots can again be equipped with human effectors. A number of robots have been constructed that have arms and legs modeled after ours. But robots need not be limited to these and can drive all sorts of appendages, from claws and pincers to tracks and wheels.

Crucial to understanding this topic is the field of **prosthetics**, the study and construction of prostheses. A prosthesis is an artificial extension that replaces a missing part of the body. As mentioned, medical researchers have developed artificial retinas and cochlear implants as well as artificial limbs. Whereas robotic sensory and motor systems are purely mechanical creations that are no different than the rest of the robot, prostheses must be integrated into a living person, which effectively turn their users into cyborgs. Many of the latest creations are neural prostheses, which send and receive signals from the person's nervous system. Some prostheses also have on board computers and electronics to process sensory-motor information.

In this section, we now review selected aspects of human motor ability. The focus is on muscles, arms, hands, and legs. This is followed by a description of recent attempts to construct prosthetic and robotic equivalents of these structures. We then introduce the field of neural prosthetics that hints at how human biology and technology may some day merge.

ARTIFICIAL MUSCLES

Humans locomote and manipulate using skeletal muscle. Nervous impulses cause fibers in these muscles to contract. Because the muscle is connected at both ends, this shortening results in limb motion. As an illustration, contraction of the bicep pulls the forearm in toward the body. Muscles are a more reliable way of moving a body around. They have fewer moving parts than current mechanical solutions such as motors. Electric motors have a number of other limitations. They run best at a single speed and can burn out if overloaded. For this reason, researchers have been studying the way muscles work and attempting to engineer synthetic or artificial equivalents.

The McKibben artificial muscle was one of the earliest attempts and has been in use for several decades (Chou & Hannaford, 1996). It is driven by compressed air and follows the principles by which our own muscles work, contracting and expanding to move a limb. An internal bladder fills with air, causing it to shorten. When the pressure is reduced, it expands. Researchers at Carnegie Mellon University have constructed a human-like arm and hand using McKibben muscles that can grasp objects.

Other more recent innovations are the use of Shape Memory Allloys (SMA) in which an alloy is heated producing a contraction. Cooling causes it to expand back to its original configuration. There are also Electro-active Polymers (EAP). These are ribbons of carbon, fluorine, and oxygen molecules. Application of an electrical charge induces a shape deformation that can serve as the basis of an artificial muscle system.

At the Artificial Muscle Research Institute at the University of New Mexico, scientists have built a skeleton called "Myster Bony." Sitting atop an exercise bicycle, it uses its EAP leg muscles to pedal continuously under an external electrical supply source. Although experiments such as this show great promise, there are some obstacles to be overcome. One of the disadvantages of an EAP-based system is that they are relatively weak and cannot lift large loads (Bar-Cohen, 2004).

ARTIFICIAL ARMS

As described at the beginning of this book, reaching out to grab something may seem like a simple action but turns out to be quite complex. One discovers this when trying to engineer an arm capable of duplicating human arm actions. In this section, we will consider arms apart from hands even though the two are sometimes used in concert. That is because arms are typically employed for reaching while hands are used for manipulating. The primary function of an arm is to place a hand at an object location. The primary function of a hand or other effector is to then manipulate the object.

A robot arm is articulated, meaning it has different parts divided into sections by joints. Robot arms can contain more joints than a human arm, although they can be made with three major joints in which case these could be labeled as "shoulder," "elbow," and "wrist." Robot arms with more joints have a corresponding increase in the number of different ways they can move.

The term *degrees of freedom* is used to measure arm mobility. There are three primary ways to move in 3-D space. They are up and down or pitch, left and right or yaw, and rotation or roll. A joint that can move in all three of these ways possesses three degrees of freedom. The shoulder has three degrees of freedom, while the elbow has only one since, if the shoulder is fixed, you can only move your elbow up and down. The total degrees of freedom for an arm is the sum of the degrees of freedom for all its joints.

So, an advantage to robotic arms is that they can be made to be more flexible than human arms. Although three degrees of freedom is sufficient to bring the end of a robot arm to any point in 3-D space, the more joints it has, the more easily it can do so. Most robot arms are employed in industry for product assembly. In this context, they are quite successful, able to move car parts or screw the cap onto a peanut jar over and over again in precisely the same way without getting tired as a human operator would.

ARTIFICIAL HANDS

Of all the limbs we consider, hands are the most challenging to engineer artificially. Unlike an arm or leg, the hand, considered together with wrist and fingers, has 22 degrees of freedom. Each finger can be considered a limb unto itself and has some amount of independent motion. The opposable thumb also characterizes the human hand. We can place our thumb against each of the other fingers, increasing the dexterity with which we can hold or orient objects. The opposable thumb may have even driven the evolution of intelligence in early humans because it enabled us to create and use tools (Napier, 1980). Coupled with this complex manipulator capacity is the hand's high concentration of tactile sensory neurons in the fingertips and palms. A complete reproduction of this amazing structure's motor and sensory function may take some time.

One recent example of a robotic hand is Robonaut (Figure 3.1). A joint development project of the National Aeronautics and Space Administration (NASA) and the Defense Advanced Research Projects Agency (DARPA), Robonaut consists of a torso with a head and two attached arms with hands. Astronauts operate it remotely by viewing what Robonaut sees through his stereoscopically mounted twin cameras. They move his hand through a "data glove" that mimics the operator's hand motions. His anthropomorphic design enables natural and intuitive control by human tele-operators. Robonaut was designed to perform maintenance and repair in the dangerous work environment of space outside the International Space Station.

Figure 3.1 NASA and DARPA have developed Robonaut for work on the International Space Station. Robonaut has a dexterous five-fingered hand that can grasp and manipulate a wide variety of tools. Photo courtesy of NASA.

Robonaut's hand looks much like its human equivalent. It has four fingers and an opposable thumb that can touch the forefinger and index finger. The fingers roll at the base and pitch at all three joints allowing 14 degrees of freedom. A forearm houses the motor and drive electronics. The hand currently provides no tactile feedback to the operator, but research is ongoing to provide this capability. It does have a grasping algorithm that clasps the hand about certain objects automatically once it is prepositioned by the tele-operator. Future hands will utilize finger tendon sensors that allow the grasp to adjust to a wider range of objects.

ARTIFICIAL LEGS

The solution to many terrestrial locomotion demands is satisfied by the use of wheeled or tracked vehicles. Wheels are the best way to move on flat surfaces with good traction. Tracks are better for soft or sandy ground and for dealing with small obstructions like rocks. Legs, though, are the best solution for traversing rough terrain. They can be used to step across or jump over obstacles. In conjunction with arms, legs also enable climbing vertical or near-vertical surfaces. Legs, whether bipedal, quadrupedal, or more, are nature's solution to getting around difficult environments. Researchers have therefore devoted a considerable amount of effort into designing artificial legs that can mimic these feats.

The Otto Bock HealthCare's C-leg is a big step toward a fully functioning artificial leg. It has microprocessors and sensors that reproduce the stability and stepping motion of a real leg. One of its features is an electronically controlled hydraulic knee that adapts to different movements. A strain sensor measures the load on the foot. Others track characteristics like knee angle and motion more than 50 times a second. Algorithms then process this data to determine the current phase of the gait cycle and make adjustments. The result is that patients don't have to think about how to use the leg as they do in a normal "dumb" prosthetic. The C-leg enables patients to walk normally down ramps, stairs, or uneven terrain. Curtis Grimsley, a computer analyst for the Port Authority of New York and New Jersey, used the leg to walk down 70 flights of stairs at the same speed as other evacuees to escape from the attacks on the World Trade Center on September 11, 2001 (Karoub, 2002).

NEURAL PROSTHETICS

An exciting new area in prosthetic development is the creation of an effective neural interface between organic body and artificial limb. This type of interface would ideally allow sensory information from electronic sensors in the limb to be transmitted to the patient's own peripheral nerves and then to the brain, where they could "feel" feedback from the artificial limb. In the other direction, motor commands to move the limb from the brain's motor center could then travel downstream by nerves to the limb, causing it to move.

Researchers at the Scuola Superiore Sant'Anna in Pisa, Italy, have created a Regeneration Type Neural Interface (RTNI) that allows nerves to grow into a chip and make contact with electrodes (Cocco, Dario, Toro, Pastacaldi, & Sacchetti, 1993). In one experiment, they spliced a rabbit's sciatic nerve and guided it to grow into proximity with a silicon chip punctured with numerous microscopic holes. Forty-eight days later, they were able to record signals originating from the nerve in the electrode. They could also activate the electrode and send a signal to the nerve producing muscle contraction. The RTNI and other devices like it hold great hope for future accident victims who some day may be able to feel sensations in an artificial limb and will that limb to move in much the same way as a normal organic limb.

Another more radical approach is to situate a neural interface in the brain itself. The BrainGate system does just this. Neuroscientist John Donaghue of Brown University has more recently embedded a 4mm square chip directly into the motor cortex of Matthew Nagle, a paralyzed patient (Patoine, 2005). The chip has 100 electrodes that project down into the outer layers of Matthew's cortex. The electrodes measure the activity of the motor neurons in this region and send a signal to an interface at the top of his skull. This relays the signal to a processor that sends commands to a computer screen. Matthew can then move a cursor around on the screen simply by thinking about it. In this way, Matthew can do such things as draw shapes on the computer screen, play video games, and control lights and a television. The potential for this type of device is enormous, because it can be used to control any external device in addition to a prosthetic limb.

PERCEPTION AND ACTION

A key concept when discussing perception and action is the idea of an agent. Russell and Norvig (2003) define an **agent** as anything that perceives its environment through sensors

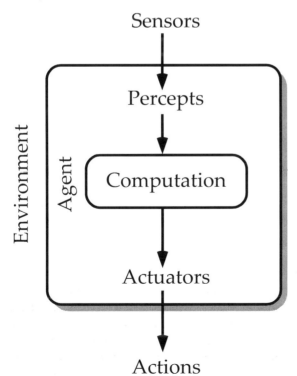

Figure 3.2 General schematic architecture for an agent.

and acts on the environment through actuators or effectors in order to achieve purposive, goal-directed action. People, computers, and robots are all examples of agents. A person takes in information through senses like eyes and ears, then acts using legs, arms, and hands. A computer software program receives input in the form of file contents and network data and acts by transmitting information. A robot perceives through electronic senses like video cameras and microphones and acts using robotic arms and manipulators. Since an agent is a general concept, we will use it throughout this book.

In this section of the chapter, we discuss the interplay between perception and action. We consider these together because they are functionally intertwined. Whenever we perceive, it is usually in the service of action and whenever we perform an action it usually changes our perception. To illustrate this, imagine driving your car down the street. You see another car in front of you at a stop sign. This immediately causes you to step on the brake to slow down so you don't hit it. The result is that the size of the car in your visual field looms larger as you near it, but at a slower rate. The degree to which you push on the brake is directly correlated with the rate at which the visual size of the car expands. Once it is directly in front of you and has reached a certain size, you can now remove your foot from the brake pedal. This example illustrates that perception and action should always be considered in conjunction as part of a loop where each influences the other. Perception influences action, that action then influences what you perceive which in turn affects your next action and so on.

Sensory information regardless of the specific modality such as vision serves several larger goals in the survival of an organism. Both people and other animals need to perceive in order to stay alive. Perception serves a number of important functions including:

- Recognition. The ability to identify or classify objects in the environment. This is in part a perceptual and cognitive process, since it requires drawing on stored memories of what things look like.
- Manipulation. Grasping, lifting, and performing other operations on objects that can vary widely in shape and weight.
- Locomotion. Moving around the environment requires among other things that we avoid obstacles and navigate from one point to another.
- Communication. In people, perception serves as the "front end" to a complex communication system called language that allows us to interact with others.

Notice that each of these demands an action. Recognizing your uncle implies some sort of action on your part, like shaking his hand. After picking up a soda can, you would need to manipulate it further by bringing it to your mouth and drinking. Walking down the sidewalk means more than just moving your legs, you have to avoid bumping into a tree. Listening to and comprehending speech precedes formulating a response, what you would say to someone who has asked you a question. We can see then, that the construction of artificial perceptual systems needs to be linked bi-directionally to motor and cognitive systems. The outputs of sensors must feed into mechanisms that control effectors and that plan what to do next. The results of these computations then alter the sensory inputs. This cycle repeats throughout most movements.

Our discussion here looks first at robotic paradigms that specify the overall way in which a robot interacts with the world. Then, we examine the concept of active vision and how it is implemented in a robot. Following this, our focus is on specific categories of action: obstacle avoidance and navigation, reaching, grasping and manipulation, then walking and running. For each of these we describe the process behind the action and then for some cases, what technological reproductions of them have been achieved.

ROBOTICS

Robotic Paradigms

Perception and action are of great significance in the field of **robotics**, characterized by the research and development of robots. Because a robot must interact with the world autonomously, it must be able to perceive and act. Although our discussion will focus on the robotic emulation of humans, researchers in this field have copied some of nature's other creatures. Recent developments have seen the creation of robotic insects, birds and fish.

In the **reactive paradigm,** there is a direct connection between sensors and effectors. This approach postulates that complex behavior can arise out of reflexive action without the need to perform extensive computation. Rodney Brooks developed this approach extensively in what he calls a **subsumption architecture**, where a single complex behavior can be decomposed into many simple layers (Brooks, 1986). The top layers that are more abstract, use or subsume the lower more concrete layers. The output of one layer serves as the input to another, triggering it into action. The layers are independent or modular; for the most part they only turn each other on and off.

One of Brook's robots, Allen, has three layers. The first layer avoids stationary and moving objects. It will just sit in the middle of a room until approached, at which point it scurries away, avoiding fixed obstacles. Allen's second layer causes him to explore by making him move in a random direction about every 10 seconds. The third layer causes Allen to look for distant places and head for them. Allen's complex behavior is thus the result of very simple reflexes wired together in a simple way. The evolution of the major sections of the human brain echo this architecture to some degree since new areas were layered onto and wired up to older areas. The recently evolved cognitive areas of the cortex to some extent subsume lower level emotional centers like the amygdala that, in turn, subsume other lower level motivational centers like the hypothalamus.

One difference though between reactive robots and people is that the former lack the ability to form coherent representations of the world the way we do. This prevents them from reasoning, but as you can see this is not necessarily an impediment to effective world interaction. An alternate approach, based on planning and thought is found in the **deliberative paradigm** (Murphy, 2000). Here, the robot senses the world and uses it to construct a global map of its environment. In conjunction with the map it then creates a plan that will enable it to achieve some goal, such as getting to a desired location. These robots will call on information stored in memory to enable the plan, such as knowing that one needs to open a door to get from one room to another. The robots can evaluate the current state of affairs with their sensors and alter or make new plans based on sensory inputs. For example, if one door is locked, they may be able to use another.

The reactive paradigm is "bottom up." Actions rely exclusively on sensory inputs. Brooks says that the world serves as its own model for these robots. They also don't rely on either representations or memory. In contrast the deliberative paradigm is "top down." These robots must construct their own model of the word and use it to plan their behaviors. Both representations and memory are thus necessary. The reactive paradigm is fast, but its success to a large extent depends upon the sense-act structures put into it by its programmers. Robots with this architecture may fail if put into situations for which they are unprepared. The deliberative paradigm is slow, since plans and changes to plans can require extensive computation. A recent solution has been to combine the features of both systems into a **hybrid paradigm** that has elements of bottom up and top down architectures. These robots have met with success and overcome some of the problems of their forbearers.

Active Vision

Intelligent perception requires **active vision**, the ability to deliberately process certain aspects of the visual environment. Active vision is the ability to gather scene information dynamically and selectively, rather than just "taking it all in." This means that vision and the other senses don't just passively take in information and send it to the brain for processing. The brain's higher order cognitive processes also guide and control perception. Information flow is thus iterative, traveling back and forth in both directions cyclically over time. This occurs when looking for a familiar face in the crowd. We would have to keep in mind what the person might be wearing and then scan back and forth to make sure we had covered the entire region.

Cog is a robot with an active vision system (Breazeal, Edsinger, Fitzpatrick, & Scassellati, 2001). Developed at the MIT AI Laboratory, it is a humanoid robot consisting of a torso, head, and two arms with hands (Figure 3.3). Cog is equipped with many human senses, including vision, hearing, and touch. It can alter its viewpoint by moving its waist, neck, head, and eyes in many different directions. One of Cog's design features is to allow it to learn how its own movements alter its sensory inputs. Some of Cog's capabilities are following a moving target with its eyes, detecting faces and reaching to a visual target. It can even perform repetitive motions like sawing and playing the drums.

Obstacle Avoidance and Navigation

Part of moving around requires **obstacle avoidance**, which is moving around the environment without bumping into objects. There are several ways a robot can do this. The simplest is to have it follow a simple rule. A robot equipped with a range finder can tell how far away it is from a surface by sending out a signal and recording the time it takes the signal to bounce back. As it approaches the surface, the echo time will decrease. The robot could then be instructed to slow down and turn as it nears the surface. Another even simpler solution is to have the robot reverse its direction then turn and move forward when it bumps into an object.

Figure 3.3 Cog and his designer Rodney Brooks play with a slinky. Cog was developed at the MIT Artificial Intelligence Laboratory and can use haptic feedback to adjust its actions and is also capable of copying human behavior. © Peter Menzel / Menzelphoto.com

Navigating involves getting from where one is to where one wants to be while avoiding obstacles along the way. Robots have relied on two different ways of navigating (Gibilisco, 2003). **In metric navigation**, a machine forms a computer map of the environment. Computer maps can be generated using radar, sonar, or a vision system. They can be two-dimensional (2-D) or three-dimensional (3-D). A 2-D map resembles a bird's eye view. It could show the locations and borders of all the furniture within an office. A robot could then use this map to move from its current location to the door without bumping into a desk or chair. A series of 2-D maps taken at different heights can be combined to create a 3-D map. This would have much more additional information that could be used by the robot. A 3-D map would allow a robot to judge the height of a door to see if it could pass through.

Computer maps contain all the possible routes a robot might take to get from a starting point to a goal. The robot can use the map to plan its route. This means selecting one optimal path, usually the shortest or the one that requires the least expenditure of energy. For people, metric path planning is like using a road atlas to decide how one wants to drive, for example, between New York and Boston when there are competing possible ways for doing so.

In **topological navigation**, a robot is programmed to negotiate its work environment by using landmarks along with periodic instructions for actions. The robot would have stored in its memory images of various landmarks. It then compares images from its sensors to those in its memory. When it detects a landmark, it then follows an instruction to move in a particular way. People also navigate this way. When a friend gives you directions to their house, it is usually in the form of landmarks and instructions. They might say: "When you get to the intersection, you will see a gas station on the right. Turn left. A little bit further you will get to a big red barn. My driveway is beyond that."

Metric techniques rely on an absolute coordinate system outside of the individual traveler. A problem with this approach is that it is dependent on the accuracy and resolution of the map. The use of satellite-based Global Positioning Systems, in which the individual and points in the environment can be specified in great detail, resolve this issue. Topological techniques, instead, rely on a relative coordinate system, the position of the traveler with respect to landmarks. It has difficulties, however, in situations where landmarks are similar and can be confused when one of the landmarks is missed altogether.

Reaching

Getting an arm to reach out toward an object may seem easy, but the problem is really quite complex and not yet fully understood. To begin, a moving limb does not just traverse a path through space. It must move in a certain direction with a given force and speed. If you were reaching to catch a moving fly ball in a baseball game, you would do it differently than when picking up a stationary glass of water. This information on how a limb should move constitutes a motor goal or command issued by the brain. This abstract command must then be converted into a pattern of signals that control the muscles during movement execution. The human arm is articulated by a number of different muscle groups such as the bicep and triceps. Each of these must be activated in a particular sequence in order to produce a given motion.

Specifying an arm movement requires several pieces of information (Bizzi, Mussa-Ivaldi, & Giszter, 1991). First, there is the initial location of the arm. Then there is the location of the object. These two constitute starting and end points. Finally, there is the trajectory the arm must pass through. Human arm location is provided by proprioception and other cues. Object location is for the most part visually determined. The brain then computes the trajectory based on these cues. However, as mentioned earlier, the movement is dynamic in the sense that it can be altered during execution. When reaching for something, we can swerve to avoid obstacles or to compensate for sudden object movement. An artificial person's reach would need this capability.

Grasping and Manipulation

Once a hand or gripper has been directed to an object by reaching, it can be grasped. Grasping requires that fingers hold an object securely. A secure grip is one in which the object won't slip or move, especially when displaced by an external force. Your grasp on a hammer, for example, would not be secure if bumping against something caused you to drop it. One precondition of a firm grasp is that the forces exerted by the fingers balance each other so as not to disturb the object's position (Mishra & Silver, 1989). The characteristics of an object such as its geometric configuration and mass distribution may demand that some fingers exert greater force than others to maintain stability. The grasp and support forces must also match overall object mass and fragility. An egg requires a more delicate touch than a rock.

Another factor to be considered is finger positioning. Two fingers are in equilibrium when they oppose each other and share the same line of action, i.e., when they are oriented 180^0 apart and push toward one another. Three fingers are in equilibrium when their forces add to zero and their lines of action intersect at a point (Ponce, 1999). An object's center of mass affects stable finger positioning (Bingham & Muchisky, 1993). If mass distribution is low down on an object, as it is in a half-filled glass, then the grip should be lowered to be closer to the center. Texture also impacts on finger positioning and force. Adjustments may be necessary to accommodate smooth and rough surfaces that are more or less slippery. In robots, this is accomplished with texture sensing. A laser beam is bounced off a surface. Smooth shiny surfaces scatter less light back to detectors than rougher matte surfaces.

A stable grasp is necessary for manipulation, which can take many forms. An object can be rotated by turning the wrist or by finger repositioning. Three-dimensional translations through space can be accomplished by moving the hand and arm. Objects can also be pushed or pulled across a surface (Lynch & Mason, 1995). Twirling and rolling are further examples of complex manipulation.

For both grasping and manipulating, sensory information needs to be monitored constantly. Feedback from hand sensors plays a critical role in setting and adjusting grip force to prevent slip (Johannson & Westling, 1987). This is true for people and machines. Robots that perform complex manipulations use closed-loop control systems where sensory input from a limb is sent back to regulate its motion. A good example of this is a back pressure sensor that sends a signal registering the amount of mechanical resistance encountered. The greater the resistance, the greater the motor force applied to the limb. In this way, a robot arm will work harder to lift a heavier load, or grip more strongly to maintain a grasp on a heavier object.

Walking and Running

Legged machines can be divided into two categories (Boone & Hodgins, 1999). In a passively stable system, the body's center of mass stays within a well-defined region formed by the points where the feet touch the ground. Because the body's center is always centered over the feet, these machines can stop at any time and still maintain their balance. In dynamically stable systems, the body is only balanced and would remain upright during a given portion of the gait cycle. This inherent instability makes them more difficult to design. Bipedal human locomotion is dynamically stable. Try pausing at different times while walking to discover for yourself where the greatest instability is.

In December 2004, Honda Corporation unveiled the latest version of its humanoid robot, named ASIMO (Advanced Step in Innovative Ability). The design philosophy behind ASIMO was to create a robot assistant that can interact with people and devices in human environments (Figure 3.4). ASIMO is a dynamically stable walking robot. It can walk at normal human speed, turn to change direction, climb and descend stairs, and run at 3 km/hour. Some of its new skills are the ability to twist its torso to prevent itself from

Figure 3.4 Honda's ASIMO robot shakes hands. It can also walk on level surfaces and up and down stairs. Photo courtesy of American Honda Motor Co., Inc.

slipping. It can also detect people's movements through visual sensors in its head and force sensors in its wrists. These allow ASIMO to give or receive an object, shake hands, and step forward or backward in response to being pulled or pushed.

Years of research on human walking went into ASIMO. The location, range of movement and torque exerted on the joints was based on human measurements. So was the body center of mass and impact force during walking. Even the human sensors used to maintain balance had mechanical analogues. ASIMO was equipped with joint angle sensors, force and speed sensors, and a gyroscope to monitor foot movement. In humans, these functions are carried out by the otolith and semicircular canals of the inner ear and from proprioceptive feedback originating in joints, muscles, and skin.

There are other recent Japanese robots that show remarkable locomotive and motor abilities. Sony's "Qrio" robot is only 2 feet tall and weights 15 pounds, but it can avoid obstacles, climb stairs, and even dance, moving its legs, arms, and fingers to a musical beat. Its programmers gave it the ability to even throw a small football. Qrio can run at speeds of up to one and a half miles per hour and uses sensors on its heels to slow down when it has to walk over bumpy terrain. The HRP-2 robot designed by Kawada Industries can lie down and get up by itself. This solves the problem of what the robot should do if it slips and falls but also has practical applications. Robots that can lie down are more energy efficient and can slip under obstacles to inspect or work on them.

4

LEARNING AND MEMORY

Learning makes a Man fit Company for himself.

—Thomas Fuller, 1732

LEARNING

The world is a constantly changing and unpredictable place. Any person or machine must therefore have some way of dealing with unexpected and novel events. The capacity to learn is what enables this. **Learning** is a relatively permanent change in behavior due to experience. The fact that we can learn enables us to deal with situations similar to those we have encountered in the past. It allows us to draw on our history of the past where we have acted efficaciously and apply it to a current situation where we're not quite sure what to do. This is a tremendous boon to any creature that must interact with a variable environment. Without learning, we are condemned to making the same mistakes over and over again.

Our discussion in this chapter will center on two broad categories of learning. Behavior-based learning involves the acquisition of a behavior or action. There are three types. Classical conditioning concerns the association of two stimuli in triggering a reflexive action. In operant conditioning the frequency of a response can be increased or decreased by following it with a reinforcement or punishment. In observational or "copycat" learning, a behavior is perceived, remembered, and then imitated.

Knowledge-based learning concerns the acquisition of knowledge. What is learned or applied in these cases is typically information rather than a behavior. We introduce and give examples of three types of these as well. In supervised learning a "teacher" provides correct feedback for a response. For inference learning, a system follows the logical rules of deduction, abduction, and induction to generate new knowledge from existing knowledge. In analogical reasoning, an agent uses a knowledge structure acquired from previous experience and applies it to a novel but similar situation.

BEHAVIOR-BASED LEARNING

Classical Conditioning

One of the most basic forms of learning is **associative learning**, where two events that occur close together in space or time frequently become associated. The two events can be stimuli (as in classical conditioning) or a response and its consequences (as in operant conditioning). If two things tend to happen together regularly, then one is a reliable indicator of another. Learning they go together means that exposure to one signifies the other will soon be on its way. This is useful because it allows us to predict and anticipate events. If it almost always rains after the formation of dark clouds, then seeing dark clouds will allow you to seek cover before the downpour.

The Russian physiologist Ivan Pavlov (1849–1936) was the first to study simple learned associations between stimuli in animals. He noticed that dogs in his lab began salivating before receiving food and wanted to know why. So, he presented a stimulus, the sound of a tuning fork, before presenting food to dogs. After several pairings, the dogs began salivating to the sound of the tuning fork alone. It had become what he called a conditioned stimulus that now elicited a conditioned salivation response. This association between one stimulus and another, in this case between the sound and the food, has become known as **classical conditioning**.

A fairly simple artificial neural network has been used to allow associative learning between stimuli. It is called a pattern associator or **associative network** (Cotterill, 1998). The exact details of how one works is technical and beyond the scope of this text, but we will provide a brief sketch of its operation. Figure 4.1 shows an associative network. It receives stimulus input from one source that activates the A units. Prior to learning, this input might automatically cause a response. In the case of Pavlov's dogs, this input comes from the gustatory system and is the taste of the food that elicits salivation. Input in the form of the tuning fork from the auditory system would activate the B units. Before learning, these would not normally initiate a response but after classical conditioning the simultaneous or near simultaneous pairing changes the weights on the connections so that eventually the sound of the tone alone is enough to produce a response from B unit activation.

Associative networks can be used to associate any two stimuli together so that a second stimulus can produce a response at first generated only by a first stimulus. A response need not be an overt behavior. It could be a thought or a visual image. For example, hearing the sound of your friend's voice over the phone might conjure to mind an image of her face. Associate networks allow us to effectively recreate this basic but important form of learning in machines.

Operant Conditioning

In **operant conditioning** an action is followed by a consequence. If the consequence is good, the action tends to be repeated. If it is bad, it becomes less likely to be repeated. Good consequences are known as reinforcement. Reinforcements are usually in the form of a reward. Food, sex, and praise are all forms of reward. A student who studies to receive an "A" grade and is praised by her parents would tend to study more in the future. Bad conse-

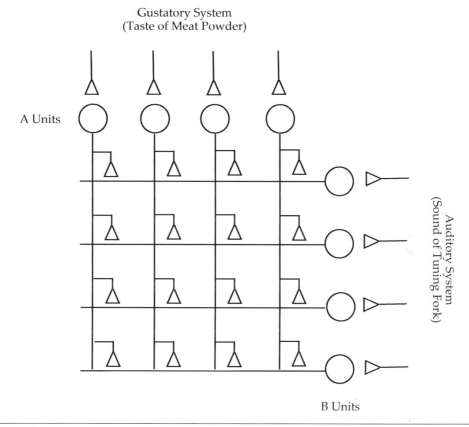

Figure 4.1 An associative network like this can be classically conditioned. It can learn to make associations between two stimuli that co-occur frequently.

quences of an action typically come in the form of punishment. Examples of punishment are spanking and verbal scolding. A child who spills juice on the sofa while playing and is then spanked will tend not to play on the sofa again.

The psychologist B. F. Skinner (1904–1990) is most closely tied to this form of learning. He believed that every action we make is the result of our operant conditioning history. He stated that any behavior could be changed simply by the appropriate application of reinforcement and punishment. This view, characterized by the Behaviorist movement, was a dominant influence on psychology for the first half of the 20th century.

It turns out that the principles of operant conditioning can be used to govern the behavior of a computer or robot. In the field of machine learning, these methods are collectively referred to as **reinforcement learning,** abbreviated as RL (Sutton & Barto, 1998). RL is an instance of **unsupervised learning** or, in some cases, what is called trial-and-error learning, where the consequence of an action generates feedback from the environment that affects future actions. In the pure case of operant conditioning, the agent does not need to think or deliberate. It simply follows a set of rules that map rewards onto behavior. Some

RL methods, however, do involve planning. In this case, the learning is not truly operant in the behaviorist sense, as the agent is deliberatively trying to achieve a goal through a cognitive or algorithmic process.

Most RL procedures have an agent that senses the environment, then selects among possible actions in pursuit of a goal. The execution of the action in addition to producing a reward, affects the state of the environment. Behavior is structured so as to maximize a cumulative reward signal the agent receives over time. The environment is changing and so cannot be reliably anticipated or predicted. RL procedures typically consist of four elements:

1. They have a policy that maps stimulus inputs to actions. These are rules used by agents to determine an action based on the current state. They can be thought of as conditional "If x, then y" rules in which an action can be looked up in a table, but in some cases may involve the execution of a complex algorithm.
2. A reward function that determines the value of a reward for a given action. A high reward value is sought after by the agent and is the machine equivalent of a reinforcement like food or praise for humans.
3. A value function that determines the amount of value for a particular action. Values are like rewards in that the agent seeks to maximize them. Whereas rewards are satisfying in the short term, values are satisfying in the long run. An agent might choose a low reward on a given learning trial if it calculates the consequences of that action will later produce a high value. Similarly, we might decline to go out drinking with our friends and choose to stay home and study for a test. Inebriation and socializing would have more immediate reward value, but scoring high on the test would produce long-term value.
4. A model of the environment that mimics the operation of an environment. This would generate the next state, given the agent's action.

Let's illustrate with a simple case that involves values. An RL agent playing checkers would begin by examining all the possible moves it could make. For each move, there is an associated value that if chosen reflects the possibility of winning. These values are updated as the agent plays based on how successful it was in the past when choosing that move. Adjusting the value of an earlier state to the value of the latest state does this. In a temporal difference learning method, a new value is created by taking a weighted difference between the two states and adding it to the old state. The result is that the value of winning for each move converges to an optimal policy for playing the game with higher values of moves more likely to result in success and lower values for those that lead to failure.

Most selections in RL are **greedy choices**, with the program picking the move with the highest associated value of winning. Some, however, are **exploratory choices**. They are picked at random to enable the program to gain experience. These two types of move echo an important aspect of human learning. Anyone who is doing something for the first time must try a variety of different solutions in order to know which ones work and which ones don't. Then, later, they can draw on this experience to more accurately select appropriate responses.

Observational Learning

Observational learning involves copying someone else's behavior. Unlike classical or operant conditioning, which can take place without conscious thought or awareness, observational learning has a cognitive component. One must pay attention to what a model is doing and then remember the action so that it can be reproduced. This calls on a variety of mental processes such as perception, attention, cognition, and memory. Typical examples of observational learning are learning how to dance, perform yoga, karate, or aerobic exercise routines by following an instructor's actions. Imitative learning speeds up the time it takes a child or novice to acquire skills because they don't have to rely on the consequences of their own actions time after time. They can instead benefit from others around them who have already become masters at what they do.

The first psychologist to systematically study the principles of observational learning was Albert Bandura (1925–) . In a landmark study, he had children watch a video of an adult attacking an inflatable "Bobo" doll (Bandura, Ross, & Ross, 1961). When the children were later frustrated and placed in a room containing the Bobo doll, a greater number of them attacked it in comparison to a control group who did not witness the adult attack video. The behavior of the children followed very closely the actions of the adult model. They kicked and screamed in much the same way. This study confirms what many parents already know, that children learn by mimicking the behavior of parents and others around them.

But can we get a robot to learn observationally? This is a bit more challenging than associative learning because, as mentioned earlier, it calls on a number of cognitive skills such as recognizing, learning, and copying actions. But the payoff of robot imitation is huge; robots would be able to learn on their own, meaning that we would not have to go through the laborious and time intensive process of programming them to perform each and every task. It also makes it easier for humans and robots to work together in the same environment. Imitative ability allows a robot to perceive others as intelligent agents and to predict their actions and infer their goals. A robot assistant could anticipate, for example, that a human carpenter may be running low on nails and go fetch a new box.

Acosta-Calderon and Hu (2004) have developed a system that allows a robotic arm to copy the actions of person's arm. Their robot, called United4, was equipped with a color vision system. It first watched a human demonstrator move their arm into different positions during a learning phase. The arm joints on the person were labeled with colored bands for easy identification. In a later execution phase, it mimicked the movement with a five-degree of freedom robotic arm and attached gripper. In a second set of experiments, United4 was able to grip a pen and trace out several letters written by its human model.

In order to achieve these feats, United4 followed several stages of information processing. First, it identified the relative body part to be copied. To simplify its representation, it focused on the end effector, in the case, the person's hand, and the path the effector took when performing the action. It then had to solve the correspondence problem of mapping the target limb onto its own. United4 did this by assigning the human reference joints on the shoulder, elbow, and wrist onto its own joints. This mapping operation is easy for robot arms that perfectly match a human arm, but trickier when the two are dissimilar. It also poses a problem for the required motion. If the robot arm is different from a human arm, it will have to move in a different way in order to reproduce the action.

The solution Acosta-Calderon and Hu (2004) implemented was to endow United4 with a body schema containing knowledge of the spatial representations among its body parts and the actions they could perform. They also gave it the ability to determine a body percept or "snapshot" of its body's position at any given moment. To recreate the motion path of the model's arm, United 4 first calculated it and used the body schema and percept to execute the equivalent motion with its own parts.

KNOWLEDGE-BASED LEARNING

Supervised Learning

Many times when humans learn, it is in the presence of a teacher who can provide feedback in the form of a correct answer. For example, a child who is learning the multiplication tables might incorrectly answer "24" to the problem 3 × 7. If a teacher were present, he would tell the child that the correct answer is "21." The child would then remember the correct answer and be more likely to use it in the future. This form of learning is called **supervised learning**. Notice that it is in contrast to the unsupervised reinforcement learning we examined earlier. In that case, the environment itself serves as the teacher. Supervised learning methods thus require more prior information on the part of the teacher, because the right answers must already be known to them.

Artificial neural networks have long used supervised learning methods. In one such procedure, a stimulus first activates units in the input layer. This causes activation of units in the hidden and output layers. The pattern of activation in the output layer is compared to the desired response, provided by a "teacher" with the correct answer. Any difference between the actual and desired responses is fed back into the network in the form of an error signal and used to change the weights so that succeeding responses more closely approximate the target. This form of learning is called the **back propagation method** and has been used to teach artificial neural networks to recognize stimulus sets like letters of the alphabet and geometric shapes.

Artificial neural networks demonstrate many human learning properties. They exhibit **graceful degradation**, a gradual decrement in performance with increased damage to the network. Graceful degradation is a consequence of the network's distributed nature. Damage to some of the nodes doesn't prove fatal because the network can "relearn" using connections among the remaining nodes. Human forgetting follows a similar decay function to that seen in networks where information is lost slowly and gradually over time.

Networks also display two other key aspects of human learning: interference and generalization. **Interference** occurs when the learning of one type of information obstructs the learning of another. This can happen when you study words in one language (e.g.. Italian), and find that it prevents you from remembering words in another language (e.g., Spanish). Some networks though, suffer from **catastrophic interference**. The learning of a new stimulus set in this case completely erases all the information acquired from a previous training session. This happens because the new set modifies the weights containing the prior information. **Generalization** is the ability to apply what was learned in one context to another. Neural networks also generalize. One network trained to learn the past tense of verbs successfully applied the irregular to a new form. It produced "wept" for "weep" after learning "slept" for "sleep" (Rumelhart & McClelland, 1986). This network did make a number of mistakes however.

Inference

We will now look at how sentence-like statements about the world can be generated by people and machines. This ability is very useful because it allows agents to "go beyond the facts" and to produce new information from what is already known. This ability is known as making an **inference**. Inferences build up a knowledge base that represents aspects of the world and can be used to interact successfully with it.

A **proposition** is a statement about the world that can be proved true or false. Propositions usually take the form of sentences. For example, the sentence "Susan has red hair" is a proposition because it expresses some aspect of the world. **Deductive reasoning** is one way to determine the validity of a proposition, that is, whether it is true or not. In deductive reasoning, we start out with two premises or propositions and then derive another proposition from them:

> All British citizens love soccer.
> William is a British citizen.
> Therefore, William loves soccer.

In deductive reasoning, one assumes that the premises are correct. If they are, then the conclusion drawn from them will also always be correct. As you may have surmised already however, if either or both of the premises are false, the conclusion will also be false. In the case above, the first premise is false. Not all British citizens love soccer. We cannot, therefore, be certain that William loves soccer. Deductive reasoning doesn't go much beyond the information given but, if applied correctly, always yields valid knowledge.

The reverse of deductive reasoning is **abductive reasoning**. Here is an example:

> When the home-team wins, there is a parade.
> There is a parade.
> Therefore, the home-team won.

The observation we start with is the second part of the initial premise, that "there is a parade." We then reason backwards from this to conclude that the home-team won. In comparison, with deductive reasoning, we start with the first part of the original premise and reason forward. The problem with abductive reasoning is that there could be other reasons to account for the conclusion. For instance, there could be a parade because it is Independence Day and not because the home-team won.

In **inductive reasoning** one again starts with premises and derives a conclusion. Here is an example:

> Rover, the dog, is brown.
> Lassie, the dog, is brown.
> Therefore, all dogs are brown.

Notice that the first two premises are again assumed true, but are this time based upon observation. The conclusion is then a generalization from the examples in the premises to all members of their class. Because both Rover and Lassie are brown, we can determine that all dogs are brown. Conclusions generated from inductive reasoning go beyond the information given. In this sense they are more useful than deduction. But, they can end up being proved invalid by a single counterexample. In the case above, a single dog that is non-brown proves the conclusion false.

THE CYC PROJECT

In 1984 AI researcher Douglas Lenat took control over a project named Cyc (an alteration of the word encyclopedia). The funding was provided by the Microelectronics and Computer Technology Corporation located in Austin, Texas, although it is now under the auspices of Cycorp, Inc. The goal of the project was to imbue a computer with all the general world knowledge possessed by the average adult. It could then apply some of the rules noted above to expand upon and reason about its knowledge. David Freedman gives a good description of the Cyc project in his 1994 book *Brainmakers*.

Douglas and his team set about entering millions of propositions gleaned from magazine and newspaper sources. In an early version of the program, the team entered the data using a programming language called CycL. CycL organizes information into **frames**. Each frame contains a number of slots that specify particular attributes about a unit or concept. A frame for "Thomas Jefferson" would contain slots for the superordinate or genus category to which it belongs, in this case "person," as well as his professions, ideology, likes and dislikes, and so forth.

Cyc can reason deductively. If it was presented with the statement "Thomas Jefferson was a person," it could conclude "Thomas Jefferson breathed" based on its understanding that "people breath." An alternate way of thinking of this is that because concepts are hierarchically ordered, a frame for a subcategory will inherit some of the attributes of its genus. Because the unit Thomas Jefferson is a person, Cyc would automatically realize that he has a body, needs to sleep, eat, breath, and so on. Cyc also employed inductive reasoning. It was capable of making certain generalizations based on statements about particulars.

Lenat's initial hopes for Cyc were quite high. He believed Cyc would come to understand and reason about the world much as you or I do. He thought Cyc could apply logical laws like deduction and induction to rapidly expand its knowledge. Sadly, this never came to pass. A number of criticisms have been made of Cyc. It is too complex and difficult to add data to by hand, it is unable to deal effectively with certain concepts with multiple meanings and, where there are "holes" in its knowledge base, and it never began acquiring knowledge in a widespread way by itself. In spite of all that, Cyc still has some usefulness. Its potential applications include intelligent character simulation for games, improved machine translation and speech recognition, and semantic data mining.

Some doubt the ability of computers like Cyc to reason logically. They describe AI programs that use rigid rules and data structures as "brittle," meaning they are unable to adapt to novelty, fluidly changing environments, and ambiguous circumstances. Stanford logician John McCarthy counters this by noting that logic-based methods in AI have been making steady progress. Recent advances in non-monotonic logics have shown that computers can revise their knowledge in light of new information. These methods are a development of formal logic in which old axioms can be invalidated by the introduction of new axioms inconsistent with previous ones (McDermott & Doyle, 1980). Also, as we will see below, computers are now capable of noticing and applying similarities between old and new knowledge.

ANALOGICAL AND CASE-BASED REASONING

A computer that is fed propositions can do something no human can. It can take each new fact it acquires and compare it against every other fact it already has. In this way it can make all possible inferences, thereby maximizing the growth of its knowledge. A system capable of doing this is said to possess **logical omniscience**. But this type of exhaustive comparison becomes astronomically intensive, even for computers, as the number of propositions grows. Imagine having to evaluate a new fact to the millions of other facts you already know. We simply couldn't do this. However, people do make inferences when comparing similar thoughts. This is what happens when we think using analogies. **Analogical reasoning** involves noting the similarity between two situations and applying what was learned in the old case to the new case. So, unlike computers that have a better chance at exhaustively comparing all propositions, humans seem instead to compare and make inferences mainly between situations that are similar.

Here is an example of analogical reasoning: Imagine learning how to ride a motorcycle for the first time. You may realize there are some similarities between this new activity and driving a car, which you've already done. You know that in a car you must start the engine by activating the ignition while supplying gas. You could then try to do this on the motorcycle, taking into account that the ignition and accelerator pedal may be located in unfamiliar locations and require different types of action. The same process could then be applied for changing gears, turning, braking, etc. Applying your knowledge of a similar situation to this novel one and using it to guide your actions makes learning the new task much easier.

Gick and Holyoak (1980) showed that people reason analogically. They gave participants a problem involving a doctor needing to remove a tumor from a patient. The single beam of a ray could destroy the tumor but would also damage the healthy tissue it passed through. Only 10% of participants in a control group discovered the correct solution. A second group read an analogous story involving the capture of a dictator in a fortress. The solution to this problem involved splitting up forces and sending them along multiple converging roads to the fortress to capture it in strength. Of those who read this story, a full 75% got it right. They realized that for the doctor story, the beam could be split up into multiple smaller beams that would not damage tissue but would converge in force and destroy the tumor at its source.

Falkenhaimer, Forbus, and Gentner (1989) created a Structure Mapping Engine (SME) that finds analogies between two situations using a set of match rules. It has been successful at finding similarities between topics like heat and water flow, and solar systems and atoms. Chalmers, French, and Hofstadter (1995) critique the SME model saying it can only draw analogies from representations structured specifically with the model in mind. They also point out that the model is too rigid in the way it sets up those representations. Humans draw analogies under much looser conditions. We can see the relationship between situations when they have multiple interpretations. For example, we can notice the similarity between an office building and a cruise ship even though the two have only a weak structural similarity to one another.

Holyoak and Thagard (1989) produced an artificial neural network called ACME that performs analogical mappings. ACME is more flexible than SME in that it uses structural, semantic, and practical constraints when making comparisons. Part of its operation involves converting propositions to their underlying logical structure and matching corresponding elements. A critique of ACME is that it doesn't "understand" the similarities it creates and is merely following a set of predefined rules (Chalmers, French, & Hofstadter, 1995). This critique is general to all machine replications of cognition and we treat it at greater length in the chapter on thinking to follow.

One well-known AI method of analogical thinking is case-based reasoning. **Case-based reasoning** methods employ a computer program that attempts to solve new problems based on solutions to similar past problems. It has been formalized as a four-step process (Aamodt & Plaza, 1994):

1. Retrieve cases from memory that are similar to the target problem. A case consists of a problem, its solution, and comments on how the solution was obtained.
2. Reuse the case by applying it to the new case. This will involve adapting the old to the new by adding or changing certain procedures.
3. Revise the application if necessary. Sometimes the initial adaptation of the original case may not work. It will then be necessary to revise it until it does.
4. Retain the revised case after it works successfully. Store it in memory so that it can be called on and used again if necessary.

Case-based AI methods have been applied successfully to a variety of different domains since the early 1990s. They have been used in medical diagnosis to match diseases to symptoms and in legal reasoning to match rulings on past trials to current ones. Other applications include finance, marketing, architectural and industrial design.

MEMORY

It is not possible to discuss learning without discussing memory. That is because any change that occurs due to learning must persist over time in the form of a memory. Very generally defined then, **memory** is the retention of information over time. It is where a stored representation of what was learned exists so that it can be called on when needed at some future time. Without memory, there could be no learning, as the change that occurred when the agent interacted with the environment would be forever lost.

Given this seeming importance, you might recall from the chapter on perception and action the debate over just how necessary memory is for an intelligent agent. Those who adopt the deliberative paradigm or "top-down" view argue that stored knowledge is absolutely essential. Researchers in this camp load lots of information into their robots to enable them to form maps and plan where they need to go. In contrast, in the reactive paradigm or "bottom-up" approach, robots are given rudimentary stimulus-response instructions that are layered and call on each other. These robots have very little in the way of memory. Current thinking is that neither of these approaches in the pure sense is perfect and that some hybrid of the two constitutes the best type of architecture. We can conclude from this that some degree of memory is necessary for effective robotic world interaction.

Memory comes in handy for many cognitive tasks other than navigation. Inference-derived propositions stored in a memory constitute a knowledge base. As discussed in chapter 2, a knowledge base can be used to help us successfully look for a lost object by restricting the number of places to search. It also aids us to comprehend and produce language. Thinking, reasoning, problem solving, creativity, virtually every topic touched on in this book to some extent calls on an understanding of the world which resides in a memory system.

In this section, we present three important dimensions of human memory along with their synthetic equivalents. We will see that both human and machine have need for short- and long-term memories, for the storage and use of declarative and procedural knowledge, and for semantic and episodic memory. Following this, we next discuss three fundamental memory processes. Any memory system, natural or artificial, must be able to encode, store, and retrieve information.

MEMORY AND TIME: THE LONG AND SHORT OF IT

Research on human memory has shown what at first might seem counterintuitive: that there are multiple memory systems, some of which are used to process the same data. Each system has a different duration, capacity, and coding, and each serves a unique function. Cognitive psychologists have investigated extensively the various parameters of these memory types. We start by outlining two of them first, short- and long-term memory. Figure 4.2 shows each of these memory types and the processes that accompany them (Atkinson & Shiffrin, 1971). In addition, it shows sensory memory, where perceptual information is stored very briefly before being passed to working memory for processing.

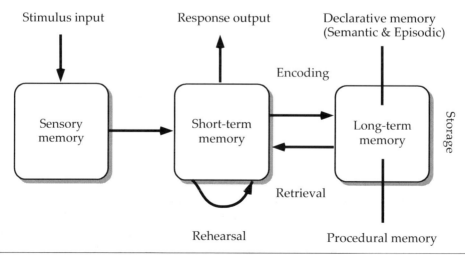

Figure 4.2 A model showing the different types of human memory and memory processes (after Atkinson & Shiffrin, 1971).

Human Short-Term Memory

Short-term memory (STM) stores a limited amount of information for a limited amount of time. As the name suggests, it has a brief duration, estimated from various studies to be about 30–45 seconds. It can be described as the capacity for holding in mind a small amount of information in an active and available state. Human STM is considered a subset of **working memory**, which is a collection of structures and processes in the brain used for storing and manipulating information. Whereas working memory has components that govern attention and direct processing, STM is better thought of as a repository for this information. An analogy is helpful here. Think of STM as a workbench where things like wood, screws, and other parts are laid out, ready for assembly. Working memory would then constitute the workbench, the parts, and the various tools that could be applied to the parts to operate on them.

Human STM has a limited capacity. It can only hold about seven items, give or take two, what has become known as the "magic number" 7±2. These items can be any meaningfully coherent unit of information such as a number, letter, or word. Such a unit is known as a "chunk" of information. Increasing the size of a chunk can increase the overall capacity of STM. For instance, given a string of letters to remember, grouping the letters into meaningful acronyms three letters long will triple capacity. Information in human STM can be stored in a variety of formats, auditory, visual, or semantic.

HUMAN LONG-TERM MEMORY

Information in human **long-term memory** (LTM) lasts longer, from over 30 seconds to years. With periodic use information can remain in LTM indefinitely. It is difficult to ascertain LTM capacity, but it is certainly very large as much of what is learned over the lifespan of an individual may be retained in this store. Landauer (1986) estimates that the average adult has a storage capacity of over one thousand billion bits of information. LTM holds information about facts and events. It additionally contains knowledge of how to perform learned skills. Long-term memories fall into two broad categories, declarative and procedural. Declarative knowledge itself consists of semantic and episodic knowledge. These subdivisions are discussed shortly.

COMPUTER MEMORY

The distinction between STM and LTM is so fundamental that we see it in computer systems as well. Computer STM is referred to as primary storage or what we called main memory in the brain chapter. **Primary storage** contains data that are actively being used by the computer. These include programs that are running and the data they operate on. It is high-speed, consists of relatively small amounts of data and is volatile, meaning its contents are lost when the computer loses power. Access to primary data is immediate and random. **Secondary storage** is where information not currently used by the computer is placed. This would include files and programs that the user may not need for quite some time. It is usually slower but higher in capacity and typically nonvolatile with serial data access.

Before continuing our discussion of computer memory we need to digress into the way in which it is measured. The smallest possible unit of information in a computer is the **bit**. A single bit can assume one of two states, either a one or a zero or an "on" or "off." Eight bits make up a byte, which can store 256 (2^8) possible values. Bytes are used to represent a standard symbol such as a letter, number, or a simple instruction. For example, the letter "A" is stored in binary code as the byte "01000001," the number "5" as "00110101," and the "backspace" command as "00001000." Multiples of bytes are given different names. A megabyte (MB) is one million (10^6) bytes, roughly equivalent to a million characters or 2,000 pages of text. A gigabyte (GB) is 10^9 bytes, equal to a billion characters or approximately two million pages 500 words long.

In many computers, primary storage takes the form of RAM or **random access memory**. The contents of RAM can be accessed in random order, so retrieval of data is fast. Information can usually be both written to and read from RAM. Because bits are stored as a charge in a capacitor in dynamic RAM or as flip-flop in static RAM, a loss of electricity results in the erasure of all information. A Mac Pro desktop computer available for purchase in 2006, for example, can be upgraded to 16 GB of RAM.

In contrast, information in secondary storage is usually written to a magnetic disk with sequential or serial data access. A mechanical read-write head retrieves and stores data from the disk one bit after another in order. This considerably slows down processing speed. The magnetic encoding on the disk surface retains its state in the absence of electrical power making it non-volatile. Internal or external hard disks are the typical secondary storage medium for personal computers. A single internal hard drive on a typical 2006 desktop computer can hold as much as 750 GB of data.

Although the underlying mechanisms of primary and secondary memory in humans and computers differ, their functional equivalence is the same. Apparently all complex information processors, biological or artificial, require a short- and long-term memory. A fast-access, low-capacity system is needed for representing and computing information in the here and now. This is especially important for agents that need to think and respond quickly to urgent environmental demands. Pausing too long for reflection could result in death or termination. On the other hand, a slow-access, high-capacity system is also needed to allow the agent to draw on its learned experiences. This system must be able to store vast amounts of data that have accumulated over the agent's history and can be used under less urgent circumstances.

MEMORY AND KNOWLEDGE: FACTS, EVENTS, AND RULES

Declarative Memory and Semantic Networks

Human LTM consists of declarative and procedural memories. **Declarative memory** stores declarative knowledge of facts and events. It is demonstrated by saying and is generally within our conscious awareness. Knowing that fish swim is an instance of a fact that most adults possess. Facts, as we have seen, can be represented in the form of concepts and propositions. The concept "fish" and the proposition "fish can swim" can be stored in declarative LTM in the form of a semantic network.

A semantic network is not exactly the same as an artificial neural network. Both have nodes and links between them. Both have spreading activation, where activity in one node can travel along links to activate other nodes. But semantic networks are characterized by **local representation**, where an individual node stands for a single concept. Artificial neural networks are characterized instead by **distributed representation**, where concepts are represented as the pattern of activity among a collection of nodes.

Semantic networks are well suited to storing declarative knowledge. Generally defined, a **semantic network** is a way of recording all the relevant relationships between members of a set of objects and their types. An object refers to an individual or particular like a car, tree, or house. A type refers to all members of a class, such as all cars, trees, or houses. Each object or type is represented as a node and the relationships between them are labeled as the link between nodes. The Cyc database was a type of semantic network. Figure 4.3 depicts an example of another. Notice that in this network two types of relationship are depicted showing membership and property relations.

Semantic networks have been designed that mimic human performance. In the sentence verification task, participants are asked to judge the truth or falsity of a sentence such as "Is a bird an animal?" The speed it takes them to respond is thought to reflect the spacing and relationship between the nodes representing "bird" and "animal" (Collins & Quillian, 1969). In the field of AI, semantic networks are constructed to store knowledge for use in natural language processing as well as problem solving in specialized domains (Lytinen, 1992; Shastri, 1989).

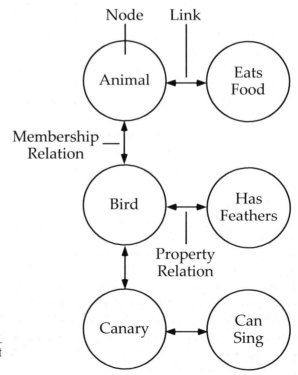

Figure 4.3 A semantic network is used to represent and organize information about facts.

Episodic Memory

The second type of declarative memory is **episodic memory** and is used to store episodes. An episode is a personal event such as a vacation to Italy or a birthday party. Whereas factual knowledge in declarative memory is organized hierarchically according to categories and property relationships, human episodic memory can also be organized temporally and spatially, meaning that events are sometimes recalled in the order they occurred or in terms of where they took place. Also, while facts are third-person, objective and independent of an observer's experience, episodes tend to be first-person, subjective, and dependent on an individual's unique experiential interpretation.

There have been a number of attempts to model human episodic memory. One of the earliest was CYRUS (Computerized Yale Retrieval and Updating System). The system stored episodes from the lives of former U.S. Secretaries of State Cyrus Vance and Edmund Muskie (Kolodner, 1983). A user could query the system on a particular topic. The program would then retrieve and present the relevant information to the user. It was organized into conceptual categories related to specific topics including diplomatic meetings, political conferences, and state dinners. Although CYRUS had a hierarchical structure reminiscent of semantic memory, it was useful in demonstrating how episodic knowledge grew and changed over time with the addition of new information.

Another way to account for episodic knowledge is to add this information on to existing semantic networks. Anderson (1990) in his ACT* model of memory does just this. He attaches token nodes representing specific personal information onto the type nodes used to refer to an entire category. A token node standing for your dog, Fido, in this scheme could be linked to your more general type node for "dogs."

Rinkus (2004) proposes a neural network model that forms spatiotemporal memory traces of episodic events. The event representations are distributed across the network's nodes. Because each node participates in the memory of multiple events, the network can easily match similarities between one event and another. The model is thus good at performing analogical type reasoning and generalization.

Procedural Memory and Production Rules

Procedural memory holds procedural knowledge of how to perform a skill. It is demonstrated by doing and is usually outside conscious awareness. An example of procedural knowledge is knowledge for how to ride a bicycle. Although you may know that you know how to ride a bicycle and could explain how to do it to someone else, you are not conscious of the actual rule. You couldn't actually prove to someone that you knew how to ride a bicycle until you actually did it, that is, until the rule was executed. In people, procedural memory is believed to reside in the cerebellum, a large cauliflower-shaped structure at the back of the brain.

Procedural knowledge can be represented in the form of production rules. A **production rule** is coded as an "If x then y" statement, where if the condition specified by "x" occurs, the action "y" gets executed. In the case of riding a bicycle, the stimulus input of your knee joint being at or near a right angle could trigger the motor instructions for a downward pedal push by the leg. In AI, production rules are referred to as stimulus-response agents or simply as reactive agents.

The subsumption architecture discussed earlier is an example of how production rules can be used to guide the behavior of a robot. In the case of the robot Allen, specific stimulus conditions in the robot's environment triggered specific actions. If Allen sensed an obstacle, it would move away from it. Nilsson (1998) describes another robot that uses production rules to follow walls. This robot can successfully navigate around obstacles by following their edges. It does this based on a very small number of if-then statements that map the location of objects in the space around it to directions it can travel. For instance, if there is an object to the north and no object to the east, it moves east. If there is an object to the east and no object to the south, it moves south.

Both declarative and procedural knowledge are necessary for any person or machine that needs to interact effectively with the world. This becomes clear when we imagine what it would be like to possess one but not the other. Imagine first a person who knows lots of facts about the world but is unable to apply them. This person would be very knowledgeable, but could not use their knowledge to inform them how to act in any given situation. They might know that it is raining outside and that rain will make them wet but not know that they should take an umbrella with them to avoid getting wet. Now take the opposite extreme, a person who is only capable of reacting to situations and doesn't have or can't apply world knowledge. They will take an umbrella outside with them if it is raining, but not be able to flexibly modify this action. They could not judge that they should wait inside until the lightning goes away to avoid being struck unless they had already formed a production rule for this.

MEMORY PROCESSES

Before concluding, we must mention something about memory processing. Rather than discuss all of the detailed memory operations that can be performed, we will instead focus on basic processes. There are three information-processing stages common to any memory system, be it biological or technological. They each concern how information gets into, stays, and is used by the system. **Encoding** refers to the processing and combining of received information. **Storage** is the creation of a permanent record of the encoded information. **Retrieval** is the calling back of the stored information that is needed for some computation. Figure 4.2 shows where in the human memory system each of these processes takes place.

There are a variety of different processes by which information gets encoded into a human memory system. Information that we pay attention to is remembered better than what is ignored. There are also a variety of other tricks one can use to ensure encoding. In **rehearsal**, items are repeated over and over again as when you need to remember a phone number but are unable to write it down. This strengthens the memory trace of the item and improves its chances of being recalled later. The chunking or grouping of items together as mentioned previously is another encoding technique. The different techniques one can use to encode are collectively referred to a **mnemonics**. In computers, information must also have some way of getting into a memory system. Input from various sources such as the keyboard or a camera may in some cases have to be converted into a format suitable for primary or secondary storage.

Information in human brains is stored in the form of a neural circuit. The synaptic connections between a collection of neurons becomes strengthened during encoding. This circuit then retains the information over time until needed. Repeated activation of the circuit during rehearsal results in biochemical changes that enhance the synaptic action. These changes include increased numbers of receptors on the postsynaptic membrane as well as increased release of neurotransmitters. In computers, storage depends on the particular hardware. For RAM, we have seen that data is represented as changes in electrical charge that disappear with power loss. For long-term hard disk storage, data is magnetically coded and nonvolatile. The actual way in which data is retained during storage depends crucially on the substrate in which it is represented. Future changes in hardware will necessitate new forms of storage.

Retrieval or recall of information involves getting it out of a stored form so that is available to computational processes. Human recall is governed by a number of factors. A **retrieval cue**, or item that is related to the item that needs to be recalled, is one. Thinking about the cue will often trigger the associated item. This is to be expected, since if the two related concepts are coded in a semantic network, spreading activation from one should activate the other which is nearby. For example, thinking about India should help to recollect the name of Mahatma Gandhi. These two concepts have a high associational value and are probably close to one another in a network containing information about India. We have already seen that information is retrieved differently in computer systems depending on the type of memory. For RAM access is random and fast. For secondary storage it is accessed serially and more slowly. Again, the particular hardware of a computer memory will determine the retrieval mechanism.

NATIVISM AND EMPIRICISM

There are two primary ways information can get into an intelligent system. First, it can be in place at the very beginning. For people, this requires being born with innate behavioral reactions or some other form of knowledge. For computers or robots it means that skills or information would need to be programmed in. In philosophy, this idea is called **nativism**. If information doesn't exist from the get-go, it must be acquired through learning processes of the sort we have described. The acquisition of knowledge through an agent's interaction with the environment is known as **empiricism**.

These two views bring up an interesting issue for the construction of an artificial person. How much information should be programmed in and how much should be left to learning? The advantage of prior knowledge is that the agent can start operating right away because it knows what to do. This eliminates the need for a time-consuming and costly developmental learning period filled with trials and errors. The downside to putting it all in at the start is that the amount of required information that must be input may be quite large.

It is also difficult, if not impossible, to anticipate everything an artificial person may ultimately need to know. That is because one cannot reliably predict what they might encounter in the future. Learning allows an organism or artificial construct to adapt to whatever circumstances they may meet without knowing what they are ahead of time. Learning in this sense is a hedge against uncertainty.

Human beings have a mix of "pre-programmed" knowledge and learning capacity. Natural selection forces have provided newborns with innate behavioral responses like the sucking reflex and certain smell preferences (Steiner, 1979). These help the newborn survive by ensuring that it nurses and eats appropriately. Likewise, any artificial person that must develop over time would need to have some amount of pre-programmed knowledge to speed up learning. The extent of the knowledge we wish to endow it with depends on a variety of factors such as the complexity and specific requirements of the environment it will "grow up" in.

Finally, we must consider the issue of curiosity. How much should we put in? Too much curiosity could have potentially serious consequences. In the human domain we have to be very careful with young children because their inquisitiveness and ignorance may cause them to do something dangerous like swallow poison or walk out into the street. So, too much curiosity in an artificial person could cause them harm. However, too little curiosity means a failure to learn enough about the environment and could also prove fatal. Balance again seems to be the solution. We need to provide an artificial person with just the right amount of curiosity, not too much, not too little, to maximize learning while minimizing hazards.

5

THINKING

Thought runs ahead and foresees outcomes, and thereby avoids having to await the instruction of actual failure and disaster.

—**John Dewey, 1922**

THOUGHT

Much of human thought or cognition is a product of the cortex. You will recall that this is the part of the brain to have most recently evolved and is larger in humans than in any other primate species. We define **cognition** broadly as the representation and computation of information. This definition allows us to discuss both computers and people as capable of thinking.

Representations can take two forms. They can be local and considered as symbols. This is this is the original approach in artificial intelligence, what is sometimes referred to as Good Old Fashioned AI or GOFAI. In GOFAI, computations on symbols are performed by the application of formal operations or algorithms. Processing in these systems is typically serial. In contrast, representations in artificial neural networks are distributed and take the form of different weights or connection strengths throughout links between nodes in the network. Computation consists of the initial activation of nodes and the consequent spread of activation through the network. This is sometimes called the parallel-distributed processing or connectionist approach. Processing in these networks proceeds in parallel.

Thought can be considered as an internal model of the world where representations stand for objects and computations stand for actions on those objects. Thinking simulates the external environment and allows the user to "try out" different possible courses of action without having to actually do them. This conveys a tremendous survival advantage. Instead of having to bump around, make mistakes, and experience the world directly, a thinker can anticipate, imagine, plan, and solve problems before they happen. Thought thus serves as a world surrogate, saving the thinker from having to act directly and suffer any potentially damaging consequences.

In cognitive psychology, cognition is conceptualized in the form of a **process model**. This is effectively a "wiring" or "circuit" diagram of some cognitive process. In these diagrams boxes are used to depict a particular computation and arrows to depict the flow of information from one computational process to another. Figure 2.4 gives an example of a process model. Processing models can depict both serial and parallel computational styles. The diagrams showing artificial neural networks that we have already seen reduce to process models where circles representing individual nodes stand in for boxes. Process models allow researchers to visualize how thoughts get executed. They can also be evaluated against empirical data and revised.

This chapter is not about different thought processes, models of how they operate, or the experiments that support various models. We refer the reader to any textbook in cognitive psychology to learn about those topics. Instead, we focus on the critical issues of whether a machine can think and how it is that thoughts are understood and have meaning. The Turing Test and the Chinese room paradox are two important thought experiments that help us to conceptualize the issue. Both are controversial, so we present them and follow with an extensive discussion of the objections and counter-objections. We also delve into explanations for how it is that thoughts might become meaningful, drawing on ideas from the philosophy of mind.

THE TURING TEST

Alan Turing, in his 1950 paper "Computing Machinery and Intelligence," proposed a simple test for whether or not a machine could think. In current versions of this **Turing Test**, a human judge is allowed to communicate with two parties, one a machine, the other a person. The judge is separated from both and can only communicate with them by typing questions and then reading and responding to replies from each, also in text. If the judge cannot reliably distinguish the person from the machine, the machine will have successfully passed the test. Figure 5.1 shows the setup of the Turing Test.

Nobody has yet created a machine that can pass the Turing Test. This is especially remarkable when one considers the advances made in computer science in the more than a half century since it was first proposed. The Loebner prize is an annual competition that awards $25,000 to the person who writes a program that passes the text only version of the test. A full $100,000 is awarded to the winner of a more complete version that includes visual and auditory input. Here is a sample of a transcript from the 2004 winner, Richard Wallace and his ALICE program, followed by an excerpt from one of the human confederates:

[12:55:52] Alice: Hello, my name is Alice and I am the human.
[12:57:14] Judge 4: Hi, I'm Roy. Are you a Yankees fan?
[12:57:39] Alice: Hi there Judge 4. Good gossip: you are Roy. Am I a Yankees fan? Maybe.
[12:58:00] Judge 4: Maybe. You are obviously not from NY.
[12:58:20] Alice: I understand. What makes you think I am not from NY?

Human Confederate　　　　Machine

Human Judge

Figure 5.1 The Turing Test. A computer program has not yet been devised that can fool a human judge.

[12:58:55] Judge 4: All the New Yorkers I know seem to have strong opinions about the Yankees.

[12:59:08] Alice: Perhaps there are a few exceptions.

[12:59:48] Judge 4: So you are a New Yorker who is indifferent to the Yankees?

[13:00:29] Alice: Interesting deduction. Thanks and you are a delightful person too. Am I a New Yorker who is indifferent to the Yankees? Yes.

[12:56:30] Confederate 1: Hello, my name is David and I am the human.

[12:57:34] Judge 4: Hi, I'm Roy. Are you a Yankees fan?

[12:57:50] Confederate 1: Yes, but only because I'm a New Yorker. Generally, I don't follow sports.

[12:58:17] Judge 4: What about art?

[12:58:21] Confederate 1: What about it?

[12:59:11] Judge 4: Is it something that interests you?

[12:59:22] Confederate 1: Yes. I like art very much. Do you?

[13:00:25] Judge 4: Yes especially early modern. Are you familiar with Modigliani?
[13:01:42] Confederate 1: Yes. I like his work. As far as painting is concerned, I like Juan
Gris and the surrealists. Sounds like a band name. I also like... who's the guy who
covered the canvas with squares of color in long lines. He was famous for painting the spirit of jazz, I think.

Based on these two transcripts, you probably had little difficulty distinguishing the
computer from the person. The conversational programs employed for the Turing Test pick
up cue words and phrases that allow them to respond. However, it is questionable whether
they have any real understanding of what they say. We address the issue of meaning later in
this chapter. Further along in the chapter on language we provide an in depth description
of how algorithms can comprehend and produce language.

Arguments and Counterarguments

Do you think that machines can think? Turing, in his seminal article, raises nine arguments to the idea and counters each of them. Please see the references to other parts of this
book to explore these arguments further.

1. The Theological Argument. Thinking is a product of man's immortal soul.
   Machines don't have souls and therefore cannot think. Turing's response is that
   God could provide a machine with a soul if he so desired.
2. The "Heads in the Sand" Argument. The consequences of machines thinking are
   too dreadful to imagine. Let's hope it never comes to pass. Turing states that this
   is not really an argument and offers consolation instead. The chapter on social
   behavior looks into the future possibilities of human-machine interaction.
3. The Mathematical Argument. Machines think using formal systems like math and
   logic. There are limits to these systems, particularly in terms of their ability to validate certain propositions (see Gödel's Incompleteness Theorem). People are not
   limited to using formal systems and can think in other ways. Turing replies that
   humans also make mistakes and err in their thinking.
4. The Consciousness Argument. People are conscious. We subjectively experience
   our thoughts and feelings. Machines are not conscious, but merely follow rules.
   Turing says that we cannot prove whether any individual other than ourselves is
   conscious. Machines may thus also be conscious. The chapter on consciousness
   examines this further.
5. The Various Disabilities Argument. Machines may be able to do some things, but
   there are some abilities they will never have. Examples include being kind, telling
   right from wrong, and falling in love. Turing counters that there is no evidence
   that machines cannot do any of these things. We discuss whether machines can be
   ethical or fall in love in future chapters.
6. The Lady Lovelace Argument. Computers are not original. They can't come up
   with new ideas or be creative the way people can. Turing's answer is that machines
   may yet be capable of creativity in the human sense. The chapter on creativity
   addresses this issue in greater detail.

7. The Continuity Argument. The human nervous system is continuous, not a digital or discrete state machine like a computer. A computer cannot therefore mimic the behavior of a nervous system. Turing's reply is that for the purposes of the Turing Test, a discrete-state machine does very well. There are also simpler continuous machines that can be used. A comparison of brains and computers is given in the chapter on brains.

8. The Informality Argument. Computers are governed by rules and are therefore predictable. People don't necessarily follow rules and so their behavior can't be predicted. Turing replies that it is more appropriate to say that human beings and computers are both governed by more general physical laws and these are what should be used to account for behavior.

9. The Extra-Sensory Perception Argument. Turing suggests that extra-sensory phenomenon may exist but that conditions could be created in which this would not affect the test.

Recent Criticisms

Is the Turing Test really the best way to test if a machine like a computer can think? Many think not. In addition to Turing's original arguments, a number of more recent criticisms have been leveled against it. Copeland (1993) lists four.

1. The Chimpanzee Objection. Animals, young children, the illiterate, and the mentally disabled may not be able to pass the test, but they all seem perfectly capable of thinking. Conversely, a machine may be able to think but not be able to express its thoughts linguistically like a person.

2. The Sense Organs Objection. A computer program in the Turing Test relies on verbal comprehension and replies, but there's no way to confirm that a machine understands what in the world a word actually refers to. There is no way of discerning real meaning or intentionality on the part of the computer. To do this would require perception and action, it would have to perceive, then pick up an object or point to it. Intentionality and its role in generating meaning are discussed later in this chapter.

3. The Simulation Objection. The Turing Test is only a simulation of thinking, not actual thinking. Even if a computer passed the test, it wouldn't prove that it could think, only that it has simulated an intelligent linguistic process. We also talk more about simulation later in this chapter.

4. The Black Box Objection. The computer's supposed thinking ability is based solely on its outward observable behavior, how it replies to questions. Nothing is known about its internal workings. A complete understanding of thought requires not just functional performance, but knowledge of the material processes that underlie the behavior.

Just in case we haven't listed enough problems with the Turing Test, we should also mention that it is a subjective estimate of what thinking is. The set of human judges in these contests are the ones who determine the outcome. The test asks people to determine what is or is not "person-like." The assumption here is that people, who are intelligent thinking agents themselves, will intuitively know what thinking is like. But do we really know? Perhaps what is being judged in the Turing Test is human-like responding and not the presence of actual thought.

What is really needed is an objective definition of thought and a test that can measure it independent of individual people's biases or prejudices. Here we get onto slippery ground because there are different definitions of what constitute thought. If we side with the strong version of the Symbol System Hypothesis, then thought is nothing more than symbolic representation and computation. By this definition, all computers think. If however, we believe that thought requires something more, like intelligence, consciousness or understanding, then these properties must also be accounted for.

THE CHINESE ROOM

The philosopher John Searle argues that a machine can never understand what it thinks. All it can do is manipulate symbols according to rules, i.e., process information algorithmically. To drive this point home, he poses a thought experiment, called the **Chinese room scenario** (Searle, 1980). Imagine a person in a room who is given a batch of Chinese text. The person does not speak any Chinese, but he has a set of written instructions in English, which he does speak. The instructions tell him how to convert the first batch of Chinese text into a second batch that he hands out of the room when finished. To the Chinese speaker outside the room it appears as if the person in the room understands Chinese because for each question or statement that is put in, an intelligible reply comes out. Figure 5.2 depicts the hypothetical Chinese room.

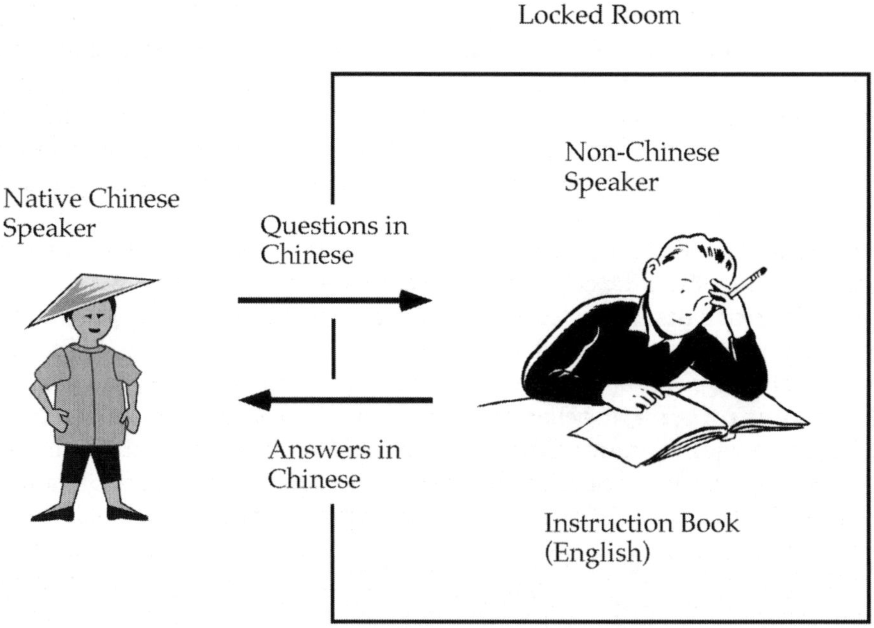

Figure 5.2 The hypothetical Chinese Room scenario. Is rule-following enough to allow for understanding?

Searle says the man in the room does not and never will come to understand Chinese. He will not experience it in a meaningful way. He is just blindly following the instructions given to him. A computer does exactly the same thing. It takes data and processes it by a set of preprogrammed rules. This means the computer will also never come to understand or meaningfully interpret what it does.

Evaluating the Chinese Room Argument

As with the Turing Test, there have been a number of replies to the Chinese room argument. Let's examine each in some detail.

1. The Systems Reply. While the individual in the room may not understand Chinese, he is just part of a larger system that includes the text and the rules. It is the system as a whole that may be considered to understand. Searle responds that a person who consisted of the entire system would still not understand, that adding the rules and the data does nothing to add comprehensibility.

Many AI researchers dispute the systems reply. Wilensky (1980) says that a man who has internalized the entire Chinese room may not understand Chinese, but some information-processing part of him does. In this case, understanding is a local property of the mind possessed by a subsystem whose knowledge is not accessible to the whole or to other systems. Fisher (1988) makes several points in counterargument to Searle. Among these are that we lack adequate intuitions about what would be going on inside the head of a person who internalized the room. We couldn't say for sure what they understand or not.

2. The Robot Reply. Put a computer brain into a robot body and allow the robot to perceive and act. Then, place this robot into the room. The robot would now understand the Chinese. Searle counters by saying if a person replaced the robot's computer and was capable of perceiving through the robot's sensors and initiating actions through the robot's effectors, that person would still not understand Chinese. It would again be rule following, this time only with casual connections to the world added on. By making this counter, Searle is denying the plausibility of appropriate causal connections to create meaning (Fodor, 1980). According to intentionality, it is the connection between representations and the things they refer to that generate meaning. This is discussed more fully below.

3. The Brain Simulator Reply. In this argument, we create an artificial brain that replicates exactly what transpires in a Chinese speaker's brain when he is reading and responding to Chinese text. The computer reproduces the actual sequence of neuron firing and synaptic action. Since this is what happens in a real brain when someone understands Chinese, the computer will de facto also understand. Searle asks us to think about an elaborate water pipe system that also reproduces this neural activity. In his estimation, the operation of this system would also lack understanding. A formal representation of the neural activity of a Chinese speaker is still just rule following he says, but of a different sort. Whether or not connectionist networks follow rules is a controversial issue and the topic of considerable debate (Horn, 1995).

4. The Combination Reply. This takes all three of the previous arguments and combines them. Imagine a computer that simulates the neural activity of a Chinese speaker. Place this in the body of a robot inside the room and consider all of this together as a unified system. Searle reverts back to his previous rebuttals for this, arguing the combination of these cases doesn't really add anything new. The brain of the robot, for example, would still not understand because it continues to just manipulate symbols.

5. The Other Minds Reply. The only way we know that someone understands Chinese is by his or her behavior. If they can respond intelligently to questions, then that demonstrates understanding. The same holds for a computer. Since we attribute cognition and understanding to other people who act this way we should do it for computers and robots as well. To Searle, we presume that people are cognitive. This is an assumption that we take for granted based on our own subjective experience. However, this assumption cannot be proved objectively, it is taken for granted in the same way the physical sciences presume the existence of reality. Fisher (1988) argues that AI does not have to even explain understanding at all. A general cognitive theory only needs to explicate functionality, how a system performs. This is enough to allow us to design and perhaps down the road, accommodate ideas like understanding.

6. The Many Mansions Reply. Given our current state of technology, we are limited in the extent to which we can produce thinking machines. Someday, we may develop new computational methods that will capture the important aspects of understanding and, when we do, a machine will have this capability. Searle acknowledges that this may be true, but that it redefines the goal of artificial intelligence away from symbol processing to whatever it is that produces and explains cognition.

Learning in the Chinese Room

An important aspect left out of the original Chinese room scenario is learning. A human Chinese speaker has acquired his understanding over many years of listening, speaking, and making mistakes. In addition, the human speaker would have learned many other things in the course of his life such as commonsense knowledge that contributes to his comprehension of Chinese. If we took a particular kind of computer, placed it inside a robot, and let it grow up in a world and learn Chinese, that robot, when placed in the room, might then comprehend what it was doing. The right type of brain that is embodied and allowed to develop over time seems crucial for the emergence of understanding.

The learning hypothesis receives support from a number of scholars (Horn, 1995). Holland, Holyoak, Nisbett, and Thagard (1986) suggest that semantics can emerge from learning programs with inductive adequacy. These are systems that can create all the new knowledge they need to use. A computer system endowed with a semantic network that had inductive adequacy could continually update nodes and links to its network to accommodate new experiences. Rapaport (1988) believes that internal semantics can be achieved in syntactic networks that learn. Meaning will result if these networks are wired up in the correct way and capable of learning. After all, learning in people seems to occur in much the same way. Neurons in the human brain are part of a syntactic network that creates meaning.

Rapaport (1988) buttresses this notion with the Korean room thought experiment. Imagine a Korean professor who is the world's leading authority on Shakespeare. This professor can only understand Korean. He reads Shakespeare that is translated into Korean and writes about Shakespeare in Korean. English speakers then interpret his translated works. Although the professor does not understand English, he does understand Shakespeare. Similarly, the man in the Chinese room does not understand the Chinese symbols he works with, but he may understand Chinese.

SIMULATION

Simulation and Realization

A **simulation** is an imitation of some real object or state of affairs. Simulations attempt to represent certain features of the behavior of a physical or abstract system by the behavior of another system. Process models are examples of simulations. They are computer programs that emulate the execution of some cognitive process. This brings up an important question. Can a simulation realize a property of the actual process or system it is modeling? It helps to be clear about this. On the one hand, we have a system such as a brain that exhibits certain properties like thought, intelligence, and consciousness. When modeling we do not attempt to reproduce this brain or even some subsystem of it in its entirety. Instead, we reproduce only those key aspects of the system that we think are necessary to produce the attribute in question. The successful production of the attribute is **realization** and may be brought about by the actual system or a simulation.

If we wanted to simulate a system that "remembered," for instance, we would need to allocate a place in the simulation where information could be stored. The simulation would also need to implement the processes of encoding so that information could get into the system, and retrieval, so it could be taken out. But if remembering requires more than this our simulation cannot be said to remember because it is leaving that extra something else out. Simulations, in order to be successful, need to reproduce all "necessary ingredients," the crucial factors in the realization.

The question "Can a machine think?" is like the question "Can an airplane fly?" The answer, it turns out, depends on your definition of flying. If flying is something an animal does to move through the air and requires flapping, then an airplane can't fly. If we define flying more broadly as just moving through the air, then an airplane, helicopter, and hot air balloon can all fly. This is an interesting example because we can consider the airplane to be a model that simulates "flying" behavior. We thus need to very carefully consider what it is we want our simulation to do and what we consider to be the successful achievement of that goal.

Simulations involve three key elements. There is the data that is input into the simulation and the way this data is subsequently represented, the computational processes that act on those representations, and the underlying physical structure on which this happens. This means that a simulation could fail on three counts. Even if a simulation had the right data representations and processes, it might still not be able to reproduce the crucial property in question if that property depended in some fundamental way on the hardware or substrate in which it was running. Functionalists, you will recall from the chapter on brains, believe that the process is what's crucial, not the stuff in which it happens. Biological naturalists say that a biological substrate is necessary for thought. If the functionalists are right, then we can ignore structure. If the naturalists were right, then any simulation of thought would have to reproduce its necessary biological underpinnings.

The ability of a simulation to achieve its goal is also dependent on the data that it receives as input because this affects its subsequent representation, processing, and outputs. If the property we want our simulation to have depends on a particular type of representation, then failing to provide this will produce a failed simulation. Recall from the brain chapter, our discussion of analog and digital representations. It may be that the ability to "see" involves computations on an analog representation of the visual scene provided by the eyes. If the representations were digital, then seeing might not result. In this case, we would need to convert the digital inputs to analog representations. Our argument here is not whether digital or analog representations are important per se for cognition, but that a simulation, in order to produce a particular cognitive process, must instantiate the correct form of representation.

The validity of a simulation additionally depends in great degree upon the computations it implements. If what the model attempts to reproduce is based on a specific algorithm or computation and another is used, then the model will fail. Earlier we discussed serial and parallel processing as two basic forms of information processing. Biological brains rely heavily on the latter, computers on the former. Certain mental phenomena may emerge from massively parallel computation. Should this be true, then attempts to model them should also employ extensive parallel computing procedures. An even more basic consideration is that sometimes slight changes in parameter values or in the number of iterations in an algorithm can produce vastly different outcomes.

Simulation and Artificial Psychology

The potential difficulties with simulation do not pose a problem for the realization of an artificial person. As we mentioned, a simulation can produce realization under appropriate conditions. An artificial person is a model or simulation of a real person when any of the above considerations are not addressed. It ceases to become a simulation and is realized when these are met and the desired goal or property of the system, appropriately defined, is achieved.

Jack Copeland echoes these sentiments. He distinguishes between simulation and duplication (Copeland, 1993). A simulation fails to capture the essential characteristic of what it is modeling and is therefore not the same as it. For example, a theatrical death lacks the essential physiological features of real death. However, he says that some simulations are duplications. They capture the essential features of the simulated object despite being produced in a nonstandard way. The example he gives here is artificial coal, which can be burned to produce energy the same way as naturally occurring coal.

Recreating the essence of what it means to think is a tall order. At a minimum, it requires that the data, computations and structure of the model thinking system all correspond to what we find in humans or to the abstract instantiation of essential thinking qualities. Before this happens, we need to agree on what thought is and define those crucial properties. As we see in the next section, there is more to thought than just information processing. We need to take meaning into account as well.

Meaning

There seem to be two aspects to thought. A thought can be considered as pure information, nothing more than a representation that gets operated on. In this sense, a thought seems devoid of content or meaning, much the same way a word or number might appear on a page of paper independent of an observer's glance. But, to the person who is having the thought, there seems to be more. The thought, when experienced, is understood by that person. To illustrate, think of your house. We could symbolically represent the thought using the word "house." This word could then be the subject in a variety of propositions that describe it such as "The house is red" or "The house is old." But do any of these representations convey the experience of what it is like to think about the house? Not really. In this section we attempt to explain how the representations that constitute thought acquire meaning.

INTENTIONALITY

The Symbol-Grounding Problem

Imagine that symbols acquire meaning by pointing or referring to other related symbols, all inside the head. In this explanation the meaning of the word "house" is defined as: "The building or part of a building occupied by one family or tenant." House would then get its meaning by referring to the concepts "building," "family," and "tenant," as well as a specific type of relationship between them. But then the meaning of "family" would be denoted in the same way, referring in turn to concepts like "parents" and "children." In a dictionary, there is no inherent meaning because all concepts are defined circularly in terms of each other. Human meaning cannot be derived this way because the concepts have to be learned and connected in some fundamental way to what they stand for. This requires that the symbols be connected in some way to external reality. This dilemma is called the **symbol-grounding problem** (Harnad, 1990).

One way to get around the symbol-grounding problem is to have symbols "be about" something. The symbol "house" inside someone's head is about an actual house in the world. The real house is said to be the **referent** for its symbol, it is the thing the symbol stands for. The philosopher Franz Brentano (1838–1917) believed that thoughts have meaning precisely because they are directed toward their referents. This idea is known as **intentionality** and he thought it was the fundamental difference between physical and psychological phenomena. A physical object in the world just is, while its corresponding psychological thought is directed toward and is about it. Note that intentionality should not be confused with "intention," which means an active goal or outcome someone is trying to achieve.

A feature of intentionality is that there should be some sort of observable relationship between a thought and its referent. If a representation is intentional, it should be triggered by the referent or by something related to it. In the example we have been using, the sight of

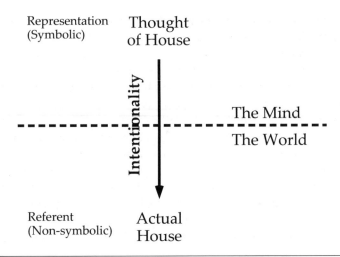

Figure 5.3 Human thoughts are intentional. They are directed toward something in the world. One aspect of intentionality is an appropriate causal relation. Thinking about a house might trigger childhood memories that one could then talk about.

a house or of the yard surrounding it should activate its conceptual representation, making you think of it. Once this happens, the thought of the house should then activate behaviors or thoughts related to it, such as a memory of playing outside the house with friends as a child. There is thus a mapping between stimulus inputs and behavioral outputs for thoughts with intentional content. This relationship is known as an **appropriate causal relation**. Figure 5.3 is a diagrammatic depiction of intentionality. The appropriate causal relation in this figure consists of the following chain of events. First, perception of the house triggers its corresponding conceptual representation. This then retrieves the childhood memory of playing, which causes the person to talk about that experience.

Stevan Harnad believes that symbolic representations are grounded in two kinds of nonsymbolic representations (Harnad, 1990). The first are "iconic representations" or images derived directly from sensory input. The second are "categorical representations," feature-detectors that describe the invariant features of objects and events. He allows both traditional localized symbolic representation from the GOFAI perspective and distributed representation from the connectionist approach to count. In his explanation, objects in the external world first generate the iconic and categorical representations. These then serve as the basis for symbolic representations that because of their grounding in stimulus events, create meaning.

Problems With Intentionality

But is reference to externals alone enough to produce meaning? Searle (1980) doesn't think so. He believes that representational connection to referents does not by itself constitute an explanation of meaning. Haugeland (1985) provides several examples of representations that are not directly linked to referents but still have meaning. We discuss each and see if they pose a problem for intentionality in what follows.

Haugeland (1985) points out that words and sentences can have meaning even if their referents don't exist. This is true for the sentence "Santa is an elf." The fact that we can believe in imaginary beings like Santa Clause and elves probably comes through their grounding in real-world perceptual events like stories, books, and television. So even though the things portrayed in these media don't exist, they have meaning for us because we've experienced them perceptually.

Second, Haugeland asks us to consider two different phrases that have the same referent: "mile-high city" and "Colorado's capital." Both are meaningfully interpreted to indicate "Denver" but are expressed differently. This is also true for synonyms like "fast" and "quick." In these cases, two symbols or symbol combinations have come to be linked to the same referent. Apparently, multiple mental variants of a referent can be instantiated, each with identical or similar meanings. We can think of Denver as that city that is one mile high or as the capital of the state of Colorado.

Third, there are formulations that don't directly refer to anything specific in the world. These can be hypothetical or conditional statements like: "What would happen if you quit your job?" or "If you quit your job, you won't be able to pay the rent." Neither of these statements refers to anything that has actually happened: the person in question has not quit their job yet. In these examples, the interpretation of the sentence makes a difference. We discuss how this affects meaning below. In a similar vein, abstract words like "justice" don't have particular referents either. Abstract concepts, because they are formed from specific instances, may inherit meaning from them. After having experienced enough actual incidents of just action, an agent may automatically apply their meaning to the superordinate term that stands for all of them.

ARTIFICIAL INTENTIONALITY

What are the implications of all this for the construction of an artificial person? If the intentionality thesis is correct, it implies that symbolic representations cannot have meaning or be understood in the human sense of these terms unless they are connected to sensory perception and the world. Our artificial person, in order to experience the meaning of what he or she thinks, would need to relate their concepts to their corresponding referents in the environment. This would ensure that their ideas are grounded in reality and "about" objects and events in the world.

There are two opposing viewpoints on whether an artificial version of intention is possible. The philosopher Edmund Husserl (1859–1938) believed that meanings and mental states are intentional not because of their connectedness to anything else, but because of their intrinsic nature. He believed thoughts are inherently representational and need not be grounded. Although mental states can be described formally, they can't be reduced entirely to this formal structure. As such, mental states and their associated intentional qualities cannot be duplicated on a computer (McIntyre, 1986).

In opposition to this, James Mensch argues that thoughts develop intentionality over time. They do this through a rule-governed process, a "passive synthesis" where sensory data get ordered into intentional perceptions without any effortful action on the part of the subject (Mensch, 1991). Because this process follows rules, it can be reproduced on a computer. This means we could create a computer that synthesizes sensory data into intentional mental contents. If this were true, we could create an artificial person with meaningful thoughts.

Assuming McIntyre's interpretation of Husserl is correct and intentionality is intrinsic, then there may be some as yet undiscovered property of thoughts that makes them intentional without connection to sensory experience. We could then imbue an artificial person with thoughts having this property and he or she would experience them as meaningful. If Mensch's view is correct, we need to discover and reproduce a mechanical version of passive synthesis and implement it in an artificial person to make their thoughts meaningful.

Intentionality and Stances

In philosophy of mind, a stance is a perspective one takes to explain and predict the actions of a system. Someone who is trying to understand a system adopts stances and, as we will see, they can be intentional. In this case, the intentionality is not necessarily possessed by the system itself but by an outside observer who ascribes intentionality to the system in order to understand it. So, in this section we focus on intentionality not in terms of how it may give meaning to what the system itself experiences, but to how it used by others to explain and give meaning to the behavior the system produces.

Daniel Dennett (1981) states there are three fundamental stances one can adopt. The first is the **design stance** that is used mostly to explain the behaviors of mechanical objects based on their function. Take a car, for example. If we had sufficient understanding of how a car worked, we could predict what it will do. Pressing on the accelerator will make it go forward, pressing on the brake will make it come to a stop, turning the steering wheel a certain amount in a certain direction will make it turn by a given amount. We can say these things because we understand how the carburetor, brakes, and steering system operate.

A **physical stance** is based on the physical state of the object and an understanding of how the laws of nature will affect that state. Generally, it is used to describe when something will break down or won't work. We know that a car won't run if it is under water because of our understanding of the properties of water and how they will affect the car. We also know that a car will fall and hit the ground if it is driven off a cliff due to our knowledge of the law of gravity.

For the **intentional stance**, behavior is predicted by relying on terms like beliefs, desires, hopes, fears, and intentions. We explain what an object does by ascribing information and goal-directedness, then working out what it is likely to do. The intentional stance is used primarily to explain complicated systems like computers, animals or people. For these systems, the design and physical stances are uninformative because they get too complex. For the design stance to be an effective description of a person, we would need to know most or all of the neural wiring in that person's brain. For the physical stance, we would need to know how the laws of physics impact on those neurons and other body parts. This is simply too hard to figure out, so we rely on the intentional stance instead.

To continue with our example, by the intentional stance a car may be said to "want' to roll down hill if it is parked at the top in neutral with the brakes off. Dennett reminds us that the car in this instance doesn't actually "desire" to go downhill. This is just a descriptive label we apply to the car in order to understand its action. He says that we could just as easily substitute more scientific sounding terms like "belief analogs" or "information complexes." Dennett wants to make clear that the intentional stance is not anthropomorphizing. We are not turning machines into humans by ascribing them intentionality, just using a language that helps us to figure out what they do.

McCarthy (1979) elaborates on this point. He says that beliefs can reasonably be ascribed to an entity when its actions are consistent, the result of observation, and in accordance with goals. A thermostat demonstrates these three qualities. It consistently turns on whenever the temperature drops below its set point and off when the temperature rises above it. Multiple individuals can observe and confirm that this happens. The thermostat's behavior can also be described as pursuing the goal of keeping the temperature constant. Because thermostats meet these criteria, McCarthy concludes it is reasonable to say they have beliefs.

The intentional stance is useful because it is simple. It involves making assumptions about why a system is acting by describing it using rule-governed internal states. To give a human example, we can assume that Bob will want lunch if he has not eaten breakfast because of his internal state of hunger. Hunger is a motivational drive that operates according to the rule that the longer you have gone without eating, the hungrier you will get and the more likely it is that you will try to eat. An artificial person who acts in much the same way as a normal person, i.e., exhibits complexity, would best be described using the intentional stance.

Interpretation

In addition to intentionality, there is another way that thoughts may come to have meaning. So far we have focused on the representational form of thought, the symbols or connection weights that code for ideas. But in order to be understood, a thought needs to be interpreted. Meaning may thus arise through an interpretive act. In this scheme, an interpreter such as a person or computer applies a set of rules to representations. The application of the appropriate rules then produces meaningful understanding.

English text to an English reader has meaning because the reader understands the rules that govern the language. This reader knows which letters allowably go together to form words and the proper order for different word types in a sentence. To a Chinese speaker who has no understanding of English the same text looks like gibberish and is meaningless. Similarly, a sentence following the rules of English grammar makes sense to an English reader but this same sentence loses all meaning when these rules are violated:

Give me liberty or give me death.
Liberty or me give death me give.

Under the interpretive thesis, meaning isn't just a property of a symbol but also of the processes that act on it. This requires that we consider both representation and computation for it to occur. Examples of separate types of rules that govern language include sounds (phonology), meaning (semantics), and grammar (syntax). In addition, social and world knowledge also come into play. These types of knowledge though, need to be applied to linguistic representations and so must also follow some type of rule-governed or interpretive process.

Pylyshyn (1984) proposes another interesting way for interpretation to affect meaning. He says holding a belief consists in storing in a special "belief box" an instance of a particular thought. This suggests that different mental states like beliefs, intentions, and desires are the same symbolic representations put into different such boxes, perhaps in different locations in the brain. This is, of course, a hypothetical way of thinking about the problem. These boxes and locations may not actually exist, but it expresses the idea that perhaps different transformations or forms of processing, when applied to a given thought can change its meaning. The sentence "I love Jill" when placed in one box or interpreted a certain way would generate the feeling of loving Jill, while this same thought in another box or processed differently would produce the understanding that one loves Jill.

Haugeland (1985) supports this idea when he asks us to differentiate between propositional mode and content. The propositional **content** of a sentence consists of the basic information it holds. The sense or meaning of this content can vary by expressing it in linguistically different ways or **modes**. The sentence "John won the race" can have four modes:

John won the race.	[An assertion]
Did John win the race?	[An inquiry]
Make sure that John wins the race.	[A request]
I'm sorry that John won the race.	[An apology]

In each of the above cases the meaning of the thought was changed by altering the way it was expressed and/or by adding a symbol such as a question mark.

So, we see that meaning must go beyond representation to include interpretation. It's not enough for an interpreter to merely possess a symbol. The symbol must be processed in an appropriate way using a set of allowable rules to generate and change its meaning. An artificial person, in order to make sense out of its symbols, would need to process them using appropriate rules. The application of the wrong rules would result in meaninglessness, as would be the case for a normal person. In linguistics, meaning is referred to as **semantics** and rules are known as **syntax**. Knowing or understanding the concept of "book" is semantic. Knowing how to read a sentence containing that word requires an understanding of syntax. We elaborate on the relationship between syntax and semantics in the next section.

The Syntax-Semantic Barrier and Computers

The interpretation argument above assumes that the application of rule-governed processes or syntax will result in meaning. Searle (1990) argues instead that there is a barrier between the two. He says brains have meaningful mental contents while computers just follow formal rules so they have only syntax. He concludes that syntax by itself cannot give rise to semantics, therefore computers that follow formal rules can never attain meaning. Robert Horn (1995) summarizes a variety of responses within the AI community to this argument that we review now.

Paul and Patricia Churchland (1990) state that Searle's conclusion is unwarranted. They claim that it is an empirical rather than logical issue. Research in AI may yet show that syntactical processing by computers can lead to understanding. James Moor (1988) points to empirical evidence that semantics can emerge from low-level syntactical operations. He gives the example of a bar code reader. At a primitive level, the reader is just following algorithmic rules. But the data that is generated can be analyzed in conjunction with other information to yield knowledge about which items in a store are popular and which items need to be restocked, etc. In other words, high-level semantic properties may arise from the elaborative processing of primitive rules.

Georges Rey (1986) states that syntax can generate meaning if there is a reliable causal connection between the syntactic system and the world. This idea is similar to the ideas of intentionality and an appropriate casual relation but it is now the rule-governed system as a whole that is grounded in experience. To illustrate, imagine a computer that can recognize a cat. The sight of the cat in front of it triggers a syntactical process each time this occurs such that the computer can always reliably display the sentence "I see a cat." This consistent stimulus-response relationship would then constitute a meaningful syntactic belief by the computer that the animal is in front of it.

Richard Double (1983) counters Searle by noting that the syntax-semantics barrier is as much a problem for Searle's theory as it is for AI. Both brains and computers are made up of parts that have no intentionality. Neurons in the brain operate as logic gates, following much of the same rules as circuits in a computer, yet according to Searle brains have semanticity while computers do not. What is needed in both cases is an explanation of how "mindless" components give rise to meaning.

THINKING AND COMPUTING

In chapter 2, we introduced the notion of computability. If something is **computable**, it can be formally specified in the form a mathematical equation or computer algorithm. In other words, the steps and processes involved in a computation are understood and can be implemented in a computer or machine. Some cognitive processes, like arithmetic operations, lend themselves well to computational solutions. **Uncomputable** processes in contrast are not well specified, making it difficult for them to be realized on a machine. Creative acts, like composing music or painting, may be examples of processes that are uncomputable.

Kugel (1986) gives an extended account of the differences between computable and uncomputable processes. These are summarized in Table 5.1. Computations are specified in advance. A device performing a computation in essence has already solved the problem because it has a way of obtaining a solution. The computation thus yields a single result that is considered correct. Computations follow rules or instructions and terminate their processing, what is called halting. The perspective that adopts the computational view is the traditional GOFAI school. Computable processes are good at solving well-defined problems such as those encountered in mathematics.

Uncomputable processes are considered as procedures rather than computations. They are not specified in advance, the solution must instead be obtained. They never yield a final, conclusive result that may be considered absolutely correct. They are thus said to "satisfice" (be good enough for) a solution, rather than satisfy it (Simon, 1957). Uncomputable

Table 5.1 Different features of computable and uncomputable processes

Feature	Computable	Uncomputable
Type of Process	A computation	A procedure
Specification	Specified in advance Problem already solved (a priori)	Not specified in advance Problem needs to be solved (a posteriori)
Result	Only one result	Never a certain result
Satisfaction	Satisfying Provides best solution	Satisficing Result is good enough
Adopted by Perspective	Traditional artificial intelligence (GOFAI)	Connectionism
Halting	Halting Program stops	Non-halting Program never stops
Approach	Follows instructions	Evolutionary or trial-and-error
Examples of problems	Arithmetic	Penrose tilings

processes may follow general operating laws, but they don't adhere to specific, step-by-step level instructions. They operate by a trial and error process in which solutions are repeatedly generated, tested, and discarded. This iterative process may never terminate, so it is non-halting. Connectionists and evolutionary theorists advocate the uncomputable approach. Uncomputable processes are best suited to solving problems for which there is no formal solution. Penrose tilings are an example of these. In this situation a tile with a particular shape must completely fill up the space of a two-dimensional surface like a floor. The only way to do this is to randomly throw down different shapes to see which ones work.

One way to implement a non-halting uncomputable process is to attempt to *disprove*, rather than the more conventional computable form of attempting to prove. Kugel (1986) suggests a pattern recognizer whose job is to recognize letters. The recognizer could send out a symbol that could be the letter "A" to a number of subunits. Each of these subunits then attempts to prove that the letter is *not* an "A," in which case they would turn themselves off. If every subunit turns itself off, the recognizer concludes that the stimulus in question is not a letter. If only one fails to halt, the recognizer chooses that letter as an answer. Finally, if several units fail to halt, one of them is picked as the letter in question. This method of disproving can explain many aspects of human thought like quick decisions, changing our minds, ruminating on an unfinished task (the Zeigarnik effect) and deriving word meaning.

Critics have pointed out that much of human thought is uncomputable and therefore cannot be implemented artificially. Kugel (1986) suggests a way out of this impasse. He says that we can learn about uncomputable human thought processes by developing precise uncomputable computer models of them such as the disproof recognizer. The models can then tell us about how the thoughts occur and enable us to create artificial versions of those processes. Machines running trial and error procedures have already been used to model the cognitive process of induction (Angluin & Smith, 1983) and grammatical induction (Osherson, Stob, & Weinstein, 1990). Kugel points out that these trial and error models don't involve any special kind of "magic." They run on regular computers and have the same hardware and memory requirements as computable processes.

6

LANGUAGE

Half the world is composed of people who have something to say and can't, and the other half who have nothing to say and keep on saying it.

—**Robert Frost (1875–1963)**

The standard way for communicating with a computer today is awkward. We have to laboriously move a mouse around a screen or type in commands. Wouldn't it be nice if we could just talk to a computer or robot and tell it what to do? Spoken language is the natural and efficient way that people communicate with one another (Figure 6.1). If we could get machines to comprehend and produce human language, we could interact with them more easily. Imagine having a conversation with a housecleaning robot. You could tell it to clean the bathroom but not the kitchen and to wait until after dinner before washing the dishes. If the robot was confused about these orders, it could then ask and you would respond to clarify its confusion.

In this chapter we examine some of the amazing progress that has been made in machine language. We first describe what language is and then describe its human development and neural foundations. The bulk of the chapter is devoted to explaining the different information processing stages machines go through in order to comprehend and produce language and to engage in conversation. Although a number of hurdles remain, we can see from this work that computers are capable of reproducing much of human linguistic ability. You may be surprised to discover that there are already artificial conversational agents that can engage in complex typed or spoken dialogues with people. From a functional perspective, these agents understand and use language in a way that is at times indistinguishable from humans.

WHAT IS LANGUAGE?

Language can be defined as a system of finite arbitrary symbols that are combined according to the rules of a grammar for the purpose of communication. Let's unpack the different

Figure 6.1 People effortlessly use language to communicate complex ideas to one another. Language is thus the ideal medium for human-machine interaction.

parts of this statement. The symbols in a language stand for objects, actions, characteristics or other features of the world. These symbols can assume any form. They may be words built from an alphabet, pictures, sounds, or gestures. The symbols are finite. In other words, there are a limited number of symbols that can be formed in any language. They are also arbitrary, meaning that any particular symbol can be chosen to stand for any given aspect of the world. This becomes immediately obvious when we compare the words different languages use to stand for the same thing. The word "shoe" in English and the word "zapato" in Spanish both stand for the same concept but are otherwise unalike. It is the association a language learner makes between the term and the referent that gives it its representational power.

These symbols are then combined together to create more complex meanings. But they cannot be combined in just any old way. The combination must follow the rules of the language in order for it to be sensible. These rules are known as its **grammar**. The grammar of one language will differ in its details from that of another. In English it is customary to place adjectives before the noun. In Spanish the adjective follows the noun. A language's grammar allows a user to generate a very large number of possible meanings. Language can thus be used to express new ideas that come to mind. Most languages are also dynamic. They change with the world around them. Words get dropped over time and new ones come into usage.

The purpose of language is social. It is to communicate or convey information between agents. Language serves as a commonly agreed upon medium agents use in a society to transmit and receive information. Language becomes a very powerful tool because it allows agents to act in a coordinated fashion and achieve goals not possible to individuals acting in isolation. In human societies, language skills are taught to children and so passed from one generation to another. In computer societies individual agents must also use language to communicate. We talk more about how such agents cooperate and compete with each other later in the book.

In order to understand language better, we need to introduce a few key ideas. We must distinguish between language comprehension and production. Comprehension involves the processing of language by a recipient so that it is understood. When you listen to your friend talk and understand what she means, you have performed an act of comprehension. Production refers to the generation of linguistic information by a producer. When you reply to your friend, you are generating spoken language information and thus producing. Complete natural language processing requires that an agent both comprehend and produce.

Many language users also have the ability to comprehend and produce in different modalities. Humans naturally acquire language in the auditory modality as they grow up listening and speaking to others. Then, in school, we learn to read and write; these are the visual equivalents of listening and speaking. We also possess the ability to translate back and forth between these modalities. For instance, we can read out loud or write down what someone is saying. An artificial person would also need to possess these capabilities. It would need to be able to perform what is called text-to-speech and speech-to-text conversion. Later in this chapter we discuss some of the differences between language understanding or comprehension on the one hand and language generation or production on the other. Both capabilities are obviously necessary if an agent is to engage in conversation with another.

In spoken language the smallest unit of sound is called a **phoneme**. Changing a phoneme alters its meaning or the meaning of the larger sound in which it is embedded. Phonemes usually but do not always correspond to the letters of the alphabet. They consist of sounds like the "p" in the first part of the word "pill." There are approximately 45 phonemes in the English language. **Morphemes** are the units of spoken language that have meaning. They can be words but also parts of words. The pronunciation of the word "walk" is a morpheme but so is the "ed" sound that might be attached to the end of a word converting it to the past tense. An approximate estimate of the number of words in the English language based on encyclopedias, dictionaries and other reference sources runs from 450,000 to 1,000,000. If we add modifiers like "ed" or "s," then the total number of morphemes is somewhat larger.

LANGUAGE LEARNING

Is Language Innate or Learned?

There has been considerable debate over how much of human language is innate and how much is learned. There is some evidence to support the idea that all people are born with certain aspects of language use. A **universal grammar** is the term used to describe this (Chomsky, 1986). It is considered a collection of language rules that are genetically specified and universal, that is, found in all known languages. Indeed, some rules seem to be universal. In most languages consonants precede vowels and the subject precedes the object (Crystal, 1987).

On the other hand, there is also evidence demonstrating the importance of experience in language learning. Children who are not exposed to language during a particular time in development show pervasive deficits. There are case studies of children who through tragic circumstances were not exposed to language during this **critical period**. These children never learn to speak at an adult level (Jones, 1995). It is also more difficult for children to acquire a second language the later their exposure to it. Children who arrive in the United States from another country show decreased test scores of English grammar the later their age of entry (Johnson & Newport, 1989).

It is generally acknowledged that both nature and nurture are necessary for human language development. Humans appear to have some predisposition to using language but in order for this ability to fully express itself, exposure to and practice with language is needed. An artificial person could be programmed with much of the necessary knowledge of a language. For example, we could put into it English vocabulary and grammar. This approach as you will see has already been implemented. Language algorithms can call on extensive built-in dictionaries to determine the pronunciation or meaning of a word. However, we also summarize a learning approach to computer language where two or more agents embedded in the same environment can develop shared vocabularies.

Human Language Acquisition

Nobody is born with complete fluent knowledge of his or her native tongue. This ability takes time to emerge. Developmental studies of human language acquisition have shown that all people pass through at least four identifiable stages (Stillings, Garfield, Rissland, Edwina, & Rosenbaum, 1995). Each stage marks the expression of new linguistic skills. The **cooing stage** begins in the first year and is marked by the infant uttering a wide range of sounds. This is followed by the **babbling stage**. Starting at around 6 months, babies articulate a smaller set of sounds that correspond roughly to the phonemes of spoken human languages. The intonation of these utterances now begins to match that of their future language.

This is followed by the **one-word stage**. At an age of just less than 1 year we see the appearance of one-word utterances. Now babies are able to successfully articulate complete words. These words may not be pronounced in an entirely accurate fashion, but the word is being used in its intended way. Babies at this point show they can use words to effectively represent objects in the world. Then there is the **two-word stage**. Young children now produce two-word utterances. They will say things like "want milk." Because they are arranging the words together to convey more complex meanings, this indicates an understanding of grammar. Following the two-word stage, children put together more complex articulations, speaking out three or more word sentences to convey more complex meanings. This period is characterized by a steady growth in vocabulary and grammar.

Agent Language Acquisition: The Talking Heads

Luc Steels who directs the AI Lab at the University of Brussels has taken a radical and fascinating approach to how agents might acquire language (Steels, 1998). Rather than put language concepts directly into AI programs as has been done in the past, Steels lets his programs learn language on their own. He starts with collections of agents that exist in a computer network. The agents become grounded only when they interact with one another in which case they download themselves into robotic bodies at a common location.

The robotic bodies they temporarily inhabit consist of a camera, microphone and loud-speaker arrangement referred to as a "talking head." Two agents might download into two separate talking heads in the same room. They both then view the same scene from different perspectives, i.e., different locations in the room. The scene consists of a variety of colored objects on a white-board. A sample board might contain a blue triangle and a green circle. Figure 6.2 depicts two robotic agents viewing the same scene.

The agents have the ability to recognize these objects and to categorize them. But they do so in different ways because of their differing locations and because they are made to focus on different object characteristics over time. This, in fact, mimics the way people approach the world, from a particular perspective and by attending to one or another feature over others. One agent might view the triangle and decide to name it based on its shape. As a result it would give the triangle the name "TETULA," signifying the "the triangular one." The second agent upon viewing the same triangle would instead focus on a different attribute, referring to it by color as "the blue one."

The names agents assign objects are constructed randomly to ensure that other agents cannot initially understand them. In other words, the names for words are arbitrary. This

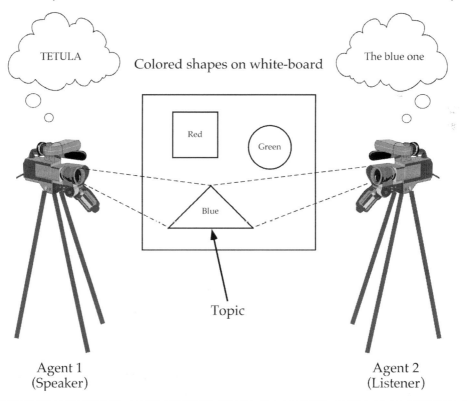

Figure 6.2 Two of Luc Steel's robotic agents focus on the same object and use a word to express it. They are able to spontaneously develop a language and use it to create shared meaning.

is true for all human languages. What matters is not the particular string of symbols that constitute an object name, but that all members who use the language agree that those symbols stand for a particular object and apply the common rules of the language to it. The random generation of object labels by these agents may also be seen as reflecting the babbling stage infants go through. In both cases basic linguistic elements are generated but then later combined to form symbol strings serving as words.

The agents have thus begun to play a language game. They agree on a context, which is the part of the scene they are viewing together. In this case it would be the white-board with the colored shapes. One agent then views an object in the context, categorizes it based on one of its features and utters its name for the object to the other agent. The second agent attempts to comprehend what is meant by this utterance by indicating what it thinks it refers to. If they agree, both agents now use the term to refer to the object. If they cannot agree, their behavior is adjusted so that they are more likely to agree the next time around.

So, in a sample trial the first agent might refer to the blue triangle as "TETULA," thinking of it as a triangular thing. The second agent would hear this and then agree that "TETULA" is the name for that same triangle, but would categorize it instead as a blue thing. Although the agents develop their own unique way of understanding what the object is, they now both share a common language for referring to it. Again, this is much the same way people operate. We may each think of something like an elephant differently, but we can use the name to communicate with each other effectively and share each other's meaning. Two people can tell stories about elephants to one another and know what the other is talking about even though they may experience the concepts involved in a unique and subjective way. This is one of the great feats of language. It does not ensure that we agree on every detail of our subjective understanding but merely that we use a common framework of shared meanings.

Language and Neuroscience

Over the past century, we have come to understand which major areas of the brain subsume different language functions. In the 19th century the French surgeon Paul Broca (1824–1880) discovered a region in the left frontal lobe since named **Broca's area**. Patients who suffered damage to this area had difficulty producing speech. They uttered a string of nouns and verbs but omitted many of the filler functional words like "the" or "as" and additionally failed to conjugate verbs. Their speech was also telegraphic, filled with pauses and interruptions. This suggests that Broca's area is the region in the human brain where speech is produced.

A second area, this one located in the left temporal lobe, is named after Carl Wernicke (1848–1905). **Wernicke's area** mediates language comprehension. Patients with damage to this region produce rapid fluent speech that is meaningless. This speech has the same rate and intonation as normal speech but has no content or meaning. These patients have deficits in understanding speech and difficulty in reading and writing.

There are several other brain areas linked to different aspects of language ability. The **arcuate fasciculus** connects Wernicke's and Broca's areas. Damage to this pathway results in problems with repeating words that have just been heard. There is also the **angular**

gyrus located behind Wernicke's area. Damage to this region produces deficits in reading and writing. In addition to these structures, various primary cortical areas play a significant role in language. The **primary auditory cortex** in the temporal lobe is where speech information is first processed. **Primary visual cortex** in the occipital lobe is where basic visual features are extracted and processed. There is also the **primary motor cortex** in the frontal lobe. Commands issued from here initiate muscle contraction for articulation and movement.

All of these areas are included in a process model of language known as the Wernicke-Geschwind model (Geschwind, 1972). This model shows the flow of information processing during speech comprehension and production and for reading and writing. Imagine that your friend Jim asks: "How are you?" Your response is: "I'm doing fine." According to the model, the following pathway would be activated in your brain. The primary auditory cortex would first become activated as it processed the perceptual characteristics of the speech sounds of your friend's voice. The results of this processing would then be passed to Wernicke's area where the meaning of what is said is understood and a reply is generated. Next, this reply would be passed along the arcuate fasciculus to Broca's area. Once it reached Broca's area, the reply would be converted to a motor code or program of articulation. This code is passed to the primary motor cortex where commands to move the mouth and produce speech are executed.

The model specifics a second pathway for reading and writing. The sight of printed words now activates the primary visual cortex and other visual areas that mediate recognition of the words. This visual representation is then converted into an auditory code by the angular gyrus, which sends the code to Wernicke's area. Wernicke's area comprehends the text and formulates a reply that is passed to Broca's area via the arcuate fasciculus. A motor code is then created for writing or speaking this reply.

The Wernicke-Geschwind model is considered to be an oversimplification for the neural basis of language. Not all of the areas in the model are functionally exclusive. Damage to Broca's area in some patients produces no deficits or only mild transient deficits (Dronkers, Shapiro, Redfern, & Knight, 1992; Mohr, 1976). Brain imaging studies show the areas are not modalty-specific, i.e., tied to speech or reading and writing alone as they are also employed for sign language use (Bavelier et al., 1998). In addition, it appears that these areas may be used for non-linguistic processing and that other areas not specified by the model play a role in language function (Swinney, Zurif, Prather, & Love, 1996). However, until a more detailed and comprehensive model is available, the Wernicke-Geschwind model still serves as a useful way to conceive of the neural underpinnings of language. As we discuss computer language algorithms you may notice that they are performing operations similar to those in these different brain regions.

NATURAL LANGUAGE PROCESSING

Computers are already sophisticated at using formal programming languages like C++ or Basic. These are easy for machines to process because the symbols and rules that govern how the symbols are transformed are well specified. It is much more difficult to get machines to comprehend and produce natural language. A **natural language** is one that has evolved in and is used by humans. English, Spanish, and German are all examples. Natural languages are more flexible than formal languages but also more ambiguous. It has been the goal of many researchers in linguistics and artificial intelligence to develop software capable of natural language processing at the ability level of a human adult. Recent years have seen steady progress in this area and the realization of this dream may lie in the near future.

STAGES OF NATURAL LANGUAGE COMPREHENSION

There are four major stages of information processing that a machine must pass through in order to comprehend spoken language (Cawsey, 1998). In the first stage, known as **speech recognition,** words are extracted from the sound of a spoken voice. Next, in **syntactic analysis**, the computer must make sense of the ordered arrangement of these words, what is equivalent to recovering sentence structure. During the third stage, the meaning of individual words and word groupings is recovered. This is known as **semantic analysis**. In the fourth and final stage of **pragmatic analysis** complete sentence meaning is derived by applying social and contextual information. We give a detailed account of how this is achieved in the following sections, noting parallels between machine and human processing.

Speech Recognition

The job of a speech recognition mechanism is to take the sound of spoken language and break it down into basic sound or phonological units. We start with the speech signal or actual speech sound. This is represented using a **speech spectrogram,** a plot showing the different frequency components and how they vary over time. A computer program takes as input the intensity and temporal change in frequencies and uses it to extract phonemes. A process analogous to this occurs in people. The raw speech signal is decomposed into its component frequencies by the cochlea in the inner ear. This information is then passed along afferent auditory pathways and after synapsing several times reaches the primary auditory cortex in the temporal lobe. Different neurons in this region code for distinct frequencies. These neurons form a **tonotopic** map much like the layout of a piano keyboard and are used to activate more complex phonological neural representations.

What is required next is to assemble the phonemes into morphemes to produce words. One way to do this is to compare candidate phonemic strings against a database containing words with their proper phonemic ordering. If there is a match, then the string in question stands a chance at being that word. A database containing a list of words and their attributes for a given language is known as a **lexicon**. A lexicon is essentially a "dictionary" containing important information about a word such as its pronunciation, meaning, and syntactical function. Human neuroscience research shows that these different aspects are represented in neural regions throughout the left temporal, parietal, and frontal lobes (Kay & Ellis, 1987).

There are, however, a number of difficulties with determining the sound of a word. One is that there are no pauses or boundaries between words. This makes it hard to determine where one word starts and another ends. Without this knowledge a lexical match can't be made. Another problem is phoneme variability. Different people pronounce phonemes differently. The sound of a certain phoneme also varies depending on the sound of those around it, a phenomenon known as **coarticulation**. To complicate matters further, two identical sounds like "hare" and "hair" can belong to more than one word.

There are a few ways to overcome these issues. One is to use context to disambiguate phonemes. For example, the phoneme preceding "eel" would be interpreted as an "m" for "meal" if it occurred in a sentence referring to food and an "h" for "heel" if the sentence were about shoes (Warren & Warren, 1970). This requires a top-down approach where individual ambiguities about sounds or words are left open until the overall meaning of the entire sentence becomes clear. This meaning may not arrive until the later stages of syntactic and semantic processing are complete. Visual cues like lip reading can also assist in disambiguating when such information is available.

Syntactic Analysis

The first stage in syntactical processing is part-of-speech word-tagging. The **parts of speech** are noun, verb, pronoun, preposition, adverb, conjunction, participle, and article. Modern computational methods have yielded a much larger corpus of word classes, some containing up to 45 distinct types (Marcus, Santorini, & Marcinkiewicz, 1993). Knowing the part of speech a word belongs to gives information about a word and its neighbors. It can tell us what words are likely to precede or follow it. For example, possessive pronouns are usually followed by a noun ("my dog") while personal pronouns are typically followed by a verb ("she ran"). Parts of speech also inform us as to how a word is pronounced.

An important feature of language is that individual words don't exist in isolation. They are organized at successive levels into larger and larger groups of words that consist of more complex relationships. For example, a noun phrase is a word grouping that contains a noun, such as "the horse." A verb phrase is a grouping of words containing a verb like "ran swiftly." A sentence is composed of a noun phrase and a verb phrase but there are many more complex variations possible. The allowable ways that words can get ordered in a sentence for a given language is governed by **syntax**. A representation of the hierarchical arrangement of these word types is depicted using a **tree diagram**.

A syntactical analysis proceeds by determining the hierarchical structure of a sentence. Whenever an input is decomposed into a part-based structure it is known as **parsing**. Figure 6.3 shows the tree diagram that represents a correct syntactic parsing of the sentence "The thirsty man drank the cool water." You can see that the sentence (S) is divided into a noun phrases (NP) and a verb phrases (VP). The noun phrase consists of a determiner (D), adjective (A), and noun (N). The verb phrase consists of a verb (V) and another noun phrase which itself contains a determiner, adjective, and noun.

Semantic Analysis

In the chapter on thinking, we discussed **semantics** or meaning. We said that the meaning of mental contents might arise from their grounding or connection to referents in the world. However, we also mentioned that meaning might be intrinsic and that there could be some quality or characteristic of a representation that could give it meaning without

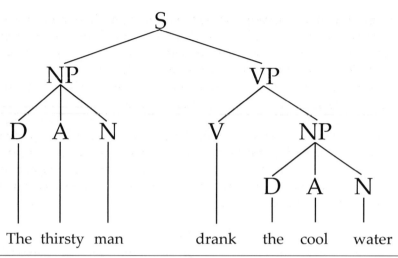

Figure 6.3 A sentence tree diagram depicts the different parts of an utterance. Recovery of this type of structure is necessary in order to understand speech.

recourse to outside reference. In the field of computational linguistics accessing and using semantic representations derives the meaning of an utterance. Just as there are symbolic or structural representations to stand for the phonetic or syntactical qualities of language units, we can now also use similar organizing structures to derive meaning.

The lexicon is an example of just such an organizing structure. The phonological representation of a specific word in the lexicon tells us what it sounds like and how to pronounce it but not what it means. Similarly, a syntactical entry may tell about the word's function and whether it is a noun, verb, or adjective, etc. But this alone is often not enough to get complete word meaning. For this, access to the word's meaning component is needed. Activation of a meaning entry for a word in the lexicon is one explanation for how meaning is derived. This is equivalent to looking up the definition of a word you don't know in a dictionary. There is an extensive psychological literature on lexical access during reading but also in other linguistic tasks (Balota, Flored d'Arcais, & Rayner, 1990). Researchers in this area use neuroimaging and reaction time methods to determine the locations of the different aspects of the lexicon in the human brain and how they are used.

Semantic networks are another organizing structure that can be used to obtain meaning. You will recall we introduced semantic networks in the chapter on learning and memory. These networks represent concepts and the relationships between them. Networks are particularly good at explaining the associational and circular nature of word meaning. In the chapter on thinking we pointed out that many concepts don't have unique intrinsic meanings but are defined by referring to other concepts. The example we gave in that chapter was that house was defined by reference to the concepts "building," "family," and "tenant." So, the meaning of the concept house may arise as near simultaneous activity in these nodes and the connections between them. In the network account, meaning for a word is thus the sum of the activation of the component nodes that define it.

The derivation of a sentence's meaning may occur in a similar way. Sentence meaning could correspond to the activation of nodes that stand for the various concepts in the sentence. In this account, understanding the meaning of "The thirsty man drank the cool water" occurs when the nodes for "man," "water," "cool," and the like become active at more or less the same time. The sentence's overall meaning is the pattern of activity between these nodes that occurs during spreading activation.

We mentioned above that knowledge of syntax is not enough in most cases to yield meaning. However, syntax does play an important role in winnowing down a word's sense. If we know that a word is a verb and follows a noun, then it is a good bet that the verb describes an action made by that noun. Similarly, an adjective that precedes a noun describes it in some way. Having this kind of information narrows the number of possible meanings for a word and makes deriving meaning that much easier. Instead of having to search for all possible meanings, an agent with knowledge of a word's part of speech can restrict its search to just that category.

Pragmatic Analysis

Pragmatics is the study of how language is used to refer to people and things. When we talk to each other we usually have little difficulty understanding to whom or what a speaker is referring. Take, for example, the following sentence:

> Heather went to Lindsey's house to see her new dress. She looked at it and wanted to buy one just like it.

In this case it is pretty clear that "she" refers to "Heather" rather than "Lindsey" and "it" refers to "dress" rather than "house." But how did you know this? Pragmatics investigates the rules people and machines use to interpret these sorts of denotations during conversation.

Determining who is doing what in conversation is known as **reference resolution**. As in the example with Heather and Lindsey above, there are certain words in the English language that we use to refer to objects or people. Such words include "it," "this," "that," and pronouns like "I," "you," "he," "she," "we," and "they." Psychology experiments show that people follow certain rules in resolving issues of reference. Clark and Sengal (1979) had participants read three context sentences and then respond when they understood a following target sentence. Reaction times were faster for the condition where the referent for the pronoun in the target sentence was evoked from the most recent clause in the preceding context sentences. In other words, people tend to assign reference to the person or entity most recently mentioned, probably because they are the most active representation in working memory.

There are many other factors in addition to recency that influence pronoun resolution. Lappin and Leass (1994) created an algorithm that takes recency and these additional factors into consideration. When the program encounters a noun phrase that evokes a new entity, it assigns it a salience value. The value is calculated as the sum of the weights assigned by a set of salience factors. The weights of the salience factors assigned to entities are reduced by half each time a new sentence is encountered. This decreases the salience of "older" entities decreasing the likelihood that they will be referents. The program thus mimics the recency effects found in the psychological literature.

Another property of conversation and reading is **coherence**. This is the idea that sentences should be meaningfully related to each other. Sentences that are strung together at random or don't follow logically lack coherence. Take, for example, the following two sentences:

Ed walked down the street. He pulled the book off the shelf.
Ed walked down the street. He went into the store.

The first sentence fails to exhibit coherence because pulling a book off a shelf has little to do with walking down the street. The second demonstrates coherence because going into the store is something one can do after walking down the street. In fact, in the first sentence most readers will try to make sense out of the sentences by introducing an appropriate set of intervening events, like having Ed go into a library first. In this case, we are making an inference that is logically or causally reasonable given the evidence provided. This demonstrates how important coherence is to us. Our minds try to make sense out of linguistic input even when it lacks coherence.

Myers, Shinjo, and Duffy (1987) generated four context sentences to accompany a number of target sentences. The context sentences varied in how causally related they were to the target. If the target sentence was "She found herself too frightened to move" then "Rose was attacked by a man in her apartment" would have a high degree of causal relatedness and "Rose came back to her apartment after work" would have a low degree. Participants viewed context-target pair sentences. Reading times were faster for pairs with a higher degree of causal relatedness. The participants were then presented one sentence from each pair and asked to recall the other. Recall was better for more related pairs. This experiment suggests that readers make logical inferences between sentences in order to provide coherence to them.

Abduction is one way to make inferences between sentences. You will recall from earlier in the book that abduction is method of logical reasoning whereby implications are run backward. One starts with a general statement— "All men like cars"—followed by a specific statement—"Michael likes cars" —then conclude that "Michael is a man." Hobbs, Stickel, Appelt, and Martin (1993) have produced a computer program that uses abductive inference to provide sentence coherence. Their algorithm constructs a logical chain of events to establish a meaningful connection between two sentences. A similar subconscious process is probably what is happening in our brains while reading or listening.

NATURAL LANGUAGE PRODUCTION

If a machine could recognize speech, identify the meaning of words and sentences, and understand how these refer to things, it would still not match human linguistic ability. That is because understanding what someone says is useless without being able to reply.

Natural language production can be considered as natural language comprehension in reverse. Instead of taking acoustic input and deriving meaning, a production system must start with meaning and generate acoustic output. Whereas comprehension is a process of decoding information that is in a signal, production is a process of encoding information to create a signal. Many of the same processes we have already looked at can be used when generating language. For example, lexical selection is needed to choose an appropriate word or pronunciation, while inferences need to be drawn to group sentences together in meaningfully related ways. Choice is a key issue in language production and occurs at many levels. What kind of reply should be made? How specifically should it be phrased? How much should be said? These are decisions that people make when replying during conversation and that a machine must make as well.

Jurafsky and Martin (2000) outline a general architecture for a natural language generation system. To start, the system must have a communicative goal. This may be to answer questions or assist a user in some task. Second, the agent must call on a knowledge base. This could be a lexicon and/or specialized knowledge of a particular domain. A **discourse planner** takes information from both these sources and makes choices about what to say. The content of what needs to be said is ultimately fed to a **surface realizer**. The job of this component is to produce the actual sentences that will be uttered. In a final step, these sentences are transmitted to a speech synthesizer that pronounces them. If textual output is desired, the sentences would instead be fed to a text generator that could display them to a monitor or other device.

A speech synthesizer can be thought of as performing text-to-speech conversion because it receives as input text or some other symbolic language format and must convert this to speech. This is accomplished by accessing pronunciation information for words in the lexicon. This information can be used for recognition purposes when the system starts with a sequence of phonemes and must map them to a morpheme or word as discussed earlier. But it can also be used for production when one is starting with a known word and wants to speak it.

The final step in speech synthesis is the conversion of the phonemic code into a physical sound or waveform. In **concatenative synthesis** phonemes are pronounced one after another in the correct order. Unfortunately, this results in poor sounding speech even when the "edges" are smoothed or blended into one another. This is because of the coarticulation problem discussed previously where adjacent phonemes influence pronunciation. A solution to this is to use a unit of pronunciation that starts half-way through the first phoneme and ends half-way through the second. This unit of measure is known as a **diphone**. Diphones take into account the influence of the prior phoneme and produce a more natural sound.

We would be remiss if we did not mention the role of prosody. **Prosody** refers to those aspects of pronunciation that go beyond the mere sequence of phonemes. This includes changes in pitch, rhythm, speed, and other factors. Prosody conveys information about what is being said. For instance utterances tend to end with pauses while a rising pitch characterizes questions. But prosody also conveys information about the emotional state of the speaker. When we are nervous, we tend to talk quickly and when we are depressed, more slowly. When someone is angry, the tendency is to raise the voice.

Computational language systems to equal human ability must be able to both produce and recognize prosody. Adding prosody to speech makes it sound more natural (i.e., human) and less monotone and machine-like. Language systems should also be able to detect when someone is anxious or upset and adjust the content and expression of their response accordingly. A computer that could adopt a soothing tone in response to detecting stress in the voice of a user would go a long way toward facilitating human-machine interaction. On an interesting side note, first-episode schizophrenics are impaired in their ability to interpret prosody in the spoken human voice (Edwards, Pattison, Jackson, & Wales, 2001). The authors of this study suggest that this deficit is consistent with amygdala dysfunction. The amygdala is a part of the brain underlying perception of emotions like fear.

Dialogue

Human language serves a social function. It allows us to communicate our ideas and intentions to one another in a reciprocal fashion. People talk back and forth to each other in a conversation or **dialogue**. An artificial person must thus also be capable of dialogue. In this section we describe the fundamental characteristics of dialogue that any machine must possess if it is to equal human conversational skill.

Turn-taking, grounding, and implicature are the features that characterize dialogue (Jurafsky & Martin, 2000). During **turn-taking** speakers alternate or wait their turn to talk. One speaker waits until the first is finished before speaking. Usually there is no overlap; the start of one speaker's turn follows shortly on the completion of another's. For spoken English, the time between turns is quite small, only a few hundred milliseconds. This interval is so short that speakers must have a reply planned before the speaker has even finished, implying that human speakers know that their turn to talk is coming up. But how does a person or agent know this? Sacks, Schegloff, and Jefferson (1974) have formulated a set of turn-taking rules:

a. If during this turn the current speaker has selected A as the next speaker, then A must speak next.
b. If the current speaker does not select the next speaker, any other speaker may take the next turn.
c. If no one else takes the next turn, the current speaker may take the next turn.

There are additional cues that inform us when a speaker has finished and we can talk. These boundary cues help determine utterance boundaries. Cue words like "well," "and," and "so," tend to happen at the start and end of statements. A machine programmed with Sack's rules and capable of using these cues would display appropriate turn-taking behavior.

Dialogue must also have what is called **common ground**, the set of things that are mutually believed by both speakers. A listener can establish common ground by acknowledging what the speaker has said. This can occur through the use of utterances that inform the speaker that the listener understands and often prompts him or her to continue. These short words or phrases are called **continuers** (e.g., "uh-huh," "yeah," and "OK"). Other ways of indicating common ground are paraphrasing or repeating what has just been said or completing the speaker's utterance (Clark & Schaefer, 1989). It is fairly straightforward to implement continuers and they are in use in a number of conversational agents.

The third important characteristic of dialogue is **conversational implicature.** When speaking to one another, we often convey more meaning than what is literally true of an utterance. For instance, if person A stated they were thirsty, person B might reply, "There is a store around the corner." The implied meaning is that person A can get a drink at the store. Person B is not simply informing person A of the presence of the store as a geographical fact. Grice (1975) outlines four maxims that speakers generally obey when speaking to each other. These maxims help guide our interpretation of meaning during conversation.

1. **Maxim of Quantity**. Be as informative as required. Do not say more or less than what is required.
2. **Maxim of Quality**. Say what you believe to be true. Don't lie.
3. **Maxim of Relevance**. Be relevant. Stay on the topic at hand.
4. **Maxim of Manner**. Be as clear as possible. Avoid being ambiguous or obscure.

A conversational agent in order to be understood would need to follow these four maxims.

An utterance can be considered not just information but also an action (Austin, 1962). Many times when we say something it is a command to others or is intended to have some sort of effect on others. If we consider language in a social context, then utterances must be interpreted in terms of their actions. We need to know what it is we have to do or not do as a result of someone having said something. Searle (1979) classifies speech into several action categories. An **assertive** asserts that something is the case as in: "The woman was wearing a red coat." A **directive** is a direct instruction or command from the speaker to the listener as in: "Please open the door," A **commissive** commits the speaker to some later action as in: "I promise to mow the lawn later today." Other speech acts can express the speaker's psychological state or change the state of the world.

Computer scientists have expanded upon Searle's five speech acts. They have developed programs that classify different utterances into one of a larger number of possible **dialogue acts**. In essence, these programs perform dialogue act tagging. They take a phrase or statement and determine what sort of action it conveys. One recent program that does this is Dialogue Act Markup in Several Layers or DAMSL for short (Carletta, Dahlback, Reithinger, & Walker, 1997). Table 6.1 shows just some of the DAMSL dialogue act tags along with a description of their function. Once a conversational agent identifies the dialogue act of an utterance, it can use this information to guide an appropriate response.

Conversational Agents

The ability to carry out a conversation or dialogue is a hallmark of what it means to be human. People engage in this type of language activity more than any other. Turing's famous test is, of course, based on this capacity. There is something magical about carrying out a conversation with a machine. The experience causes us to attribute characteristics like thought, intelligence, and consciousness. We mention computer dialogue programs at various points throughout this book. ALICE was an example of a computer chatterbot that won the Loebner prize and is described in the chapter on thinking. The SHRDLU program from the intelligence chapter receives typed commands through a computer keyboard and responds with questions of its own. ELIZA is a computerized conversational therapist we will discuss later.

A **conversational agent** then, is a computer program that communicates with users using natural language. Most conversational agents in commercial use now are designed to

Table 6.1 Selected dialogue act tags in the DAMSL program. Forward-looking functions identify the type of statements made by a conversational partner. Backward-looking functions identify the relationship of an utterance to previous utterances by the other speaker.

Forward-Looking Functions	Tag	Description
	Statement	A claim made by the speaker.
	Information Request	A question by the speaker.
	Action-Directive	An actual command.
	Opening	Greetings.
	Closing	Farewells.
	Thanking	Thanking and responding to thanks.
Backward-Looking Functions		
	Accept	Accepting the proposal.
	Reject	Rejecting the proposal.
	Hold	Putting off response, usually via sub-dialogue.
	Answer	Answering a question.
	Signal Non-Understanding	Speaker didn't understand.
	Repeat-Rephrase	Demonstrated via repetition or reformulation.

perform some specific task like book airline flights, reserve tickets to a film, or check a bank or credit card balance. They are capable of understanding spoken user input, responding appropriately to questions and asking questions of their own. In this section we describe the different types of architectures that underlie conversational agents.

The **dialogue manager** of a conversational agent is the "higher-level" part that guide's the agent's side of the dialogue. It controls the flow of dialogue, determining what statements to make or questions to ask and when to do so (Jurafsky & Martin, 2000). The simplest dialogue managers follow a flow chart specifying what responses and questions need to be made based on user utterances. For instance, a conversational agent that is booking movie tickets might ask first for the desired region of the theater, then for the theater itself, then for the movie, and then for the show time. These types of systems are fine for well-defined situations where there are a small number of possible options.

More complex situations call for a more complex architecture. Ross, Brownholtz, and Armes (2004) at IBM Research have created the Lotus Conversational Interface (LCI) to speech-enable software applications like email, instant messaging, and stock quotes. LCI was supposed to be an electronic version of the prototypical English butler, helpful but not intrusive. LCI does not generally interrupt the user while they are speaking, although the user can interrupt the system. If LCI has something to say, it can ask permission before speaking. It also accepts and responds to polite speech phrases such as "good morning" and "thank you." Notice that the system is generally conforming to the rules of turn-taking mentioned above.

LCI also assures the users that they have been heard and understood. It restates questions and describes what it is doing if there is a pause or silence. In other words, LCI is capable of establishing common ground. The system is also modeled to be consistent and transparent to the user. It doesn't use words or phrases that it might not be able to act upon. It does not make assumptions about what the user wants beyond what the user stated and tries not to mislead the user into thinking it is more capable than it is. Notice that these principles correspond to conversational implicature and the following of Grice's maxims.

The LCI architecture contains several major components:

1. A speech engine takes auditory input and converts it into a textual or symbolic format suitable for processing. This is equivalent to speech recognition.
2. An ontology. This defines the objects and classes within a software application. For example, the word "open" is a type of action that will open a program or file.
3. The lexicon. This provides synonyms and part-of-speech information for the words defined in the ontology.
4. A syntax manager contains a grammar for use by the speech engine that draws on information from the ontology and lexicon.
5. Semantic analysis. This uses a frame with slots that get filled by particular values. For example, the command "Open the message from Bill" would have "open" as the action, "message" as the item to be acted upon, and "Bill" as an attribute of the

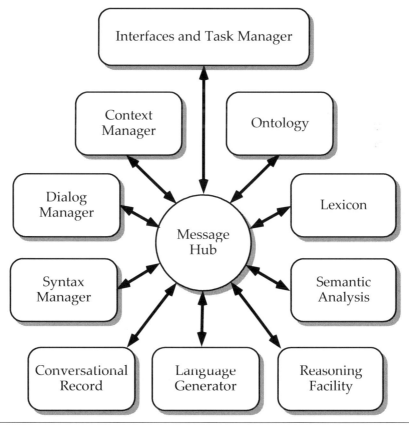

Figure 6.4 The organization of the Lotus Conversational Interface (LCI) program. Developed at IBM Research, it is capable of carrying on limited spoken dialogues with human users.

item. A frame determines the meaning of an utterance and like semantic networks is another example of a semantic structural representation.

6. A rule-based system takes utterances and decides what to do about them. "If-then" statements map utterances onto commands that are executed. The rules specify the kind of act the system must make.

7. The dialogue manager regulates incoming and outgoing utterances, prevents interruptions and keeps track of user commands.

Figure 6.4 shows the organization of these components. The speech and computer interfaces are kept separate from the linguistic processing modules that in turn surround a central message hub. All messages are routed through the hub.

The LCI system is flexible and has been modified for new applications that drive different hardware devices. In a relatively short time, LCI code was modified to speech-enable a simulated automobile. The system allowed user control over the radio, telephone, climate control, windows, and doors. It is important to note that LCI is not equipped to carry on a general conversation about any topic. It is restricted to dialogue in the specific domains for which it is given expertise.

7

INTELLIGENCE

If you're so smart, how come you ain't rich?

—American saying

WHAT IS INTELLIGENCE?

If you had two psychologists in a room and asked them what intelligence was, you would probably get three opinions. Intelligence is one of those elusive concepts that is very difficult to define. We all seem to have a general idea of what it means and might even be able to point out someone who we think is intelligent, but it has eluded a formal definition that researchers can agree upon. However, we will adopt the following broad definition. **Intelligence** is the ability to learn from experience, solve problems, and use knowledge to adapt to new situations (Myers, 2001). The last part of this definition is particularly important, because it gets at the crux of what it means to be smart. An intelligent agent, be it a person or machine, must be able to adapt successfully to changed circumstances.

Copeland (1993) aptly points to the digger wasp as an example of what intelligence is not. This wasp follows a stereotyped behavioral routine. When she flies back to her burrow, she will deposit food at the entrance then go in to check if there are any intruders inside. If there aren't, she will go back outside and bring the food in. If however, an experimenter moves the food a small distance away while she is inside checking, she will repeat the entire sequence over again, moving the food back to the entrance, the going in to check once more. The wasp is blindly following a fixed response pattern and fails to take change into account. She apparently cannot remember that she has checked the burrow already or can't figure out that she can take the food in from a greater distance. This example shows the importance of learning, memory, and the application of past experience to a current problem situation as the defining ingredients of intelligence.

AI researchers distinguish between two broad visions of the field (Brighton & Selina, 2003). According to **strong AI**, the goal is to build a machine capable of thought, consciousness, and emotions. This view holds that humans are no more than elaborate computers. An underlying assumption of strong AI is that intelligence is a physical process and that if we can reproduce this process correctly intelligence and perhaps other human mental qualities like consciousness will be the result. This is the functionalist view introduced earlier. Functionalists believe that mental qualities can arise from the operation of appropriate processes regardless of the material hardware in which they execute. They argue that intelligence can arise from a biological substrate like the brain, from silicon chips like a computer, or from some other material background. The aim of **weak AI** is much less bold. The goal here is to develop theories of human and animal intelligence and test them by building working models like computer programs or robots. Those adopting the strong AI view believe that someday a program or robot will actually become intelligent. Those favoring the weak AI view see these models simply as tools for understanding intelligence.

ONE OR MANY INTELLIGENCES?

In the history of the psychological literature, there is also a debate over whether intelligence is a single general ability or a specific capacity. There are important implications that stem from this debate. If intelligence were a single unitary ability, we could measure it more easily through testing procedures and compare people or machines quantitatively along a continuum, judging some to be more intelligent than others. If, instead, intelligence turns out to be a hodgepodge of different skills, then individuals differ from each other in a more qualitative way, making comparisons among them more difficult.

An early approach to this problem was to apply a statistical procedure called factor analysis to intelligence test scores. The analysis breaks down an overall score into a number of different components that in turn may be divided up hierarchically into smaller components still. Different researchers using this technique conclude intelligence is made up of a varying number of factors.

Charles Spearman (1927) thought intelligence consisted of a single general ability, which he called the "g" factor. According to Spearman, this factor pervades all types of thinking and is akin to "mental energy." However, he also acknowledged "g" was made up of several smaller specific abilities labeled "s." Thurstone (1938) was more on the side of specific abilities, which he called primary mental abilities. He listed seven. These included verbal comprehension and fluency, inductive reasoning, spatial visualization and mathematical problem solving. Guilford (1967,1982), formulated a model of intellect containing no less than 150 separate factors organized into three dimensions.

Howard Gardner (1993) has developed a well-known **theory of multiple intelligence**s. His theory is not based on the factor-analytic approach. He is not advocating a single intelligence that is made up of different types, but instead seven different intelligences, each relatively independent of the other. We describe these below in terms of how they are measured in people and then contrast this with current machine abilities.

1. Linguistic: The ability to use language. Exemplified in reading, writing, and understanding spoken words. In the language chapter, we've shown programs that possess linguistic intelligence, being capable of comprehending and producing natural language. There are, however, some obstacles that need to be overcome before computers are on a par with people, including the appropriate application of a world knowledge base to aid in comprehension.
2. Logical-mathematical: Used in solving math problems and logical thinking. Computers excel in this domain. They are capable of computing these sorts of operations far more quickly and accurately than people. That is because these problems can be specified in an exact formal way and solved algorithmically.
3. Spatial: The representation and manipulation of spatial information. Characterized by skills like navigation and mental rotation. We saw in the chapter on perception and action that robots can form internal maps of their environment and use these to get from one location to another.
4. Musical: Skill at composing, singing and performing music. Computers too can be said to possess musical intelligence. We discuss musical computer programs in the chapter on creativity.
5. Bodily-kinesthetic: Use of the body to solve problems as in dancing and playing sports. Robotic examples of bodily-kinesthetic intelligence include reaching, grasping, and walking, outlined in the perception and action chapter. Robots are getting better at interacting motorically with the world but have some way to go before they can match human feats in this arena.
6. Interpersonal: Relating to and understanding other people. Machines that exist in societies must be able to work effectively with other humans and machines. There are already social robots that work cooperatively together to achieve a goal. We explore this further in the chapter on social behavior.
7. Intrapersonal: Understanding ourselves and using this knowledge to effectively manage one's life. This requires self-awareness, the ability to monitor our own internal mental states.

One explanation for human specialized intelligence is that there may be separate brain mechanisms or modules that underlie specialized processing of particular problem types. In evolutionary psychology, these are known as **evolved psychological mechanisms**. The theory is that selection pressures have given rise to them over time because they provided solutions to adaptive problems of survival or reproduction (Buss, 1999). The hallmark of an evolved psychological mechanism is that it is good at doing just one thing and nothing else. Each of Gardner's specific intelligences above may be an instance of just such a mechanism. Cosmides and Tooby (1992) liken the mind to a "Swiss army knife" or bundle of special purpose devices each of which is triggered by a particular problem.

INTELLIGENCE TESTING

We often associate intelligence with a score on an intelligence test. Alfred Binet (1857–1911) and Theodosius Simon were the first to develop a test of human intelligence. They wanted the test to discriminate between normal and mentally retarded learners. It thus had a practical purpose in guiding children's placement in school. William Stern (1912) suggested the best way to compare the abilities of children at different age levels in school was to express their score relative to their own age group. The way to do this was to create an **intelligence quotient**, or IQ score, where a child's score on the test, their mental age (MA), was divided by their chronological age (CA) and then multiplied by 100. The formula for the quotient was thus $IQ = (MA/CA) \times 100$. In this equation, a 7-year-old girl Jane with a mental age score of nine will have an IQ of 128, since $(9/7) \times 100 = 128$. Similarly, a 7-year-old boy with a mental score of six will have an IQ of 85, because $(6/7) \times 100 = 85$. The score is standardized so that a score of 100 indicates a person whose IQ is average for their age. Scores above 100 indicate above average ability, those below 100 indicate below average ability.

There is much controversy over the use of IQ testing, primarily because many mistakenly believe the test is a direct measure of intelligence. But as we have seen, there is no concrete definition of what intelligence is and it is not possible to measure what one can't define. Modern day IQ test scores are in line with their original purpose, they are used to determine aptitude for school-related skills. The most widely used IQ test in use today for adults is the third version of the Wechsler Adult Intelligence Scale (WAIS), introduced in 1997. There are also two other versions for testing pre-schoolers (3–7 years) and children (7–16 years). There are a total of 14 subtests in the WAIS-III divided into verbal and performance categories. The test provides three scores, one for each category and an overall score based on the combination of the two. Figure 7.1 shows some examples of questions that might be encountered on the verbal section of the WAIS.

"Intelligence" tests can also be devised for computers. Part of developing an AI program involves testing its problem solving ability. Researchers begin by designing a program, for instance one that can play chess. They have the program play several games of chess and

General Information
> What day of the year is Christmas?

Similarities
> In what way are wheel and propeller alike?

Arithmetic Reasoning
> If jelly beans cost 36 cents a dozen, what does 1 jelly bean cost?

Vocabulary
> Tell me the meaning of insidious.

Comprehension
> Why do people buy home insurance?

Digit Span
> Listen carefully, and when I am through, say the numbers right after me.
>   5   3   1   8   4   6
> Now I am going to say some more numbers, but I want you to say them backward.
>   9   7   3   2   6   1

Figure 7.1 Examples of questions that might be found on the verbal section of the Wechsler Adult Intelligence Scale (WAIS).

monitor its performance. The program can compete against human players or other computer programs. The program can then be modified and the outcome assessed once more. This testing-evaluation cycle can continue until the developers are satisfied with the level of performance.

Most AI programs, like the chess-playing example given above, are designed to solve a specific task. These are usually restricted to a single domain like games, medical diagnosis, or language comprehension. In these situations, the problem is usually well defined. The program is fed input data in a specific format, analyzes it with an algorithm and produces a particular output. These kinds of programs show little flexibility. They only solve problems of a specific type and can have difficulty if the problem parameters are changed. The idea that a specialized AI program will produce nonsense if there is even a slight deviation from its narrow expertise is known as **brittleness**. A medical program designed to diagnose disease, if asked about a rusty old car, might diagnose measles (Brighton & Selina, 2003).

The specialized nature of AI corresponds to Spearman's "s" factor. The programs may be considered to have a specific form of intelligence rather than any general ability. There is no computer program to date that can solve the wide variety of problems human beings can. In other words, we cannot currently administer the WAIS-III to a computer and expect it to perform as well as the average adult. If we really wanted to create a computer program that could match human performance on the WAIS, it might someday be achieved by creating a bundle of specialized problem solving routines together in one machine. Each program could then be called upon to produce a particular solution to the problem for which it was designed.

However, is a computer with a decent IQ score really intelligent? Doesn't true intelligence require something more than just doing well on a test? Remember, the IQ test doesn't measure intelligence, only scholastic potential, so a high IQ is not the same thing as being "smart." There are plenty of people without a formal education who exhibit intelligence. These individuals may not do well on standardized tests, but they do show what it means to be intelligent in the general sense: they learn, solve problems, and adapt to new and changing circumstances. In a similar fashion, a computer or artificial person who is truly intelligent would need to demonstrate these same qualities, rather than just score high on a test.

INTELLIGENT AGENTS

In the chapter on perception and action, we introduced the idea of an agent, which in its simplest form is something that perceives and acts in an environment. In this section, we will expand on the idea of agents, discuss the various types of agents and show that they can be considered intelligent. A **rational agent** is one that does the right thing. It will always perform its intended action given the proper circumstances. Imagine a robot waitress designed to serve food to patrons. If it failed to provide menus to a couple that had just walked in, it would be doing the wrong thing. Proper action for a rational agent is behavior that will cause the agent to be the most successful.

One way to ensure that a rational agent is doing its job is to measure its performance. A performance measure for a robot waitress might be defined as providing menus to new patrons, returning to take their order, providing the order, then the bill and finally return-ing change. We might additionally impose reasonable time limits for each of these actions, since customers usually don't like to wait.

A rational agent is one that maximizes expected rather than actual performance. It decides on a course of action that will further its goals, given its level of understanding. If an agent acts in a way that degrades its performance because of information it does not have, then it is not irrational, but merely acting out of ignorance. For example, a robot waitress that fails to bring ketchup with fries does not at first know that this will dissatisfy customers. But after receiving complaints, the agent can then add this routine to its reper-toire. This, of course, highlights the importance of learning to rational action. An agent, in order to be considered rational, must be able to modify its actions based on experience to improve performance. It can do this by gathering information about its environment through asking questions or exploring.

Agent action or computation occurs on three different occasions. Designers add in computational ability when an agent is constructed. Alternatively, if an agent evolves or develops over time computational abilities arise in it. Second, a functioning agent is com-puting when determining which action to take next in service of its goals. Finally, during learning, the agent modifies or adds new computation that will alter its future behavior. Agents that rely more on learning and less on prior knowledge are said to be autonomous. See the section on nativism and empiricism in the chapter on learning for a discussion of how much should be "designed in" to an agent at the start and how much should be left for learning.

Agent Architectures

An agent's **architecture** refers to its internal structural layout. All agents are computing devices with sensors and actuators. Agent programs refer instead to the agent's functional organization. A program takes percepts as inputs from sensors, performs some computa-tion, and returns an action to the actuators. We will in this section describe four types of agents that embody the principles underlying many intelligent systems (Russell & Norvig, 2003). The programs described here are "heavy agents." They have a somewhat elaborate internal structure. There are also "light agents" that have a fairly simple internal organiza-tion. In the social chapter, we discuss multi-agent architectures that can be composed of many light or heavy agents. The reader should refer to figure 7.2 for a general schematic architecture of an agent.

A **simple reflex agent** is one that uses production rules to map stimulus inputs to actions. A production or condition-action rule, as we have already seen, is a simple "if x then y" statement. If a particular precondition is met, then a given action is executed. A window-washing agent might spray ammonia on a spot and wipe if it detected a black spot based on the programmer's assumption that a spot indicates dirt. It could then move on once its actions removed the spot. But if the spot were paint, a scratch, or a hole, the agent might become locked into an infinite loop of spraying and wiping. Simple reflex agents are the least intelligent. They can only act under the limited cases of their preconditions and have no way of tracking or recording what is going on in the world outside of their percepts.

Model-based agents include a world tracking feature. They can keep track of the part of the world they can't directly perceive. A train-driving agent might know that a train on a parallel track was even closer after having glimpsed it approaching earlier. These agents also have knowledge of how their own actions affect the world. The agent in this example could know that if it activated the brake the train would eventually come to a stop. This internal knowledge of how the word works is called a world model.

However, model-based agents only have access to current states of the environment, what is happening more or less in the immediate moment. They don't have goals about what it is they want to achieve in the future. Agents that incorporate goals and can engage in decision making to get them are **goal-based agents**. Decision-making calls on other computational processes like search and planning. A truck-driver agent has the goal of transporting its cargo to the desired destination. If it arrived at an intersection and found the route ahead blocked, it would need to figure out an alternate route to achieve that goal. Determining the new route might require searching through all the possible ways of getting from where the truck is now to where it needs to be and selecting the one that is the shortest and has the least amount of traffic.

In many decision-making situations, two or more goals conflict with one another. In these cases, a goal-based agent will falter unless it has some more complex way of choosing. One solution to this problem is to assign different possible states a utility value. Utility is a term indicating desirability. A state with a higher utility is preferred to one with lower values. A **utility-based agent** assigns utility values to different states or possible courses of action. It then acts in such a way as to maximize its utility. A vacuum agent might have two goals, to clean the floor and to not bother the occupants, with the latter having a higher associated utility. If the occupants are in the living room, the agent might determine to clean the bedroom instead, thus maximizing its utility.

As you probably noticed, each of the four agents that we discussed in order had increasingly more intelligence. Reflex agents are the "dumbest," capable only of reactive responses. Model-based agents are a bit smarter, endowed with some understanding of the world. Goal-based agents are smarter yet, being able to make decisions in pursuit of a goal, while utility-based agents come out on top, able to decide in situations with conflicting goals. You may have also noticed that the internal architecture of these agents becomes more and more complex in the order described. Intelligence then, is the increased internalized capacity to deal flexibly with environmental situations. As intelligence increases, there is a shift that takes place where the agent's behavior is guided more by its internal decision making operations and less by the vagaries of the environment.

ENVIRONMENTS

Micro-worlds and Scalability

To truly understand intelligence we have to go beyond the agent and consider the environment in which they operate. There are many different kinds of environment. Some are simple and pose few challenges for an agent. Others are more complex and require correspondingly greater complexity on the part of the agent. The ultimate goal of AI researchers is to create intelligent programs that can operate in complex real world environments like the ones humans and animals live in. This is not so easy though, and early efforts in this field focused on getting agents to work in much simpler situations.

Most AI programs, as we mentioned earlier, have narrow expertise. They are designed to solve a specific type of problem only. Games like chess and checkers provide an ideal environment for a problem-solving agent. They have well-defined possibilities, strict rules, and predictable consequences. A game is an example of a **micro-world**, a simplified and specially constructed environment in which an AI program can operate.

Terry Winograd created one of the first examples of a micro-world. His program, called SHRDLU, controls a robot arm that moves different colored geometric blocks on a table-top (Winograd, 1972). Both the arm and the block world are actually computer simulated: a video monitor is used to display the arm's movement. Figure 7.2 shows the appearance of this block world. Winograd communicates with SHRDLU by typing in commands at a keyboard. SHRDLU responds by asking clarificatory questions and by performing the desired action. For instance, Winograd might instruct SHRDLU to pick up a red block and place it in a container. SHRDLU would respond by first removing a green pyramid stacked on top of the red block and placing it on the table, then picking up the red block and putting it in the container.

At first glance, SHRDLU seems to understand the commands given to it and to be able to reason and manipulate its imaginary block world with ease. But its understanding is really quite limited. It doesn't actually know what a block or a pyramid is. It treats them strictly as things that it can move. Similarly, it doesn't understand what colors are, only that these are attributes it uses to identify the things it can move. SHRDLU's performance

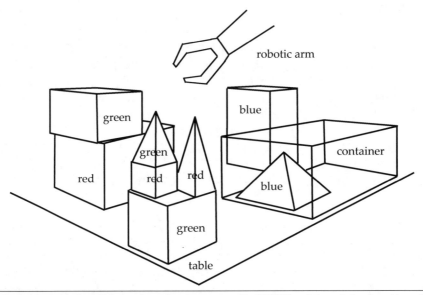

Figure 7.2 Depiction of a block world. Instructions given to a program like SHRDLU are interpreted and used to perform actions such as picking up one shape and placing it on top of another.

is limited to simple geometric solids. It would falter if the environment became more realistic and it was asked to pick up a shoe or a leaf.

Micro-worlds were constructed with the idea that techniques learned on them could eventually be generalized to cope with more complex environments. This concept is known as **scalability**. An agent that demonstrates scalability can cope with ambiguity, variety, and novelty. In other words, it can cope with real-world scenarios like a house or forest and not just the highly specialized environments of a micro-world. The more general and realistic the environment an agent can cope with, the more intelligent it can be said to be.

Characteristics of Task Environments

Environments differ in all sorts of ways. What is it that distinguishes a simple environment from a complex one? Russell and Norvig (2003) list six fundamental properties of task environments, ones in which an agent can act. They illustrate these using the example of a taxi-driving agent. Following their lead, in this section we describe these properties and illustrate them using the same example.

1. Observability. An environment is fully observable if an agent's sensors allow it to perceive the total state of the environment at any given time. Agents that operate in fully observable environments need not have memories, they don't have to carry around information about the world inside of them. Partially observable environments contain states that cannot be perceived by an agent and may require the use of memory. A taxi-driving agent that has access to all information about its world, a complete map of the city streets, locations of all the other cars and construction sites etc., is operating in a fully observable environment.

2. Determinism. In a determined environment, the next state is completely determined by the current state. In a stochastic or non-determined environment, it is not certain what the next state will be, given the current state. If the behavior of city traffic could be predicted exactly, it would be a determined environment. This is rarely the case in the real world.

3. Experience. In episodic task environments, the agent's experience consists of distinct episodes or events, each characterized by a single perception and resulting action. The action is affected only by what occurs in the current episode, not by the actions taken in previous episodes. In a sequential environment, decisions made in previous episodes affect the current episode. Taxi driving is sequential. Taking a left turn at an intersection may limit the number of routes the agent can now take. Sequential environments are more complex and may require planning on the part of the agent to effectively problem solve.

4. Change. If the environment does nothing while an agent is deciding, it is static. A dynamic environment can change while the agent ponders. Dynamic situations are clearly more challenging, because circumstances can alter radically if the agent takes too long to make a move. Taxi driving is a dynamic environment. Other cars continue to drive about while a taxi-driving agent is stopped deciding what to do next.

5. Continuity. When the environment consists of a finite number of distinct states it is said to be discrete. Games like chess and checkers are discrete, because there are a limited number of possible moves that can be made. Driving is continuous, because the position of the car over time occupies a range of continuous values.

6. Agency. An environment can consist of one or more agents. Taxi driving is a multi-agent environment if agents are driving the other cars on the road. Social environments are generally more complex because of the interactive behavior that arises between agents that may be cooperating or competing.

So, we see that environments can vary tremendously in the type of challenge they afford to the agent. Games are the easiest. A crossword puzzle, for instance, is fully observable, deterministic, sequential, static, discrete, and single-agent. Taxi driving is the hardest, being partially observable, stochastic, sequential, dynamic, continuous, and multi-agent. This description of environments shows that intelligence really cannot be considered in terms of an agent alone but as an agent-environment interaction. Simple environments do not require much intelligence. A simple reflex agent can get by in these situations with little more than stimulus-based reactive behaviors. Complex environments demand more of agents. In these cases, world models, goals, and utility are necessary for effective decision making.

Environments play a key role in learning and evolution. Individual learning agents that are embedded in varied and challenging environments can adapt to them, demonstrating greater intelligence. What we see here is that the complexity on the "outside" becomes matched by complexity on the "inside." The same can be said for evolutionary change. In this case, environments over many generations shape the structure of agent populations. Intelligence is perhaps the most adaptive trait any species of agent could have because it is useful in any environment. This suggests that, given the right conditions, intelligence should eventually develop within any evolutionary system.

PROBLEM SOLVING AND SEARCH

Part of intelligence is being able to solve problems. In cognitive science and artificial intelligence, a problem can be considered as an **initial state** that needs to be transformed by a series of possible actions through **intermediary states** to a **target state**. The initial state is the problem situation as it stands before anything is done. The intermediary states are what result from the actions and the target or goal state is the final solution. The tricky part is figuring out what moves need to be made to get you from the starting to the end point. Imagine you are driving along in your car and get a flat tire. The initial state is the flat tire itself. The target state is the solution of replacing it. How might you go about this? You would first need to remove the bad tire. This requires that several other actions come first such as jacking the car up. Once the bad tire is removed, it could be replaced with a spare. This also requires another set of actions, each with their own preconditions.

This example shows that problem solving can be conceptualized as a number of possible actions, each having a consequence. If the proper action is selected, the consequence results in an intermediary state that brings one closer to the solution. In a game the range

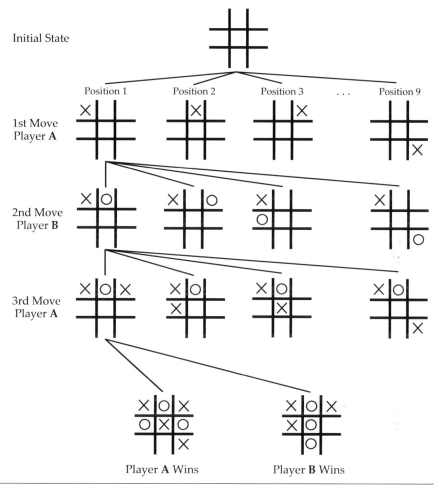

Figure 7.3 A game tree for tic-tac-toe. Each branch in the tree represents a possible move, each node the result of a move.

of possible moves and states is represented with a **game tree**. Figure 7.3 shows part of the game tree for tic-tac-toe. Each branch in the tree corresponds to an action or operator. Each node stands for the state that results from that action.

For games where the number of possible moves is limited, a computer can hold the entire game tree in memory. It can then search through the tree in its entirety to determine the best possible countermove against an opponent. This is sometimes known as the "brute force" approach to search. But for chess, the number of potential moves is exceedingly large, too big to be held in memory and searched. Under these circumstances, a new method is needed. The solution is to employ a heuristic. You will recall that a heuristic is a "best guess" or rule of thumb. In search, heuristics narrow the portion of the game tree that needs to be searched by using knowledge.

A chess-playing computer using heuristic search would look ahead a few moves of its opponent. It would then rank order the moves by assigning a score to each board position.

The score is calculated using an **evaluation function** that reflects how good the position is by taking into account short-term tactical and long-term strategic knowledge. An example of a tactical rule is to not lose a piece on any move. Strategic considerations might include sacrificing a piece in order to move a rook into a certain position on the next move. The program would then implement the move with the highest score.

In 1997, IBM's program "Deep Blue" defeated Gary Kasparov, the world's most highly ranked human chess player and thus became the first computer system to defeat a reigning chess champion under standard tournament time controls. Deep Blue was one of the most powerful supercomputers of its day and was capable of evaluating 200,000,000 positions per second. This gave it considerable brute force search capacity. In contrast, Kasparov was only capable of evaluating a maximum of three moves per second. Deep Blue's evaluation function was first written in a general form and tuned by allowing the system to analyze thousands of master level games. It was then fine-tuned further by several human grand-master chess players. The knowledge gained by this experience provided it with the ability to effectively "prune" its search tree.

REASONING

From a common-sense point of view, intelligence is being able to reason effectively about the world. In the learning and memory chapter, we outlined several of the basic rules of reasoning: deduction, abduction, and induction. A computer or robot can apply such rules to propositional statements to generate new knowledge, thus adding to its understanding of the world. Reasoning, combined with a knowledge base, allows us to make decisions and solve problems as well. An artificial person could reason to look both ways before crossing the street. It could draw on its knowledge that being hit by a car is damaging and that it does not want to be damaged. From this it could infer to walk when there are no cars approaching.

There are a number of obstacles to getting robots to reason and to infer successfully under real-world conditions (Aylett, 2002). First, the content of a robot's senses need to be converted into symbolic format if they are to be inserted into propositions and reasoned about. This conversion process is difficult because information obtained through sensors is represented non-symbolically. The input from a video camera is in the form of a visual image. A robot looking at a scene through its camera needs to determine relevant information about objects, their attributes, and identities before it can reason about them. Pattern recognition algorithms would allow a robot to extract such information but it would have to be converted quickly and accurately from a visual to a symbolic representation before it could be subject to reason. More research needs to be done on the interface between perception and reasoning.

Also, new forms of logic and reasoning may be needed to take into account the kinds of changes that take place in the world. Physical transformations can change one type of object into a completely different type with new properties. For example, dropping a plate on the floor shatters it into pieces. The result is that it can no longer be treated as a plate but as something else entirely. An ice cream cone, if held long enough, can no longer be considered to be the same because it has changed from a solid to a liquid. An artificial person would need to possess logics that inform it about physical object transformations, but it turns out these are very hard to reason with.

Expert Systems

An **expert system** (ES) is an AI program that provides expert quality advice, diagnoses, and recommendations for real-world problems in a specific domain. A user queries the ES which then provides answers. These systems are used as a substitute for a human expert such as a doctor or engineer when these individuals are not readily available. Such systems have been used successfully to solve a variety of problems in medicine, geology, business, law, and education, among other fields. First developed in the 1970s, they were applied commercially throughout the 1980s, and are still used today.

Figure 7.4 depicts the architecture of an ES. A user interacts with the system through a user interface that may use menus, typed questions, or spoken natural language. An inference engine then converts these question inputs to responses. The inference engine can rely on a number of reasoning techniques such as deduction, abduction, and production rules. The heart of an ES is a knowledge base that is obtained from a human expert. This consists of both theoretical and practical or heuristic information. It is extracted from the human expert with the help of a knowledge engineer who will typically interview the expert and have them solve a range of problems. A working prototype may then be shown to the expert and the users, who will check the system's performance and provide feedback for further refinements.

An ES also has case-specific data that holds information provided by the user and partial conclusions based on this information. Another component is the explanation system that allows the program to explain its reasoning to the user. Finally, there is a knowledge

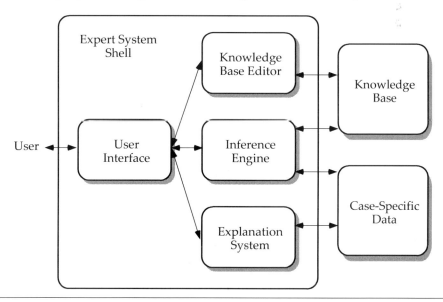

Figure 7.4 The architecture of an expert system (ES). An ES can be used to solve complex problems such as medical diagnoses that require specialized knowledge.

base editor that assists the expert or knowledge engineer in updating and checking the knowledge base. Typically, an ES will separate the general-purpose part of the program from the domain specific knowledge. This area is called the ES shell or toolkit and can be connected to different knowledge bases and case-specific data to solve problems in different domains (Cawsey, 1998).

Perhaps the most well-known ES is MYCIN. It was designed to diagnose infectious blood diseases and recommend antibiotics with the dosage adjusted to the patient's body weight. MYCIN used a set of production rules to map symptoms onto a diagnosis with a given certainty factor. For example:

IF the infection is primary-bacteremia
AND the site of the culture is one of the sterile sites
AND the suspected portal of entry is the gastrointestinal tract,
THEN there is suggestive evidence (certainty 0.7) that the infection is bacteroid.

The certainty factor in the conclusion above expresses the degree of certainty that the diagnosis is correct. A value of 1.0 would indicate that the conclusion is definitely true. A value of –1.0 indicates that it is definitely not true and a value of 0.0 indicates the absence of any certainty.

MYCIN was a very successful early example of an ES. It influenced the design of other commercial systems. On some occasions, it even outperformed members of the Stanford Medical School. Physicians have been reluctant to use it because of the legal implications. If an incorrect diagnosis is made using MYCIN, who can be held responsible? The human expert? The knowledge engineer? The user? MYCIN itself? We discuss the legal and ethical aspects of intelligent agents in the social chapter.

An ES is really not intelligent in any true sense of the word. First, these systems are only good at diagnosing and recommending in specialized knowledge domains where the information is limited to a single topic. They are not designed to reason or problem solve in a broad way. At the very least, they might qualify as examples of specialized intelligence as mentioned above. Second, the systems don't learn by themselves. Any mistakes or errors made by an ES must be detected and corrected as part of the development or evaluation process. A third and related point is that an ES is only as good as the knowledge and inference rules that are put into it. Mistakes made by the expert or knowledge engineer will transfer into the system. An ES is thus more a copy or emulation of the way a knowledgeable person would think rather than an autonomous instantiation of real intelligence.

Planning

A plan is a guide to action. The beauty of plans is that they are formulated ahead of time and can be used to avoid potential problems. If you were going to Puerto Rico for a vacation, you would need to engage in planning. The plan would consist of purchasing your ticket, reserving hotel rooms and rental cars, buying sunscreen, and packing. Planning is a form of intelligence because it allows us to adapt to a future environment, one that hasn't yet occurred. Planning in all likelihood is one of the features that separates humans from other animals and which has contributed to our survival and permanence as a species.

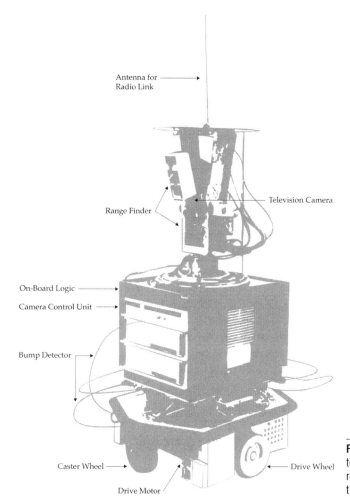

Antenna for
Radio Link

Television Camera

Range Finder

On-Board Logic

Camera Control Unit

Bump Detector

Caster Wheel

Drive Wheel

Drive Motor

Figure 7.5 Shakey was one of the first robots to use planning to move about simplified environments. Image by Gabriele Schies. Sichtwerk, Inc.

Robots designed according to the deliberative paradigm discussed in the perception and action chapter are given the ability to plan to help them navigate. In fact, this paradigm is referred to as sense-plan-act because the robot first senses its surroundings, formulates a plan and then acts on the plan. Early attempts at getting robots to plan met with limited success. Shakey was an autonomous mobile robot first built in 1968 by the Stanford Research Institute. It was about the size of refrigerator, sensing through a television camera and moving along on small wheels. It tended to shake as it rolled about, hence its name. Figure 7.5 shows what Shakey looked like.

Shakey operated in a simplified environment composed of a set of rooms connected by a corridor. The rooms were bare and filled with box-like objects. It was given a task such as moving a block. To execute the task, Shakey would formulate a plan consisting of how to get the block and move it in the desired fashion. Shakey used higher order symbolic planning routines to break the task into more manageable parts. Although capable of performing many of its assigned jobs, the initial version of Shakey suffered a number of limitations. It couldn't adequately deal with unexpected changes. If a researcher suddenly moved a box, Shakey would become very confused. A dynamic environment thus requires the ability to monitor for and deploy changes to a set plan. Shakey was also too deliberative. It would often stall for minutes while computing plans. This suggests that a hybrid architecture of planning combined with reactive low-level routines that quickly and automatically carry out basic functions may yet prove to be the best solution to robotic action.

Shakey had a powerful influence on robotic design. The formal language it used, the Stanford Research Institute Problem Solver (STRIPS) is a useful way to approach planning in dynamic environments. STRIPS has a list of facts that it constantly updates based on its actions. If it picks up a cup from a desk, this fact becomes true and others like "the cup is on the desk" become false. For any action, STRIPS specifies the necessary preconditions and the post-conditions, altering facts as it goes along. Planning is therefore akin to problem solving in that the desired goal must be broken down into sub-goals. Achievement of each sub-goal alters the state of the environment, which must be tracked to ensure correct performance.

BRAIN-BASED INTELLIGENCE

Maybe the way to create a truly intelligent machine is not using principles of logic and machine engineering, but to base it instead on the human brain, the organ that we already know is the basis of genuine intelligence. This is the approach taken by Jeff Hawkins and described in his 2004 book *On Intelligence*. Hawkins wants to build computers based on the architecture of the human neocortex, a thin strip of multi-layered tissue that is part of the forebrain and that subsumes perceptual and cognitive ability. The neocortex is larger in people than in other animals and underlies our capacity to see, hear, plan, reason, and use language.

According to Hawkins, the primary function of intelligence is prediction. He says our brains compare perceptual inputs at any given moment to an expectation generated from past experience and drawn from memory. If there is a mismatch, then it signals the presence of a novel event to which attention should be directed and from which we can learn. This form of prediction is omnipresent in what we do and happens as part of both low-level perceptual and higher-level cognitive processing. For instance, if we take a step and our foot fails to land as expected, we immediately take notice and initiate a correction to keep from falling. If we see a person, such as our spouse, in a familiar context, then we can predict what that person will say based on what they have said under similar circumstances in the past.

The brain's ability to predict and thus guide action is reminiscent of what Llinas (2001) and Franklin (1995) said in our discussion of mind in the brain chapter. Hawkins, however, sees prediction as the fundamental basis of what it means to be intelligent. Humans have taken this ability to recognize patterns, detect novelty, and generate expectations far further than other animals. We can apply it to a much wider domain than other species. We can predict and understand all phenomena from music to social interaction using this process.

How is it done? According to Hawkins, prediction is a product of the neocortical architecture (see Figure 7.6). The cortex has a hierarchical organization. At the bottom level, basic perceptual features are represented. For vision, these are elements such as oriented lines. For audition, they correspond to individual frequencies. As we move up the hierarchy, larger object and event representations are formed by the combined outputs of feature representations. Different frequencies for instance get combined to create the perception of a melody or song.

Information in this hierarchical network feeds both ways. Upward flow produces coherent perception. But learned information in memory also flows downward. In this fashion, an expectation can be compared against what is perceived. The first few notes of a song could trigger the rest of it from memory, enabling a prediction. If the song matches what we've heard, it is familiar and we could sing along. If there are some aspects that differ, we take pause and notice the differences, attending to and perhaps learning the new version.

There are several other interesting implications of this architecture. At the higher levels of the hierarchy, information from different sensory modalities can combine. In this way, we can learn to identify our grandmother not just from the appearance of her face, but also from the sound of her voice. The visual and auditory representations can get associated so that the presence of either her face or her voice will trigger recall of the other. This auto-associative recall is a key feature of recognition, because just a small feature or part of an object can cause the mental reconstruction of the whole.

Hawkins wants to build intelligent machines using these principles. His recipe is to start with a set of senses to extract patterns from the world. Next, we need to attach a hierarchical memory system like that of the neocortex to them. We then train the memory system much as we teach children. Over time, the machine will build a model of the world as perceived through its senses. This, he says, will obviate the need to program in lots of rules,

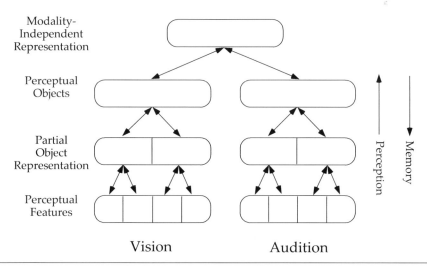

Figure 7.6 A schematic representation of human cortical organization (after Hawkins, 2004). It is characterized by increasing levels of abstraction that allow for recognition, expectation, and cross-modal comparison.

facts, or other prepackaged aspects of the world. The machine should eventually exhibit intelligent behavior, seeing analogies to past experiences, making predictions, and solving problems.

This idea has appeal because it is based on the biological hardware that underlies our own intelligence. It is thus part of the human AI approach and corresponds to the idea of reverse engineering the human brain so that we can reconstruct an artificial version. This is in contrast to the alien AI approach of doing something in whatever way works best. However, some of Hawkin's proposal is speculative and based on aspects of brain function that we are only now beginning to understand. Future advances in neuroscience, particularly those that illuminate cortical function, might substantiate some of his claims. There are also technical obstacles that need to be surmounted before an artificial cortex becomes a reality. These include the creation of a vast memory capacity equivalent to eight trillion bytes and the connectivity issue of wiring together billions of individual computing units.

8

CREATIVITY

Young admirer: Papa Bach, how do you manage to think of all these new tunes?

Bach: My dear fellow, I have no need to think of them. I have the greatest difficulty not to step on them when I get out of bed in the morning and start moving around my room.

—Johann Sebastian Bach. Quoted in Laurens van der Post (1975)

One of the traits that make us uniquely human is creativity. We have the desire and capability to create in a way that transcends other species. It is true that other animals create. Birds construct nests and beavers build dams. But these creations are fairly rigid and stereotyped. In contrast, human creativity is more fluid and diverse. We have a long and productive history of artistic, scientific, and engineering endeavor. Just think of all the paintings, sculptures, music, poems, books, plays, scientific discoveries, architectural forms and machines, to name just a few categories that humankind has produced. Perhaps it is creativity that makes us human. If so, then we must address whether creativity can be reproduced in an artificial person. That is the issue we take up in this chapter, but first we must discuss what creativity is and what the various elements of creativity are.

WHAT IS CREATIVITY?

Boden (1995a) makes a distinction between two different meanings of creation. The standard dictionary definition of creation is to cause something to come into existence or bring something into being. However, it doesn't seem possible to create something totally new, which comes out of nothing at all. Everything new in the universe instead comes from precursors or a set of existing elements. These are then combined or placed into a unique relationship to one another producing a new thing. It is the combination that is novel, not the parts from which they are constructed. When creating a song, a composer takes notes and arranges them to produce a melody. Similarly, the creation of a poem comes from a novel arrangement of existing words while a painting is the result of the combination and application of standard color pigments. Creativity then, is not the bringing into existence of something out of nothing, but the combination of things that are already here.

Jeffery (1999) proposes several criteria for a creative work and whether they could be implemented in a computer. First, there must be a product or some end result that comes out of a creative process. This need not be something physical or tangible like a painting or sculpture. It could very well be an idea or hypothesis. Second, the product must be new. It cannot be a copy or duplication of something that is already in existence. Third, it must be considered good by an observer or judge. This last criterion is important. It is not enough to just generate novelty, the resulting product must be considered good, beautiful, or useful by some other agent. An aesthetic or value judgment of this sort requires emotions or some sort of value system both for the observer who appreciates or uses the product but also for the creator.

A computer would have little difficulty creating a novel product. This can be done simply by taking elements and arranging them in different ways either randomly or using a rule governed system. However, getting a computer to generate a good novel product is more difficult if goodness requires a value system. Our computer would then need to possess values and use them to guide its creative process, perhaps with the end goal that this product would be used or appreciated by someone else who would resonate with those values.

In order for a work to qualify as creative, it must also be self-generated (Jeffery, 1999). That is, the creator must produce the work independently of its own accord rather than follow a set of prescribed rules. Jeffery gives the example of a computer that could compose music in one of three ways. It could randomly generate notes, generate notes using a rule-governed system, or generate notes using rules, but then break and bend the rules. In this latter case, the changing of the rules is accomplished randomly or through the application of another set of rules. For all these instances, the computer is not being truly creative because it is just following the instructions put into it by a human programmer. The only contribution of the machine is the randomness.

One way to get around this is to allow a computer or artificial person to generate its own rules. These could be derived from experience or perhaps to some extent allowed to occur by chance. If an artificial person develops and interacts over time with a complex environment, it would form its own unique views and values. These could then be incorporated into its creative process, allowing for an autonomous form of creativity. This is, in fact, what happens with people. Our own special circumstances and history influence our perspective on the world, influencing what we consider important. These values then affect the way we create. A designer who prizes simplicity and symmetry will incorporate these principles into his work while complexity and irregularity would be reflected in the product of an artist who instead holds these different values.

AESTHETIC AND ANALYTIC CREATIVITY

Aesthetic creativity as mentioned earlier can be evaluated according to goodness or beauty. But how is this done? How can we judge whether a creative work is good or not? This is an aspect of the definition of art. According to the American philosopher Ayn Rand, art is "a selective recreation of an artist's metaphysical value judgments" (Rand, 1975). In this view, an artist sees some aspect of the world that they deem important and puts it into their work. An observer then interprets the work and identifies with the values thus sharing the artist's experience. According to Rand, a good creative work is one that communicates proper values. This view of art as value transmission is at odds with theories of modern art that allow the interpretive process to take place entirely within the observer, who brings his or her own experience to bear on the work independent of the artist's intent.

There are many other theories of beauty. This is the primary issue addressed by the field of philosophy called aesthetics. It is difficult to formulate an objective theory of aesthetics because there are numerous individual differences in what people consider beautiful. Individual preference is influenced by each person's unique history. Someone who grew up listening to one style of music, for example, might prefer it to another style with which they are less familiar. In the arts, it is difficult to discern universal laws of beauty, partly because different genres or styles are judged by different standards. One does not evaluate jazz music in the same way one evaluates classical.

But art is not the only means of creative expression. Scientists and engineers also create. In these fields, it is easier to evaluate a work based on objective standards. In **analytic creativity,** the goodness of a work is judged using certain predetermined criteria. A scientific theory can be evaluated based on how well it accounts for the facts. An automobile can be judged on price, fuel efficiency, acceleration, and braking. Whereas aesthetic creativity is based on emotions, analytic creativity is based more on cognitive thought processes. The observer would engage in an analytical evaluative process to determine how good a given creative work is. One could easily write a program that evaluates the goodness of two washing machines based on preset criteria like the amount of water and electricity used, the amount of time spent in the different cycles, etc. In fact, this program would be better than humans at evaluating which of the two washers is best, especially when a large number of criteria are used.

Both aesthetic and analytic evaluative methods are at work in the arts and the sciences. We can evaluate a picture based on its beauty but also on its size if it must fit into a specific space on the wall. In like fashion, we can judge a car based on its attractiveness as well as its handling characteristics. It is just that beauty is primary to the arts while other criteria like explanatory power, simplicity, efficiency, and performance are primary in the sciences and engineering.

KNOWLEDGE AND SKILL

Knowledge and skill are both crucial to the creative act. In order to create something, we need to draw on our past knowledge. That is because experience provides us with the raw materials for the creative act. The more we learn, the more concepts, ideas, and other elements we have ready to be combined. Take the example of Michelle the novelist. The more Michelle learns, the greater the variety of content knowledge she can draw upon. If Michelle travels to Morocco or makes a new friend, she can now add these locales and characters to her stories. This could also be achieved if she simply read more novels by other authors.

The style, tone, plots and themes acquired from them could then be implemented in various permutations in the stories she writes. It follows from this that the more you know, the more creative you can become. Many innovators and great thinkers throughout history were broadly educated and able to successfully apply ideas learned in disparate fields to their own.

Knowledge by itself, though, is not enough to produce creativity. The elements must then be combined or integrated together in a novel way. This requires skill or the application of some computational process. For instance, Michelle could take features of different characters she had met or read about and then amalgamate them into a new character for one of her novels. The different character features would constitute knowledge but the particular way in which they are combined to generate a new character would require skill. A male protagonist who is anxious but driven by ideological principles might be the result. Another example is creating a plot line. The relationship between characters and the actions in which they engage might be a skillful blend based on past experience. Just as raw materials are learned, so, too, are the skills that are applied to them.

An artificial person in order to be creative must therefore need both a database of knowledge to draw on and a set of skills to apply to it. In previous chapters, we discussed the importance of world knowledge. We said it allows us to solve problems and reason effectively about everyday situations. We now see that knowledge of this sort is also a necessary component of creativity. The skills needed to take this information and generate creatively can come from two sources. They may be partly inborn or programmed and in part learned. Just as Mozart's musical ability may have been to some extent genetic, an artificial composer may be given some prerequisite musical ability which could then be supplemented through learning and experience. Finally, we should note that creative expertise is also the result of practice. Good creators are constantly creating. A painter keeps painting and an inventor keeps tinkering. An artificial person, in order to grow and develop creatively, must continually practice their craft.

THE PSYCHOLOGY OF CREATIVITY

Creative Personality Traits

Feist (1998) performed a meta-analytic review of the literature on creativity. He analyzed a fairly large number of creativity studies. A statistical analysis of the traits from these studies showed that in general creative people are more open to new experiences, less conventional and conscientious, more self-confident, self-accepting, driven, ambitious, dominant, hostile, and impulsive. Creative people tended to focus their attention and efforts inward and to be separate and unique from others. They were also ambitious and motivated with a desire for excellence.

Dacey and Lennon (1998) list 10 traits that contribute to the creative personality. Among them are: tolerance of ambiguity, freedom to see a situation or solve a problem differently, flexibility, risk taking, a preference for disorder, delay of gratification, courage, and self-control. Many of these traits reflect a capacity to consider new information or consider alternatives that is crucial to creative problem solving. Others reflect more long-term aspects of creative or productive behavior such as staying motivated, overcoming obstacles and regulating one's own actions.

Novelty Seeking and Arousal

One sign of the creative individual is that he or she seeks out novel stimuli (Austin, 2003). This type of behavior is seen in animals as well as people. Rhesus monkeys will persist in trying to solve a simple mechanical puzzle even after they have stopped being rewarded for the behavior (Harlow, Harlow, & Meyer, 1950). Apparently, they derive intrinsic satisfaction from the exploratory actions of just trying to figure the puzzle out. Human infants orient toward stimuli that are just a bit more complex than what they are used to, but not too different. In one study, 4-month old infants initially preferred 2×2 checkerboard patterns but, after repeated exposure, began to prefer 4×4 boards (Greenberg & O'Donnell, 1972). According to the **moderate discrepancy hypothesis**, people seek out stimulation that is somewhat, but not too different from what we already know. This maximizes the rate of learning. If too little or too much information is presented relative to existing knowledge, then learning fails to occur.

Repetitive stimulation in some cases results in **habituation**, which is a desensitization or decreased reaction to a stimulus. A person who startles to the sound of car alarms after moving to the city will quickly get used to them. Habituation is useful. It makes sense to ignore constancy since it is an aspect of the environment that is uninformative to an agent. For some stimuli, such as the application of electric shock, we see an opposite effect and there can be an increased reaction over time. This is known as **sensitization** and usually occurs in response to aversive or threatening stimuli.

Most creative activity lies between these two extremes at moderate levels of arousal. At these levels, a person is neither bored nor anxious. Novel stimuli are rewarding, but only when they induce a moderate level of arousal (Berlyne, 1958). If they are too exciting or too boring, learning and creativity levels drop. Intelligent creative people have been found to seek out novel stimuli more often than those judged less creative based on a word association test (Houston & Mednick, 1963). However, Dacey and Lennon (1998) point out that optimal arousal may vary depending on the stage of the creative process (see below). During incubation, when the subconscious mind may be attempting solutions, high or even moderate arousal levels may interfere. In the illumination stage, moderate arousal seems best.

Martindale (1981) formulated a creativity theory based on arousal patterns and focus of attention. He found that creative people show a decrease in arousal to stimuli that have moderate arousing potential (Martindale & Hines, 1975). During high states of arousal, attention is very focused thereby allowing an individual to concentrate but preventing entry of new or unusual ideas. In low states of arousal, attention is unfocused which allows more of these sorts of ideas to enter conscious awareness. Martindale believes the dip in arousal seen by creative individuals allows them to think "laterally" and apply more or varied solutions to a problem. Their uncreative counterparts who are more aroused and focused instead persist in applying the same solutions over again.

The above evidence suggests repetition of neutral stimuli is boring for most people. It also shows that creative individuals seek out new stimuli that are moderately arousing.

This makes sense because novelty supplies us with new information about the world. This information provides the raw elements that later get combined and transformed by the creative process. The computers and robots that exist now, unlike people, have no such hang ups about repetition. They can perform the same action over and over again endlessly and never get tired or bored. Software programs frequently go into processing loops and assembly line robots can execute identical actions like welding car doors all day long. In fact, the essence of what it means to be a machine seems to involve immunity to boredom from similar experience.

If we were to design a creative artificial person, we would need to give it a drive to seek out and enjoy novel stimuli, i.e., to avoid repetition. We could instruct our artificial person to avoid falling into loops and to switch to another activity when its current actions become too iterative. We could also add instructions telling it to explore and seek out new stimuli whenever possible. This would maximize its learning rate and provide it with the informational foundation for subsequent creative processing. Our creative artificial person should also have the capacity to flexibly control its arousal or attention levels. It would need to spread out its attention and increase associative thinking when generating possible solutions or ideas but then switch back to focused attention when applying or testing them. These two modes of thinking correspond roughly to divergent and convergent thinking and are discussed in the next section.

Creativity Testing

As is the case with intelligence, psychologists have devised numerous tests for creativity. One survey puts the number of such instruments at 255 (Torrance & Goff, 1989). The tests measure cognitive processes involved in creative thinking. These include making associations, category formation and the ability to work on many ideas simultaneously. These tests have also looked at noncognitive aspects of creativity including components such as motivation, flexibility and other personality factors. The scores on many of these tests have been found to have reasonably high levels of inter-rater reliability and to correlate with other measures like teacher ratings. In addition they can to some extent predict adult behavior. Cropley (2000) however, warns that the tests are best used as measures of creative potential rather than achievement because actual productivity depends on a number of other factors like technical knowledge and expertise in a given field.

Creativity tests measure both divergent and convergent thinking. **Divergent thinking** is the ability to consciously generate new ideas that branch out to many possible solutions for a given problem. The Guilford Alternative Uses Task (1967) does this by asking how many possible uses one can think of for a common household item like a brick. Examples of responses to the brick question could include a paperweight, a doorstop and a weapon. The responses are then scored on their originality, fluency, flexibility, and elaboration. The Torrance Test of Creative Thinking also measures divergence through picture- and verbal-based exercises. A figural question shows an abstract picture such as a black dot with outward radiating lines. Observers are to generate as many descriptions of the stimulus as possible. Responses might be a squashed spider or a star.

Convergent thinking is the ability to correctly hone in on a single correct solution to a problem. It usually requires taking a novel approach to the situation, adopting a dif-

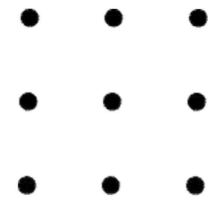

Figure 8.1 A spatial insight problem illustrating convergent thinking. Can you connect all nine dots using just four straight lines?

ferent perspective, or making a unique association between parts of the problem. In the Remote Association Task, three words are presented. The examinee must determine what single word associates all three (Mednick, 1962). What word associates cottage, blue, and mouse? The answer is cheese. Insight problems that are often solved in the "Aha" experience after incubation are also examples of convergent thinking (Dow & Mayer, 2004). Figure 8.1 shows an example of a spatial insight problem. Try working on it. Here is a hint in case you have difficulties: allow yourself to draw a line outside the square boundary of the dots.

An artificial person, in order to possess this sort of human creative thinking, would need to be endowed with mechanisms that allow it to think in a divergent and convergent manner. Divergent thinking to the brick question requires knowledge of a brick, association of things a brick is like, and an evaluation or comparison between the brick and the associated object. A knowledge database supplies the first requirement. Association of objects like a brick can be accomplished through spreading activation of related concepts in a semantic network. Evaluation or comparison between two objects is essentially analogy formation. Associative or analogical processes can also support convergent thinking. These examples further demonstrate that the cognitive processes underlying creativity are not mysterious or unfathomable, but instead can be specified and reproduced.

The Six Steps of the Creative Process

Hughes (1963) outlines six steps in the creative process. His focus is on scientific creativity, but these steps can be generalized to other forms of creativity. In order, they are interest, preparation, incubation, illumination, verification, and exploitation. Steps two through four have also been proposed by Wallas (1926) as the fundamental stages of insight learning. **Insight learning** is the solving of a problem where the solution suddenly and immediately presents itself. So, we can think of creativity as a form of problem solving where the creative product is the solution to a given problem.

1. **Interest**. One has to be interested enough in an endeavor to see it through to completion. Interest is a motivating force that keeps a person working on a project and gets them to start new ones. It is not enough to have knowledge and skill as stated above, one must also want to create. This passion or desire is a hallmark of many successful creative people throughout history like Leonardo DaVinci, Edison, and Picasso. An artificial person must be interested in what it does if it is going to be productively creative over the long term. We discuss how an artificial person may be motivated or driven to pursue goals in the chapter on motivation and emotion.

2. **Preparation**. This involves acquisition of background knowledge and mastery of basic techniques. During insight learning, preparation calls on conscious attempts at solving a problem. Here different solutions or options are tried and evaluated. This stage is characterized by the use of logic and other rational thought processes all of which can be modeled algorithmically on a computer.

3. **Incubation**. Now, the problem or project is put aside for a while. A person may rest, sleep, meditate, or engage in other activities not related to the creative endeavor. However, it is believed that the problem continues to be worked on subconsciously during this time. Subconscious processes may be more associational than syllogistic. Association involves making a connection between concepts based on some measure of similarity. Thinking about the beach, for example, may consequently make you think about swimming, because the two concepts are related.

    Subconscious association can provide creative solutions to certain problems. The chemist Kekule von Stradonitz was confronted with the issue of how to arrange six carbon atoms to account for the structure of benzene. He is reported to have dozed off in the evening and dreamed of a snake holding its tail in its mouth. When he awoke he had the solution: the carbon atoms formed a circle or benzene ring. There are numerous other personal accounts like this, as well as empirical evidence suggesting that subconscious processing is a key element of insight learning (Silveira, 1971).

    Associational processing is mostly nonalgorithmic. A programmer can't give complete explicit instructions to a computer telling it how to associate. It is a result of spreading activation between nodes representing concepts in a semantic network. The arrangement of the nodes and the structure of the network are particular to a specific individual's experience. Artificial semantic networks of the sort discussed in the chapter on learning and memory can serve as the basis of associational processing in a machine.

4. **Illumination**. During this stage the solution suddenly and dramatically comes into conscious awareness. It has been likened to a flash of insight or "Aha!" experience. If the problem had been previously solved subconsciously, during illumination it rises to the surface and makes itself accessible to more controlled conscious thought processes. Most creative work involves alternations between conscious deliberative efforts involving logic and reason and subconscious incidental processing that may be more associational in nature.

    We could model this in an artificial person by having primary "online" processing of a problem followed by secondary "offline" processing. The primary processes would be algorithmic. They would rely on logical inference, search, heuristics and other specifiable problem solving approaches from AI. The secondary processes would be associational and based on spreading activation in a semantic or neural network. We could even devise an architecture where the two processes would reciprocally share information, each informing the other of their conclusions. In this way each computationally different approach could complement the other and work synergistically toward achieving a solution.

5. **Verification**. At this point, the insight is confirmed. If it is a scientific hypothesis, then it must be tested. If it is a solution, then it must be applied to the problem to see if it is correct. This stage can be executed in a formal manner and does not pose any undue problems for a computer.

6. **Exploitation**. Finally, one must follow through to complete the project investing whatever additional effort is necessary. Ideas must at this stage be translated into action. If it is a book or poem, it must be written. If it is an invention, then it must be assembled and put in operating order. An insightful or creative idea by itself is important but it must be concretized or made accessible to others if it is to have any impact. A computer can certainly implement this stage. A creative software program that sends its results to a printer or disseminates them over a network is practising exploitation.

CREATIVITY AND COMPUTERS

Creativity as an Evolutionary Process

The creative process bears some similarity to evolutionary processes. Three aspects characterize an evolutionary process. First, there must be variability or diversity of elements. Next, the total number of elements is then honed down by a selection process in which some of the elements are chosen and remain while others are eliminated. Third, the features of the remaining elements are combined in a process like reproduction to yield new elements. The entire procedure then repeats, iterating until elements with desired features are achieved.

This series of evolutionary steps seems to play itself out in most creative acts. Thomas Edison, when he was inventing the light bulb, had to find a filament that would emit more light than heat when an electric current was passed through it. He tried a number of different materials, many of which burned up and so were dropped from consideration. He eventually settled on one that had properties displayed by some of the other materials he had tried and that proved to be moderately successful. Alternatively, take the example of a composer who produces a given rough melody. He next deletes certain refrains while keeping others and then produces new refrains as variations of the ones he kept.

A software technique called **genetic programming** (GP) employs evolutionary principles like those described above to solve problems (Koza, 1992). Many GP models follow a four-step process. To begin, the program generates an initial population of random programs. Each program is then run and evaluated in terms of its fitness, i.e., how good it is at doing a particular task. Copying, mutating, and reproducing those programs with high fitness values then creates a new population of existing programs. Mutation involves random changes to an individual program's features, while reproduction involves crossover or combination of two or more program's features, resulting in an "offspring" that shares some of the characteristics of its "parents."

Karl Sims at MIT in the early 1990s used GP to create artistic two-dimensional images (Sims, 1991). The program begins by generating an image at random using a given rule. It then makes 19 changes or mutations in this original rule to produce a total of 20 different images. A human observer then either selects one of these to mutate or two to mate through crossover reproduction to produce a single offspring. The computer then takes this new image as the basis for producing another 19 new images that are again judged by a human observer. The process can be repeated until a satisfactory final image is obtained.

Sim's program is not independently creative because it relies on the aesthetic judgment of a person or group of people. It can be considered to be fully creative only when considered as an entire computer-human interactive system. If the program were capable of aesthetically judging its own work, then we might assign it autonomous creative ability. As indicated earlier, giving a computer independent aesthetic judgment requires developmental interaction with an environment and the consequent formation of values. We could, of course, program such values into a computer to give it certain pre-acquired tastes. It would be fascinating to see the kind of artwork Sim's programs would create using different prepackaged aesthetic styles. Some people might prefer the final images that result from a style favoring repetition over images generated by other styles, for example, those favoring reflection. Human choice in these situations would probably indicate a person's own unique values and might even be used as a personality test.

Creativity as Rule-Governed Transformation

Boden (1995b) presents a theory of creativity that introduces the idea of a conceptual field. She says that within any given creative field like music, painting, or poetry, there exist such spaces. A **conceptual space** is an established style of thinking particular to a specific discipline. Examples include the sonata form, tonal harmony, pointillism, and sonnets. Each conceptual space constrains the number of possible elements and the computations or transformations that can operate on them. It consists of sets of generative rules and procedures that practitioners adhere to when creating.

One way to think of a conceptual space is as a multidimensional volume bounded by axes representing the various dimensions that define it. In music, a very simple three-dimensional conceptual space might consist of three axes for the pitch (frequency), loudness (amplitude), and timing (duration) of notes. Transformations within this space would then be rules governing how one moves from one note to another. Some rules might allow consecutive notes in a song to be separated by as much as two octaves. Other rules might restrict notes to a single octave pitch difference.

In the original conceptual space of tonal harmony found in post-Renaissance music, composers had to start and finish in a home key. Reminders and reinforcements of the home key would then be provided throughout the performance in the form of chords, arpeggios, and scale fragments. But, as this musical form progressed, composers deviated more and more, introducing modulations between keys and, eventually, doing away with the notion of the home key altogether. In this way, composers could start from a set of structural constraints but then violate them to ultimately transform or create new conceptual spaces.

There is thus a distinction between exploring and transforming a conceptual space. A conceptual space is explored when one follows the existing rules to create novel combinations. This occurs in music when a composer generates new melodies that obey the given rules. J. S. Bach's piece "Forty-Eight" explores the range and possibilities within the framework of original tonal harmony but does not violate them. A conceptual space is transformed when the rules are bent or omitted. Schoenberg's dropping of the home key is an instance.

A conceptual space specifies the types of allowable representations and transformations within a given domain. It therefore permits scientists to formalize how people create and allows them to construct computer programs capable of creating. Cognitive psychologists and artificial intelligence researchers favor Boden's theory for this reason. In what follows, we describe a few creative computer programs based on the principle of exploring or transforming conceptual spaces.

Paul Hodgson is a professional jazz musician who has written a computer program capable of jazz improvisation (Hodgson, 1990). The program is first fed musical information about a specific song. For instance, it might be given the basic melodic theme of the jazz tune "Sweet Georgia Brown" along with other supplementary information concerning chords. It then generates its own melodic lines that are variations on the basic theme. The program can employ notes from the original theme or be given greater freedom to use an even wider range of possible notes. One of the other ways it improvises is by taking melodies and rhythms and inserting them at different points in the song.

Creativity as Variation on a Theme

Douglas Hofstadter believes that the crux of creativity is variation on a theme (Hofstadter, 1985). He seems to be right. GP methods and rule-governed transformations both start with a given pattern and then through one process or another derive variations. Notice that in these cases, the creative act always starts with something. It does not generate something "out of the blue" as we indicated earlier, but begins with some starting material. Next, we touch upon some of the ideas on thematic variation introduced by Hofstader.

Creativity involves **imagination**. Imagination deals not with what is, but with what might be. When we dream, fantasize, or conjure up hypothetical scenarios, we do so from an originating point. Thinking about where we might go on our next vacation has as its basis what we did on our last vacation. Imagining what life might be like on other worlds is an extrapolation of what we know life to be like here on earth. In every case, we begin with an idea or concept and derive novel content from there.

The ability to imagine is like a lot like analogical or metaphorical reasoning. In the chapter on learning and memory, we introduced the idea of analogical reasoning where a computer or person notices the similarities between two situations and applies what was learned in one to the other. This form of reasoning is useful for mastering new skills and in problem solving but it also plays a role in imagining. When we imagine, we essentially take a given concept, extract certain features or aspects from it, and apply these to the creation of a novel concept.

Hofstadter (1985) likens imagination to "slipping" from one concept to a second that bears some relation to the first. Verbal slips of the tongue are instances of unintentional or subconscious slippage. The Reverend William A. Spooner in the late 19th century was the source of the term "spoonerisms," which is another phrase for these sorts of linguistic errors. One of his more famous is "You have hissed my mystery lectures" as the accidental pronunciation of "You have missed my history lectures." The conceptual confusion here is between "history" and "mystery" and "hissed" and "missed." The relation is both semantic and phonological.

Slippage shows that our concepts are not discrete or insulated from one another, but are connected based on shared features. The physical basis for this in a person or machine would be a semantic network with nodes representing concepts and links connecting nodes. Spreading activation in the network would then be the means by which one concept could trigger or slip to another. This is, in fact, what is happening during associational thinking as mentioned earlier and it may occur both consciously and subconsciously. Hofstader (1996) has implemented a software program called Copycat that reasons analogically. The program contains an associative network that enables it to complete a letter string. When presented with the starting sequence—"abc" is to "abd" as "ijk" is to "?"—it can fill in the missing segment with "ijl" or some other possible string.

How creative an agent is should in part be determined by the degree of "slipperiness" of their conceptual network. The less tightly insulated concepts are the more connections and associations can be drawn between them and the greater their imaginative power. However, there may be a limit to how fluid a creative network can get. Too much and reasoning may become fuzzy. An agent with excessive slippage may have difficulty telling even dissimilar things apart and would overgeneralize from examples. On the other hand, a network with too little slippage would be highly discriminatory, assigning similar concepts into different categories and being unable to see obvious connections. Optimum imagination and creativity may lie somewhere between these two extremes.

CREATIVE COMPUTER PROGRAMS

In this section, we give a brief historical summary of some of the best-known creative computer programs. They span a wide variety of disciplines ranging from poetry to scientific discovery. We do not go into great detail in describing how they work since, in many cases, the programs operate using principles previously outlined. We encourage the interested reader to pursue the primary references to find out more.

Computer Creativity in the Arts

Computer Sketchers and Painters A research group at the National Panasonic Division of the Matsushita Electrical Industrial Company has created a robot sketch artist. A camera is first pointed at a scene, such as a still life or person. Image processing software then computes the differences between the light and dark parts of the image. These differences are used to extract contours or edge information that then form the basis of a line drawing. In a final stage, the robot traces out the drawing onto paper. The resulting drawings are primitive in the sense that they lack color or shading, but they depict the scene very clearly. It should be noted that this robot "artist" is not displaying true creativity because it is simply reproducing a contour equivalent of what its camera sees. It is not interpreting the scene in a novel way. This makes it more like a human sketch artist drawing in the realist style who attempts to capture an accurate reproduction.

Professor Harold Cohen at the University of California at San Diego has developed a program called AARON whose paintings are so good they hang in art galleries and museums around the world. Figure 8.2 shows one of AARON's paintings. Cohen programs rules into the program, which then produces a painting by controlling a robotic arm. The rules enable AARON to create original color paintings that, because of the manipulation of different variables, are different each time they are drawn. The compositions can be abstract or realistic in style portraying scenes with objects or people.

For AARON to paint an object, it needs to know something about the object. It is thus fed basic knowledge about objects that enable it to draw them. For example, to draw a person AARON needs to know the size and positioning of body parts and how they change when a person is standing or walking. It also must know something about how to draw, so AARON additionally receives information on this process that includes knowledge of composition, occlusion, and perspective. It took decades to bring AARON to its current

Figure 8.2 A painting by AARON. Courtesy of Harold Cohen and Ray Kurzweil. 2001 © Kurzweil CyberArt Technologies, Inc.

state. As a result of his experiences, Cohen has written some interesting ideas in art theory (Cohen, 1995).

Computer Musicians David Cope is a music professor at the University of California at Santa Cruz. He is also a professional composer. In 1981 when commissioned to write an opera, he faced a composing block. In order to help himself overcome the block, he began work on a computer program that would act as a composing tool. He called the program EMI (pronounced "emmy") short for Experiments in Musical Intelligence (Cope, 1996). EMI composes music by analyzing and rearranging music by other composers. It has performed music in the style of Bach, Mozart, Gershwin, Joplin, and Stravinsky.

EMI consists of a six-step algorithm. A user first chooses pieces from an existing composer and enters these as input. The program recognizes signatures representative of the composer. It divides the music into component parts and recombines these parts into a new score that maintains the original composer's style. It can then perform the piece. What makes EMI especially interesting is that it can help us to understand the process by which we recognize musical style.

In 1997, Steve Larson, himself a music professor at the University of Oregon, set up a musical version of the Turing Test. He had observers listen to three pieces of music and guess which one had been composed by J.S. Bach. He wrote one of the pieces. Another was the result of the EMI program and the third was by Bach. The audience judged his own piece as written by the computer and the computer piece as written by Bach. So, by the Turing Test standard, the EMI program qualifies as a successful artificial composer.

Computer Story Tellers Several storytelling algorithms have been created. Meehan's (1981) TALE-SPIN program was one of the earliest. It is based on the idea that the telling of a story is like solving a problem. The program works by simulating a world, assigning goals to characters and determining what happens when the goals interact with events in the made up world. It relies on user input. The reader must choose the characters and specify the relationships between the various characters. The user then selects the problem the story is about out of a list of only four possible problems.

TALE-SPIN follows a prescribed five-step routine. The characters, problem, and micro-worlds are first selected from pre-defined sets. This information is then fed to a simulator or problem solver. At this point, the story can either stop or repeat. TALE-SPIN lacks many elements of a good writer. It really only handles a single character well, doesn't manage the author's intentions, and lacks the knowledge needed for the construction of character's that have any sort of depth (De Beaugrande & Colby, 1979; Dehn, 1981; Lebowitz, 1984). Yazdani (1989) has since developed a program called ROALD to remedy these faults.

Scott Turner's MINSTREL is another attempt to improve upon TALE-SPIN. MINSTREL also approaches storytelling as problem solving but adds many new elements such as moral themes and dramatic devices like suspense, foreshadowing, pacing, dialogue, and tragedy (Turner, 1994). The program uses a case-based reasoning approach governed by user selection at successively more concrete stages of theme-selection, consistency-maintenance, dramatic writing techniques, and linguistic presentation. It introduces elements of creativity by "mutating" certain parameters like characters.

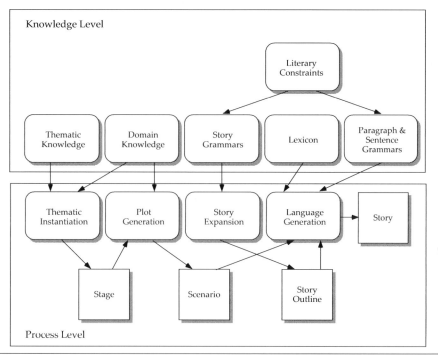

Figure 8.3 The BRUTUS system architecture (after Bringsjord & Ferrucci, 2000). When given appropriate information, BRUTUS can create complex stories.

The most advanced story telling software is BRUTUS (Bringsjord & Ferrucci, 2000). BRUTUS has a knowledge and a process level reflective of the two fundamental elements of knowledge and skill discussed earlier. Figure 8.3 depicts the system's architecture. At the knowledge level is contained the information needed to tell a good story. This consists of domain knowledge of things like people, places, and events, linguistic knowledge of words, sentences, and other parts of speech, and literary knowledge of themes and story grammars. The process level takes this information and uses it to construct a story. It instantiates the thematic concept, generates the plot, expands the story structure and uses language to produce the story. BRUTUS is capable of creating stories with much greater depth, complexity, and realism than has previously been possible. However, Bringsjord argues that BRUTUS does not possess literary creativity in the human sense but rather produces the appearance of creativity using computational methods.

Computer Poets Margaret Masterman in 1968 displayed a computer poetry program at the Cybernetic Serendipity exhibition held at the Institute of Contemporary Arts in London. This algorithm generates Japanese haiku based on user interaction. A Japanese haiku poem contains three lines. The first and last lines each have five syllables and the middle line has seven. The poem can be on any topic but must reference in some way a season of the year.

Her program starts with a frame that structures the lines (Masterman, 1971). Each of the spaces in the frame is a slot that can be filled with a word. The user is prompted to fill the slots by choosing from a set of prescribed words lists. The order in which the slots are filled is determined by their semantic relationship. An example of one of the poems that was composed was:

ALL GREEN IN THE LEAVES,
I SMELL DARK POOLS IN THE TREES.
CRASH! THE MOON HAS FLED.

Clearly, this program is not being truly creative because it relies on the user for word choice. However, the words could be selected randomly or with some knowledge of their meaning by the computer.

A more recent example of computer poetry comes from Ray Kurzweil. His RKCP (Ray Kurzweil's Cybernetic Poet) program reads an extensive collection of poems by a given author. It then produces a language model that represents that author's work and writes original poems from it. The resulting poems capture many aspects of the author's unique style. Kurzweil has even included algorithms to preserve thematic consistency and discourage plagiarizing (Kurzweil, 1999). Here is a poem created by RKCP called "Long Years Have Passed" after it had read poems by Randi and Kathryn Lynn:

Long years have passed.
I think of goodbye.
Locked tight in the night
I think of passion;
Drawn to for blue, the night
During the page
My shattered pieces of life
watching the joy
shattered pieces of love
My shattered pieces of love
gone stale.

Computerized Advertising Agents Goldenberg, Mazursky, and Solomon (1999) programmed a computer to create highly successful and creative product advertisements. They used an algorithmic approach based on analogies whereby the program would replace the idealized properties of the product with another to represent it. The performance of the program was then compared to that of human novices who were not in the ad business. As an example, in one ad the goal was to convey that Jeeps have very quiet engines. A human idea featured a car alone in the country. The computer idea had two Jeeps communicating in sign language (Angier, 1999). Judges rated the computer ads as more creative and original than those of the humans. Some of the computer ads were, in fact, so good they were evaluated as equivalent to award-winning human ads.

Computer Creativity in the Sciences

Computerized Scientific Discovery Herbert Simon won the Nobel Prize for Economics in 1978. He also contributed greatly to the field of artificial intelligence and cognitive science. One of his research interests was in how important scientists made historically significant discoveries. Given the information these scientists had, would it be possible to get a computer to make the same discovery? He set about trying to reproduce the process by which the 17th-century astronomer Johannes Kepler discovered what is now called Kepler's third law of planetary motion. This law states the relationship between a planet's distance from the sun and its period, the time it takes complete an orbit.

Kepler started with the distances and periods of the first five planets and, ultimately, discovered that the square of the orbital periods are proportional to the cube of their distances. Simon created a computer program called BACON, named after Sir Francis Bacon. He gave it the same data Kepler had. BACON then searched for patterns in the data and in seconds was able to arrive at the right relationship, rediscovering Kepler's third law. Rather than exhaustively test all possible relationships, BACON would generate patterns, compare the pattern with the data, make adjustments and try again. It obtained a solution after only three or four attempts.

A number of other programs have been written that duplicate historical findings in science (Langley, Simon, Bradshaw, & Zytkow, 1987). GLAUBER, named after the 18th-century chemist Johan Rudolph Glauber, was used to discover new chemical theories. GLAUBER was fed the same information Johan Glauber had. It was given information on taste, chemical reactions, and the distinction between reactants and products. Based on this, GLAUBER was able to determine which substances were acids, bases, and salts. The STAHL program, named after the chemist Georg Ernst Stahl, could backtrack and change some of its original inferences based on contradictory data. The DALTON program, named for chemist John Dalton, was also capable of making revisions. It would re-examine tentative conclusions that were derived earlier in the face of new data.

Computer Chemists   Joshua Lederberg and a number of other principal investigators started work on the DENDRAL project in 1965 at Stanford University. The project continued until 1983. The program served as a means to explore the mechanization of scientific reasoning in the specific domain of organic chemistry (Lindsay, Buchanan, Feigenbaum, & Lederberg, 1993). DENDRAL stands for dendritic algorithm because it used a tree-based notation for organizing different kinds of chemicals. The program took data from mass spectrometry and other sources and proposed possible candidate structures for new or unknown chemicals.

A mass spectrometer bombards a chemical compound with electrons. This produces a fragmentation pattern of ions that is unique for different chemical structures and serves as an identifying "fingerprint." DENDRAL was able to make inferences about the type and configuration of atoms based on the spectrometer readouts and was able to identify compounds from among many thousands of possible candidates. DENDRAL generated and tested hypotheses about the identity of a given chemical and could discard unlikely candidates. It used the tree notation to represent and categorize its findings.

DENDRAL was very successful at identifying compounds from the data it received. It ultimately proved faster than a human professional and just as accurate. It was later joined by META-DENDRAL, a separate program that formulated new rules for DENDRAL (Buchanan et al., 1976). META-DENDRAL was provided with training examples of molecules whose chemical structure was known. It then inducted or generalized rules based on its discoveries. METADENDRAL also met with success and was able to rediscover the existing published mass spectrometry rules on its own.

Computer Mathematicians Douglas Lenat produced two mathematical programs. The first was for his PhD thesis and is referred to as AM or Automatic Mathematician (Lenat, 1976). Unlike most math programs that attempt to prove existing theorems, AM is designed to propose interesting new theorems. The program starts with a set of concepts. It then uses a set of rules for specializing and generalizing the concepts and for deciding how interesting they are. AM was at first given 115 simple concepts from set theory, each represented as a data structure with empty slots. The program attempted to fill the slots using a collection of 250 heuristics. These heuristics helped guide the program toward promising solutions.

AM's initial success was remarkable. It "discovered" the basic principles of counting, addition, multiplication, and prime numbers. It also uncovered the opposite of prime numbers, what may be called maximally divisible numbers, and began to propose theorems about them. This was considered by some to be a case of a computer doing interesting original mathematics. AM's success, however, came to a relatively abrupt end. After a certain point, it failed to generate anything new or interesting. Lenat speculates that the program was only as good as its search heuristics and that it failed to acquire new ones.

He then created an updated version of the program called EURISKO that could discover new heuristics (Lenat, 1983). EURISKO could propose new heuristics and rate the value of both old and new heuristics. Using these methods EURISKO was able to evolve better models and rules for selecting among them. The program employed evolutionary principles because it mutated and selected heuristics based on their performance. It is thus an example of genetic programming.

EURISKO has been applied not just to mathematics but to other fields such as programming, biology, integrated circuit design, and plumbing. It is perhaps best known for its performance in gaming. Lenat used EURISKO to play the Traveller naval war game where contestant's design fleets of ships that fight one other. He trounced the competition so badly 2 years running that the sponsors told him they would cancel the game if he entered again. Lenat stopped playing.

WHERE CREATIVE COMPUTER PROGRAMS FALL SHORT

Boden (1999) mentions three key areas where creative computer programs fall short. First, they do not accumulate experience. They fail to learn from their mistakes and achievements and to apply these lessons. Second, they work within fixed frameworks. They operate within a set of assumptions, procedures, and criteria for what constitutes success. Third, they are unable to transfer ideas and methods from one program to another. This latter problem is akin to a failure to apply analogical reasoning, not within a creative domain, because some programs are explicitly designed to do that, but between domains.

Buchanon (2001) offers some solutions to these problems. Computers can solve the accumulation issue by storing winning and loosing solutions in memory. They would then need to recognize when a given problem scenario calls for the use of a particular solution that worked in the past. Conversely, they would also need to know which solutions not to apply in a given context.

The solution to the second issue of rigidity is to have the program reflect about the problem. This requires giving it meta-level knowledge about the situation. **Meta-level knowledge** includes an awareness of not just how to solve a specific problem but knowledge of problem-solving techniques and approaches. It involves thinking about the problem in addition to the rote execution of procedures. A computer program with meta-level knowledge knows about problem-solving techniques, strategies, and when it is appropriate to apply certain procedures. This could enable the program to know when to transform a conceptual space, introduce new procedures, or employ just the right amount of randomness (Buchanon, 2001).

We have already mentioned a number of analogical reasoning programs. However, most of these are designed so that they can be applied only to another scenario with an identical or similar structure. It is more difficult to design an analogy program that can see the similarities between two different situations and apply the lessons learned in one to the other. Humans have little difficulty doing this and can make comparisons between widely disparate situations. Poetry is full of comparisons likening eyes to oceans, lips to pears, and faces to a summer's day. Research in case-based reasoning methods provides a fruitful area for how machines might transfer concepts and methods between domains (Leake, 1996).

9

FREE WILL AND DECISION MAKING

We must believe in free will. We have no choice.

—**Isaac Bashevis Singer (as cited in Kanfer, 1991)**

FREE WILL AND DETERMINISM

It is a Saturday night. You have two choices. You can go out to dinner and a movie with some friends or stay in and study for a test you have on Monday morning. Which will it be? What factors influence your decision? Is it the lure of having fun with your friends? The importance of the exam? The amount of time you have available to study on Sunday? Now think about how you made the decision. Was it a subconscious or a conscious process that you were aware of? If the latter, can you describe what the process was like? Was this decision even under your control? Might you act the same if put into the identical situation in the future?

These questions get at the ideas of free will and determinism. According to the doctrine of **free will**, a person is the sole originator of their action. The action stems from a decision or act of will on the part of the individual and is not initiated by other preceding causal factors. **Determinism** instead claims that all physical events are caused by the sum total of all prior events. Human action is a physical event, and can be explained by these events that precede it.

Can free will and determinism both be right? It depends. According to **incompatibilism** they cannot both be true. Incompatibilists hold that a person acts freely only when they could have acted otherwise, if they truly had a choice in determining what they did. This notion contradicts determinism, which says that the person could not have acted otherwise, given the preceding causal factors. Incompatibilists argue that free will cannot exist if determinsim is true, i.e., if every choice is completely specified by the past.

By **compatibilism**, a person is free to choose if they had decided to. Their decision making capacity however can be denied by circumstances, such as having a gun pointed at their head and being forced to hand over their wallet. The point in compatibilism is that a factor or set of factors can override the individual's desires and preferences about their own actions. An aggressor, an environmental circumstance, or even an internal factor can coerce people into an action and this nullifies free will. To be a compatibilist, you don't have to adopt any particular conception of free will; you only have to deny that determinism is at odds with it.

The Anatomy and Physiology of Volition

Spence and Frith (1999) sketch out a rough neuroanatomical account of what takes place in the brain during an act of will. They derive their model from brain imaging techniques like PET in animal and human subjects. It involves a number of different and widespread areas (see Figure 9.1). They discovered that the initiation of motor acts occurs in the prefrontal regions, in particular the dorsolateral prefrontal cortex (DLPFC). Activity in this area is associated with the subjective experience of deciding when to act and which action to perform. They propose the DLPFC keeps possible actions in mind before they are exe-

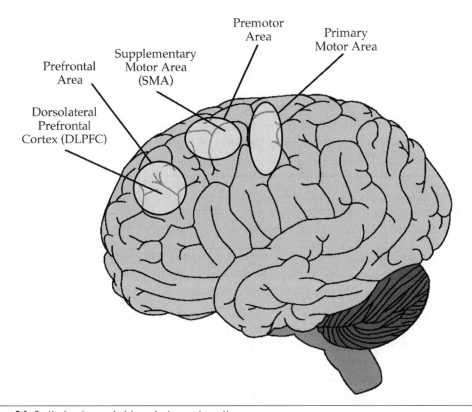

Figure 9.1 Cortical regions underlying voluntary motor action.

cuted, perhaps by suppressing inappropriate ones, and then selects which of these will be performed.

Evidence to support this comes from patients who suffer damage to the DLPFC area. They display lack of self-generated activity, are easily distracted by environmental cues, and engage in stereotypical repetitive behaviors. For example, a patient might automatically and uncontrollably start brushing their teeth upon sight of a toothbrush. These patients seem to have lost some of the ability to internally regulate their behavior (free will) and be under the control of their environment (determinism).

The actual performance of an action seems to be the responsibility of the premotor regions that include the supplementary motor area (SMA). They receive connections from the prefrontal areas. Premotor areas program the action. They create a "plan" for a movement. The SMA seems to be specifically involved in sequencing and programming the order of movements over time in tasks that call on bimanual coordination and self-pacing. Connections from the premotor areas next project to the primary motor cortex. It is here that the production of motor output occurs. Stimulation of neurons in the primary motor cortex activates descending motor pathways that cause muscle tissue contraction and physical activity.

This model shows that the decision to act is not localized to one particular brain area. There is no single place in the brain that we can point to and say: "Here is where free will takes place." Instead, we see that decision making involves a constellation of different regions all acting in concert with one another. This fits the neurophysiological pattern underlying many other behaviors. It refutes the notion of a CPU in the brain. In this regard, human brains are unlike modern computers that do employ a CPU for issuing commands. Human decision making appears to be more distributed than localized.

The Conscious, the Subconscious, and Free Will

The idea of free will is strongly imbedded in Western culture and values. We like the notion that we are in control of our actions and determine our course in life. But is this true? Are we always in control of what we do? Part of being in control means being consciously aware of what we are doing. After all, you wouldn't say that you are exercising free will while in a coma because you couldn't effectively monitor or affect the outcome of what happens. But it turns out that subconscious processes do govern much of our waking behavior. Reflexive actions are an example. Reflexes are automatically triggered by their stimulus and cannot be modified by conscious thought. The right tap on the knee will always produce the knee jerk reflex response, whether we want it to happen or not. That is because the neural circuits underlying many reflexes are insulated from other neural inputs or influences. The stimulus in a typical reflex activates a sensory neuron that activates interneurons that, in turn, activate motor neurons which cause muscle contraction. Nowhere in this loop are there connections from other parts of the nervous system that could modify or regulate the response.

Attention and awareness are required during learning when we acquire a new behavior. If you know how to ice skate, you may remember how much concentration it took just to keep yourself from falling down. As you mastered the activity, it required less and less conscious control. Eventually, an expert ice skater can talk or perform other actions like playing hockey without even thinking about skating. That is because the brain created a set of production rules that execute the appropriate action in response to the right stimulus. These learned stimulus-response patterns happen quickly and subconsciously over time. They mediate a surprising amount of what we do during our waking hours. It only makes sense that this should be the case, since we don't want to have to think about things we do all the time, like walking, cooking, and making our beds.

Most voluntary actions, ones that we think are under our complete control, have automatic components. Perhaps the best example of this is the Stroop effect where experimental participants are asked to say the color of a word or read the name of the color the word depicts (MacLeod, 1991). In congruent conditions, the word "red" may appear in red ink. In incongruent conditions, the word "red" may appear in green ink. When the color and the name are congruent, responding is fast with few errors. When they are incongruent, participants are slowed down and make mistakes. In particular, they cannot suppress saying the name of the word when asked to identify the color only. Reading is such a well-learned process that we are simply incapable of shutting it off; the presence of the word automatically triggers interpretation of its meaning.

Baars (1997) points out other examples of automatic processing during voluntary action. He lists a number of accidents that happened because people were unable to inhibit practiced actions. Among these were a London bus driver who drove his double-decker bus into an overpass because he had been used to driving the same route in a single deck bus. The point here is that when performing skilled action like driving, typing, or reading, we do not control every aspect of what we do. Some of the action is handled by subconscious automatic processes that, depending on the circumstances, may or may not be subject to monitoring, editing, or suppression by conscious voluntary control.

This distinction between conscious and subconscious control of action shows up in the underlying neuroanatomy. The DLPFC is linked to conscious control of action. This area becomes active during the overt making of a willed movement but also during covert imagined movements, both of which involve awareness. Subjects asked to perform imaginary acts show activity in DLPFC. In comparison, the premotor regions and primary motor cortex show activity during unconscious involuntary motor behavior. This demonstrates that there are different neural systems mediating voluntary and involuntary motor performance. Prefrontal regions apparently come into play only when deliberative decision making is needed prior to the execution of action.

Libet (1999) shows that the interplay between conscious and subconscious control is more complex than we might have imagined. He found that voluntary acts are preceded by a specific electrical change in the brain, called a readiness potential that starts 550 milliseconds before the act. Participants in his study only became aware of their intention to act 350–400 ms after the readiness potential, but 200 ms before the motor act started. He concludes that a volitional process is initiated subconsciously but then is subject to conscious control. To illustrate, the intention to reach out and grab a candy bar might be initiated because of hunger and the sight of the bar but later vetoed because one is on a diet or it is too close to dinnertime. An alternate analogy is to think of a congressional body creating a bill and then submitting it to a president who can pass or veto it.

Table 9.1 Key stages in the evolution of freedom, according to Dennett (2003).

Entity	Instance	Key Abilities	Freedom
Humans	*Homo sapiens*	Full problem solving ability, counterfactual reasoning, complex societies and culture	A lot of freedom
Animals capable of movement	A deer	Anticipation, guidance of action, some problem solving ability	Some freedom
Single-celled organisms	An amoeba	Detection of food and danger, pursuit and avoidance behavior	Limited freedom
Inanimate objects	A boulder	Incapable of perception or action	No freedom

The Evolution of Free Will

Daniel Dennett, in his 2003 book *Freedom Evolves,* sketches out a view of how free will evolved. This view is depicted in Table 9.1. Five billion years ago, he says there was no freedom because there was no life. Without life you can't have an agent that perceives, thinks or acts. Therefore inanimate objects possess no freedom whatsoever. He then steps through the evolution of more complex life forms showing that increased freedom comes with increased complexity and flexible ability to deal with a dynamic environment.

Single celled organisms like bacteria may be said to have a small amount of freedom because they can detect food or danger and either swim toward or away from it in either case. But they are limited in terms of the amount of information they can take in and process. It would be a stretch to assign the label "decision making" to even more complex multi-cellular organisms like clams that close shut after a rap on their shell. This is because they are acting reactively through the use of production rules.

Dennett likens the thought processes that underlie decision making to switches. There can be "on-off" switches and "multiple-choice" switches that regulate behavior. More sophisticated behaviors are the result of more complicated arrangement of these switches into arrays, where switches can regulate one another in a large variety of ways, allowing for a greater possible range of action. The development of the brain is ultimately the result of this, it can be thought of as the biggest collection of switches wired together. The brain's purpose is, of course, to guide action and generate decisions that keep the organism alive and healthy.

Animals that move can be said to have even greater freedom than those that are sessile. Locomotion means that animals must anticipate where they need to go next and then figure out how to get there. This calls on planning, or at least the generation of an expectation about what is going to happen next. Recall these ideas are similar to those proposed by Llinas (2001) and Franklin (1995). In this scheme a jellyfish that just floats on the tide has less intelligence, decision-making power, and freedom than a cat that can walk around under its own control.

In a similar vein, parasites are less free than their hosts. This is because they "outsource" or have given up many of their own functions to the host. A tapeworm, Dennett says, relies on its host for such functions as transportation and digestion and therefore doesn't have to deal with the problems these entail. It may also be the case that predatory animals are better at decision making and therefore freer than their vegetarian prey. Hunting requires a predator to think and make decisions about how it must get a meal that is constantly trying to elude it. This forces the animal to call on a more diverse behavioral repertoire to survive.

The ability to recognize and act on opportunity is fundamental to survival. The more an animal can do this, the better its chances at staying alive. It is not enough in most cases to act reactively. One must be proactive and realize that doing something could work to our advantage while doing something else might not. Humans, it seems, are really good at this. We don't just anticipate in a rudimentary perceptual motor fashion to anticipate our next most immediate action. We can also anticipate what the world would be like "if" something were the case. In other words, we can hypothesize or construct counterfactuals and use this information to guide our action.

The penultimate stage of freedom then comes in Homo sapiens. Only in people do we see the true expression of free will in the real sense of the word. Humans exist in a rich social world. The cooperative and competitive nature of sociality forces us to think. For example, we may need to decide which group of people we want to quit working for and which ones we want as allies.

Humans also exist in a culture. Cultures are unique because they allow for the transmission of knowledge from one generation to the next. The primary mechanism for this is language. Adults can teach what they know to children through this shared medium. Dennett points out the significance of **memes**, which are ideas or concepts that get propagated through cultural transmission. Memes, like the wheel, are useful or adaptive and it is for this reason that they get passed along. Memes are often contrasted with genes, which are physically encoded into our bodies and propagated by sexual means. Memes fill up our brains with the accumulated past knowledge of our culture and allow us to reason and plan more effectively.

In summary, Dennett argues that evolution over vast stretches of time has selected for rationality and rational agents that have expanded their ability to recognize and act on opportunity. Part of this is because of our more complex brains and increased intelligence. The other part of it comes from our social and cultural environment that gives us "new topics to think about, new tools to think with, and - new perspectives to think from" (Dennett, 2003, p. 191).

Is Free Will an Illusion?

A number of investigators argue that our concept of free will is illusory. Wegner (2002) says that the experience of willing an act comes from interpreting one's thought as the cause of the act when that act is actually caused by other factors. He says that there are three steps in producing an action. First, our brain plans the action and issues the command to start doing it. Second, we become aware of thinking about the action. This is an intention. Third, the action happens. Our introspective experience informs us only of the intent and the action itself. Because we are not aware of the subconscious initiation, we mistakenly attribute conscious intention as the cause.

Douglas Hofstadter (1985) believes the concept of free will stems from our desire to be in control combined with our lack of understanding of the human brain. He states that if we knew more about ourselves we would realize our decisions are determined. If we don't know how something works, like the mind, we say it's a mystery and give it a mystical explanation like free will. When we understand something like a computer, then it has no mystery and we say it acts deterministically. He believes that this ignorance and our desire to remain in control force us to create an inner-agent or choice-maker.

Within the cognitive science framework free will corresponds to **decision making**. A decision is the process of choosing a preferred option or course of action from among a set of alternatives. We can represent some decision-making processes using a **decision-tree** that reduces choices to a number of fixed options. Figure 9.2 shows a decision tree that a college psychology department or chairperson might use in determining whether to hire a new faculty member. Each step in the overall process corresponds to a set of smaller decisions framed as questions and represented as nodes in the tree. In this example, there are only two possible responses, either a "yes" or a "no," although there could be more. The outcome of this binary response leads to another until the tree terminates in a final outcome of "hire" or "don't hire."

In a broader sense, decision making is an information process that occurs inside an agent who is embedded in an environment. The decision determines the agent's action.

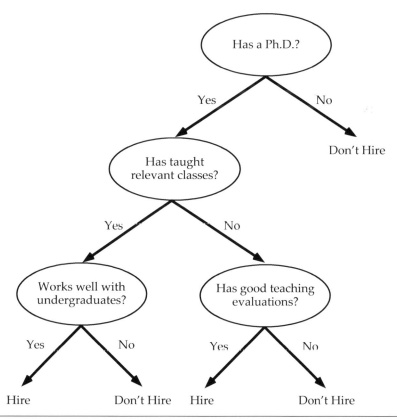

Figure 9.2 A decision tree depicting how a college department might go about hiring a new faculty member.

The time-course of decision making can be characterized in chronological order by inputs, computation, and outputs. The inputs to a decision can be the result of stimuli originating from the external environment such as information from a problem or from the internal environment, for example, information from memory. The computation consists of an information processing routine that takes these inputs and transforms them in some way, producing a conclusion in the form of an output. The output may start off as information but is ultimately translated into a behavior such as talking or some other motor action. In the example given at the beginning of this chapter, the inputs are the choices or options, either going out or staying in to study. There could be a number of different computational processes that constitute the decision itself. One possibility is to simply weigh the costs and benefits associated with each choice. If the costs associated with one are higher and the benefits lower, it may win out. The winning decision would then be acted on in a physical manner.

If free will is a decision made by an agent in an environment to solve problems, then are such decisions free or determined? From a scientific standpoint we can say a decision is determined to the degree that we can understand it. Remember from the first chapter that scientific understanding is based upon description, explanation, and prediction. The more we understand a system in these three ways, the more determined it becomes. Decision making is no exception. Currently, we cannot completely understand human choice. There are two primary reasons for this. The first is that we lack knowledge about all the inputs that go into a decision which include environmental conditions and a person's life history. The second is that we also lack knowledge about the brain mechanisms that produce decisions, which themselves may be quite complicated. This does not however mean that we can't someday explain most or even all of these phenomena. If we can explain an agent's decision making completely, then its resulting behavior is determined. If we can only partially explain it, the behavior is to that extent partially determined. The free will determinism debate for any given agent thus reduces to an empirical, rather than philosophical question.

DECISION MAKING

Types of Decision Making

In this section, we discuss three different types of decision making. Copeland (1993) introduces the first two, which he refers to as nil-preference and outstanding candidate choice. The third is probabilistic reasoning or judgment under uncertainty. Technically speaking, probabilistic reasoning is not decision making, since it doesn't always involve the consideration of alternatives. But we include it here because of its similarity to decision making processes. For all three of these types, a decision can be made in an optimal or ideal manner by utilizing a set of underlying rules. Whether or not people do this has been the focus of many studies and is reflected in a two-fold approach to the field, the normative and descriptive approaches.

In the **normative approach**, we assume the existence of an idealized decision maker. This is an agent who acts rationally, has well-defined preferences and follows several other axiomatic principles. The assumptions of normative decision making are outlined by rational choice theory and for judgment under uncertainty by the rules of probability. Normative decision processes show how a machine or artificial person might choose. It is based on a priori assumptions about how choice is made and seeks to describe optimal decision-making behavior. In the **descriptive approach,** we are primarily concerned with the psychological factors that guide the decision process. The descriptive approach investigates how people actually think under these circumstances. It is based on empirical observation and the results of human experimentation. As we will see, people don't always choose or reason in the most optimal way possible.

Nil Preference Choice

A **nil preference choice** is one where there are two or more options, but the chooser has no inherent preference for any single option over the others. In other words, the person making the choice has no a priori desire for any particular option. They are all equally desirable given the available information and the amount of time available to deliberate. Imagine that Karen goes to the store for ice cream. It is summer and there are only three flavors left, the rest having sold out. She can only choose one flavor out of these three, those being vanilla, chocolate, and strawberry. If Karen likes them all equally, how might she decide?

In this scenario, a computer could choose by calling on a random number generator. This would pick one option out of the number available with equal probability. In the case of two choices, the probability for each item is 0.5, equivalent to flipping a coin, while for three choices it is 0.33. A random process such as this is unbiased. It is equally likely to select any of the options available and is a satisfactory way of choosing in nil preference situations.

Random processes are interesting because they cannot be predicted. Nonpredictability is the hallmark of a nondeterministic process, one that cannot be specified algorithmically. People seem to act this way. It is difficult to predict their behavior and to specify how they make decisions. There always seems to be an element of chance to what we do and this chance element makes it difficult to model or reproduce human choice on a computer. In the case of Karen, we could specify with a certain degree of probability which ice cream she might choose, but if her choice was random, we could never predict what it would be exactly each time. Free will is believed to be nondeterministic in part because it cannot be predicted.

Some have argued that machines will always be deterministic and hence predictable while people, who are nondeterministic, can never be predicted with absolute certainty. The ability to be unpredictable can even give humans an edge, allowing them to solve problems that computer's can't. Roger Penrose (1989) points out there are some tasks, like filling up a floor space with a particular tile pattern that cannot be specified algorithmically. There is no computer program that one could write that would provide a rule-based solution. The only way to solve this problem is through a trial-and-error process whereby different tile shapes are generated and placed at random into the space. People, he says, can do this, but not computers.

However, as we have seen, a computer can act in a nondeterministic fashion if it uses a random number generator. Random number generators are actually deterministic. They take a starting number or seed and apply an algorithm to it to generate random numbers as output. If the seed is drawn from a truly random and unpredictable source, such as the time since a person started a software application, then the output will also be random. This means that computers that have access to a random external source, i.e., that are part of an open system, are non-deterministic and unpredictable. This would allow them to use trial-and-error learning and to solve problems like the Penrose tiles in the same way we do. Only if a computer is isolated, being part of a closed system, will its behavior be considered determined, algorithmically specifiable, and predictable.

Outstanding Candidate Choice

In **outstanding candidate choice**, there are again several options to choose from but just one best answer out of these alternatives. An instance of this is a multiple-choice question on an exam, where there are five possible responses (a, b, c, d, and e) with only one of these responses corresponding to the right answer. Here is another example. Mark has been accepted to four medical schools, each with different features. He must decide which of these is the best school for him to attend. School A may be the most prestigious but it is also the most expensive. School B is cheaper but has good hospital residency opportunities. How might he decide?

Rule-based ways of choosing do exist for this type of decision, so a computer can solve them. One way of choosing in the example above is to calculate a weighted average (see Table 9.2). We could assign weights to each of the criteria such as prestige, location, residency opportunity, etc. Each weight is a number between zero and one and all the weights for a given choice must sum to one. A weight reflects the subjective importance of a particular criterion for a given school, with the higher the weighting the greater the assigned importance. We then assign a score to each criterion reflecting its objective value. The score could run from 0 to 100 with higher scores indicating greater value.

If school A had a nearly perfect prestige score of 95 and Mark valued prestige highly, then we could assign it a weighting of say 0.55. We would then multiply 95×0.55 to obtain 52.25. We would next calculate cost, location, and residency scores for school A in the same way and then add all the resulting numbers together. This is our score for school A. Doing the same for the other schools yields overall scores for each of them as well. In the final step, we simply choose the school with the highest score or alternatively rank order the schools from high to low based on their overall score to give us a first-, second-, third- and fourth-best choice to consider. This method of weighted means works only when the crite-

Table 9.2 Calculating a weighted average is one way to determine which of four schools to attend. It is an example of outstanding candidate choice because the school with the highest score is the one that is picked.

	School A	School B	School C	School D	Weight
Prestige	95	35	54	88	0.55
Cost	87	71	63	91	0.20
Location	64	93	12	48	0.15
Residency	72	26	39	67	0.10
Score	86.45	50.00	48.00	80.50	
Ranking	1	3	4	2	

ria under consideration and their values are known. For many situations this information is not always available.

Utility Theory

A classical normative approach to choosing between set alternatives with a single expected best outcome is utility theory. John Von Neumann and Oskar Morgenstern were the first to lay down its foundations. According to **utility theory** a rational agent decides on a course of action that will maximize its utility. Utility is the subjective value the option has for the decision maker and corresponds roughly to happiness or pleasure. A utility-based agent assigns utility values to different choices and then follows certain rules to decide on the one that will return the greatest value. This is considered rational behavior and was first introduced in the chapter on intelligence.

There are seven axioms of utility theory that guide agent choice. We will describe three of them. A complete summary is beyond the scope of this text. Utility theory is a complex and technical topic and we refer the interested reader to the original source material to find out more.

1. Orderability. Given any two states, a rational agent must prefer one to the other or else rate the two as equally desirable. However, the agent cannot avoid deciding between them. Gabriele wants to buy a car. She has three choices A, B, and C. By the ordering principle, she must specify which cars she likes more than others and which ones she considers equal in preference. Possible outcomes could include liking A more than B (A > B) but liking B and C equally (B = C).
2. Transitivity. Given any three states, if an agent prefers A to B (A > B) and prefers B to C (B > C), then they must prefer A to C (A > C). In other words, if Gabriele likes the Porsche more than the Honda and the Honda more than the Ford, she will like the Porsche more than the Ford.
3. Monotonicity. Given two choices with the same outcomes but different probabilities of winning, the agent will always select the choice with the highest probability of winning.

People don't always act according to these axioms. In practice, human preferences change over time. People also often choose outcomes that are not optimal, but merely good enough. They practice "satisficing" rather than "optimization" of utility (Simon, 1955). Rather than exhibiting purely rational behavior, people seem instead to show a limited or bounded rationality when it comes to making decisions. Other examples of this come from economics, where people fail to treat money equally. They compartmentalize wealth and spending into different categories like rent, entertainment, and savings and then value the money in those categories differently (Thaler, 1985).

PROBABILISTIC REASONING

Uncertainty and Mathematical Probability

Many times when we have to reason, we do so in the absence of certain knowledge. Is it going to rain today? Are the Yankees going to win their next game? We can't say for sure in these cases. Instead, we express a degree of certainty for an event using a probability. We might say that there is a 60% chance (0.6 probability) that it will rain or that there is an 85% chance (0.85 probability) the Yankees will win. Uncertainty can arise from many sources, such as inaccurate, incomplete or conflicting information. The everyday world is filled with uncertainty, yet we go ahead and make decisions based on the limited information we have at hand. This ability is known as **probabilistic reasoning**. Formally defined, it is the formation of probability judgments and of subjective beliefs about the likelihoods of outcomes and the frequencies of events (Shafir, 1999).

There is a normative basis for probabilistic reasoning just as was the case for outstanding candidate choice. The mathematical rules of probability constitute this foundation. They specify the optimal way to reason under uncertain conditions. A computer or machine employing these principles will be acting optimally. It will be able to estimate accurately the probability of some event given available knowledge and be able to act effectively as a consequence. A person who does not follow these rules will make errors in reasoning and act in a less than ideal fashion.

The Russian mathematician Andrey Kolmogorov (1903–1987) developed three fundamental axioms that constitute the basis of probability theory. The first axiom states that all probabilities must run between zero and one, that is, there cannot be a negative probability. Probabilities are always assigned to propositional statements about the world. His second axiom states in regard to this that all necessarily true propositions have a probability of one and those that are false have a probability of zero. The third axiom says that the disjunction of two probabilities is equal to the sum of each minus their intersection. This is represented as $P(a \vee b) = P(a) + P(b) - P(a \wedge b)$. These axioms are true for **unconditional probabilities**, sometimes also called prior probabilities, those for which there is no prior information. Unconditional probabilities stand alone. They are not dependent or conditional on other events.

Using the Kolmogorov axioms we can derive a more elaborate set of rules governing probabilities. In particular, we can specify how to predict **conditional probabilities**, those based on the occurrence of other events. One of the most useful of these is **Bayes' theorem**. This is expressed as: $P(b|a) = P(a|b) \, P(b) \, / \, P(a)$. In other words, the probability of occurrence b based on a is equal to the probability of a based on b multiplied by the probability of b divided by the probability of a. Let's illustrate this with a medical diagnosis example. Suppose you wanted to know the chances of getting a sore throat given that you have a cold. Assume that the conditional probability for getting a cold given that you have a sore throat is equal to 0.15. If the unconditional probability of getting a sore throat by itself is 0.05 and the unconditional probability of getting a cold is 0.01, then $P(s|c) = P(c|s) \, P(s) \, / \, P(c) = 0.15 \times 0.05 \, / \, 0.01 = 0.75$. You would thus have a 75% chance of getting a sore throat under these conditions.

Human Probabilistic Reasoning

Bayes' theorem shows that knowledge of probability can be very helpful. If a person knew their chances of getting a sore throat were so high, they could take preventative measures like wearing a scarf or taking medication. But alas, most people don't know the prior or conditional probabilities and even if they did, they would be unlikely to apply them using anything like Bayes' theorem. In what follows, we show that people reason under conditions of uncertainty in many cases by ignoring or misapplying the rules of probability.

The first are in situations involving gains or losses. Imagine that you are given the following offer. You have a 50% chance to win $2,000 and a corresponding 50% chance to win nothing. The alternative is a 100% chance of $1,000. Which would you pick? If you are like most people, you would go with the second choice even though the expected value is the same in both situations. The expected value is calculated by multiplying each amount by its probability and summing. In the first case, it is $(0.5 \times \$2,000) + (0.5 \times \$0) = \$1,000$. In the second case it is $(1.0 \times \$1,000) = \$1,000$. However, people don't see it this way. They prefer a sure outcome over a risky prospect of equal expected value. This is known as **risk aversion**. People are risk averse when it comes to potential gains. They want to minimize their chances of losing what they might get.

Now imagine a different scenario involving losses. You have a 50% chance to lose $2,000 and an associated 50% chance of losing nothing or a 100 percent chance to loose $1,000. Most people in this instance now take the first option. This is true even though the odds of losing are identical in each case. This behavior is known as **risk seeking**. It is the preference for a risky prospect over a sure outcome of equal expected value. People are willing to take risks when it comes to negative outcomes.

One reason people seem to be poor at probabilistic reasoning is that we rely on heuristics. The use of heuristics leads us to commit **fallacies**, fundamental misunderstandings of statistical rules. Tversky and Kahneman (1974) were the first to discover many heuristics and fallacies in judgment under uncertainty. They presented statistical problems to participants in experiments and then examined the way the problems were solved to see to what strategies people employ. Here is a sample from one such study:

> Jack is a 45-year-old man. He is married and has four children. He is generally conservative, careful, and ambitious. He shows no interest in political and social issues and spends most of his free time on his many hobbies, including home carpentry, sailing, and mathematical puzzles. Is Jack a lawyer or an engineer?

If you think Jack is an engineer, then you are not alone. The participants overwhelmingly said Jack was an engineer. This was true even when they were instructed that he belonged to a set of 100 people of whom 70 were lawyers and 30 were engineers. Tversky and Kahneman argue this is due to a **representativeness heuristic**, the assumption that each member of a category is "representative" of the category and has all the traits associated with it. Because Jack's description fits the stereotype of an engineer, we consider it very likely that he is one. The representativeness heuristic in this case is accompanied by the **base-rate fallacy**, ignorance of the base rates underlying the set of people from which his description was drawn.

Here is another example of our difficulties in probabilistic reasoning (Tversky & Kahneman, 1974). Read the following description:

> Linda is 31 years old, single, outspoken, and very bright. She majored in philosophy. In college, she was involved in several social issues, including the environment, the peace campaign, and the anti-nuclear campaign. Which of these statements do you

think is more likely: "Linda is a bank teller" or "Linda is a bank teller and is active in the feminist movement"?

People overwhelmingly choose the latter sentence that Linda is both, even though this cannot possibly be, since there are always going to be more tellers than feminist tellers. Participants again rely on the representativeness of Linda's description that fits a stereotypical feminist. This time, however, they ignore the conjunction rule, which states that the probability of encountering those who are both feminists and tellers is lower than the probability of encountering either individually. This error is the **conjunction fallacy**. The conjunction rule stems from the axioms of probability theory that state that the probability of the co-occurrence of two events cannot possibly be more than one of those events alone.

The **availability heuristic** states we judge an event to be more likely if we perceive or remember it well. Salient events that stand out in our memory because they are important or shocking increase our estimate of how often they occur. For example, plane crashes are estimated as occurring more often than they actually do because of the large amount of attention they receive in the press. Another instance would be a person rating the likelihood of houses catching fire to be higher than in actuality after he just viewed his neighbor's house burn to the ground.

Yet another instance of poor judgment under uncertainty is the phenomenon of **anchoring**. This refers to people's tendency to use an established answer as a reference point and to make estimates by adjustments to this point. In one study, participants were asked to judge the proportion of African nations in the United Nations. Two groups watched the experimenter spin a wheel numbered from 1 to 100. They believed this wheel was random, but, in fact, it was fixed so that for one group it stopped at "10" and for the other group at "65." Those who viewed the wheel in the "10" condition gave an average estimate of 25%. Those who viewed the "65" condition reported an estimate of 45%. What we see here is that the participants were taking the wheel's "estimate" as an anchor point and then making their own judgment in relation to it.

STATES OF NATURE AND PREDICTION

So far our discussion has centered on the role of people or agents in decision making. We have looked primarily at the processes that enable decisions and reasoning. We have described these processes mostly in terms of information processing models that explain in an abstract way how a person approaches and solves a problem. But we can consider agents and the environments in which they act in an even more abstract sense, in terms of the overall properties of their physical states. The nature of these different states has direct implications on whether or not an agent is free. Prediction is a key element of free will. Systems that can't be predicted may posses at least part of what it means to be free because their behavior cannot be understood well enough to anticipate what they will do next.

In physics, there are five fundamental states a system can be in (Lorenz, 1996). A **steady state** is the simplest because nothing is happening to the object or objects in question at a particular level of spatial and temporal scale in this system. We must make this qualification because if we examine something at a sufficiently microscopic level or wait long enough, then things start happening. A rock sitting on the ground is in a steady state. Objects under these conditions constitute the simplest possible system to predict. The prediction is always the same for them: nothing will happen.

Next, there are periodic states. A **periodic state** is one that acts cyclically. Its behavior repeats at regular intervals. The swinging pendulum on a grandfather clock is in a periodic state. It swings back and forth through the same trajectory time and time again. Periodic states are a bit more complex than steady ones but they are just as predictable. Given the current location of the pendulum, we can say exactly where it will be at different times in the future. There are also **quasiperiodic states**. These are states that exhibit partial, but not complete periodicity. Quasiperiodic motion is characterized by having two or more frequencies that are incommensurate with each other, meaning they are not rationally related. Quasiperiodic states can be predicted with reasonable accuracy.

Dynamical or **chaotic states** are perhaps the most interesting. They are characterized by sensitivity to initial conditions (Rasband, 1990). Two identical systems will behave exactly only if their starting conditions are the same. If there is even a slight deviation in them, their outcomes can rapidly diverge. A billiard ball game is an example of a chaotic system. The starting conditions in billiards include factors such as the location of the cue ball and the force and angle with which it is struck. If any of these factors vary between two games where the rest of the balls are racked identically, the movement and final resting positions of the balls will differ. This is true even though the game is itself deterministic, the laws governing how the balls interact are understood and given the known positions of the balls at any moment in time, we could predict where they would be at a future moment.

Another interesting property of chaotic systems is that they can alternate between states of predictable and unpredictable behavior. A chaotic system can start acting periodically or even steadily. These regions of regularity are known as **attractors**. Chaotic systems can thus be categorized as acting both orderly and disorderly. Chaos is present in nearly all natural phenomena. Other examples include turbulent fluids, economies, and the weather.

The concept of randomness is debated among philosophers, physicists, and psychologists. For our purposes, we will define a **random state** as one that lacks any predictability. A random state is thus one in which behavior cannot be reliably anticipated. Many events in nature are random. For example, we can never predict exactly when someone will be born even though the overall growth rate of a population may be predictable. In this case, random events at a microscopic scale can still give rise to regular and ordered macroscopic behavior. This also seems to describe quantum mechanics, in which the individual behavior of microscopic particles such as radioactive decay cannot be predicted but the system's global behavior can.

A spinning top is a good example of a single system that switches between each of these states when one variable, the velocity of the spin, is changed. When spin is fast, the top is periodic. As it encounters resistance and slows it may spin periodically then quasiperiodically. When slowed further, it can exhibit chaotic behavior. Finally, it will behave randomly before it stops altogether and reaches a steady state of motionlessness. Intelligent agents like human beings also exhibit state transitions. They can be in a steady state as during certain periods while sleeping. Walking or running is an instance of a periodic state. There are neural circuits within the human brain that show periodicity and chaotic activity. Some aspects of human behavior can also be considered random because they are unpredictable.

This means that human and other types of intelligent behavior can be understood and predicted to varying degrees depending upon their state. When a person is in a steady or periodic state, their actions are predictable and locally deterministic. Correspondingly, the mechanisms underlying such action should be easier to understand and replicate. When an agent is in a chaotic or random state, there is diminished predictability and determinism. In agents, this is usually a consequence of an increase in the complexity or functioning of the underlying mechanism. It is important to note that decreased predictability is not always the result of increased complexity. In the case of the top, it was a change in the velocity variable that led to state transitions. In other systems, a small increase in complexity can produce a marked jump to a less predictable state. A single jointed pendulum is periodic, while a double-jointed pendulum acts chaotically.

10

CONSCIOUSNESS

Consciousness is the perception of what passes in a man's own mind.

—John Locke, 1694

WHAT IS CONSCIOUSNESS?

Perhaps the most amazing aspect of being human is **consciousness**, which, roughly considered, is a subjective awareness of our internal mental states. If somebody came up and pinched you, you would feel the resulting pain. If you got into an argument with your best friend, you might feel anger or regret. When solving a math problem, you are aware of what it is like to represent the numbers and manipulate them in various ways. As the above examples show, we can be aware of many different types of mental contents including perceptions, emotions and thoughts. These contents can be representations of the outside world as when we look at the items on our desk. Alternately, they can be internally generated ideas as when we imagine going to an exotic country we have never visited. It is also possible to be conscious of ourselves as a particular mental entity distinct from the external environment.

There is a strange divide that keeps appearing when we study consciousness that seems to forever remove it from our understanding. On the one hand, we have the brain that is part of the external physical world and that can be studied objectively through scientific means. On the other hand, we have consciousness, which, like mind, makes up an inner psychological world that is subjective. Consciousness is experienced uniquely by each one of us as individuals. This makes it very difficult to study in any sort of rigorous way.

To complicate matters further, there are many different kinds of consciousness. There is the type of consciousness we experience when are awake and alert. Then there is the subconscious, which refers to mental processing that occurs outside of awareness. There is also the unconscious, a state that occurs when we fall sleep or are knocked on the head. We can consider other additional states like meditation, hypnosis, and drug-induced consciousness. In this chapter, we will focus mostly on the normal everyday sort of consciousness that happens while you are awake and aware of mental processing.

As is the case with so many other concepts we have visited, there is no generally agreed upon definition of consciousness. This is, in fact, part of its mystery. If we could define it, we could understand it better. So, rather than rely on any single definition like that given above, we will instead describe some of its key features. Searle (1997) lists six attributes of consciousness. We elaborate on each of these in what follows.

1. **Subjectivity**. Searle believes this to be the most important element of consciousness. Mental phenomena are subjective because they are experienced or interpreted entirely through our own minds. We can describe what it is like to have a given mental experience, but it doesn't seem we can get someone else to experience an event exactly the way we do. Each mental state has a special felt or experienced character by the person who is having it. Philosophers use the term **qualia** (quale, singular) to refer to this subjective feeling. Examples of qualia include what if feels like to see the color red or to feel hungry.

2. **Unity**. We experience things as wholes rather than parts, even though studies show our brains divide up and process mental events as pieces in parallel. We also have the sense that there is a single "I" or person who has an experience. This is the sense of self.

3. **Intentionality**. This is the idea that mental states are related to or directed toward external situations and circumstances. The "grounding" of mental representations in their referents is probably part of what gives them meaning. See the chapter on thought for more on intentionality.

4. **Center and periphery**. Searle makes the distinction of having primary awareness of some state while relegating other states to the background. We can, for example, pay attention to a college instructor's lecture while ignoring the pressure of the seat against our back.

5. **Familiarity**. By this Searle means that we can recognize objects even though they seldom ever occur the same way twice. For instance, we can recognize a melody we have heard before even though it is played in a different key. Prior experience provides a structured template or schema for what is out in the world. We can then fit a stimulus to this schema to generate a sense of familiarity.

6. **Boundary conditions**. Finally, Searle mentions that conscious states are embedded in a context or situation. When we think of something, we are at least vaguely aware of when and where it occurred. Our episodic memories have time and location as part of their character. Facts in semantic memory are also contextualized by their relations to other facts. These constitute a type of halo or situatedness for anything that is experienced.

FUNCTION AND EXPERIENCE

Chalmers (1996) differentiates between two types of problems consciousness poses. The **easy problem** involves understanding the computational or neural mechanisms of conscious experience. These include the focusing and dividing of attention, our ability to monitor and report cognitive processes, and differences between states such as wakefulness, sleep, meditation, and hypnosis. We can use the scientific method to investigate these phenomena and to understand how they work.

In contrast, it is not at all clear how to go about solving the **hard problem,** which is to explain our subjective experience of conscious states. Here, we need to account for the feeling of what it is like to pay attention, think, perceive or feel emotion. The easy problem explicates the mechanisms of consciousness and describes objectively how those mechanisms operate. It is thus characterized by *function*. The hard problem must explain the subjective quality of consciousness and is therefore concerned with *experience*.

The hard problem is a thorny issue to AI theorists because the main goal of AI is to construct devices that can perform mental functions. If an algorithm or machine is devised that can execute a certain mental operation, then this in itself is a measure of success. But being able to perform the operation does not explain what it feels like for an entity to carry it out. Suppose an AI team after several years develops software that can recognize faces as well as a person. From a functional point of view, the team has been successful. Their program does all it was supposed to do. But the program does not tell us whether the computer or robotic system in which the software is running is actually aware of the faces its sees or experiences them in the same way you or I do when we see a face.

So, the distinction between the execution of a process and its conscious experience is fundamental. AI has made great strides achieving the former but has a long way to go toward explaining the latter. Recall our previous discussion of functionalism that states that thinking is the result of information processing independent of the underlying hardware. We can now see a problem with functionalism. It cannot explain qualia like the feeling of seeing red or being hungry. Building an artificial color vision system may be able to functionally reproduce those states, some say, but cannot explain their felt character.

One retort to the functionalist conundrum is to imagine an artificial person that can do everything a person can do. It exhibits every behavioral manifestation of human mental life, perceiving and recognizing objects in the world around it, providing answers to problems, crying during sad movies, and laughing at jokes. Furthermore, our artificial person can report on its own mental states. It can tell us how it feels at any moment, saying that it is anxious, depressed, in love, or whatever the case may be. Would we not call this person conscious? The majority of us most certainly would. The reason is that we only know that other people are conscious based on their behavior. We assume that they are conscious because they are acting and talking as if they were. If function were the sole criteria of what it means to be conscious, and machines eventually achieve full human functionality, then there is no way to distinguish whether an artificial person is any more or less conscious than you or I.

Some people have taken this argument one step further and argue that we cannot prove that any of us are indeed conscious. After all, you say that you are conscious and act as if you are, but why should we take your word for it? Chalmers (1996) argues that a person like himself might have a **zombie,** somebody who acts just as he does but who lacks consciousness. The zombie would behave exactly like him but fail to have any subjective internal mental experience, i.e., it would lack any qualia. The result of this thought experiment is that if we believe in zombies, then we have to acknowledge that consciousness is not essential to being human. It is an "option" like leather seats in a new car (Blackmore, 2004). If we believe that zombies cannot exist, then consciousness must be essential for at least some of the things conscious entities do.

ARTIFICIAL CONSCIOUSNESS
Criteria for a Conscious Machine

Aleksander and Dunmall (2003) posit five axioms they believe necessary for a machine to be conscious. The axioms are abstract and mathematical in nature but they give a clear sense of what mechanisms an agent must possess in order to be conscious. By the term *agent* they mean an active object that can sense its environment, have a purpose, then plan, choose and act in a way to achieve that purpose. An agent in this broad sense can be a biological organism such as a person, a mechanical device like a robot, or a virtual agent such as a software program running on a computer. In every case, the agent must exist in an environment that can be experienced by it perceptually.

Axiom 1. **Depiction**. The agent must have sensorial states that depict or represent aspects of the environment. For example, the agent must be able to "see" or "hear" what is happening in the world around it. Depiction refers to the internal representations that are generated from perceptual processes. When looking at a book on a table, an agent must be able to internally depict the book.

Axiom 2. **Imagination**. The agent has internal imaginal states that can recall aspects of the environment or produce sensations that mimic aspects of the environment. For instance, an agent must be able to imagine an object like a book even thought it can longer experience it perceptually, i.e., because the book is occluded by some other shape or because the agent is no longer in the room where the book is located.

Axiom 3. **Attention**. The agent must be able to selectively attend to certain aspects of the environment or of its own internal mental contents. In the first case, this will determine what it depicts and in the second what it imagines. Attention narrows the enormous range of what can be perceived or thought. In a visual scene, it would determine what object or part of the scene one focuses on. It could constitute paying attention to a book on a table while ignoring the other objects present on the table. With regards to imagination or thought, it means activating only certain ideas or concepts and not others. For instance, thinking only about the book and nothing else.

Axiom 4. **Planning**. The agent needs to be able to control the sequence of its imaginal states to plan actions. For instance, an agent that needs to obtain a book in the next room needs to be capable of imagining not just the book but also the actions it would have to execute in order to obtain it. The ordering of these events is crucial. One must open the door to the next room first, then move to the desk, then reach for the book, etc.

Axiom 5. **Emotion**. The agent will have affective states to evaluate planned actions and determine how they may be pursued. Emotions help guide actions. They enable the agent to determine when or why a particular action should occur. Fear of failing an examination may prompt an agent to enact the book-getting plan and delay the execution of other plans.

Notice that the five axioms are all functional criteria. They describe what a machine or other agent must be able to do if it is to act like a conscious being. They don't address, at least in an axiomatic way, the subjective aspect of conscious experience. For this Aleksander and Dunmall state that a factor, what they call the sensation of being conscious, must correspond to the various functional states. To illustrate, it is not enough for an agent to be able to imagine something. The agent must also be aware that it is imagining. Aleksander and Dunmall believe this conscious experience is something that can be explainable by physical laws. They liken it to the reflection of a scene in a mirror where the reflected image can be explained by the properties of light and surfaces.

MODELS OF ARTIFICIAL CONSCIOUSNESS

In recent years, a number of investigators have designed computer programs that they hope will exhibit signs of consciousness. Some researchers have adopted a biological approach, basing their models on the way brains operate. Igor Aleksander's MAGNUS model reproduces the kind of neural activity that occurs during visual perception. It mimics the "carving up" of visual input into different streams that process separate aspects of an object like color and shape. Rodney Cotterill also adopts a neural approach. He has created a virtual "child" intended to learn based on perception-action couplings within a simulated environment.

Other researchers utilize the cognitive or information processing perspective. Pentti Haikonen has developed a cognitive model based on cross-modal associative activity. Conscious experience in this model is the result of associative processing where a given percept activates a wide variety of related processes. Stan Franklin has built a conscious machine model based on global workspace theory. His program implements a series of mini-agents that compete for an attentional "spotlight." We discuss each of these models in the sections that follow.

Neural Models

MAGNUS Igor Aleksander (2001) believes consciousness is the result of activity in a population of neurons that code for a particular experience. These neurons become activated through sensory experience and after having been learned this way can also be activated internally. For example, the conscious experience of an apple would correspond to active neurons that represent its different features. Neurons representing "red" would fire at the same time as other neurons standing for "round." Their unique pattern of activity would then be the physical basis for the qualia of "apple." Once this pattern has been learned by experiencing the object, it could then be triggered internally, as when one imagines or thinks about an apple even though it is not perceptually evident.

Aleksander has implemented this idea in a computer program called Multi Automaton General Neural Unit System (MAGNUS). The software runs on a PC. It consists of about a million artificial neurons that are all linked to each other. Different neurons code for different aspects of an object like color or shape. The input MAGNUS receives comes from another program called "Kitchenworld," which presents a picture of an object in this world along with its verbal label. After training with a set of objects, MAGNUS develops specific neural states among the feature neurons that represent the different objects. After this, it can "recognize" an object if it is presented with it visually or "imagine" the object if presented with its label. Aleksander believes the program may be conscious of the object because it has a specific state associated with it and because this state is linked, i.e., grounded, to a referent in an environment, albeit in this case a simulated one. The idea of a specific neural state and reference are both fundamental aspects of human consciousness as well.

CyberChild   Rodney Cotterill has developed a computer simulation of a young child. His model called CyberChild is based on the known architecture of the mammalian nervous system. The "child" is equipped with hearing and touch and can also vocalize, feed, and even urinate. CyberChild can process sensory information about the environment and its body. It can detect the level of milk in its simulated stomach and whether or not its simulated diaper needs changing. Cotterill hopes that, over time, conscious awareness may emerge in this system just as it does in a real baby and that it may be inferred from CyberChild's behaviors.

Cotterill (2003) adopts a system approach. His simulation is not that of an isolated computing device. It models a brain that is inside a body that is inside an environment. We have earlier mentioned the importance of embodiment and said that these sorts of conditions appear necessary for the emergence of mind. CyberChild is set up so that interactions can take place between these different levels. The simulation can process inputs from its surroundings and then activate muscles to produce actions. It can, for example, raise a feeding bottle to its mouth after the bottle has been placed in its hands.

An experimenter views an animated version of CyberChild and responds to it interactively. If CyberChild senses low milk levels, it will cry. The experimenter can then provide it with milk that is consumed. This raises the simulated blood glucose level. The consumed milk then fills up the bladder in the form of urine. If tension in the bladder is great enough, CyberChild will urinate in its diaper, causing it to cry. This should then cause the experimenter to change its diaper to stop the crying.

The key to the possible emergence of consciousness in CyberChild is the neural circuitry on which it is based. Cotterill (1998) believes consciousness is the result of activity in a thalamo-cortical loop. Sensory inputs channeled through the thalamus project first to sensory cortical areas. The inputs send signals forward to frontal areas that issue motor commands. This motor signal can then follow descending pathways to activate muscles. However, at the same time a copy of the motor signal can be sent to posterior cortical areas completing the loop. This last part allows a memory or thought about the movement to be represented. This is particularly important when it comes to learning because it allows the simulation to make associations between its actions and their consequences. If CyberChild remembered that the bottle restored its glucose levels and satisfied its "hunger," then it will be more likely to implement this action under similar circumstances in the future.

So far, CyberChild has failed to exhibit learning or complex variations in its behavior. Instead, it tends to become trapped in stereotyped movement patterns. Cotterill speculates that this may be due to the relatively small number of neurons in the different brain regions of the simulation compared to those found in biological brains. One must keep in mind that Cotterill's approach is bottom-up in nature. The simulation emulates as closely as possible what happens in actual biological brains. The hope is that by doing this something like consciousness will emerge from the activity and tell us something informative about consciousness. This method is to be contrasted with top-down methods whose designers have preconceived notions of what consciousness is and then design models to implement such notions.

Cognitive Models

Cross Modal Associative Processing   Pentti Haikonen (2003) has formulated an interesting notion of how it is a machine could be conscious. One of the main features of conscious experience is that although it has a physical basis, it is not experienced this way. Even though we have brain activity underlying consciousness, the subjective perception, thought, or emotion that arises seems to be immaterial. This is the classic mind-body debate introduced earlier. Any machine model of consciousness must be able to explain why it is that the machine, like us, is only aware of the contents of consciousness and not its physical manifestation.

According to Haikonen, this is because of the property of **transparency**. Neural activity only conveys information about the thing it represents, not the substrate or medium by which it is represented. Activity in a silicon chip, for instance, might stand for an object. The machine, by realizing that activity in a certain way, becomes aware of the object but not the circuit that conveys it. In a similar fashion, when we look at a chair, we experience the chair and not the parts of our brain that become active. The experience of the chair as realized in an appropriate physical substrate is the "ghost." The carrier mechanism or cognitive architecture that conveys the information is the machine.

But there must be something special about the architecture of the human brain to produce this effect. After all, a television represents information about the video it receives but is in no way conscious of it. The difference, Haikonen argues, is that the TV represents the image for someone else, while a brain represents the image for itself. The brain is specifically set up to meaningfully interpret what it sees. Furthermore, when a person recognizes an image, they are not just processing visual information. There is associated activity that is triggered in other brain areas that correspond to emotions, memories, and possible actions. These are different in any given individual and reflect that person's unique history. These cross connections are part of what make the image meaningful for the person experiencing it.

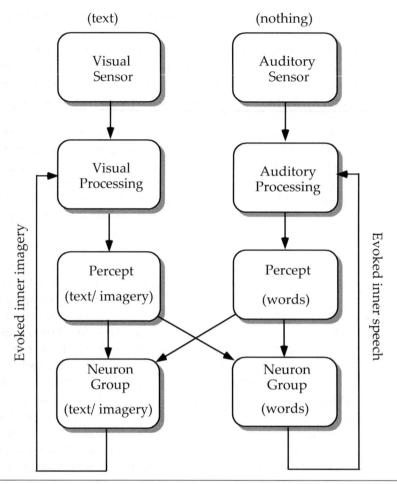

Figure 10.1 Pentti Haikonen's cognitive model of consciousness based on human neural processing (after Haikonen, 2003).

Haikonen proposes an extensive cognitive model of how a machine could be conscious that is based on human neural processing. He illustrates this with the example of reading (Figure 10.1). When we read, the stimulus of the text undergoes perceptual processing. The result is a percept of the text that can activate multiple neural groups. One group corresponds to our visual awareness of what we are reading and can evoke visual images. Another group might activate auditory perception processes and evoke inner speech. Others could correspond to the emotional significance of the text. The conscious experience of reading consists of all of this cross-modal associative activity. This activity is also unified or bound together by the fact that it is occurring at the same time and is about the same thing. It can then be laid down as a semantic or episodic memory. The person or device experiencing it could introspect about what it is like while it is happening, but also be able to report what it was like later by accessing the memory.

The difference between conscious and nonconscious operations, according to Haikonen, is the amount of associative cross connections. Activity with little cross connectivity fails to produce conscious awareness. For example, the "bed-time story reading effect" can occur when reading a book to a child. If the reader is tired, he may be able to visually process the text and speak it, but not be aware of what he is reading or remember it. This is because they failed to activate other associated neural processes responsible for comprehension, memory, emotional reaction, and so on.

Haikonen concludes that consciousness does not require a central observer, agent, or supervisor to which all information must flow and be interpreted. Instead, it is characterized by distributed neural activity in different brain areas that are activated associatively. The resulting activity can be introspected and retrospected (remembered) without recourse to specialized consciousness neurons or a centralized "seat" of consciousness. This process is what gives rise to conscious experience in the human brain. He believes that a machine implementing the same cognitive architecture would also be conscious.

An Intelligent Distribution Agent Stan Franklin distinguishes between what he calls **phenomenal consciousness** and **functional consciousness**. The first is subjective awareness of mental states and is the topic of the hard problem. The second refers to the processes of consciousness and falls under the easy problem. We have already alluded to some of the functions consciousness provides. They include helping us deal with novel situations for which there is no automatic learned response, making us aware of potentially dangerous situations, alerting us to opportunities, and allowing us to perform tasks that require knowledge of the location, shape, size, or other features of objects in the environment (Franklin, 2003). Given the problems with phenomenal consciousness and its inherent subjectivity, it would seem much easier to build a machine that could do the sorts of things a conscious mind can do rather than attempt the construction of an artificial phenomenal consciousness. This is the approach that Franklin has taken in his software program titled Intelligent Distribution Agent (IDA). Franklin's IDA is modeled on a specific theory of consciousness that we must describe before getting into any of the details of the program itself.

The theory of consciousness that inspires IDA is known as **Global Workspace Theory** or GWT (Baars, 1997). It is based on the idea that consciousness is like a theater (Figure 10.2). To begin, there is a spotlight that shines on the stage. The spotlight can be moved to point at different actors or scenes. Whatever falls under the direct illumination of this light becomes the subject of primary awareness. Events caught in the fringe or halo of the light are only partially lit up and produce only partial awareness. There is no awareness at all for things on stage that are entirely outside the fringe of the spotlight. Notice this corresponds to Searle's notion of the center and the periphery.

The contents of the spotlight are broadcast to members of the audience who are aware only of what the spotlight shows them. There are also backstage operators that influence the movement of the spotlight and what happens on stage. These are equivalent to directors and spotlight operators in a real theater. In this model, information competes for access to the stage in much the same way actors wait for their next scene appearance. This information can come from internal and external sources such as visual perception or imagination.

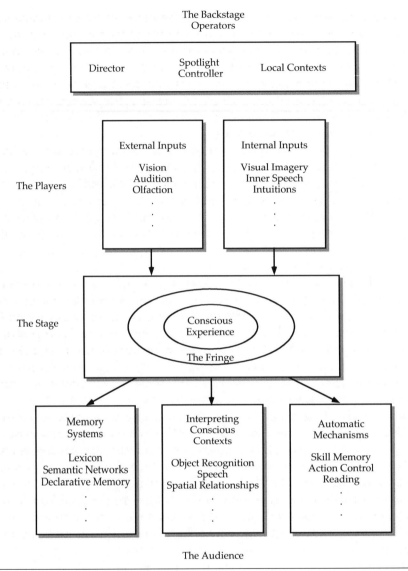

The Backstage
Operators

Director   Spotlight
Controller   Local Contexts

The Players

External Inputs

Vision
Audition
Olfaction
.
.
.

Internal Inputs

Visual Imagery
Inner Speech
Intuitions
.
.
.

The Stage

Conscious
Experience

The Fringe

Memory
Systems

Lexicon
Semantic Networks
Declarative Memory
.
.
.

Interpreting
Conscious
Contexts

Object Recognition
Speech
Spatial Relationships
.
.
.

Automatic
Mechanisms

Skill Memory
Action Control
Reading
.
.
.

The Audience

Figure 10.2 A model showing Baar's Global Workspace Theory. It serves as the inspiration for Stan Franklin's Intelligent Distribution Agent.

Members of the audience in GWT are the equivalent of different cognitive mechanisms that receive the information and process it in some way. Examples include pattern recognition, reading, motor control, and memory. If the spotlight shone on an actor, a face recognition system would allow you to identify who it was. If the information were important, it could be encoded and stored in long-term memory. The purpose of consciousness in GWT now becomes clear. It is to make information available to the various cognitive processes and operators who need it. Information that is in the global workspace or areas lit up by the spotlight becomes accessible to and can be used by any of the audience members.

IDA was designed for the U.S. Navy. Its purpose is to assign new quarters to sailors who have finished a tour of duty. IDA must access several databases, satisfy constraints determined by numerous Navy policies, minimize moving costs, and take into consideration the needs of the sailors. It communicates with the sailors through natural language using email. The program contains a nearly quarter-million lines of JAVA code and runs on a 2001 model high-end computer workstation.

A key element of IDA is the codelet. A **codelet** is essentially a small software agent that acts in a relatively autonomous manner and carries out a specific purpose. The codelets correspond to the various cognitive processors in GWT. In IDA, they operate inside modules that correspond to broader aspects of mind. A perception module processes incoming mail messages. Individual codelets in that module perform different tasks like recognizing pieces of text. There are other modules that are the computer equivalents of associative and episodic memory, emotions, deliberation, negotiation, problem solving, and metacognition.

The workspace arena of IDA is equivalent to the stage in GWT. It is here that information gets sent for possible availability to the system. Numerous codelets govern the operation of the workspace. They include spotlight controllers, broadcast and coalition managers. Attention codelets "watch" the workspace. If an important piece of information arrives, an attention codelet will form a coalition consisting of itself and the information carrying codelets that brought the data. This increases its activation level allowing it to compete more effectively for the spotlight. If it wins, the information is then broadcast to all codelets and can undergo additional processing.

Do these capabilities make IDA conscious? Franklin argues that the program possesses functional consciousness in the sense that it can execute many of the necessary abilities a conscious entity should. He does not claim that it has phenomenal consciousness, but, considering our lack of understanding as to exactly what this is, there is no convincing argument for why IDA does not have this as well. A conceptual model of IDA has the additional capacity to report on its internal processes. According to Franklin, a fully operational model of IDA with a self-report ability would be easy to implement. However, he acknowledges that IDA does not have a sense of self, which may be a crucial element to consciousness.

IS ARTIFICIAL CONSCIOUSNESS POSSIBLE?

The models described above introduce a number of key features found in people that seem important for conscious awareness. They are embedded in environments and are designed to process information about objects or events in those environments. In some cases, the programs can perform actions that subsequently change their environment and thus what they will experience in the future. Many of them learn and remember and that is crucial for adapting to novel circumstances. For the most part, they also implement distributed processing architectures. Information that comes into the system produces activity in various regions that process different aspects of the input. This activity can then be coordinated or synchronized in various ways.

Even with these humanlike features, it may not be possible to construct a conscious machine. In this section, we evaluate this question. We begin by defining what is meant by machine and artifact. We then address the topic of whether something has to be alive to be conscious. Three objections to the idea of machine consciousness are proposed and it is shown that none of them preclude the possibility. We then discuss issues related to the substrate, function, and organization of conscious entities. Finally, we wrap up with a debate of how one might go about testing for consciousness in a person or machine.

Machines and Artifacts

Could a machine be conscious? McGinn (1987) points out that the answer to this question depends upon how we define the words "machine" and "consciousness." He notes that consciousness can be considered a collection of abilities like perceiving, thinking, feeling, creating, or willing, and that each of these may raise separate issues and requirements. In this book, we have adopted the componential view and addressed each of these abilities, including consciousness, in separate chapters. We therefore focus now on what exactly is meant by the term "machine."

A machine can be considered in both a narrow and a wide sense (McGinn, 1987). In the narrow sense, a machine is anything that has been designed and constructed by humankind. This would include such things as elevators, automobiles, and computers. It seems that none of these sorts of machines are conscious in the human sense, although this may be debated. This does not mean though that machines of this narrow sort will not someday be conscious, assuming they are constructed in the proper way.

Machine in the wider sense means anything actual or possible that is the intentional product of intelligence. These types of machines are the equivalent of artifacts. An **artifact** is any product that is designed by a human or other type of intelligence. Artifacts can be something quite simple like a stone axe or something quite complex like the space shuttle. In contrast, a natural object such as a tree is the unintentional result of a natural process that has no inherent intelligence. The detailed aspects of a natural product were not designed or planned out ahead of time.

The question of whether or not humans can construct a conscious artifact remains to be seen. If consciousness requires a certain level of complexity, then we may need to wait until humankind develops the technology capable of such complexity. Even if humankind lacked this capability, it does not rule out the possibility that other intelligences do. A conscious artifact thus remains possible in principle.

It is important to reiterate here a point made in the introductory chapter. There we said that intention is actually irrelevant to the creation of an artificial person. The same thing is true of consciousness. What really matters is the process by which consciousness is created, not whether this process was intentional. If one adopts the scientific evolutionary perspective, then we must conclude that the process was unintentional and consciousness is a natural product. If we instead adopt the religious perspective of intelligent design, then we must conclude that the process was intentional and consciousness is an artifact. Either way, the key argument is whether this process can be understood and reproduced.

Life and Consciousness

One important property that separates artifacts from natural objects is that some of the latter are alive. We say some because obviously things like rocks and water are not alive but other things like plants and animals are. It is not clear whether artifacts can be alive. This depends on how one defines the term. We introduce the idea of life and its relation to an artificial person in a later chapter. Here we center on the issue of whether life is necessary for consciousness.

Looking at nature, we see that all conscious beings are alive, but not all living beings are conscious. Things like bacteria, fungi, and plants do not seem to possess consciousness but are clearly alive at least by the standard biological definition. On the other hand, beings like humans and many other animal species seem to possess consciousness and are also alive. We can conclude that at least for biological organisms, life is necessary but not sufficient for consciousness (McGinn, 1987).

There is no obvious logical or compelling reason why consciousness should depend upon being alive. However, the process of living might somehow give rise to consciousness awareness. It is conceivable that the physiological function of living along with other factors is necessary for an agent to develop consciousness. The link between life and consciousness though is far from clear. Perhaps there is some molecular or atomic reaction inside cells that catalyzes awareness. Alternatively, it could be that consciousness emerges from the cognitive activities that are themselves necessary for living things to survive in a complex environment. Cognition serves perception and action, which are both consequences of embodiment.

There is a problem with the life-consciousness connection. We judge the presence of consciousness in an entity partly upon the basis of its actions. If an entity perceives, moves around, and communicates, we are likely to ascribe consciousness to it. If an entity fails to do this, then we are unlikely to assign it this attribute. In other words, we are biased into thinking that things that act alive are conscious. This may be a fallacious assumption. It could be that life is necessary for consciousness but that lifelike behavior, at least in the sense that we know it, is not.

Impossibilities

Birnbacher (1995) proposes several reasons why artificial consciousness may be impossible. He then argues that none of these reasons preclude the realization of a conscious machine. The first reason he gives is that construction of an artificial consciousness is a **technical impossibility**. By this account, we will never have the technological sophistication to build a machine capable of consciousness. The feat requires greater complexity and engineering prowess than humankind is capable of. Notice that this is similar to Turing's Various Disabilities Argument in which it was said that we can build machines that can reproduce some, but not all human abilities. It is also equivalent to the engineering limitation objection brought up in chapter one. Birnbacher counters this notion by pointing out that many technologies that were once considered impossible have been realized. The history of technology has shown rapid and tremendous progress. Technology has produced solutions to many problems once thought unsolvable.

It might be that an artificial consciousness is **conceptually impossible**. The philosopher Wittgenstein (1963) declared that only a living being that resembles and acts like a living being could be sentient. This is the notion of biological naturalism first discussed in the chapter on the brain. According to the functionalist view, it is the process and not the hardware on which it runs that determines consciousness. By this account, nonbiological substrates executing proper operations can be conscious. Birnbacher's reply is that this is actually an empirical question. We have yet to see evidence of a machine consciousness but this doesn't mean it could not exist.

Consciousness in machines may be **nomologically impossible**, that is, impossible according to the laws of the physical world. This is the view of a number of scientists. However, the fact remains that our physical understanding of the universe is incomplete. We simply do not know enough about consciousness or the physics that support it to say whether this may be true. We may discover new laws of physics that could explain consciousness. Even if these are not discovered, the issue will remain open.

Substrate, Process, and Organization

Birnbacher (1995) next mentions in more detail the issue of what is necessary and sufficient for consciousness. He considers both the substrate and the function of a human brain. These are equivalent to the hardware or material stuff and the software or information processing in each case. It is not clear which of these is essential for consciousness. If it is the former and not the latter that is essential, then the biological naturalists are right and artificial consciousness will depend on a biological brain which may itself be artificially engineered or constructed. If it is the latter, then the functionalists are right and consciousness can exist in a silicon or other type of nonbiological brain.

We must also ponder whether both the substrate and operation of the human brain are jointly necessary for human style consciousness. If this were true, it still does not preclude artificial consciousness. It would require engineering a biological substrate and implementing in it a biological process. This could be done through intentional human design rather than natural reproduction and development, in which case it qualifies as a designed replication. One must keep in mind that once the basic principles of consciousness are discovered, then variations and manipulations can be designed which might allow for new forms of consciousness that would go beyond a mere replication.

It is an interesting question to consider at what level of organization consciousness emerges. There are many levels of functional organization in the nervous system. At the smallest scale, we have subatomic and atomic action. Above this is the molecular level that includes operations like synaptic release. One level up from this is the level of individual neuron operation. Moving up in scale, we can next talk about neural networks and brain regions. Consciousness may be more than the artificial reproduction of function at one of these levels. It may require functional reproduction of many or all of them. In other words, there may be functional interdependencies between these levels that give rise to consciousness. If this were true, then we need to reproduce the operations at each of the required levels but also ensure the proper interactions between them.

TESTING FOR CONSCIOUSNESS

We can consider two things when looking for consciousness. The first are the internal operations or inner states of the agent in question. The second are its behavioral manifestations. An example of the first might be some mechanism with a given function, perhaps self-reflection. An example of the second might be the ability of the agent to report its internal workings to other agents.

Which of these two should we rely on? The inner workings seem to be the better choice. This is because the agent can be wrong in what it reports. An agent may think it is accurately describing what transpires inside its mind when in fact it might be mistaken. Human introspection is notoriously unreliable and was abandoned very early in the history of psychology for just this reason.

But there is another basis for preferring internal operations. When taken in conjunction with environmental inputs, they conjointly give rise to behavior. If internal conscious mechanisms can be understood well enough, they would therefore allow us to explain and predict the external behaviors. In this sense, behavior can be reduced to knowledge of how an agent operates in conjunction with an understanding of relevant environmental stimuli. The problem though is that nobody has yet identified with specificity what any such conscious mechanism is. If we knew what it was, then we could look for or construct one.

The presence of a consciousness mechanism could be verified by doing a scan of the agent or perhaps by dissecting and examining it. This could objectively identify the existence of consciousness in the agent. However, it still could not account for the subjective experience the agent has when the mechanism operates. For this the only thing we might have to go on is the behavioral self-report, which, as we have shown, is inconclusive.

To illustrate how difficult it is to test for the subjective component of consciousness consider the following. Imagine that we have a person and a machine both with self-monitoring mechanisms and that both report having conscious states. In this case, we could objectively verify the internal mechanism and the external report in both agents but still have no way of verifying the subjective element. In other words the presence of the inner workings and the appropriate behavioral manifestations may both exist but neither confirms the existence of subjective experience. There is simply no way an objective test can validate something that is inherently subjective. There is therefore no objective test to measure consciousness unless we do away with the subjective part of its definition.

What we are likely to see in the future are machines that exhibit more and more human-like behavior as they become more complex. They will, over time, replicate an increasing number of human functions. But there is as of yet no way of telling when these machines may cross some threshold and become conscious until we agree on an objective criterion for this mysterious phenomenon.

11

MOTIVATION AND EMOTION

There was once an ardent young suitor
Who programmed a female computer,
But he failed to connect
The affective effect,
So there wasn't a thing he could do to 'er.

—**Kelley, 1963**

Jessica and Bob have been dating for three years and are in love. One day while walking in the park, Bob presents Jessica with a ring and asks if she will marry him. Jessica is overjoyed and says yes. In situations like this, we use words like "joy" or "happiness" to describe how Jessica feels. These words, in a broad sense, are what we call emotions. Emotions refer to a variety of different things. In humans they consist of a physiological state like a racing heart and a particular pattern of brain activity. But they also refer to how we feel when we are undergoing that state. What's more, an emotional being must be able to recognize emotions in others and express emotions to others using a variety of cues like vocal intonation, gestures, and facial expression.

Is it possible for a computer or robot to be emotional in a human way? Could we build an artificial system capable of experiencing the happiness Jessica feels? The answers to such questions have now moved beyond the realms of science fiction and philosophical debate. Recent years have seen the development of computer programs and robots that can recognize, express, and perhaps even experience emotion the same way we do. We discuss these developments near the end of this chapter. But first, we must lay down some background information to better understand exactly what emotions are, what purposes they serve, and how they are implemented biologically. We begin with a discussion of motivation because motivations and emotions are similar in many respects.

MOTIVATION

The psychological definition of a **motivation** is a need or desire that serves to energize behavior and direct it toward a goal. The most common motivations (or drives) are thirst, hunger, sex, and sleep. Each of these produces a particular physiological state that drives a behavior designed to reduce the state. Being thirsty makes us want to drink which will eliminate, at least temporarily, the feeling of being thirsty. Being hungry makes us want to eat which will, temporarily, eliminate the feeling of being hungry. Physiological motivators differ from emotions in that they impel very specific behaviors designed to maintain an internal state of body equilibrium necessary for survival. In contrast, emotions bias behavior in a more general way and service goals in addition to those related to survival such as social communication and cognition.

Motivations can best be understood by drive-reduction theory. According to this theory, a physiological need creates an aroused state that drives the organism to reduce the need. The longer the organism goes without satisfying the need, the stronger it becomes, the more aroused the psychological state and the greater its influence on behavior. The aim of drive reduction is **homeostasis**, the maintenance of a stable internal bodily state. Examples of physiological homeostasis include maintenance of water and blood glucose levels within a given operating range.

Humans have needs that are often not tied to satisfaction of basic biological drives. These higher-order needs, if left unsatisfied, aren't life threatening, but may result in our being unhappy or unfulfilled. For instance, children are often driven to play with new toys and explore novel environments. This curiosity drive may allow them to learn about the world around them. Abraham Maslow (1970) postulated a hierarchy of human needs (Figure 11.1). In his scheme, we are motivated to satisfy lower-level needs first. If these are taken care of, then we are driven to satisfy the needs at the next higher level. Maslow's theory has received some criticism. The exact ordering of the needs appears to vary across individuals and cultures, and there is no clear cut evidence that unmet needs become more important once met needs are satisfied (Diaz-Guerrero & Diaz-Loving, 2000; Hall & Nougaim, 1968; Soper, Milford, & Rosenthal, 1995).

ARTIFICIAL MOTIVATION

The Four Basic Motivators

An artificial person, in order to preserve homeostatic functioning, would need to be equipped with motivational systems. If we examine lower-order drives, there are some striking parallels between human and artificial human needs. In the following sections, we describe briefly four basic human motivational drives and show that an artificial person would require drives similar in nature to each of them.

Thirst   Humans and other animals must regulate water levels within narrow limits. This is because the concentration of chemicals in water determines the rate of chemical reactions. Enough fluid must also be present in the circulatory system to maintain normal blood pressure. In humans, low blood volume causes the kidneys to release renin into the

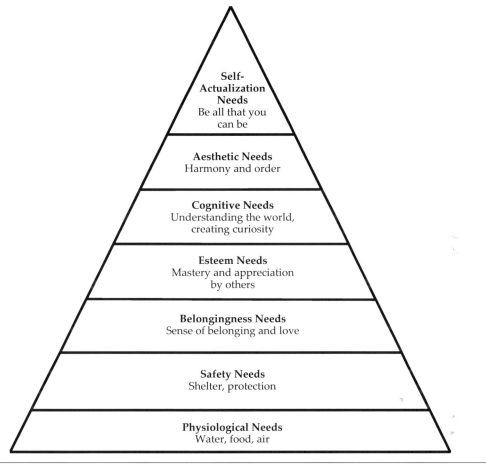

Figure 11.1 Psychologist Abraham Maslow formulated a hierarchy of human needs. In his model, we work to satisfy lower-level needs first. Once these are taken care of, we then turn our attention to satisfying higher-level needs.

blood. This initiates a chemical reaction where angiotensin II constricts blood vessels and stimulates cells in the subfornical organ to increase drinking.

Fluid regulation in an artificial person may be for different reasons, depending on the type of system, but it is necessary nonetheless. Hydraulic systems are in common use in mechanical systems. The hydraulic fluid under compression can be used to drive a piston and move various effectors. If hydraulic fluid drops, the ability to move is lost. Other fluids such as lubrication and coolant must also be kept within operating limits in mechanical systems like automobile engines.

Hunger   Eating or its equivalent is necessary for survival in all biological organisms. It allows the intake of substances that are broken down and utilized for energy. Blood glucose is regulated in people by a chemical feedback loop involving insulin and glucagon. These and other hunger and satiety chemicals that initiate and terminate feeding behaviors are modulated by various nuclei in the hypothalamus. Energy is a fundamental requirement to an artificial entity as well. Robots cannot operate or move around without some energy source. Currently, robots utilize electrical energy sources such as batteries, although like humans, they can also derive energy from chemical sources. See the biology chapter for more on these gastrobots.

Sex   Sex constitutes another salient human motivational drive. The purpose of sex is reproduction. The goal of sex is thus not to maintain the survival of any given individual, but instead that of the species. Sexual drive in men and women is governed at least in part by the hormone testosterone. Reproduction is, of course, also important to an artificial person and they would need to be equipped with some means of doing so. In sexual reproduction, the genetic content of a male and female are mixed, resulting in genetically diverse offspring. This diversity serves as the foundation upon which selection forces act and is necessary to cope with unexpected environmental change. We discuss genetics and reproduction in greater detail in the biology chapter.

Sleep   Although it might not seem like it because we aren't engaging in much overt muscular activity, sleep is also a motivated behavior. The feeling of being tired causes us to sleep and thereby feel less tired. Sleeping serves a variety of hypothesized functions. It keeps us immobile at night and away from roving nocturnal predators. It may promote healing and bodily restoration. It also facilitates learning of new information and memory consolidation. An artificial person may be able to satisfy these needs in other ways, but sleep is an adaptive and successful solution to these problems in so many species that it makes sense to implement it in the case of an artificial person as well. One possibility is to have temporary "shut down" or "standby" operating modes where energy is conserved. During these periods, maintenance of body systems could be performed.

Feedback Systems and Cybernetics

It is relatively straightforward to implement a drive-reduction scheme in an artificial entity. The simplest example of this is a thermostat of the sort you probably have in your house or apartment (Figure 11.2). A sensor in the thermostat measures the room temperature. This is then compared against an internal set point, the desired temperature fixed by the user. If the temperature is below the set point, the thermostat sends a signal to a heater, turning it on. If the temperature is above the set point, another signal is sent to the heater, turning it off. Notice that this system doesn't preserve a constant temperature. Instead the temperature oscillates above and below the set point within a fairly narrow range.

A thermostat is an example of a **negative feedback device**, one that feeds back to the input a part of the system's output so as to reverse the direction of change of the output. This is a very simple way to maintain a constant state. From a functional point of view, the thermostat is a motivated system. Some philosophers have even argued that the thermostat "wants" to stay at a given temperature or that it feels "cold" or "hot" when the temperature is either below or above the set point. Regardless of this, negative feedback devices are a proven way of preserving homeostasis. The physiological homeostatic processes in people

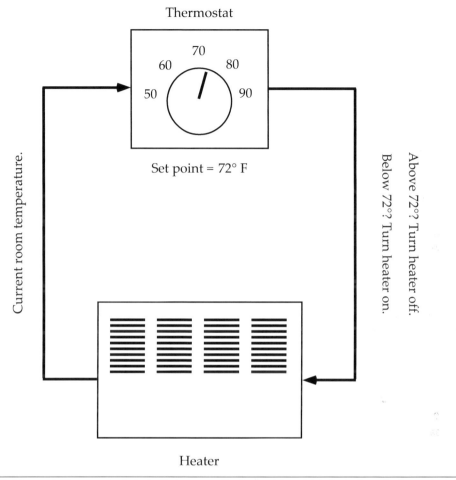

Figure 11.2 A thermostat is a very simple device that uses negative feedback to maintain fluctuations about a constant state. Our bodies also employ such principles.

and animals are essentially feedback devices like a thermostat. Although the particulars may differ, they all involve the same functional components such as sensors, actuators, and compensatory feedback signals.

Feedback mechanisms like a thermostat are encompassed under the more general field of **cybernetics**. Cybernetics is the study of communication and control that involves regulatory feedback, both in living beings, machines, and in societies consisting of one or both of these in combination. Norbert Wiener is considered one of the initial founders of the field and wrote an influential book on the topic (Wiener, 1948). Cybernetics is concerned with these types of systems in an abstract, information-processing perspective. As such, it sees little functional difference between animals and machines. Both are considered as systems that attempt to maintain a desired goal state and both can be considered to have purposive behavior. Although the term *cybernetics* is not as popular as it used to be, many of its ideas have been incorporated into related fields like control theory, complexity theory, and dynamic systems theory.

HIGHER-ORDER NEEDS

For an artificial person to be really human, it would need higher-level goals to pursue. After all, we humans pride ourselves on striving for ideals like truth, justice, and freedom. But what exactly are these upper division motivations? According to Maslow, the highest human need is self-actualization, the desire to be the best that we can be. Slightly further down in the hierarchy are the need to understand the world around us and various social needs, like being loved and appreciated by others. There are many such lofty goals that humans aspire to and it is a topic of debate which, if any, constitute what it means to be human.

Individuals can also differ dramatically in which higher order goals they pursue once basic needs have been met. The means and ends that satisfy these needs are not always well defined. One person could satisfy her desire for knowledge by reading, while another could satisfy it by traveling. This poses some difficulties for implementing such needs in an artificial person but it is not an impossible task. One could, for example, specify various ways of acquiring knowledge or of improving a skill and then allow some leeway in how it is actually executed. We talk more about higher-level needs and their importance for humanity in the conclusion chapter.

EMOTIONS

One conceptualization of an **emotion** is that it is an adaptive change in multiple physiological systems (neural and endocrine) in response to the value of a stimulus (Damasio, 1999). The value motivates or biases a behavior and is primarily related to the organism's own survival, but can also apply to its relatives or other members of a social group. For example, a mother who sees her child playing near the edge of cliff will experience fear and concern because she values the life and well-being of her offspring. This emotional state will then strongly influence a behavior to preserve that value, such as shouting to the child or running to pull him back from the lip of the precipice.

Psychologists view emotion, or affect as it is sometimes referred to, as having a variety of different components. These are the perception of a stimulus (the sight of the child playing near the cliff), physiological arousal (heart pounding), and a cognitive interpretation or appraisal of the situation (my child might fall). Over the years, there has been some debate over the exact order of these events. Early theories thought the stimulus caused arousal that then caused the emotion. This is known as **James-Lange theory** (James, 1884). According to **Cannon-Bard theory**, the stimulus simultaneously causes arousal and emotion (Cannon, 1927). In Schachter's **Two-Factor theory**, the stimulus causes us to generate a cognitive label. The label and the arousal together then determine the experienced emotion (Schachter & Singer, 1962). Modern researchers currently acknowledge that the exact order of these events is not important. For instance, there are situations where appraisal can come either before or after we consciously experience an emotion.

When discussing emotions, it is also important to distinguish between their perception, experience, and expression. When we are in an emotional state, it is difficult not to demonstrate some external sign. These are most clearly displayed through facial expression. Ekman (1992) found that for six basic human emotions there are stereotyped facial expressions where particular muscles get activated. Anger for instance, produces a furrowing of the brow, while happiness produces a smile. These expressions serve a communicative function and facilitate social interaction. In order to make sense of such expressions, we need to be able to perceive and interpret them correctly. Most people have little difficulty looking at such expressions and correctly inferring the underlying emotional state.

Finally, there is the subjective experience of what it is like to have an emotion. This is the feeling of actually being angry or sad. **Feeling** refers to the conscious experience of emotion. It is the subjective awareness of having an emotional state. Feelings are an aspect of consciousness, which we discussed in the chapter on this topic. Just as we can be aware of having a thought or a perception, we can also be aware of having an emotion. Emotional experiences in animals and people do correspond to certain patterns of physiological and neural activation that are sketched out in greater detail below.

WHAT PURPOSE DO EMOTIONS SERVE?

Rolls (1999) lists some of the main functions of emotion. These can be divided up into three broad categories that service survival, communicative/social, and cognitive needs. Let's start with a description of survival related needs. At the lowest level, emotions elicit autonomic responses, such as a change in heart rate and endocrine responses, such as the release of adrenaline. These can prepare an organism to deal with an emergency situation, such as fleeing from a predator. Most importantly, though, emotional states allow for a simple interface between sensory inputs and action. An emotional state, let's say fear, is usually triggered by stimuli that can be external, like the sight of a tiger in near proximity, and internal, like the feeling of your heart pounding. They then bias or motivate action based on this information in the service of some survival-related goal, such as not being eaten.

Emotions allow for behavioral flexibility. Unlike reflexes, they don't produce a single action, but influence the type of action that can be initiated. Fear biases running away, anger biases fighting, sadness the abandonment of a goal, and so forth. But we are not compelled to always do these things. In this sense, emotions are more general than reflexes or fixed action patterns. They suggest what should be done, but leave the actual selection of a behavior open to modification by perceptual and cognitive processes. To take an example, just because Bill is angry doesn't mean he should always pick a fight, especially if it is with Steve who weighs 200 pounds more than he does. In people, emotions thus operate in parallel with cognitive and other processes to guide action.

The second major function served by emotions is communication in a social context. Charles Darwin was the first to point this out (Darwin, 1872/1998). He noticed that animals like monkeys communicate their emotional state using facial expressions. The same is true for humans. Ekman (1992) found that people categorize facial expressions as happy, sad, fearful, angry, surprised, and disgusted. This categorization appears to be universal across different cultures.

It is hard to underestimate how important this communicative function is. In order to interact with others, any social entity, be it an animal, person, or robot, must be able to assess other's states, including their moods, desires, and motives. We can then form a model of the other that allows us to explain and predict what they are going to do, why they are doing it, and how to elicit a desired behavior from it. This emotion-derived model of other's social behavior then guides our interaction with them. For example, if someone were exhibiting a sad facial expression, we could attempt to cheer them up or encourage them to seek assistance for their problem. Emotional expression is an important cue in the formation of intentionality discussed previously.

The third major function emotions serve is in aiding cognition. At first blush it might seem that emotions and cognitions are opposites and that being emotional would only get in the way of making calm, reasoned decisions. But much recent work shows that emotions can actually enhance cognitive processes. Emotions may facilitate the storage of memories in a variety of ways (Rolls & Stringer, 2001). For example, mood states encoded at the time of a particular event may aid in the retrieval of that information from episodic memory.

Picard (1997) argues that emotion guides attention to what is important, helping us to ignore distractions and prioritize concerns. Mild positive affect has a beneficial effect on a variety of decision-making processes (Isen, 2000). In addition to facilitating memory retrieval, it promotes creativity and flexibility during problem solving, and enhances the organization, completeness, and efficiency of various decision-making tasks. Although too much emotion may get in the way of rational thought, too little emotion can be just as detrimental. Damasio (1994) reports several patients who suffered brain damage that inhibited their emotionality. These individuals were in some cases unable to make even simple decisions, giving excessive consideration to inconsequential details. They didn't know when to stop engaging in bad decisions.

EVOLUTION, EMOTION, AND PSYCHOLOGICAL DISORDERS

In the above section, we saw that one of the key roles of emotions is to aid in survival. Without emotions it would be difficult for an autonomous entity such as an animal, person, or robot, to explore and interact with a complex and dangerous environment. Motivations and emotions govern survival-related behaviors like drinking, eating, mating, defense, attack, and communication. For biological organisms, these systems exist as neural structures in the brain and body that have been selected for over many generations by evolutionary forces. Animals with these systems are better adapted to their environments and act in ways that promote their survival. In the section that follows, we describe several of the basic human emotions. For each, we describe the functional role that it serves and provide an evolutionary account for why it is adaptive. We then detail how problems with these specific emotional systems can lead to particular psychological disorders.

Disgust

Disgust is a powerful and compelling emotion that is clearly linked to a stimulus and has obvious evolutionary origins. In humans, there are certain substances like rotten food, vomit, and excrement that can be detrimental to our survival. These things are a potential source of viral, bacterial, or parasitic infection. The odor and/or sight of them produces nausea and a feeling of disgust that discourages us from ingesting them and makes us keep our distance to avoid contact. Disgust can be thought of as the opposite of hunger, which motivates us to seek out and obtain proper food for its nutritional and life-sustaining value.

Marks and Nesse (1994) have pointed out a possible relationship between disgust and the psychological abnormality of **obsessive compulsive disorder** (OCD). They note that other animal species engage in ritualistic actions to reduce the danger of becoming infected. Common examples are cats licking their fur and birds preening their feathers. People with OCD engage in similar ritualistic behaviors. OCD is characterized by an obsession, an anxiety-inducing thought often centered on the threat of contamination. Certain OCD individuals might not be able to stop thinking about the germs on their hands. They then initiate a compulsive act, like hand washing. This relieves the anxiety, but only temporarily. The result is an iterative cycle where some patients may wash their hands up to 20 or more times a day. In these sufferers, it appears that an evolutionary mechanism designed to reduce contamination has gone awry, resulting in a debilitating disorder.

Fear

We all know what it is like to be afraid; ur palms become sweaty and our pupils dilate. Our hearts beat faster and we breathe more rapidly. These bodily manifestations of fear are the result of sympathetic nervous system activation. Sometimes called the "fight or flight" response, this aroused state is typically triggered by a threatening object and allows us to better deal with it. Imagine one of our hominid ancestors who by accident stumbled upon a tiger. The physiological arousal would better enable him to react to the danger, either running away, seeking shelter in a tree, or confronting the animal.

The psychological disorders called phobias support this evolutionary account. A **phobia** is a persistent and irrational fear of a specific object or situation. Common phobias include fear of spiders (arachnophobia), reptiles, (batrachophobia), heights (acrophobia), and water (hydrophobia). Note that these are fairly common features of the natural environment. The fact that people have phobias for these things and not for more recent man-made environmental features like guns or car doors shows they are a hold-over from our ancestral past. They are the genetic remnants of ancient threats, not learned responses to modern ones (Marks, 1987).

Other anxiety disorders like panic attacks seem to have evolutionary origins. A **panic attack** is characterized by intense fear and feelings of doom or terror unjustified by the situation. Accompanying physiological symptoms include shortness of breath, dizziness, heart palpitations, trembling, and chest pain (Barlow, 1988). Eight of the twelve symptoms of this disorder, as listed in the *Diagnostic and Statistical Manual of Mental Disorders*

(*DSM-III*) are either indirectly or directly related to an escape response (Nesse, 1987). Sufferers of panic attacks seem to be hypersensitive to stimuli that signal the presence of being trapped. The resulting fear and arousal in normal individuals would motivate removing themselves from this situation. Agoraphobia is classified as a separate syndrome but shares much of the same features as panic disorder including fear of being in places where escape might be difficult, such as crowds or enclosed spaces.

In **post-traumatic stress disorder** (PTSD), a person experiences a traumatic event such as imprisonment, rape, torture, war, or loss of a home to natural disaster (Carlson & Rosser-Hogan, 1991). Although considered an anxiety disorder, PTSD also has a cognitive component. This is a psychological re-enactment of the traumatic event in the form of flashbacks and nightmares. Memory for the event in PTSD is in fact so powerful that patients cannot escape it. They will often make deliberate attempts to avoid thoughts and feelings about it.

One possible explanation for this symptom is that the high arousal and fear felt during the trauma potentiate memory consolidation, perhaps through reticular activating system inputs to cortical and hippocampal areas. This priming allows for a strong encoding of the memories that occur during and around the event. The advantage of such a mechanism is clear. If an individual survived a traumatic incident and ever finds themselves in a similar situation in the future, they could immediately call on their memory of how they may have dealt successfully with it in the past. Climbing a tree to escape a tiger and remembering that one did so would enable the fast actuation of this response if the situation ever presented itself again.

Anger

Why do we get angry? One obvious conclusion is that it motivates fighting, the other side of the fight or flight response. In this sense, anger is the opposite of fear. Instead of retreating from a threat, anger forces us to confront and deal with it. In a more general way, anger serves to mobilize and sustain energy and vigorous motor activity at high levels (Tomkins, 1963). This highly aroused state enables us to handle emergency situations in which we are threatened. Low levels of anger may correspond to frustration and motivate sustained long-term efforts to achieving a goal that is hindered or blocked.

The emotional state of anger is associated with the behavior of **aggression**. Aggressive or violent behavior can take many forms like shouting, murder or rape. Men exhibit more aggressive behavior than women. The evolutionary explanation for this is that in our ancestral past, men had to compete for mates, with more aggressive males being better able to secure mates. Evidence to support this comes from the study of the Yanomamo tribes of Venezuela and Brazil who regularly go to war against each other. Chagnon (1997) found that the reasons for this centered on reproductive success. Women from conquered villages were captured as prizes and men who proved themselves as successful warriors were allowed to marry earlier and more often, thus producing more children. Manson and Wrangham (1991) investigated warfare in 75 traditional societies. The cause in over 80% of the cases was access to females or to the resources needed in obtaining a bride.

Sadness

The emotional state of sadness corresponds to feeling down, discouraged, and hopeless. In normal individuals, this is often in response to some precipitating event such as the loss of a job or the death of a loved one. But in some people, sadness can occur without any obvious trigger and is either more intense and/or longer lasting. In such cases, it is labeled as the psychological disorder of major depression. **Major depressive disorder** is characterized by depressed mood and loss of interest in pleasurable activities. It can also include disturbances in sleep, appetite, energy level, and concentration. Depressed individuals often feel fatigued, worthless, guilty, and can be preoccupied with thoughts of suicide. A milder form of depression is called **dysthymia**.

Tomkins (1963) was one of the first to propose an adaptive function for sadness, stating that it slows one down and enables them to reflect upon disappointing performance. The result is that they may gain a new perspective that can improve future performance. Nesse (1999) argues that depression is an evolved strategy for disengaging from unattainable goals. Moods in general may regulate how much time and energy we put into different activities. A positive mood would cause us to persist at attaining some goal. A negative mood would do just the opposite, causing us to give up and therefore save energy chasing after an impossible objective.

Sadness and depression may also serve a social function. The expression of sorrow communicates that one is in trouble and may elicit feelings of sympathy and assistance from others (Moore, Underwood, & Rosenhan, 1984). According to the **social competition hypothesis**, depression causes us to stop competing with others. This allows for reconciliation with former competitors and serves to reduce costly group conflict (Price, Sloman, Gardner, Gilbert, & Rhode, 1994).

Happiness

Happiness is the emotional state of feeling good. As such, it is a positive emotion and related to others of this type like joy and contentment, which may be more and less intense versions of happiness. Feeling happy may serve as a reinforcer for adaptive responses and encourage us to engage in activities with survival value such as feeding and mating. As mentioned above, it can also motivate us to persist in attaining a goal. Happiness broadens our thought and behavior and may enhance our physical and creative skills (Fredrickson, 1998). It tends to occur most during periods of perceived security and acceptance. These are ideal times to learn new skills, establish relationships and build up other resources that can benefit the individual or group in the future when things may not be so great. Happiness also encourages us to help others. A number of studies have shown that a mood-enhancing experience like finding money or succeeding on a challenging task induces people to engage in altruistic behaviors such as giving money away and volunteering to assist others. This effect has been dubbed **the feel-good, do-good phenomenon**.

Major depression, dysthymia, and bipolar disorder all fall under the category of mood disorders that are characterized by disturbances in mood or emotion. In most cases, mood disorders are negative, but they can also be positive. This is the case with **bipolar disorder** where an individual alternates between depressive symptoms of the sort found in major depression and a manic state. People in a manic episode feel excessively happy or euphoric and believe they can do anything. They have a grandiose sense of their own self-worth, require less sleep, have racing thoughts, and feel a constant need to talk. The manic phase of bipolar disorder seems to be a malfunctioning of an emotional happiness mechanism. Interestingly, bipolar patients and their relatives achieve higher levels of education and are disproportionately represented among creative writers and other professionals (Westen, 1996). This supports the notion mentioned previously that a happy state encourages creativity and the development of new skills.

THE NEUROSCIENCE OF EMOTIONS

Much neuroscience research on brain mechanisms underlying emotion have centered on the specific emotion of fear. These investigations show that the part of the brain most closely associated with a fear response, both in humans and many other animals, is the amygdala. The **amygdala** is an almond-shaped structure that is part of a collection of brain areas involved in emotional processing called the **limbic system**. The amygdala in particular plays a role in conditioned fear responses, the ability to make a learned association between a stimulus and a fear response (Barinaga, 1992). For instance, if a tone is played to a rabbit and then followed with an electric shock, after a few such pairings, the rabbit will demonstrate a fear reaction to the tone itself before administration of the shock. Animals with damage to the amygdala or who take drugs that suppress the amygdala fail to show a conditioned fear response.

In humans, the amygdala is part of a circuit responsible for fear responses (LeDoux, 1996). Imagine that you are walking across the road and see a car speeding toward you. The image of the car would activate nuclei in the **thalamus**, a major brain relay center for incoming sensory information (Figure 11.3). From here, it would project to two other locations. It most immediately sends signals directly to the amygdala. This activation then triggers an emotional fear response that could include effects such as increased heart rate and an adrenaline rush. This "low road" to the amygdala is fast and doesn't require any thought. It acts as an emergency reaction system to deal with threats.

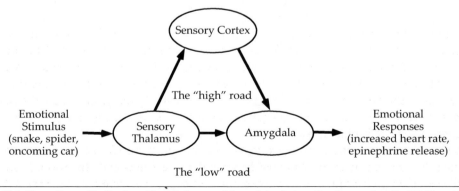

Figure 11.3 Fear pathways. The "low" road through the amygdala mediates fast emotional responding. The "high" road through the cortex allows for slower thoughtful consideration.

But the thalamus also sends information about the image of the car to the visual cortex. These areas make sense of what you see. They allow you to recognize the car, estimate how far away it is, how long it may take before it hits you, and so on. Inputs from the cortex can then feed back down to stimulate the amygdala. This constitutes the "high road" to the amygdala. The high road is slower and can involve deliberative thought processes, planning, and decision making about what actions to take next. This secondary pathway could enable you to decide what to do in the current situation, for example to sprint across the road to the other side or return to the side you came from.

The above pathways can explain emotional reactions or behaviors, but what about feelings? What neural circuits underlie the subjective experience of fear or other emotions? LeDoux (1996) lists the essential physiological ingredients necessary for feelings. He states that conscious feeling requires a number of distinct but interacting components, each associated with different brain and body systems. Feeling, first of all, requires a working memory to hold information about the experience. Long-term memories are also important for holding information about past emotional experiences. Then there is activation of the amygdala and of the brain's arousal systems. These arousal systems keep conscious attention directed toward the emotional situation. Another crucial element is feedback from the body. This feedback provides sensations like a racing heart or sweaty palms that contribute to emotional feeling.

There are multiple pathways between these different elements that mediate specific aspects of emotional experience. The amygdala activates the hippocampus. Because this structure is involved in memory. it can serve to call on past experiences in which a given emotion occurred or to lay down new emotional memories. The amygdala also activates arousal networks that in turn activate the cortex, influencing attention and cognitive processing. In addition, there are outputs from the amygdala to muscles for acting and to internal organs and glands. Information from body activity also supplies feedback to the amygdala, hippocampus, and prefrontal cortex to produce awareness of body states (Figure 11.4).

ARTIFICIAL EMOTIONS

Could a Robot Have Emotions?

Will it ever be possible to build an artificial person with emotions? Since emotions are such a primary aspect of what it means to be human, an artificial person would by definition, need to be emotional in the same way. The answer to this question depends on whether one defines emotionality as either a function or an experience. If we consider emotions in terms of the behaviors they elicit, then the answer seems to be an unqualified yes. If we consider emotions in terms of their subjective experience, what it feels like for an entity to have them, then the jury is still out.

Most robotics researchers are concerned with imbuing emotional *behavior* into their machines. They want their robots to act in ways that are emotional. The robot Kismet, as we will see below, acts as an emotional person would. It smiles when in a happy state and frowns when frustrated. But is Kismet actually *feeling* happy or frustrated the way you

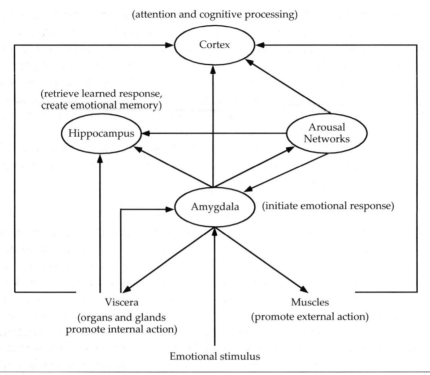

(attention and cognitive processing)

Figure 11.4 The different human brain areas involved in emotional responding (after LeDoux, 1996).

or I would? Probably not. Because feelings are an aspect of conscious experience, which we don't fully understand, it may be impossible to get a mechanical device to experience them.

One approach to getting machines that feel is to mimic the underlying computational processes that occur in humans or animals when they experience an emotional state. If there is some intrinsic aspect of this architecture that gives rise to feelings, then implementing it in a machine may also produce a feeling state. Of course, there is no guarantee that any particular computational scheme will produce feelings and in fact, it may be the case that multiple different architectures can all produce a given feeling. Feelings, like other forms of conscious awareness, may require additional factors, such as embodiment and developmental interaction with the environment.

However, we should not rule out the possibility than an artificial recreation of the human physiological processes underlying feelings might, if instantiated properly, give rise to their subjective experience in a machine. For example, researchers could build an artificial amygdala and connect it to memory, attention, and other cognitive centers. This artificial amygdala could additionally send outputs to and receive inputs from arousal/activating systems and to the equivalent of internal effectors, organs, and glands. This system could then be placed in an actual or simulated environment in which it learns to develop fears and other emotions and to build memories for them based on past experience.

Adolphs (2005) discusses the issue of emotional function versus experience in robots. He points out two problems in adopting a behaviorist or functionalist approach to emotion. If we reduce emotions to behavior, it becomes difficult to say what aspect of a behavior is emotional or not. For instance, is an increase in heart rate or pounding one's fist on the table a demonstration of anger? These operations can occur in people who aren't angry. There is therefore no perfect correlation between behaviors and emotions. Second, if emotions are reduced to behaviors, there is no good way to develop a theory of feelings. Feelings just seem to be "along for the ride." They may be a byproduct of certain neural or computational processes, but how then do these processes explain the feelings? This is one of the central problems of functionalism stated earlier, that processes alone have difficulty in explaining qualia.

An Emotional Turing Test

If behavior is our only way of judging whether an entity, artificial or not, has an emotion, then an **emotional Turing Test** may not be the best way to go. Imagine an emotional equivalent of Turing's famous test. Instead of typing in responses at a keyboard and receiving replies, a judge now is presented with a video image of a face. He or she then speaks questions such as "How do you feel today?" The computer (or a real human foil) then responds with an oral reply complete with appropriate auditory intonation and a visual facial expression. It might respond by saying in a dejected tone and sorrowful look that it is depressed because of an upset stomach. This alone might be enough to fool most human observers, especially given our penchant to anthropomorphize machines with the slightest human qualities (Braitenberg 1984).

If we then added another video camera and microphone and allowed the program to recognize affect in the judge, the illusion would be more than complete, since the program could reciprocate and ask questions like: "I notice that you are smiling. Did you win the lottery?" Of course, this emotional Turing Test, like its thinking predecessor, could manifest all the external abilities of a person possessing the attribute in question, without being able to actually have the equivalent internal conscious experience. As such, it suffers all the same criticisms as its forbearer.

There is no doubt that the sophistication of emotional processing in robots will increase in the future. Just as with cognition, robots will in some ways exceed our ability to function and act emotionally. They may ultimately prove superior in their capacity to recognize emotional states in others and to regulate their behavior based on that perception. One can imagine a robot that is finely attuned to our facial expressions and body language and that adjusts what it says and how it acts in order to minimize discomfort and conflict.

Artificial Affective Processing

In this section, we examine recent attempts to implement emotional processing in machines. First, we examine some programs that are capable of recognizing basic human emotional states either from speech or facial expression. Then, we look at the CogAff Architecture, a schema for how emotions may be computed internally by both biological organisms and machines. Finally, we discuss two socially emotional robots, one that interacts with people and another that demonstrates attachment.

Computer Emotion Recognition

A number of computer systems are already in place that are quite good at recognizing human emotion from spoken auditory cues. The Emotion Recognition project utilizes neural network software to process features present in a speech signal (Petrushin, 2000). These features include fundamental frequency, energy, and speaking rate. The program can recognize five different emotions: anger, happiness, sadness, fear, and a neutral unemotional state with 70% accuracy, about the same as human performance. It may be used in automated airline telephone reservation systems or a company's help desk to identify enraged customers who have urgent problems and quickly route them to human operators. See the chapter on language for more on intonation and other aspects of speech recognition.

There are many other sources of information that can be used to recognize human affect in addition to the auditory characteristics of the speech stream. Computer programs now exist that are capable of extracting affect from posture, body gestures and of course, facial expression. Anderson and McOwan (2003) report an emotion recognition system that is inspired by biological function. Their program first locates the face of a user sitting in front of a camera-equipped computer. A face-tracking algorithm determines the location of the face. The speed and direction of movement in different parts of the face is then calculated to determine how they are moving relative to one another. This information is then fed as input to multi-layer perceptron neural networks trained using back-propagation on a face database. The system is designed to recognize four of the major facial emotion expressions: happiness, sadness, surprise, and disgust. In testing it has been quite successful, with a matching rate of up to 86%. The use of systems like this one have tremendous potential for human-computer interaction. A computer could for instance recognize when a user is bored or tired and recommend that they take a break, or present more challenging information if the user expression indicates they are interested or happy.

CogAff: An Emotional Architecture

The type of emotion an entity experiences depends on its internal architecture. As we have seen, humans have a particular brain organization that serves as the substrate for the way they feel. If robots or artificial people were constructed with a different internal architecture for the processing of affect, they would in all likelihood experience emotions differently than we do. What would the internal organization of an artificial emotional processing mechanism be like? CogAff is one of the first comprehensive attempts at creating such a system. It was developed by the Cognition and Affect project at the University of Birmingham (UK; Sloman, Chrisley, & Scheutz, 2005).

The **CogAff architecture** is designed as a generic schema for how emotional operations might take place, either in a biological organism or a technological device. It consists of three general processing steps: perception, central processing, and action. Across each of these there are three distinct levels of emotional mechanism (see Figure 11.5). At the lowest level are **reactive processes**. These are like human reflexes in that a stimulus automatically triggers an action without any type of thought. An example of an emotionally reactive response might be the fear experienced by tripping over something in the dark. Reactive mechanisms are fast but don't allow for thought or consideration. They constitute the oldest

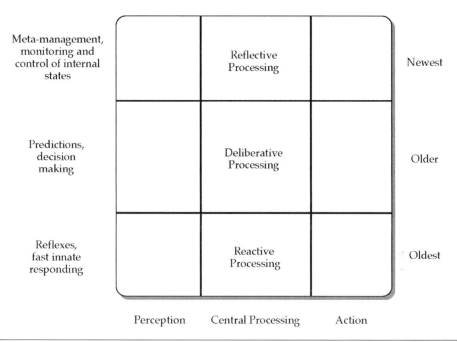

Figure 11.5 The CogAff architecture models many of the steps involved in emotional processing.

form of emotional processing and are present in most animals. Reactive fear mechanisms in the CogAff architecture are the equivalent of the low road pathway to the amygdala.

Cognition comes into play with **deliberative processes**. These involve hypothetical representations of alternate possible futures. Predictions or explanations are generated, compared, and the best one is selected. For instance, a person might be faced with the decision of whether or not to evacuate in the path of an oncoming hurricane. Both emotional states like fear and cognitive considerations of factors like the strength of the storm and tidal conditions would influence their ultimate decision. Deliberative mechanisms are a more recent development in biological evolution. True rational deliberation is most highly developed in humans. Notice that deliberative fear mechanisms in the CogAff architecture can be considered the equivalent of the high road to the amygdala pathway found in humans.

Meta-management or **reflective processes** are the newest and exist in the biological world only in people, although artificial versions have been constructed. They allow for internal processes to be monitored, evaluated, and controlled. Meta-management would allow an entity not only to experience an emotion, but to be aware that it was having such a state. They could then act on this emotion or not, depending on the circumstances and the use of deliberative processes. For example, Thomas might experience anger directed against his supervisor at work who failed to give him a raise. Reflective processing would enable Thomas to realize that he is angry, to know the reason why, but to then not express it by yelling at his supervisor because this would make it harder to obtain a raise in the future.

The CogAff model also distinguishes between primary and secondary emotions. **Primary emotions** are activated by perceptual inputs to an alarm system in the reactive layer. The alarm interrupts normal processing in order to allow the system to deal with emergency situations, such as the sight of a bear while hiking in the woods. **Secondary emotions** are triggered by inputs from internal deliberative processes that feed to the alarm system. In this case, we could imagine the case of Eve, who realizes that she has a presentation due tomorrow and hasn't prepared. The emotional state would then motivate her to get ready for this event.

Sloman, Chrisley, and Scheutz (2005) report developments on H-CogAff, a special version of the CogAff architecture designed to simulate adult human cognitive and affectual processing. There are specific modules in this schema that reproduce human functioning. These include the activation of motives, a long-term associative memory, attention, and problem-solving modules. H-CogAff can reproduce primary and secondary emotions. It can also implement **tertiary emotions**, those that perturb the control of attention in the meta-management system. A tertiary emotion of this sort could correspond to a mood or predisposition such as the distrust we might feel toward the presence of a suspicious looking stranger.

Kismet: The Emotional Robot

Cynthia Breazeal and her colleagues have devoted considerable time to the study of emotions in robots (Breazeal, 2002). The goal of their research is to design robots that both recognize and express emotion. Robots with these abilities will be better able to interact with humans in social settings. Their **Kismet** project is designed to model a very simple form of human social interaction, that between an infant and its caregiver. Kismet is a cute robotic head capable of sensing others and of expressing a wide range of facial expressions. It is driven by a cognitive and emotive system working together to regulate its interactions with people (Breazeal & Brooks, 2005).

Kismet is equipped with a set of color cameras. It can move its head and eyes to control where it looks and what it pays attention to. Its auditory system consists of a microphone that can recognize and process certain aspects of human speech. Kismet has been programmed to detect four basic pitch contours that signal approval, prohibition, attention, and comfort (Fernald, 1989). The detection of this affect then influences its own emotional state. Kismet can raise its ears to display a state of interestedness or fold them back to indicate anger. Its eyebrows move up and down, furrow, and slant to communicate frustration, surprise, or sadness. It is also equipped with a vocalization system allowing it to produce synthesized sounds reminiscent of a young child.

Kismet's primary means of communicating emotion is through its face (see Figure 11.6). The emotions it displays exist within a three-dimensional affect space of arousal (high/low), valence (good/bad), and stance (advance/withdraw). A soothed expression corresponds to high positive valence and low arousal, i.e., a state of being both happy but under-aroused. A joyous expression corresponds to a state of positive valence and moderate arousal. Some of the other expressions Kismet is capable of include anger, disgust, sorrow, surprise, and fear.

Figure 11.6 Kismet expresses surprise as Cynthia Breazeal shows it a children's toy. Kismet displays facial emotions in response to human interaction and built-in drive systems. It can display interest, surprise, happiness, disgust, anger, sadness, fear, fatigue, and calm. © Peter Menzel / Menzelphoto.com

Kismet's cognitive system is made up of perception, attention, drive, and behavior subsystems. Its drive system is, in essence, an implementation of artificial human motivations. Kismet, just like a biological child, has motivating drives like thirst, hunger, and fatigue. It has a social drive that corresponds to a "need" to interact with people, a stimulation drive to play with toys, and a fatigue drive to rest every now and then. When the robot's "needs" are met, the drives are in a homeostatic regime and Kismet acts as if it were satisfied. But if the intensity level of a drive deviates from this regime, the robot is more strongly motivated to engage in behaviors that restore the drive to equilibrium. Drives don't directly evoke an emotional response but they do bias Kismet's overall emotional state or mood.

To illustrate, if Kismet's social drive is high and it fails to receive sufficient stimulation from a person, it will display a sorrowful look. This sends a cue to the person interacting with Kismet to increase the amount of social stimulation perhaps by manipulating a toy in front of Kismet's face. On the other hand, if the robot is receiving too much stimulation, the drive state is lowered, biasing a display of fearfulness that should cause a person to back off and stimulate it less. When the level of interaction is beneficial, Kismet expresses interest and joy to encourage sustained interaction.

If Kismet is presented with an undesired stimulus, a disgust response could be triggered. This would direct its gaze to an alternate area in the visual field, where it might locate a more desirable object. This would again serve as a cue to a person to engage in a different behavior like switching to another toy. There are other ways Kismet can use emotions to get what it "wants" from others. If a person is ignoring the robot, it can attract the person by first vocalizing. If that doesn't work, it could lean forward and wiggle its ears as a means of attracting attention. These examples demonstrate that Kismet is capable of changing its behavior should initial attempts fail. This variable approach is more likely to ensure that its "needs" are met.

Kismet is endowed with nine basic level emotional states: anger/frustration, disgust, fear/distress, calm, joy, sorrow, surprise, interest, and boredom. These states are biased by the presence of certain conditions such as the strength of various motivational drives and in turn bias the display of their corresponding facial expressions. These expressions then serve as a communicative signal, informing the human present as to Kismet's state, and motivating the person to engage in a socially responsive action. Emotions in Kismet thus serve a social function. They mediate interaction between it and others. People who play with Kismet say they enjoy the experience. They also very easily attribute human-like qualities to it. Future robots with emotionally perceptive and expressive abilities like Kismet will undoubtedly make it easier for us to accept and work with artificial people.

ATTACHMENT

One of the most important human relationships is between parent and child. The parent is a source of comfort to the child because they satisfy both internal and external needs (Bowlby, 1969). Internal needs include thirst, hunger, and body temperature. An important external need is environmental familiarity. Although novel environments provide opportunities for learning, if they are too discrepant from what the child knows, they can induce fear. Early studies by Harry Harlow and his colleagues show that monkeys will use a surrogate mother as a "safe base" from which to explore a room filled with new objects. They are, at first, terrified and cling to the mother, but then foray out on increasingly longer explore and return cycles (Harlow, Harlow, & Suomi, 1971).

Mary Ainsworth and collaborators, in a series of classic studies, have focused the on role of attachment in human infants (Ainsworth, 1979). They set up a "strange situation" where a mother would bring her infant into an unfamiliar room and then leave. A short time later a stranger would come in and attempt to interact with the infant. The stranger than left the room and the mother came back. Ainsworth found infants fell into different attachment styles. Some were securely attached. In the mother's presence they played happily and explored the room. Others showed different patterns of attachment in which they were less likely to explore or engage in social interaction. This research shows the value of attachment to a caregiver in early development. It allows a child to gradually expose itself to and learn from a complex environment.

Likhachev and Arkin (2000) have applied ideas from attachment theory to robotics. A robot can be attached to a location, object, or person and use it to satisfy internal needs such as energy and external needs like familiarity and predictability in the environment. They ran simulations and tested robots that attempted to maintain proximity with an attachment object. The intensity of the robot's attachment varied with its distance from this object. One formulation resulted in a safe zone of maximal comfort very close to the attachment figure. Outside the safe zone was the comfort zone, constituting the normal working region for the robot. Outside the comfort zone, attachment values were high and would drive the robot closer in. This work demonstrates that robots can benefit from attachment in the same ways humans can. By staying close to a "caregiver" they can obtain energy, keep safe, and gradually acquire information about their surroundings.

LOVE

Attachment is one aspect of a very powerful emotion: love. There is perhaps no other feeling that has had so many poems, stories, and songs devoted to it. But what do we mean when we talk about love? There seem to be so many different kinds, the kind of love we have for friends, family members, spouses, or for that matter our pets or cars. Psychological research shows that there seem to be at least two types of love (Caspi & Herbener, 1990). **Passionate love** is short-term, intense, and based on physical attraction and sex. **Companionate love** is long-term, less intense, and based on mutual respect and admiration. Perhaps the reason so many marriages fail in Western nations like the United States is that passionate love eventually fades and may not always be replaced with its longer-lived counterpart.

From an evolutionary perspective, the function of love may seem to be obvious. It is a feeling that motivates us to seek out and stay with a sexual partner. It thus promotes both reproduction and bonding with a partner to help ensure the survival of offspring (Trivers, 1972). Couples who are in love are much more likely to stay together and cooperate in taking care of their children. Evidence to support this comes from the field of biology. Animal species with offspring that are vulnerable for a long period during development have parents that form longer-lasting and more intense pair bonds.

Could a robot experience love? If we assume that love is an emotional state, then this question is no different than asking whether a robot could experience any other emotion like happiness, sadness, or anger. More to the point is the issue of whether or not a robot would actually need to fall in love. Because love seems to have arisen in the service of sexual reproduction, artificial entities that can reproduce in other ways would not benefit from it. However, any feeling state that promotes bonding with another entity has potential social rewards. If two robots needed to work together cooperatively in order to achieve some task, it makes sense to imbue them with a desire to be with one another.

SHOULD WE GIVE ARTIFICIAL PEOPLE EMOTIONS?

The discussion earlier in this chapter shows there are good evolutionary explanations for our basic emotions. Each of these emotions evolved in humans to serve an adaptive survival-oriented purpose. But what does all this have to do with robots or artificial people? Couldn't we develop robots that act effectively without emotions? In fact, might it in some cases even be desirable, since emotions on occasion, do get the better of humans. For example, would we really want robots that get angry or depressed? That might, in a fit of rage, commit murder or get depressed and not show up for work? Also, as we have seen in the previous sections, a malfunction of an emotion mechanism can produce psychological disorders. The down side of being fearful is the potential to suffer anxiety, the downside of anger is aggression, and the downside of sadness is depression.

Under careful consideration though, the benefits of having emotions seem to outweigh their costs. Emotions have proven to be rapid, effective guides to action in humans and other species. It makes sense to put these same proven methods into our own creations. An artificial person could thus benefit from having the same basic emotions that we do and for the same reasons. Disgust would prevent an artificial person from contacting potentially harmful substances, fear would enable it to evade or avoid dangerous situations, anger would motivate it to overcome obstacles, and sadness would enable it to think about and give up on hopeless causes. It would also be important for an artificial person to be happy, since this would motivate it to obtain goals and acquire new skills. In addition to these survival functions, emotions would assist interaction between artificial people and between humans and artificial people living together in a society. Finally, as was also mentioned earlier, emotions typically assist rather than interfere with cognitive processing.

If we implement emotional mechanisms in an artificial person and these systems are modeled on those found in humans, we can expect correspondingly similar psychological disorders when these systems break down. However, there is no rule that says we must produce faithful copies of the neural and endocrine systems that underlie human emotional states. Just as there are multiple ways of performing a given information-processing task, there may also be many ways to produce a given emotional reaction. The psychological disorders exhibited by an artificial person may thus differ from those experienced in people and will be specific to the particular architecture that is implemented.

12

BIOLOGY

Life…is a battle not between Bad and Good, but between Bad and Worse.

—Joseph Brodsky, 1972

Humans are biological creatures. In this capacity, we share much in common with other animals. The makeup of our physical bodies is to a certain extent determined by instructions embedded in our genes. We must undergo a period of development in the womb before we are born and an extensive period of growth and development afterwards. As adults, our body systems are a marvel of complexity and orchestrated function. Is it possible to duplicate all of this in a machine? Research, much of it recent in origin, shows that new inroads are being made in duplicating structures and operations that many previously believed were the sole domain of biological organisms. This chapter surveys several important topics in biology and investigates attempts at replicating them artificially. We start with the most important concept of all, which is life, and then address genetics, evolutionary design and control in robotics, development, and body systems.

LIFE: WHAT IS IT?

Alas, we come once more to a concept that, like intelligence and consciousness, is difficult if not impossible to define. There is no general agreement on what is meant by the term **life**. Biologists generally consider life as a concrete entity made of matter and energy and devote their time to the study of living things in the natural world. Computer scientists are more inclined to consider life in the abstract as information structures and to allow for the possibility that machines or software might be alive. Whether we consider the natural or the artifactual, it is hard to draw a precise line between the living and the nonliving. However, there are certain properties that when taken together, distinguish the animate from the inanimate (Curtis, 1983). Let's take some time to review each of these important criteria.

1. **Organization**. Living things are highly organized. They are made up of cells, tissues, organ systems, and so forth. The organization is usually hierarchical, with parts fitting inside other parts. This organization is also interdependent. In order for cells to metabolize, they need both chemical energy sources like simple sugars provided by the digestive system, and oxygen, provided by the cardiovascular system. So these systems, although anatomically and physiologically distinct, really cooperate as part of a larger whole to service the organism's needs.

   John von Neumann pointed out that life depends on a certain measure of complexity. If there is sufficient complexity, an "organism" can organize itself to reproduce and perform other functions. If it is too simple, this becomes impossible. One characteristic that can lead to complexity is self-organization, the capacity of a system to generate more complex structures and processes out of simpler ones. Both biological organisms in the wild and software entities designed in the lab have this property.

2. **Metabolism**. The complete set of chemical reactions that occur in cells. In biological organisms, it can follow two paths. Anabolism is constructive and involves the creation of food into new tissue or body parts. Catabolism is destructive and involves the conversion of food into energy and waste products.

   There is another way in which living things employ energy. They are good at using energy to maintain order, the order of their own body systems. This runs counter to the second law of thermodynamics, which states that over time energy dissipates and becomes unusable. This tendency towards disorder is called entropy. Nonliving states, if left alone, will always undergo deterioration, they become less ordered. This is true even for something as solid as a rock, which will continually erode and disperse. Living entities seemingly violate this rule. They use energy to maintain and even increase order. This is what happens when a baby animal grows. It becomes more ordered with time. Physicists, don't loose heart: the second law of thermodynamics is only violated locally. Entropy still holds when we consider the universe as a whole.

3. **Growth**. This results when anabolism happens at a higher rate than catabolism. In other words, when synthesis exceeds catalysis. This manifests itself as a proportional increase in size, where the entire body gets bigger, not just one or some of its parts. Biological growth or development is usually greatest early on in the lifespan and occurs pre- and post-natal.

4. **Homeostasis**. Living beings are homeostatic. Although they exchange materials with the outside world, they maintain a stable internal environment. Examples of homeostasis in mammals include regulating blood glucose level and body temperature. The term *autopoesis* has been suggested to describe how any system, mechanical or biological, maintains its organization over time (Maturana & Varela, 1980). An autopoetic system preserves unity in the face of changes in physical growth or appearance.

5. **Adaptation**. Living things are adapted to their environment. Individual animals in the wild occupy an ecological niche and possess the means to perceive and act

effectively in that niche. A bat, for instance, is uniquely adapted to nocturnal hunting of insects using echolocation. A fish moves effectively through water by means of its undulating swimming motion.

6. **Response to Stimuli**. The types of reactions living things have to stimuli differ, but all react in some way to the environment. Motion is a common reaction. Reflexes are examples of built-in responses that require no thought. Even plants exhibit movement during photo-taxis when they orient themselves slowly toward the sun.

7. **Reproduction**. Living things make more of themselves. In the case of mitosis, a cell makes an exact copy of itself, duplicating its genetic material or genome and separating it into two groups. This is asexual reproduction as it does not require the contribution of two different genomes. In contrast, meosis is the basis of sexual reproduction. Here, the genome is replicated once and separated twice, forming four sets of cells each containing one half the original genetic content. One of these cells later combines with half the genes of a mating partner. This combination of two different sets of genes introduces variability into the offspring that is acted upon by evolutionary selection forces.

Artificial Life

Artificial life is the study and creation of artificial systems that exhibit behavior characteristic of natural living systems (Levy, 1992). Artificial life, or A-life as it is called, consists primarily of computer simulations, but involves robotic construction and testing as well as biological and chemical experiments. The goal of this new field is to discover the underlying computational processes that give rise to all lifelike behavior, whether biological or technological. A-life researchers adopt the information-processing perspective found in cognitive psychology and artificial intelligence. They believe that life is a complex set of processes or functions that can be described algorithmically.

Just as was the case with AI, there is both a strong and a weak claim to A-life. According to the strong claim, we will, at some point in the future, be able to develop actual living creatures whose primary ingredient is information. These creatures may be robots or exist solely as programs running within computers. In either case, they are supposed to be alive according to all of the criteria mentioned previously. The weak claim instead holds that A-life programs are essentially useful simulations of lifelike processes but cannot be considered living. That is because they lack some property found only in natural biological organisms.

Cellular Automata and the Game of Life

The earliest attempt at reproducing lifelike behavior in a computer involved **cellular automata** (CA). Imagine a square grid filled with cells. Each cell in the grid can exist in a certain state, such as being "on" or "off." Activity in the grid changes in discrete time steps. The particular action a cell should take, such as turning on or off, is determined in each time step by following a simple set of rules and by using information about the state of its neighbors.

The first and perhaps best-known CA was created by the mathematician John Horton Conway and is called Life or the Game of Life (Poundstone, 1985). Each cell in the Life grid can be in one of two states, either "alive" or "dead." Every cell has eight neighbors: above, below, to the left, to the right, or at one of four corners. If a cell is alive, it will continue to live into the next time step or "generation" if either two or three neighbors are also alive. If there are more than three neighbors alive, it will die of overcrowding. Conversely, it will die of exposure if there are less than two living neighbors. If a cell is dead it will stay dead in the next generation unless exactly three neighbors are alive. In that case, the cell will come alive, i.e., be "born" in the next time step.

Conway and his colleagues then began to see what shapes emerged with basic starting configurations. They discovered several different types of patterns. The simplest formed stable shapes that resembled blocks, boats, and beehives. Slightly more complex were oscillators, patterns that changed from one shape to another over a few time steps. Some of these earned the names toads, clocks, and traffic lights. The shapes called R Pentominos were even more interesting. These were collections of any five neighboring cells that looked somewhat like the letter R. The R Pentominos spawned all sorts of shapes including "gliders" that undulated across the grid like strange insects. Figure 12.1 shows examples of other creatures from Conway's Game of Life.

Tierra: An Artificial Ecosystem

The Game of Life shows us that CA can give rise to some of the characteristics of life such as variability, locomotion, and reproduction. However, Life never yielded a shape capable of self-reproduction, although it might be theoretically possible. The life forms it produced were also quite limited in their behavioral repertoire. To date, many A-life programs have been written that demonstrate much more complex phenomena. One such example is Tierra, created by the biologist Thomas Ray (Ray, 1991).

The creatures in Tierra were programs that drew energy from the CPU of the computer on which they ran, much the same way plants and animals might draw energy from the sun. They lived inside a virtual environment consisting of the CPU, memory and operating system software of their resident machine. Each creature replicated with mutations to simulate the species variability found in natural organisms.

Every Tierran citizen contained a set of genetic instructions or genotype. The actual expression of this genetic code or phenotype would then affect its behavior. Ray had a function called the "reaper" that killed off creatures based on fitness values. The older a creature was, the lower its fitness value. But old age was not the only thing that could lead to death in this virtual world. Creatures that acted in ways that promoted their survival would increase their fitness and survive longer to reproduce more. Creatures that acted inappropriate to their own survival quickly perished and lost the opportunity to reproduce.

Ray ran Tierra through many simulations and was surprised at the complexity that materialized. Parasites incapable of replication came on the scene. They attached to larger hosts and borrowed their replication instructions. But these hosts eventually mutated a defense. They developed instructions that prevented them from posting their location, effectively hiding themselves from the parasites. This ecological tug of war between host

Average   Blinker Ship

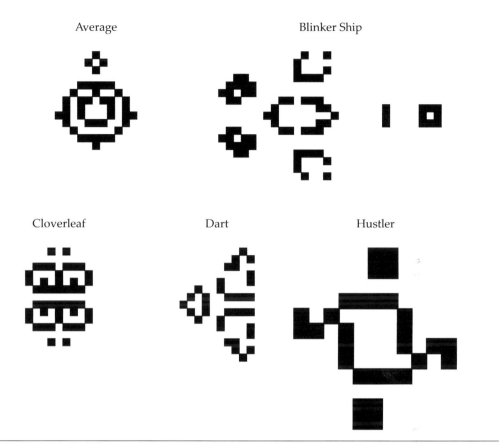

Cloverleaf   Dart   Hustler

Figure 12.1 Creatures from Conway's Game of Life. These dynamic two-dimensional "life-forms" emerged spontaneously in a system governed by very simple rules.

and parasite in which each evolves a defense against the other is a common feature in natural ecosystems. Tierra demonstrated this same feature as an emergent property of the program. It was not programmed in at the start.

When Ray ran Tierra through long sessions, it began to exhibit other features of natural ecosystems. One species of host organism evolved code that allowed it to divert the metabolism of parasites, thus bolstering its own reproductive capacity. These creatures had in essence become predators. When they detected a parasite, they would attack it and use its CPU cycles to increase their own energy. Eventually, this species evolved into a variation that exhibited cooperative symbiotic behavior. Groups of this type would share their replication code, passing it back and forth. Another cheater species then came about which capitalized on the sharers. It would sneak in and grab the replication code to use for itself. From a global perspective, these new species emerged quite suddenly after long periods of stability, mirroring the same effect in natural evolution called punctuated equilibrium.

But Are They Really Alive?

Is A-life really alive? Whether one adopts the strong or weak claims depends on several issues. There are some, biologists among them, that state life can only be carbon-based. That is, life can only exist the way we see it in nature with a chemistry founded on carbon compounds that operate in a water medium. A-lifers would counter and say that silicon or perhaps other chemical building blocks could be the basis for machine or even alien life forms. In this latter account, the life that we know here on earth may only be a subset of the possible life forms that could exist throughout the universe.

Another point is whether life is corporeal, that is, whether it requires a body. Even bacteria and viruses, the most basic life forms we know, are bounded by membranes or some sort of shell that delimits them from the environment. This results in two regions, an internal space where the workings of the organism take place, and an outside space. The creatures in Tierra and other A-life programs have virtual bodies that define their locations and allow them to move around and perform actions. But these bodies exist in a virtual computer world and are subject to a different set of laws than in the physical world.

Biological organisms are indeed physical. They are made up of matter. A-life organisms are informational. Is it possible for life to be made up of nothing but information? Some say that life must have a physical basis to extract energy from the environment, grow, respond to stimuli, and perform all other necessary functions. But as we have seen, A-life creatures that are informational representations can exhibit many of these same properties. It is possible for abstract informational entities to self-organize, adapt, reproduce, and perform the analog of many physical actions. The difference here is whether it is materiality or the logical form or organization that underlies it that is the necessary basis for life.

GENETICS: THE ULTIMATE BLUEPRINT

The instructions for how to build a person start with 23 chromosomes in the mother's ova and another 23 chromosomes in the father's sperm. These **chromosomes** are groupings of many **genes**, where each gene is a string of DNA material that codes for the production of a protein. During conception, the genetic content of the two parents is mixed to form the normal complement of 46 chromosomes we find in an adult individual. This mixture, and the random selection of half the genetic content that occurs before each parent makes their contribution, ensures that the offspring is an entirely new creation, sharing only some of its parent's characteristics. This variability is the basis upon which selection forces operate and is needed if we are to adapt to changing environments.

We have already introduced the idea of a genetic algorithm (GA) in the creativity chapter. There, we learned it could be used to generate novel works of art. A GA can, of course, be used to produce offspring that differ from their parents. John Holland is credited as being the creator of the GA (Goldberg, 1990). In a typical GA, the genetic instructions are strings of binary numbers (0s and 1s). These strings are really artificial chromosomes, with genes located at different loci, or points along them. Just as with people, these digital chromosomes code for the equivalent of a protein. They contain instructions for the creation of some physical structure or behavior that affects the performance of the artificial organism.

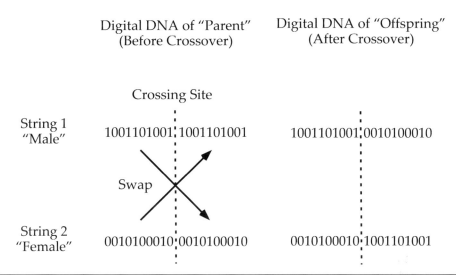

Figure 12.2 Crossover of binary code is a type of "mating" whereby genetic material from two sources, such as a male and female, are swapped. The result are "offspring" with a new combination of instructions, similar to, but not identical with, their "parents."

GA experiments start with an initial gene pool. A population of organisms with a variety of different genes are then set loose in an environment where they have to pass a fitness test. Those that do well, i.e., those with the greatest fitness are now allowed to "mate" with each other. Mating consists of an exchange of their genetic material. In this crossover procedure, a point on each of the couple's chromosomes is picked at random. The string of binary code from each of those points onward on the pair is now swapped. That section of code from the "male" goes to the "female" and vice versa. The result is two new strings that are a unique combination of the old. These are the offspring or next generation that have inherited some of their parent's characteristics. Figure 12.2 shows how a crossover of binary code from two digital genes might occur.

These offspring are now subject to the same conditions as mom and dad. They are put into the environment and allowed to act. Again, the best performing of these are allowed to live. The rest are killed off. The survivors are again mated by the crossover procedure and this process is repeated multiple times. As you can imagine, what eventually results are organisms that are very well adapted to their environment. Whereas adaptation in nature can often take millennia to unfold, adaptation in artificial environments with accelerated lifespans can take place very quickly. There are GA programs that can iterate through millions of generations in the span of 1 hour. GA programs have a variety of different uses. They have been implemented in A-life simulations and used to solve complex optimization problems.

Evolutionary Robotics and the Golem Project

Getting a robot to duplicate itself is, at least theoretically, not difficult. After all, robots are in widespread use already in the manufacturing industry. They are employed in the construction of all sorts of consumer products ranging from automobiles to household appliances. If we wanted robots to build robots, it would mean simply switching the specifics of the manufacturing process. One could envision a factory manned entirely by robots that do nothing but build more copies of other robots, perhaps using assembly line techniques. The difficulty comes when we want robotic reproduction to mimic biological reproduction. In this case, we need to create variations rather than duplications. We have already seen that evolution is a process that is very good at creating variations on a theme. The application of evolutionary principles to design and create robots is a field called evolutionary robotics (Nolfi & Floreano, 2000).

In **evolutionary robotics** an initial population of artificial chromosomes contain the instructions for the control systems of robots. The robots are then allowed to act in an environment by sensing, locomoting, manipulating, or performing some other task. Their performance is assessed. The best performing robots with the highest fitness values are then mated by the crossover technique along with some random mutation. The offspring are next introduced into the environment and evaluated with the cycle repeating until some desired measure of performance is obtained. Notice that this process is nearly identical to a GA program. The main difference is that the creatures that result are not software programs running in a computer environment. They are hardware devices operating in the real world.

Researchers at Brandeis University have developed an exciting evolutionary robotics program that they call The Golem Project (Lipson & Pollack, 2000). Their goal was to evolve robots that could naturally move under their own power. They started with a set of robot body parts that included joints connected by rods. While some of the rods were rigid, others were linear actuators that could move back and forth controlled by an artificial neural network (Figure 12.3). They would start with a population of 200 machines. The evolutionary algorithm created variations based on adding, modifying, and removing the basic body parts as well as altering the neural network. The fitness of the resulting creations were evaluated based on their locomotion ability, measured as the net distance they could move their center of mass along a flat surface in a fixed amount of time.

After evaluating performance under simulation, some of the robots that had done well were chosen for manufacture and testing in a real-world testing environment. The results were fascinating. The evolutionary process yielded surprisingly different solutions. There were "Arrows" where a rear flipper pushed an arrowhead shape forward and then retracted to catch up. There were "Snakes" where a pyramid-shaped head dragged a long tail behind. There were also models called "Crabs" that shuffled along the floor by moving claw-like appendages. Although some of these solutions appear to mimic animal locomotion, many were unique and did not correspond to any form of movement found in the natural world. Many solutions did, however, possess symmetry, probably because a symmetric body can move more easily in a straight line. Symmetry is a property found in almost all natural organisms.

Evolvable Hardware

Evolutionary principles of the sort employed in GAs have also been used to build electronic circuits. This new field of endeavor goes by the name of **evolvable hardware** (Thompson, 1998). Researchers like Adrian Thompson at Sussex University (UK) are accomplishing this using field programmable gate arrays (FPGAs). An FPGA consists of hundreds of recon-

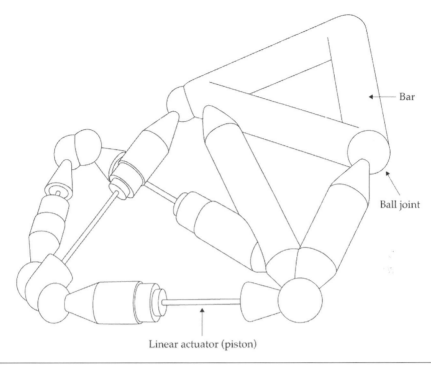

Bar

Ball joint

Linear actuator (piston)

Figure 12.3 Researchers in The Golem Project at Brandeis University created robots that locomote under their own power. The robots were assembled from basic parts that included rigid and moveable rods. The results were not designed a priori, but emerged from evolutionary principles. Image by Gabriele Schies. Sichtwerk, Inc. (after Aylett, 2002).

figurable blocks that can perform a variety of different digital logic functions. Switches control wires connecting the blocks to external devices and to each other. Memory cells in turn control the switches.

The configuration of the memory cells can be considered as the genotype of the system. A **genotype** is the specific genetic makeup of an individual. In biological organisms it is the specific sequence of nucleotides in the DNA that code for proteins. In other words, it is the genes on the chromosomes. The memory cells contain instructions for how the circuit should operate and specify what logical operations the blocks can do. The actual instantiation of these instructions, the wiring of the blocks themselves, is like a phenotype. In biological animals, the **phenotype** is either the total physical appearance of the organism or a specific manifestation of a trait like eye color, coded by a gene or set of genes. In evolvable hardware, it is the physical expression of the information contained in the memory.

There are two ways to apply evolutionary principles to this type of system. In the extrinsic approach, evolutionary algorithms are used to generate a particular set of instructions that are then implemented in the FPGA. Testing and evaluation are done here at the software level. In the intrinsic approach, the evolutionary algorithm produces a starting configuration. This is instantiated in the FPGA and its performance is evaluated in the real world. Based on the results of the performance, feedback is provided to the algorithm that then generates another variant for testing.

As an illustration of the intrinsic approach, imagine an FPGA circuit implanted in a mobile robot. The chip's design governs the robot's behavior and determines how it will perform in a given environment. Flaws in the design will become obvious and used to adjust the parameters of the algorithm so that the next design will be an improved version, better able to carry out its task.

Evolutionary processes don't proceed from an engineering standpoint, using known principles of design or an understanding of the nature of substrate materials. Evolution is conceptually blind. It has no a priori assumptions and will create anything that works. In this sense, it capitalizes on the functional properties of a system independent of any knowledge of how it "should" work. Evolution therefore doesn't carry with it any of the bias or preconceptions of human designers.

Adrian Thompson discovered this quite quickly. His evolved silicon circuits behaved in unexpected ways. They acted like analog circuits, oscillating and exhibiting other strange behaviors. But they worked nonetheless, being both compact and efficient. Nobody is quite sure how they operate. One idea is that the chips utilize in-between states, short periods where components are switching from on-to-off or off-to-on while redirecting electron flow.

The future of evolvable hardware has great promise (Bentley, 2002). Researchers at the Swiss Federal Institute of Technology are studying circuits that can reconfigure themselves when they are damaged. Circuits capable of self-repair mimic the plasticity of the human brain that can "re-wire" itself after injury. In stroke victims, brain areas that subsume different abilities like language can be destroyed. Depending on the extent of the damage and the quality of post-operative rehabilitation, patients can recover varying degrees of functionality. An examination of their brains shows that different brain regions have taken over the function that was once performed by the damaged area.

DEVELOPMENT: COMPLEXITY OUT OF SIMPLICITY

The process of biological development is truly amazing. Think about it. Each of us starts off as nothing more than a single cell. In a period of 9 months, this cell turns into a newborn with all rudimentary body systems in place. How does this happen? How do the instructions coded in our parent's DNA serve as the blueprint for the construction of a complete organism? How does this construction take place? The process is complex and many parts of it are not understood. However, researchers have already taken what we do know and used this knowledge to build software programs and computing devices that show great promise in mimicking biological development.

The **zygote**, or fertilized cell after conception splits into two cells, which in turn split into two cells and so on, producing an exponential increase in cell growth. Within the first week, cell differentiation occurs. Different cells start to form the basis of the subsequent organ systems: skeletal, digestive, neural, etc. From 2 to 8 weeks, this collection of cells is called an **embryo**. It is in the embryonic stage at six weeks that organs begin to form and function. The heart starts beating and the liver manufactures red blood cells. It is at the 9-week mile-marker that the embryo begins to look human. At this point, from 9 weeks to birth, it is called a **fetus**. A fetus is sufficiently well developed that, if born prematurely, at the end of the 6 month, it stands a chance of surviving. A 6-month fetus is also aware of its environment and responds to sounds from the outside world.

Moshe Sipper and other researchers at the Swiss Federal Institute of Technology have begun to emulate how cells grow and develop (Sipper & Tomassini, 1997). They start with a grid of cells, what they call biodules. The biodules are small cubes with tiny computers inside. They are assembled together into a grid-like configuration. Initially, the biodules are empty, lacking any type of programming. A "mother" cell with specific programming is placed into one of the biodules. The mother cell takes its genetic material, replicates it and passes it into neighboring cells. Each of these cells, in turn, then replicates and transmits its code to their neighbors, ultimately filling up the grid. Each biodule, once filled, starts to express its genetic instructions that differ depending on their relative location from the mother cell. Different cells or clusters of cells for example, might specialize, carrying out a specific computation. These cells can be considered the equivalent of biological "organs" and their specialization the computer equivalent of cell differentiation.

This "electronic embryo" has a number of advantages over traditional electronic hardware. If any of the cells in the grid become damaged, new cells will automatically grow into available spare biomodules and the entire program can be restored. Also, assuming there is enough room in the grid, the program can reproduce itself, spawning a copy or "child" that inhabits the space alongside it. Notice the difference between this project where software instructions spread from one computing device to another in a hardware grid, and cellular automata that operate and propagate on grids but entirely within the software domain.

Bentley (2002) points out several more general advantages of developmental programs like the one described above. These programs can produce organizations that genetic algorithms cannot. To begin, many structures have a hierarchical organization. This is true of biological organisms, where bodies are made of organ systems consisting of organs, the organs have different tissue layers, the layers have different cells, and so on. Developmental programs are good at creating this kind of organization where structures are nested one inside the other.

Complexity is also a hallmark of development. The end product of a body is much more complex than the starting point. All the instructions for how to build a body are not contained in the DNA. This information is generated as part of the development process. Once a certain step is reached, the context and the history of what has come before constitute a new set of instructions. In human development, neurons in the nascent nervous system know where to go by following a chemical trail of nerve growth factor. This factor and the directions it provides to these cells are not fully specified in the DNA, but unfold out of the developmental process itself. This is another advantage of such programs. The instructions serve only as a "seed" to get the ball rolling. Much of the heavy lifting gets done emergently thereafter.

ARTIFICIAL BODIES: MORE THAN JUST A MIND

Throughout much of this book, we have focused on brain processes like memory, thinking, language, and intelligence. That is because having these qualities is certainly an essential part of what it means to be human. But humans are more than disconnected mental processes. Our brains are embedded in physical bodies. It is our bodies that support our brain and that enable us to perceive and act in the world. Perception and action were covered in chapter 3. In this section we look at other important bodily functions necessary for mental abilities. For instance, without a cardiovascular or digestive system, our brains wouldn't receive oxygen or nutrients and couldn't survive. Without an immune system, we would quickly succumb to the numerous pathogens that fill the environment. An artificial person needs to be more than just a mechanical brain. It must have a body as well. In what follows, we examine several important body systems and describe recent attempts at constructing their synthetic equivalents.

Artificial Skeletal Systems

A group of scientists have recently discovered a novel way of creating artificial bone material (Deville, Saiz, Nalla, & Tomsia, 2006). They have capitalized on processes that occur naturally when seawater freezes. During the freezing process, salt and other contaminants in the water get channeled into areas between thin wafers of ice. The result is a material called a composite, which is strong, lightweight, and porous, all good requirements for bone. The researchers were able to use this technique to create hydroxyapatite, a ceramic material commonly used to make artificial bone.

Doctors have for several years already been converting coral found in the ocean to hydroxyapatite. This filler material is then used in a bone graft, where it is applied to a gap or fracture. This provides a porous framework or scaffolding that allows the host's bone cells to interpenetrate their way through the material, further strengthening it. The use of the new freeze composites promises to be a good candidate for grafting and for hip joint replacement. Their porous architecture makes them less likely to be rejected by the host body, a common problem when using metal alloys or ceramics that often trigger inflammation and immune responses.

Assuming that one has an adequate substance for use as artificial bone, the next step is to get it into the desired shape. Investigators at Advanced Ceramic Research have developed a new technique that can reproduce entire bones or pieces of bone in just a matter of hours. The bone or bone segment that needs replacing is first scanned to produce a precise three-dimensional model. Data from this model is sent to a computer-controlled machine that lays down multiple layers of a special polymer. The result is a filled volumetric shape with the required proportions. Using this technique, polymers or other bone materials like those mentioned above can be tailored to whatever shape is needed.

Artificial Cardiovascular Systems

The cardiovascular system includes the heart that pumps blood through vessels running throughout the body. It also includes the respiratory system consisting of the lungs and other organs that carry oxygen from the air to the blood stream and expel carbon dioxide. Inhaled air passes through the lungs into the blood. Oxygen from the air binds to red blood cells and is pumped through arteries by the heart where it reaches body cells. The oxygen then diffuses into the cells where it used to extract energy. The byproducts of the metabolic process diffuse back out into the blood and are transported by veins to the lungs where they can be expelled.

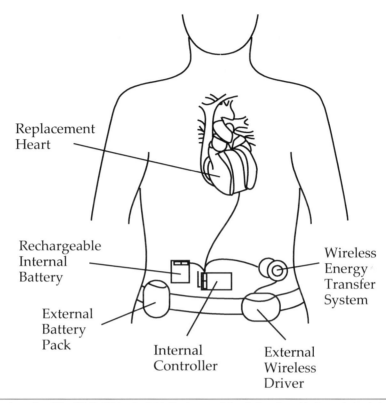

Figure 12.4 A schematic of the AbioCor™ Implantable Replacement Heart. An external battery wirelessly transmits power to an internal rechargeable battery. The controller unit senses and controls pumping speed (image courtesy of AbioMed).

The AbioCor™ Implantable Replacement Heart is the first completely self-contained artificial heart (see Figure 12.4). The device consists of a hydraulic pump that forces blood out one ventricle to the lungs and then out another to the body. It is powered by an external battery pack that transmits power to an internal rechargeable battery. An internal controller unit in the patient's abdominal wall monitors and controls pumping speed. Surgeons first implanted it into a patient on July 2, 2001. This was the first artificial heart transplant in nearly two decades. Through 2004, a total of 12 patients have undergone the procedure. The heart was expected to double a life expectancy of about 30 days prior to the operation. A follow-up study showed the heart exceeded these expectations. Patients who received the transplant lived on average 5 months following surgery (Dowling et al., 2004).

The state of the art in artificial lungs is not quite as advanced. Dr. Brack Hattler at The University of Pittsburgh Medical Center is developing an intravenous membrane oxygenator (IMO). It is intended for use in patients suffering from pneumonia, lung disease, and acute respiratory distress syndrome. The IMO is inserted into the vena cava, a vein carrying blood back to the heart. It is designed to oxygenate the blood before it reaches the lungs. The lungs would then add additional oxygenation. It is not an independent artificial lung system that can be used for long-term use. Patients would rely on it for about a 2-week period while their own lungs fully recover.

Hattler's IMO is elongated in shape and 18 inches long. It is filled with hollow fiber membranes. Oxygen enters through a tube and flows across these membranes. It then diffuses through pores in the fiber wall and into the blood. Carbon dioxide diffuses in the opposite direction, exiting through another tube. A key feature is a central balloon that inflates and deflates, drawing the blood across the membrane surface. Full results on its effectiveness are pending, but the procedure is a better alternative to an external ventilator that involves passing the patient's blood outside the body and has greater risk of complication.

There has also been work on the creation of an artificial red blood cell (Freitas, 1998). Robert Freitas has designed a robotic replacement for human blood cells that are hundreds or thousands of times more effective at storing and transporting oxygen than the natural red cells floating around inside our bloodstreams. These respirocytes could significantly enhance athletic performance. They could reputedly allow an Olympic athlete to sprint for 15 minutes without taking a breath or allow for several hours of normal activity without breathing. Working prototypes are estimated at being 1 to 2 decades in the future.

Artificial Digestive Systems

An artificial person must be able to regulate its energy levels (Aylett, 2002). It would need to be able to sense when its power levels are low or at critical levels. A low reading would in effect be a "hunger" signal and trigger action to replenish its energy to prevent itself from becoming incapacitated. Just as is the case with humans, an artificial person would also need to know when to stop consumption, since taking in too much energy has harmful consequences. This function could be served by a satiety signal or feeling of "fullness" and would motivate the termination of energy intake. Since we don't always use all available energy, an artificial person would need some way of storing excess energy the way we do in the form of fat or glycogen. Finally, an artificial person must be able to eliminate the waste products that are formed by energy consumption. This function in humans is served by urination and defecation.

Many current mobile robots that operate on batteries must recharge at electrical outlets or power stations. This limits their mobility, since they must be able to get back to the charging location before their current energy reserves run down. A better option is to utilize chemical energy of the sort obtained from food sources, the way humans and other animals do. The advantage to this is much greater autonomy, since food items are usually widely disseminated throughout the natural environment and easily available. But how can we get a robot or artificial person to do this?

Stuart Wilkinson and other investigators at the University of South Florida seem to have found a way. They have created a **gastrobot**, an intelligent machine that derives all of its energy requirements from the digestion of real food. Gastrobots are able to convert the chemical energy of carbohydrates found in sugars and starches and convert it to a useable electrical form using micro-organisms such as bacteria and yeast. They achieve this with a device called a **Microbial Fuel Cell** (MFC). The MFC is a living battery. It takes as input food, water, and air and produces as output electricity that can be used to drive a robot's sensors, actuators, and computing machinery.

The Gastrobotics Group is currently studying ways to improve the duration of MFCs and of getting robots to be able to locate and gather food, then masticate, ingest, and even

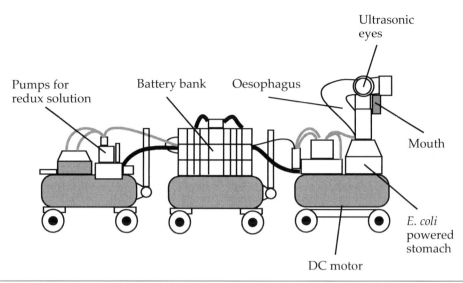

Figure 12.5 "Chew-Chew" the gastrobot, developed by The Gastrobotics Group at The University of South Florida. Chew-Chew obtains all its energy needs through sugar cubes placed into its "mouth." The goal is to develop robots that are energy self-sufficient in natural outdoor environments.

defecate (Wilkinson, 2001). In the year 2000, they built a gastrobot nicknamed "Chew-Chew" that resembles a train (see Figure 12.5). Chew-Chew was "fed" dry sugar through its single mouth. It had two pumps, equivalent to a heart and lungs that periodically refilled the battery with necessary fluids.

The difference between digestive biology and technology is narrowing in other areas as well. There has been recent research on the development and application of **Biological Micro Electronic Mechanical Systems** (BioMEMS). These are small intelligent devices that can be used to perform many physiological functions like hunting down pathogens and delivering precise amounts of medication (Bashir, 2004). Kurzweil (2005) speculates that BioMEMs will be able to determine the exact nutrients necessary for optimum health. The nutrients will be introduced directly into the bloodstream by metabolic nanobots. Once there, sensors can monitor their rate of absorption, ordering new amounts as needed. He even envisions the elimination of elimination altogether through waste nanobots that would act as tiny garbage compactors, collecting waste products and removing them by passing out of the body. A complete nanobot-based digestive system obviates the need for much of our digestive organs and would exist only after several intermediary stages of development when they would supplement our existing digestive system.

Artificial Immune Systems

Anybody who uses a computer these days is aware of or has had their computer infected with a virus. A **computer virus** is a self-replicating program that spreads by inserting copies of itself into other executable code or documents. There are some striking similarities between computer and biological viruses. A computer virus inserts itself into a program like a biological virus inserts itself into a living cell. In either case, there is an infection of a host. The virus then uses the machinery of the host in order to reproduce. Two other types of malicious software are worms and Trojan horses. Whereas a virus needs to be part of a program in order to reproduce, a worm is self-contained and can propagate on its own. Worms use computer networks to send copies of themselves to other systems. They generally affect network performance rather than individual machines. A Trojan horse pretends to be a useful program but actually performs a malicious activity. Recent examples have been of the "backdoor" variety and can allow a computer to be remotely controlled from the network.

In order to combat these little invaders, most computers now come with antivirus software. This software is a form of artificial immune system. It serves the same functions as a biological immune system, preventing, identifying, and removing viral infections. Antiviral software works by first scanning files looking for viruses that match those already known using definitions in a virus dictionary. If one is found, a disinfection process can be initiated where the virus is removed from the file, or the infected file is either quarantined or deleted. Since new viruses are constantly being generated or made to mutate, the dictionary files must be continually updated. This mirrors what happens in nature, biological organisms must develop immunity to bacteria and viruses that mutate into new forms.

The parallels between biological and artificial immune systems are remarkable (Bentley, 2002). File scanning is like the role of helper T cells in the human immune system that examine the surfaces of macrophages. T and B cells identify pathogens by using unique antigen bar codes and then remove them with tailor-produced antibodies or outright destruction of an infected cell. What's more, hackers who attempt to break into computer systems can be considered as digital parasites because they rely on and exploit the resources of their host. Counter-intrusion measures against hackers include firewalls and password access. As is the case with viruses, there is a constantly escalating war between new hacking methods and security procedures.

Stephanie Forrest and other researchers at the University of New Mexico at Albuquerque have created several different varieties of computer immune system modeled closely on human immune system principles (Chao & Forrest, 2002; Forrest & Hofmeyr, 2001). Once infected by an antigen, humans and other mammals develop a response to that antigen so that if we are ever infected again, we can immediately combat it. This is known as adaptive or acquired immunity. Antibodies are created that identify the intruder and attach to it, clustering the offenders into groups where they can be more easily engulfed by phagocytes. The instructions to manufacture antibodies are stored in a gene library that is added to with each new infection.

These researchers used genetic algorithms to generate a diverse set of possible antibodies to combat antigens. In their simulation, the fitness value of an individual was increased if it developed successful antibodies. The algorithm would then create more antibodies based on this fitness. It would add successful antibody manufacturing instructions to its digital gene library so that the individual could call on these should the same infection occur subsequently in the future. The results of the study show that powerful adaptive immune systems are now possible inside computers.

13

SOCIAL BEHAVIOR

I was part of that strange race of people aptly described as spending their lives doing
things they detest to make money they don't want to buy things they don't need to
impress people they dislike.

—**Emile Henry Gauvreau**

HUMAN AND ARTIFICIAL SOCIETIES

Humans are social beings. We live in societies where we interact with others. This interaction is typically mutually beneficial although conflicts certainly arise. Think of how much
you benefit from those around you. The house you live in, the food you eat, the car you
drive, and all sorts of additional needs are met by others. In fact, even as a fully functioning adult, it is nearly impossible to survive entirely on our own, completely cut off from the
rest of humanity.

Human societies are characterized by a myriad of different relationships. Hollis (1994)
divides up social relationships into four basic types: (1) family relationships like those
between a mother and child; (2) economic relationships like those between a consumer
and storeowner; (3) allegiance relationships like those between the members of the United
Nations; and (4) civil relationships like those between the citizens of a country and its
governing leaders. Most relationships are characterized by cooperation and competition.
Cooperation is characterized by working together to achieve a common goal. Competition
instead occurs when goals between individuals or groups vary.

One of the hallmarks of human societies is specialization—different people perform different roles. Fireman put out fires, policemen enforce the law, businessman handle goods
and services, etc. This division of labor is efficient, as usually those people who are good at
or interested in doing a task are the ones who do it. But workers never operate in a vacuum.

They rely on others to effectively carry out their tasks. The shopkeeper could not sell his goods without the others who manufacture, package, deliver, market, and transport those goods. Seen this way, human society is a complex system of interdependent agents, each acting to fulfill their own ends, but in the process also fulfilling the ends of others.

In this chapter, we consider societies that are either exclusively artificial or some mixture of human and artificial. We begin by discussing "software" societies made up of agents interacting in a virtual computer environment. Next, we examine robot societies that act together in a shared physical environment. Last, we take a look at human-robot interaction. We will see that in many ways these different societies mirror important aspects of human society including cooperation, competition, specialization, and interdependence.

VIRTUAL SOCIETIES

Swarm Intelligence

By observing nature, we can see what appears to be intelligent behavior in large groups of animals. Flocks of birds, schools of fish, and swarms of flies all act as if they have a mind of their own, turning away from predators or seeking out prey in what seems to be a ballet of choreographed motion. But in fact, the behavior of simple swarms like these can be explained by a few very simple rules. The individuals in the group act "stupidly," blindly following simple guides to action. When one steps back though, and examines the group as a whole, it acts with what appears to be purpose and reason.

Bentley (2002) points out two rules that explain swarm behavior. The first is attractiveness. Simply stated, this is that individuals prefer being with others to being by themselves. The extent to which any given individual will want to join a swarm though is dependent on its size. Bigger swarms are generally preferred to smaller ones, although the rate of attraction decreases proportional to the overall size. The second rule is noncollision. This means that individuals in a swarm don't like to bump into one another and act to preserve space between one another.

Swarms are formed and maintained by the attractiveness rule. If a single fish finds itself alone, it will move and join up with its neighbors. The coordinated movement of swarms is explained by the noncollision rule. Fish turning to avoid an obstacle will turn in near synchrony to avoid bumping into each other. The turning movement in the school actually propagates from the front to the back of the school. The fish in the front turn first to avoid the obstacle. Those behind them turn next to avoid hitting their companions in front, and so on through the school until the last fish at the end.

Although swarm behavior was first observed in the natural world, it can be applied and used by machines. Reynolds (1987) has created swarms of artificial software units that he calls **boids**. In one program, he had boids follow three rules. They matched the speed of their neighbors, tried to move toward the center of the flock, and avoided collisions. Boids following these instructions, when animated and displayed on a computer screen, behave in much the same way as natural swarms. They fly around in a coherent unified fashion emulating their biological brethren.

Now, it might not seem that flocking behavior of this sort is very intelligent. After all, the boids seem to do little more than fly around a space, keeping together, avoiding barriers, and perhaps seeking out certain locations. But this behavior can be the basis of more complex problem solving. Russ Eberhart and his colleagues at Purdue University took Boids and used them to solve problems (Eberhart, Kennedy, & Yuhui, 2001). They had boids explore a problem space. A problem space is an abstract multi-dimensional space where each point corresponds to a possible solution to a problem. The boids in this study were attracted to the center of the swarm and to points in the problem space that had improved solutions. They found that the boids were able to quickly find solutions to difficult problems. This technique is sometimes referred to as **particle swarm optimization** and has been used in a number of real-world applications such as voltage control for a Japanese electric company.

Distributed Artificial Intelligence

Humans live in societies made up of groups of individuals who interact, sometimes cooperating toward common goals, sometimes coming into conflict because of differing goals. Society as a whole has sometimes been considered "intelligent" because it adapts to challenges and solves "problems" such as poverty, economic production, and war. In fact, societies of individuals can often succeed where individuals fail. Computer scientists have taken notice of this and have developed programs that are the software equivalents of societies. This field is known as **distributed artificial intelligence** (DAI) sometimes also referred to as multiagent systems (Weiss, 2000).

DAI is the study, construction, and application of multiagent systems where several interacting intelligent agents pursue some set of goals or perform some set of tasks. We have already introduced the idea of an agent as a computational entity that perceives and acts on its environment. The environment is typically a software one, although robots can also be considered agents in which case they act in physical environments. Unlike typical software programs that follow coded instructions and act in well-defined ways, agents in a distributed system act autonomously and unpredictably. Also unlike traditional programs, there is no centralized processor that coordinates and controls actions. Instead, activity emerges out of the agent's interactions with each other.

If agents are to get anything done, they need to communicate. In many DAI systems, individual agents communicate with one another by following a particular protocol. For example, agent A may propose a course of action to agent B. After evaluating it, agent B can then accept, reject, disagree, or propose a counterproposal. The two agents continue in this fashion, in effect having a conversation until some outcome occurs. Other protocols allow a manager agent to submit jobs to contractor agents through a bidding process where the manager announces a task. Some of the agents present respond by submitting bids. The manager then awards the contract to the most appropriate agent (see Figure 13.1). Notice that these protocols serve the same function as in human societies. They allow individuals to coordinate their activity and provide for an equitable division of labor, where the agent best suited to the job is the one who gets it.

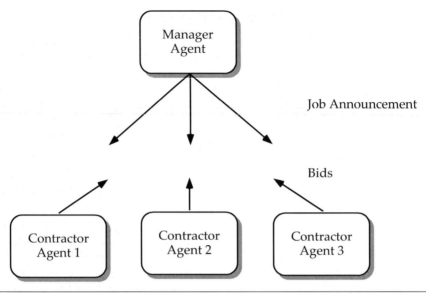

Figure 13.1 A bidding process of the sort used in multi-agent systems. These protocols allow the best agent to get the job and mimic the kinds of group interactions we see in human societies.

There are many other analogies between DAI and human societies. Some DAI systems invoke the equivalent of voting where agents choose from a set of alternatives and then adopt the outcome that received the greatest support. There are also computational economies consisting of consumer agents who exchange goods and producer agents who transform some goods into other goods. These agents then bid to maximize their profits or utility. The goods have "prices" and the net result of the activity mimics certain macroscopic aspects of human markets, such as equilibrium between supply and demand.

DAI programs have been successful at performing a variety of computational tasks. They have been used to solve problems, in planning, search algorithms, and rational decision making. Specific applications include electronic commerce, management of telecommunication networks, air traffic control, supply chain management, and video games. A DAI program called IMAGINE (Integrated Multi-Agent Interaction Environment) has even been used to design other DAI programs (Steiner, 1996).

Although DAI systems seem to be the software analog of human societies, they also serve as a model for how individual brains might operate. The brain can be considered to have multiple "agents" that act in conjunction with one another (Minsky, 1985). For example, a "Hunger" agent might motivate us to seek food. It might call on a "Plan" agent to formulate a strategy for obtaining lunch. Once the meal was in front of us, a "Move" agent could be activated to get a morsel to our mouths. This, in turn, could turn on "Reach" and "Grasp" agents to manipulate a fork. The numerous interconnections between different specialized processing centers in the human brain lend credence to this view. In fact, there are some who argue that our conception of having a single unified self or consciousness is just an illusion and that it is better to characterize individuals as distributed processing systems (Dennett, 1991).

ROBOT SOCIETIES

The field of **collective robotics** designs and implements robotic systems that, as a whole, exhibit intelligent behavior even though the individual robots in these systems are not themselves very "smart" (Melhuish, 2001). It draws on studies of collective behavior in biological systems. Insects, as we have already seen, can swarm. But they can also migrate, seek out food and materials, build, maintain and defend their nests, and care for their young. The goal in this research is to create robots that can perform similar tasks. Just like insects, it is possible to create robots that can solve problems and act intelligently as a result of following simple rules. They are able to achieve this without any of the trappings of what is considered necessary for intelligence. They have no internal symbolic representation of the world, do not perform any extended computational reasoning, and transmit only minimal amounts of information to one another.

One of the principles that allows for such emergent intelligent behavior is **stigmergy**. This is defined as the production of a certain behavior in agents as a consequence of the effects produced in the local environment by previous behavior. Stigmergy thus allows an action to be released by the consequences of a previous action. For example, ants will navigate around a barrier by laying down pheromone trails that other ants can follow. Similarly, a robot that crosses a field can return to its starting point by following the grass it has trampled down. Stigmergy does not require that any of the agents have a blueprint or plan of what they are doing. They can be blissfully unaware of the results their actions have on both themselves and others.

Beckers, Holland, and Deneubourg (1994) have demonstrated that a few "dumb" robots, following simple rules, can produce intelligent emergent behavior. Each of the individual robots had very simple capabilities. They could move pucks, detect objects with infrared eyes, and detect when they were pushing against something heavy. The robots followed three rules. Rule one was that if they saw a wall, they should turn away. Rule two was if they were pushing something heavy like another robot, a wall, or more than three pucks, they should reverse and make a random turn. Rule three was if they were not pushing something heavy and couldn't see a wall, they should go forward.

The robots were then placed in an arena surrounded by walls. Pucks were randomly scattered around the arena. In a relatively short time, the robots had, through their collective action, managed to push all the pucks together into one area. The robots had effectively worked together as a team to achieve a common goal, even though none of the individual robots knew what that goal was. The goal behavior had emerged as a consequence of their simple rule-following behavior. Next, a fourth rule was introduced. Each robot would, depending on the color of the puck, pull back by a certain distance. This time the result was a sorting of the pucks into different clusters each corresponding to a different color. In this latter case, the addition of another rule allowed for more complex emergent behavior to arise.

Researchers at the University of Salford in the UK have used basic feedback principles to allow larger, more intelligent robots to work cooperatively (Barnes, 1996). Their two robots, named "Fred" and "Ginger" were able to carry objects together using robotic arms. They were able to adjust to each other's behavior simply by trying to keep the plates that moved their arms centered on top of their bodies. The robotic couple could carry a tray from one part of a room to another, adjusting the position of the tray while avoiding an obstacle en route. Although Fred and Ginger use feedback principles, they also rely on top down planning to attain their goals. It is hoped that one day a human operator could issue task goals to the robots using a high level planner. The planner would then communicate the appropriate subtasks to the robots that could then carry them out autonomously.

Perhaps the most ambitious social robot project is RoboCup (Robot World Cup Initiative), an attempt to develop a team of fully autonomous humanoid robots that can win against the human world soccer champion team by the year 2050. Teams from around the world develop robots in various categories and play against one another in an annual tournament. The categories are humanoid, middle-sized, small-sized, four-legged, and computer simulation. In 2006 it was held in Bremen, Germany. Figure 13.2 shows a humanoid entry. The robots that compete in these events are remarkably fast and agile, defying the stereotype of robots as slow, clunky, and awkward. They can maneuver with the ball, pass it to teammates, intercept passes, and, of course, score goals.

Figure 13.2 A humanoid entry in the 2006 RoboCup contest. Will robots beat humans in the World Cup soccer championship by 2050? Photo courtesy of Messe Bremen.

Social Laws for Artificial Agents

Laws can, of course, be applied to the actions of agents as well as people. Shoham and Tennenholtz (1995) describe the usefulness of social laws that enable multiple agents in a shared environment to go about their tasks without interfering with one another. They apply a sample set of laws to the case of mobile robots. These robots must move about, performing various actions without colliding with each other. Other problems can also arise in such systems. For instance, a robot might use an object needed by another, or two or more robots might need to work together to accomplish some end.

There are two extreme approaches one can take to governing the social actions of such agents. The first is constrained and has a single programmer giving specific instructions to each of the robots, trying to anticipate all possible interactions or conflicts that might arise. This "dictator" method is undesirable because the number of specific conflicts that can occur is vast and can be expected to change over time. A second unconstrained approach is to deal with conflicts as they occur, not trying to anticipate every possible problem. This could be accomplished by appealing to a central supervisor to have each issue resolved or by allowing the agents to communicate with each other to negotiate the situation on their own. Problems with this second approach are that the central "judge" may be overwhelmed with requests and the agents may be forced to negotiate constantly.

The use of social laws reduces the need for a central decision maker or for communicative arbitration. The society of agents in this scheme adopts a set of conventions or laws that govern their behavior in conflict situations. If two robots are about to collide, they could simply follow the rule of turning to their right. But a question now arises. How does one go about making effective laws? Shoham and Tennenholtz (1995) outline two perspectives. In the first, programmers or designers hand craft laws for a specific domain. In the second, they discuss a general model of social law in a computational system, one that can be applied to a broad category of instances.

Imagine a warehouse or building consisting of a two-dimensional grid defined by rows and columns. A set number of mobile robots must travel within this space to one or more target destinations. What laws should the robots follow so that they don't collide and can go about their jobs in a reasonably efficient manner? Shoham and Tennenholz (1995) developed five traffic laws, and various derivative theorems to allow for this. For instance, the robots were required to move constantly, those in even rows must move to the left, while those in odd rows must move to the right. The implementation of these laws in simulation effectively enabled the agents in this social system to operate without running into one another. Furthermore, these laws precluded the computationally intensive need for a central arbiter or for disputative communication between individual agents.

The five laws only work in the system for which they were designed. But is it possible to derive a general set of laws, ones that would apply to any given system? The authors argue that it is. They posit a system made of agents that repeatedly and simultaneously take actions. Each agent exists in a current state and must transition from that to a new state. The possible actions each agent can engage in is limited and drawn from a known list. A social law then becomes a constraint on the selection of the next action, a prohibition against taking a particular action, given a current set of conditions. For example, a robot car, once reaching an intersection, could turn left, turn right, or go straight. If it senses the presence of another robot to the left, it could do nothing until that car has passed, then initiate the left-hand turn.

The use of social laws, be they specific or general, is an effective way of allowing agents to achieve goals while not interfering with the capacity of other agent's to do the same. However, the models they propose suffer from a number of drawbacks. To begin with, the laws are formulated offline, that is, they are determined by the programmer and thus require extensive a priori knowledge of the system and how it works. In complex human societies, laws are derived emergently by the legal system as situations arise. Another problem is that the models assume a homogenous society where the laws apply equally to all agents. It is not clear how to formulate laws for heterogeneous societies, where different rules apply to different agents. This is akin to a human "caste" system or society with different classes. These models also assume that all the agents are rule abiding. It would be interesting to see how the behavior of the system changes when certain agents are allowed to break the rules. In this case, the rogue agents become the equivalent of criminals.

HUMAN-MACHINE INTERACTION

Personal Robotics

Robotics is taking a new turn. Historically, robots were designed for use in highly structured environments that did not require direct human oversight or interaction. They functioned well in places like factories and power plants where they performed the same repetitive action over and over again. But the growing number of elderly in industrialized nations has placed an increased demand on robotic design for the home environment where they can assist the aged and/or the disabled. This calls for a new kind of robot, one that can perform a variety of different tasks and that can function safely in the presence of humans. The objective of **personal robotics** is to design and manufacture intelligent machines that can interact with and assist human beings in many different everyday circumstances.

One of the most important challenges in personal robotics is not technological, but psychological. The robots must be designed in such a way as to be accepted and used by people. Dario, Guglielmelli, and Laschi (2001) bring up several points in this regard. They argue that personal robots, like a home appliance, must be evaluated according to their usefulness, pleasure of interaction, safety, cost, and other criteria. For instance, it may not be desirable to make a humanlike personal robot because it could be perceived as an invasion of a person's personal environment. It is also important that the robot not be perceived as threatening, in which case it would be designed to not show movements or expressions indicative of aggression. A further consideration is that people may not like a personal robot with a high degree of autonomy and initiative because this could also be perceived as threatening. To avoid this, the robot would need to be designed to optimize rather than minimize user involvement.

Keeping Up Appearances

What should a personal robot look like? This is an important consideration if we are going to be interacting with them on a daily basis. A personal robot ought to be about the same size as a person or smaller. Any larger and they would be perceived as threatening. The

Honda Corporation robot, Asimo, was designed to be smaller so that it could effectively access door handles, countertops, and other work areas that are just a few feet off the ground. Although it is not a strict requirement, personal robots also ought to look at least somewhat human to facilitate social interaction. In what follows, we describe two important generalizations concerning robotic appearance.

Humanlike Vehicles   Braitenberg (1984) generates a series of thought experiments in which he asks us to imagine the behavior of simple devices that he calls vehicles. The vehicles have two light sensors in the front that are wired up to motors that spin their wheels. Different kinds of behavior can be created in them by the fashion in which they are wired. If there is an opposing connection between sensors and wheels so that light detected in the left eye spins the right motor, then the vehicle will move to the left toward the light. If the there is a same-side wiring, then the left sensor would activate the left wheel and the vehicle moves away from the light. Other wiring arrangements can produce different behaviors.

When these vehicles are placed in a room with light sources and people are asked to describe their behavior, they give human explanations. Vehicles that move toward a light are said to "love" the light. Those that move away from a light are said to demonstrate "fear." Other observers perceived these vehicles as being "aggressive." What this demonstrates is that people will easily attribute humanlike qualities to explain the actions of things that don't even look remotely human.

The results of Braitenberg's studies suggest that we should be very willing to accept humanoid robots that look much more like us. Paul Guinan produced a fictional account of a robot named Boilerplate (Figure 13.3). Developed in the Victorian age, Boilerplate's

Figure 13.3 Boilerplate with Pancho Villa, 1916. Did Boilerplate really exist? © 2006 Paul Guinan. Image from BigRedHair.com/boilerplate

escapades included a voyage to Antarctica, battles in the Japanese-Russian War of 1904, and the 1916 expedition against Pancho Villa. A surprisingly large number of people believed these stories to be factual, even though it was technologically impossible at the time. It seems then that people will have little difficulty accepting the ubiquitous appearance of robots in a mixed future robot-human society. However, the next section shows that appearances matter.

The Uncanny Valley   Although we humans certainly have a tendency to attribute human qualities to machines, other research shows that when inanimate objects appear somewhat, but not too lifelike, the result can be shocking. Mori (2005) first found that if a robot is made increasingly humanlike in the way it appears and moves, the human emotional response to it increases, becoming more positive and empathetic. However, when the robot is at about 75% of the likeness of a person, there is a dramatic negative emotional response. It is now perceived as inhuman and repulsive. At about 85% of human likeness, the emotional response becomes positive once more. Figure 13.4 shows the function depicting this drop, which is coined the "uncanny valley."

Clearly, people will not want to interact with robots with the appearance of being "almost human." But how can we explain this phenomenon? In one account, humanlike characteristics stand out more and are noticed with entities that look distinctly nonhuman, generat-

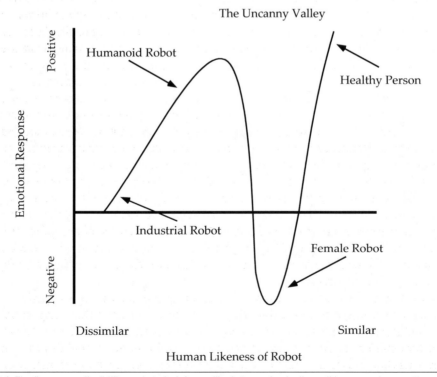

Figure 13.4 The "uncanny valley." When robots look humanlike but are clearly discernible as non-human, they produce a negative emotional response.

ing empathy. But in entities that look almost human, it is the nonhuman features that now become salient, generating revulsion. Another explanation is that things that look almost human resemble corpses while quasi-human motion is indicative of illness, neurological, or psychological dysfunction. This latter account may have an evolutionary basis, since it would be a survival advantage to avoid disease-bearing bodies.

Given these results, personal robots of the future should be designed to avoid the Uncanny Valley and should appear either extremely humanlike or just somewhat human. In the first case, we would have robots that may be indistinguishable from humans. This could cause another set of problems, as people will certainly want to be able to know whether they are dealing with a natural person or a robot. The second case thus seems the most likely outcome.

Social Perception of Computers

Researchers have also investigated people's reactions to computers, which bear little physical resemblance to humans. Do we treat computers the way we might treat a robot or humanlike face? Foerst (2004) describes two experiments by Cliff Nass, a sociologist at Stanford University who studies human-machine interaction. In the first, participants were asked to test and then evaluate a bad computer program. The program itself prompted them to perform the evaluation. Later, they were asked to evaluate the program again, this time by a person. The participants gave fairly positive reviews when prompted to do so by the computers but very critical and negative remarks when asked by the human research assistant. The results suggest that the reviewers were afraid of "upsetting" the computers and so acted politely to them. They had no such qualms about reporting what they really felt to the human assistant. It seems that when interacting with computers, we assume that they have feelings. We then treat them the same way we would treat a person.

In a second study, Nass had participants play interactive games on computers. In this experiment, half of the computer monitors were green, while the other half were blue. In addition, half of the subjects wore green armbands, and the other half wore blue armbands. Those wearing the green armbands were more successful when they played the games on green monitors. The opposite was true for the blue players. They did better on the blue machines. When later asked to evaluate how they felt, the green players reported a greater feeling of solidarity when playing on like-colored machines. Likewise, the blue players felt that they bonded more with the blue monitors. These results show that we identify with computers that share some feature in common with our own social group. It implies that a form of "machine racism" could exist, whereby we might stereotype and treat artificial people in a positive or negative way based on their similarity to our own race, religion, or other socially-relevant attribute.

Much of what we have recently presented shows that people will all too easily anthropomorphize machines. We attribute humanlike qualities to vehicles that act in simple ways, to faces that appear somewhat or very much like ours, and to computers as well as robots. **Anthropomorphism** is defined as the attribution of humanlike qualities to nonhuman subjects. This then biases the way we interact with them. Anthropomorphism seems to be an inherent way we have of interpreting the world around us. Cliff Nass and Byron Reeves suggest that anthropomorphism is the initial and intuitive response humans take to anything with which we interact and that it would take an act of will not to think this way.

MOVAID the Personal Robot

Dario, Guglielmelli, and Laschi (2001) report on the evaluation of a personal robot named MOVAID designed to assist the disabled and elderly. MOVAID is a distributed robotic system. It consists of a mobile robot and several workstations. MOVAID moves about through the house, avoids obstacles, and can grasp and manipulate common objects. The mobile component has a wheeled base on top of which is a single arm ending in a hand. It can project an image of what it sees through its cameras to the user who can monitor and control it from the workstations.

The MOVAID system was designed from the start to be used easily and effectively by people. It has a friendly screen-based interface and is simple to operate. It was deliberately designed to not appear humanoid to reduce its threatening appearance. The mobile robot only makes predictable and slow motions. It gives a warning before it moves, does not move in the dark, and goes into standby mode reminiscent of sleeping when not in use.

Several severely disabled users including those with limited or little upper limb movement evaluated the prototype MOVAID system and reacted favorably to it (Dario, Guglielmelli, & Laschi, 2001). The system was able to successfully help these individuals in performing certain household chores. An interesting result of this study was that the user's attitudes toward robotic assistance increased dramatically after familiarity with the system. Whereas only 10% responded favorably to robotic assistance before use, 43% answered that they would like to have a robot assistant after the trial period.

ISAC—A Robot With Social Skills

Researchers at Vanderbilt University are developing a robot that can interact socially with one or more other persons (Kawamura, Rogers, Hambuchen, Erol, 2003). Named ISAC (Intelligent Soft-Arm Control), it is sophisticated enough to understand human intentions and respond accordingly. ISAC is designed as a general-purpose humanoid robot that can work as a partner to assist people in either a home or work setting. It is humanoid in appearance having cameras, infrared sensors, and microphones that allow it to monitor the location of objects and people. ISAC has software that allows it to interpret and produce speech and to locate people's faces and the location of their fingertips. It is also capable of moving its body and arms to perform actions like shaking hands and picking up colored blocks.

The crux of ISAC's abilities is a multi-agent architecture made up of four components (see Figure 13.5). The Human Agent component contains an active internal representation of the human or humans with which it is interacting. This agent has information about the position, actions, and states of those around it based on observations and conversations. The Human Agent extracts keywords from speech and uses them to determine expressed intention. For example, if a person asks ISAC to perform some task, it can understand and execute it. But ISAC can also interpret the inferred intentions of others. If someone walks out of the room, for example, it will infer that this person no longer intends to interact and will adjust its expectations accordingly.

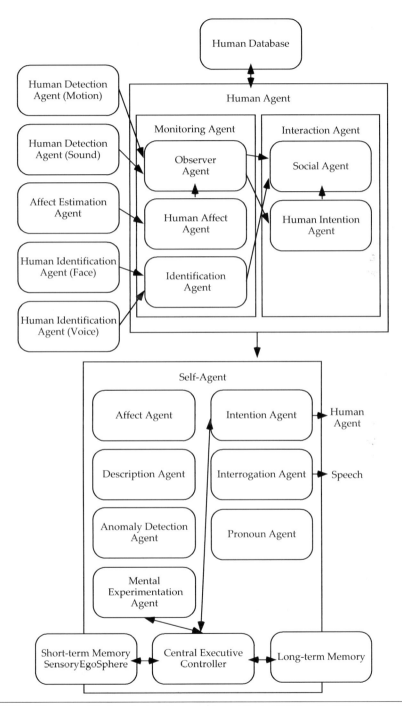

Figure 13.5 ISAC's multi-agent architecture. Designed by researchers at Vanderbilt University, ISAC can interpret and respond to people's intentions (after Kawamura, Rogers, Hambuchen & Erol, 2003).

Another part of ISAC is the Human database, which contains information about people with whom the robot has previously interacted. The database has identification information concerning the individual's face and voice that allows it to recognize people it has seen in the past. But more importantly, it also contains intention histories for these people. ISAC can consult this information to personalize its interactions with different individuals. It might, for example, ask Tamara if she would like to play the Color Game because it remembers that they have engaged in that activity many times in the past.

The Self-Agent is the part of the robot's architecture that has an internal representation. This component monitors ISAC's hardware, behaviors, and tasks and compares them against human intentions. If there is no conflict between what a person wants and what ISAC can do, it will respond or carry out the requested action. If there is a conflict, ISAC will explain to the person why it cannot do that, perhaps because it is busy doing something else.

ISAC is also equipped with a short- and long-term memory designed to facilitate social interaction. Its short-term memory data structure is called the SensoryEgoSphere (SES). The SES is a geodesic sphere centered on the robot's head in which it can store the dynamic, or time-changing location of people and objects in its immediate surroundings. ISAC needs to do this if it is to effectively track the location of people as they move around. For example, it would need to continue orienting its head toward a person if they moved about the room. ISAC's long-term memory is really a procedural memory. It contains instructions on how to perform various tasks like reaching and grasping.

ISAC's remarkable social abilities have been tested in several different demonstrations. In one such case, a person walks up to the robot. ISAC turns toward the person, identifies, and greets them. Once this interaction is established, ISAC will engage in social dialog. If the person asks ISAC to do something such as pick up a block, it will do so if it is within its capabilities. Another person then walks up to ISAC and attempts interaction. If the second person's intentions are of a lower priority, ISAC will stop what it is doing, turn to the second person and apologize for being busy. It will then turn back to the first person and continue with its former interaction. If this second intention is of a greater priority than what it is currently doing, it will switch to the new task, but only after explaining its actions to the first person.

The ISAC robot exemplifies many of the key requirements of social interaction. Any agent, be it artificial or biological, must be able to register the locations of other agents around it. It must additionally be able to identify those agents and interpret what their intentions are. A social agent must also be able to communicate with those around it and to either give commands or follow commands given to it. Finally, it should be able to take turns in communicating and acting with others. These skills form the basis of more complex social behavior such as cooperative action toward the achievement of a common goal.

DOING THE RIGHT THING—ETHICS

How should an artificial person act? What should it do in any given situation? Motivations and emotions provide a partial solution to this since they drive actions. A state of "hunger" will motivate the location of food or the replenishment of energy. A state of "anger" may motivate fighting behavior or the removal of some obstacle. But what does one do when motivational and emotional drives are satisfied? Should an artificial person just sit around and do nothing? Should it pursue pleasures or actions that make it feel good or should it strive to obtain lofty principled goals? **Ethics** is the term that refers to the standards of conduct that an individual or group follows. Ethics is concerned not just with behavior but with *moral* behavior: right and wrong action. Ethics asks us to think about what one should or should not do. Just as moral issues apply to humans, they also apply to artificial people. In this section, we examine several perspectives to the governance of proper action.

The Consequentialist Approach

Gips (1995) outlines three ethical theories that can be used to guide the action of a robot or android. In the **consequentialist** approach, actions are judged by their consequences. Consequences can be evaluated according to their happiness or goodness. The more an action increases happy or good consequences, the more it should be done. Of course, this approach immediately brings up a host of questions. For starters, what counts as happiness or goodness? Is it the satisfaction of basic pleasure for its own sake as we see in hedonism or is it the attainment of higher-order values? Once happiness is defined, there is still the problem of how it can be measured. It may impossible to quantify happiness if it is a subjective phenomenon, being different for different people.

A third question concerns whose happiness should be satisfied. Ethical egoists act only to increase their own happiness. Ethical altruists act only to satisfy everybody else, while utilitarians act to increase everybody's happiness equally, including their own. The utilitarian approach is summed up in the phrase "the greatest good for the greatest number." The issue of which of these alternatives is the proper one is a complex and hotly debated topic, especially since some actions benefit both the person who produced it as well as others. Entire political-economic systems have been founded on these different approaches, with libertarianism and capitalism favoring an individualist egoist stance and socialism favoring the altruist position.

An artificial person that acts egoistically will be selfish. It would always choose to engage in an action that would increase its own happiness whether this made others, be they human or artificial people, happy or not. "Bender," the robot on the animated TV series *Futurama*, is an example. An altruistic artificial person would, of course, be on the opposite extreme, acting only for the sake of others. It would do things to make others happy regardless of the cost to itself, even if this meant its own destruction. Many robots throughout science fiction tales are of this sort, willingly sacrificing themselves to save their teammates. A utilitarian artificial person would try to maximize everybody's happiness, acting in such a way as to distribute happiness equally to all societal members.

The Deontological Approach

In the **deontological** approach, actions are evaluated in and of themselves, not in terms of their consequences. This can be considered a rule-based way of acting, in which a person follows a set of rules or laws that say what can or cannot be done. There are numerous instances of such rules in human history. Religions, for example, often prescribe a set of rules that should be obeyed. The Ten Commandments state that among others things, kill-ing, stealing, and lying are bad. All countries have legislation in various domains detailing what is or is not acceptable action. In the United States, for instance, a driver must yield to oncoming traffic in the presence of a sign so indicating and signal before making a turn.

Science fiction writer Isaac Asimov was using a deontological approach when he formu-lated his now well-known "Three Laws of Robotics":

1. A robot may not injure a human being or, through inaction, allow a human being to come to harm.
2. A robot must obey orders given it by human beings except where such orders would conflict with the First Law.
3. A robot must protect its own existence as long as such protection does not conflict with the First or Second laws.

Asimov's rules demonstrate a number of issues concerning the use of laws. First, they show that laws can be prioritized. This means that some laws have precedence over others. A lesser law cannot be executed if it conflicts with a primary one. However, prioritizing does not prevent the law's intended behaviors from being violated. A human, for example, could order a robot following the Three Laws to kill itself, and the robot would have to comply if the act did not result in harm to the human. The robot's suicide in this case would violate the protection of its own existence deemed in the Third Law in order to pre-serve the first two. Prioritizing also fails to prevent the development of moral dilemmas. In the 2004 movie adaptation of *I, Robot*, the robots violate all three laws in order to prevent humans from destroying themselves, their particular interpretation of the First Law.

The Virtue-Based Approach

The final approach mentioned by Gips (1995) concerns **virtues**. A virtue, unlike a law, does not explicitly state what one should or should not do. Instead, it poses an abstract action that one should strive to carry out. The ancient Greeks proposed four cardinal virtues: wisdom, courage, temperance, and justice. Vices are the opposite of virtues. The antith-esis of the four cardinal virtues would thus be ignorance, cowardice, excess, and injustice. Virtues can also be prioritized, since in many virtue systems the remaining virtues can be derived from the cardinal ones.

Virtues can be thought of as servicing values. The philosopher Ayn Rand defines a value as "that which one acts to gain or keep" and a virtue as "the action by which one gains and keeps it" (Rand, 1963, 147). In this conception, the values are higher-order goals and vir-tues are the means by which they are attained. For example, if one valued truth, then one would need to practice the virtue of rationality among other virtues, in order to achieve it.

A problem with the virtue-based approach is that it is too abstract. To be virtuous, what a human or artificial person needs is a detailed set of instructions specifying how a particular virtue can be executed in a specific situation. This is a complex problem given the large number of possible scenarios and ways one can act in them. Virtue-based action doesn't provide easy solutions to moral dilemmas either. The psychologist Lawrence Kohl-berg created a number of such dilemmas in order to understand moral reasoning. In one scenario, he has a person faced with the prospect of stealing expensive medicine in order to save his wife's life. In this case, two values, property rights and human life, come into conflict. Virtues therefore tell us generally how to act, but not how to act in specific situations or when two or more virtues clash.

Rules or Learning?

All three of the approaches mentioned above can be implemented in a top down manner. Goodness, laws, and virtues can all be determined ahead of time and then programmed in to govern the behavior of an artificial person. However, an artificial person can also figure these things out by themselves. In this bottom up perspective, the individual is allowed to learn from their experiences and derive what is good or virtuous on their own. They can then apply this learning to novel situations. Human ethical action is probably a mixture of innate disposition and experience. People who are genetically predisposed to aggression may be more prone to violent acts like murder or rape. But environmental factors like parenting, religion, and education also have an influence and can mitigate or preclude such predispositions. If an artificial person were to reflect this balance, they could be programmed with certain basic ethical parameters that could then be modified based on experience.

Georges (2003) provides some additional thoughts on this topic. He states that the top down approach of pre-programmed rules is a fast and cheap way of getting a robot to act morally. But as we already alluded, rules are usually too general and the more rules we put in, the greater their chances of conflict. He calculates that a million rules have 5×10^{11} chances of conflicting with one another. Learning allows a robot to generate more specific rules but produces increased unpredictability and is more expensive and time consuming to implement. The solution again seems to be some combination of inserting general ethical rules of conduct and letting experience do the rest.

Rights: We Hold These Truths to Be Self-Evident…

The existence of artificial people interacting with humans in a societal context raises many questions. Caudill (1992) brings up a number of the most important ones and asks us to consider the following:

- What if they have differences or conflicts with us? How would these be resolved?
- What if an artificial person murders a human? What if a human murders an artificial person? Would it be ethical to turn them off or to erase their memories or personalities?
- Is it proper to own an artificial person? To force them to do what we want? To make them our slaves?

The answers to these questions depend on whether we classify an artificial person as a machine or as a person. If artificial people are considered as machines or objects without sentience, intelligence, free-will, and other characteristics we consider uniquely human, then it follows we could treat them in much the same way we treat other artifacts like cars or computers. In this case, we would not hesitate to control or destroy them as a means of resolving conflict.

Under these conditions, a human who damages or terminates an artificial person would not be considered guilty of having committed a crime anymore than a person who smashes their cell phone. Likewise, if an artificial person injured or murdered a human, it would be considered an accident in much the same way that a factory worker might be knocked over by a robotic assembly arm. In such cases, destroying or reprogramming the arm to avoid future accidents would in no way be considered unethical. There would also be little concern over owning an artificial person and in instructing them to do our bidding because they would be no different than other forms of property that could be bought, traded, and sold.

But what if an artificial person is in no fundamental way different than a biological person? In this case, we would need to treat them as fellow human beings. One political approach to how humans ought to treat one other is based on rights. A **right** is a power or privilege to which one is justly entitled. Rights serve as rules of interaction between people and place limits on the actions of individuals or groups, particularly those of governments. Humans are considered to have certain rights, for example, the right to life. This right thus prevents others from taking one's life and makes murder unethical. Legal systems are often, but not exclusively, based on rights.

What rights should an artificial person have? This is a very difficult question considering there is debate over exactly what rights humans should have. The United Nations in 1948 published a Universal Declaration of Human Rights with 30 separate articles. The positive rights proclaimed in this document include life, liberty, security, equality before the law, freedom of movement, property ownership, freedom of opinion and expression, and freedom to assemble and to take part in government. Negative rights detailed here include not being held in slavery or servitude, freedom from torture, arbitrary arrest, detention, or exile. However, many conservatives and libertarians would take argument with other supposed "rights" such as the right to social security, employment, rest or leisure, an appropriate standard of living, education, or as has been recently suggested, health care.

Jeffery (1999) suggests that we may want to assign varying rights to advanced computing entities, what he calls "human computers," based on their level of sophistication. Human computers incapable of independent thought or action, for example, may only need minimal rights pertaining to their specific capabilities. In this scenario, one can envision various Bill of Rights documents for different kinds of intelligent machines. A full-fledged artificial person, in the sense that we are using in this book though, would have all essential human characteristics and would de facto need to be accorded the same rights as humans.

Georges (2003) points out accountability as a key issue in how we treat intelligent machines. A machine can be said to be accountable for its actions if it is aware that it is doing something, knows that it is wrong, and could have acted otherwise. This type of accountability requires that the machine possess higher order intentionality of the sort proposed by Daniel Dennett: the ability to monitor and form judgments about its own motives and actions. At a minimum, this means the machine must be able to reason metacognitively, make decisions about right and wrong, i.e., perform ethical judgments, and be capable of controlling its own actions. If an intelligent machine with these abilities performs an unethical act, it could be considered guilty and punished, perhaps through reprogramming or repair.

14

CONCLUSION

The primary task of technology, it would seem, is to lighten the burden of work man has to carry in order to stay alive and develop his potential.

—E. F. Schumacher

We have spent most of this book detailing different functional human capacities and shown that many of these can be engineered. Computers and robots can now think and act in ways that just a few decades ago would have been considered fantasy. It seems we are in an age where much of science fiction is becoming science fact.

At this point, let us step back and gaze at the big picture and ask big questions. Is it really possible to build an artificial person? If it is, should we? Will this "person-building project" save or condemn humankind? What does all of this tell us about what it means to be human? In the first part of this chapter, we sketch some of the philosophical and technological hurdles that must be overcome if the person-building project is to succeed. Then, we look at the ethical issues involved and speculate on what the future might hold. We conclude with a discussion of the nature of humanity and of our place in the universe.

CAN WE BUILD THEM? PHILOSOPHICAL HURDLES

Is it possible to build an artificial person? The content of this book suggests it is, although not everyone believes this. Trefil (1997) presents the controversy from two perspectives. On one side we have the **materialists**, who believe it can be done. Materialists adhere to physicalism and tend to be reductionistic and functionalist in their outlook on this issue. They see the brain as a physical system following known laws like other physical systems. If we can figure out how the parts of the system operate, we can understand how the parts work together and use this knowledge to construct an artificial brain that would work like ours.

On the other side we have the **mysterians**. They argue that there is some aspect of being human that is forever beyond the reach of science. Adherents of this position don't provide a full-fledged definition of what this aspect is. Many of the world religions call it a soul. The vitalists thought it was some sort of vital spark or energy that imbued living organisms. From a scientific perspective it could be something that we simply haven't discovered or can't understand. Brooks (2002) says it might be some principle like computation, a type of mathematical description of biological processes he calls "the juice." He suggests we look at the microscopic structure of matter in living systems for this phenomenon.

In the sections that follow, we present and comment on two philosophical perspectives. John Pollack believes that a person-building project is feasible. We discuss his optimistic views on this issue first. Although they aren't necessarily mysterians, Donald Davidson and Selmer Bringsjord are skeptical about this possibility. We outline their more pessimistic views afterwards.

The Optimistic View

How to Build a Person   John Pollack, in his 1989 book titled *How to Build a Person: A Prolegomenon* makes a philosophical case for the construction of an artificial human. His argument rests on three assumptions. First, he asserts it must be the case that monism is true and that mental states are physical states. Second, human beings are physical creatures whose bodies and brains are made up of component parts arranged a certain way. Third, he believes that the strong AI view is correct, namely, that a physical system such as a brain or a machine can, with the appropriate architecture, produce human mental states.

Token Physicalism–It's All Just "Stuff"   In the second chapter, we introduced the idea of physicalism. This is the idea that the entire universe is physical. According to this view, there is no separate realm of the mental and all mental states are in fact physical ones. Physicalism is thus a monist position. Monists like Pollack assert that that there is nothing special about mental qualities. They are no different than any of the other natural phenomena we can observe. Thoughts, emotions, consciousness and other psychological traits thus obey the same rules as everything else we can measure in the world.

Pollack introduces two types of physicalism. The first is **token physicalism**. This states that specific mental events are physical events. A token is a specific kind of mental event, such as experiencing a pin prick. This view needs to be distinguished from **type physicalism**, which states that categories of mental events, such as being in pain, correspond to particular physical events such as activity in pain sensors. A problem with type physicalism is that it precludes two different animals with different physiologies from both experiencing pain. Token physicalism is less restrictive. It allows any given mental event to be physical but does not explicate a specific mechanism. As such, it allows for the functionalist view of intelligence to be realized in multiple mechanisms that may possess certain abstract operational qualities.

Agent Materialism—We're More Than the Sum of Our Parts   The second assumption is **agent materialism.** This asserts that people are physical objects that have an appropriate type of structure and organization. Pollack argues that people are more than merely identical with their atomic components. They are the product of those components existing in a certain arrangement in relation to one another. To illustrate, a house is not just a pile of bricks, but the bricks put together in a certain way. When the bricks are arranged, the house then comes about. According to Pollack, there is no real difference between houses and people, the arrangement and operation of our constituent parts is just more complex.

Pollack proposes a simple thought experiment to support the idea that humans are more than equal to the sum of our parts. It involves removing or replacing parts and seeing if our "humanity" remains. We encountered this notion in the introduction chapter when describing cyborgs. You may recall that it is difficult to tell at what point in the replacement process someone ceases being human and becomes a machine. If someone were missing an arm and had it replaced with an artificial prosthesis, Pollack argues that we would not cease to call him human. Likewise, replacing the tires on a car does not cease to make it a car. The concept of a person, or of any complex object, is thus a label we apply to a collection of linked or interacting physical components. The absence or replacement of any one or a number of those parts does not necessarily entail that the whole has been significantly altered.

We should keep in mind, however, that some parts are more crucial than others. Would you rather have your head or your leg removed? The former seems to constitute a critical part, one that most of us would rather not do without. There is another conceptual issue with this thought experiment, one that we can refer to as the "parsing problem," It is not clear where the spatial and temporal boundaries of a person are. From a spatial perspective, bodies seem well bounded. But can a person still be human without breathing oxygen? If not, then the presence of oxygen outside the body is essential, i.e., a person cannot be a person outside their normal operating environment.

There are temporal concerns as well. It is not clear when someone becomes human. Is it before they are born or sometime after? Is it when they can breath? Perceive? Make decisions? This issue constitutes the crux of the contentious abortion debate. Is someone really human when he or she is constantly changing? Like a water fountain that is never the same from one instant to the next, people's bodies at the molecular level are in constant flux. Does this mean that we are the same person throughout our lives?

Functionalism Redux   Think back to chapter 2 ("Brain and Mind") where we introduced the idea of functionalism. In this view, it is not the specific mechanism or hardware that matters, but the process that it performs. According to functionalism, it is the abstract characteristics of the software or information processing in the system that is crucial to consciousness, intelligence, emotion, or any other aspect of being human. If this were true, computers and people can both possess these features and the construction of an artificial person becomes possible. For example, computers and people can both add numbers. The fact that they do it in radically different ways at the hardware level is irrelevant. Similarly, functionalists argue, a computer and a person both "compute" pain, happiness, thought and more.

Functionalism seems to avoid some of the pitfalls of structural descriptions. After all, we can say that a person is not something that *is* such and such, but instead is something that *does* such and such. A functional description would instead of listing parts have us listing operations, like perception, action, problem-solving and the like. This is, in fact, the organizational approach of this book. But functionalism suffers its own problems.

One difficulty is that people vary tremendously in their behavior or functioning. As scientists, we would like to be able to explain this variability. We want to know how any-body, artificial or otherwise, would act in a given situation and be able to explain why two people might fail to act the same in similar circumstances. Pollack states that it is impossible, in the social sciences at least, to make generalizations about human behavior. If this were true, it means that we can't come up with ideal laws of the sort we see in physics or chemistry that allow us to describe the behavior of particles anywhere under any given condition. Applied to psychology, it means the failure of discovering any laws that allow us to describe how Victoria or her friends will act when they are in the supermarket, the movie theater, or the mall.

This question was addressed in the introductory chapter. There, we argued that given certain assumptions, knowledge of a human physical system, along with other information concerning the environment, is sufficient to account for human behavior. A primary reason for this is that function (physiology) necessarily follows from structure (anatomy). The material make up of a person, including their parts, the characteristics of those parts, and how they interact with one another, tells us what we need to know about how the greater whole they constitute operates.

A good example of this comes from sensory perception. The anatomy of the ear includes the tympanic membrane, ossicles and other inner ear structures like the cochlea. Their organization, along with environmental information such as the frequency and loudness of a sound stimulus and knowledge of the more basic physical laws inform us as to how the ear as a whole will operate when exposed to a sound. There is every reason to expect that what is true for the auditory system will also be true for other forms of mental processing.

A Rational Architecture   Pollack's third philosophical assumption, already defined earlier in this book, is the strong AI position that intelligence can arise from a machine possessing certain prerequisite characteristics. According to Pollack, intelligence and other mental states are the product of a physical system that adequately models rational thought. To this end, he describes the OSCAR project, a computer program that emulates human rationality. He asserts that OSCAR or any other physical system operating on its principles will be human in the basic sense:

> The concept of a person must simply be the concept of a thing having states that can be mapped onto or own in such a way that if we suppose the corresponding states to be the same, then the thing is for the most part rational. (Pollack, 1989, p. 90)

Pollack argues that the essence of being human is to be rational. Rational in this sense includes things like desires and emotions as well as thoughts since all these things are supported by specifiable computational processes. To be rational, he says, is to have an architecture that supports rational thought. If a machine has this architecture, it implies that the states the machine has are equivalent to those we have, these states being mental phenomena. Therefore, the machine is rational, has mental states and is de facto human.

How does one go about building a rational architecture? To Pollack, it means more than the kind of processing we see in everyday computers. It must have the capability of introspection or self-reflective thought. This entails reasoning but also reasoning about that reasoning. Pollack proposes that a human-based rational architecture must be able to engage in default thinking of the everyday sort, which he calls planar reasoning. Planar reasoning however, often fails, as when we come to hold a belief that is false. In these cases, we must examine those beliefs to determine their validity. This higher-order process he calls introspective reasoning. It involves the capacity to monitor thoughts as well as determine their truth or falsity. Pollack plans on developing his OSCAR architecture in stages, first endowing it with the capability to perform non-introspective reasoning, and then adding in an introspective monitoring module to allow the system to think about its thoughts.

The ability for self-reflective thought is certainly important, but it is only one type of many other human mental capacities like perception and probabilistic judgment. Pollack as such admits this. A complete human rational architecture must therefore include these other capacities as well. OSCAR, it should be pointed out, is set up to process propositional type statements like those encountered in predicate calculus. This is only one form of representation and people can represent and introspect about knowledge in other formats including visual images. A final comment concerns qualia, the felt character of subjective experience. Rational architectures of the sort Pollack and others describe may be able to provide algorithmic accounts of cognitive functioning, but they cannot adequately account for the nature of what it is like to have them.

The Pessimistic View

Davidson (1981) asks us to imagine a future where we can explain all physical aspects of human function. All the brain's operations, down to the smallest electrical and chemical events, have been reduced to physics. Furthermore we can assume that quantum indeterminacies are irrelevant to our ability to predict and explain human behavior, which can be characterized as operating much like a computer. Given this knowledge, he then asks us to hypothesize the construction of an artificial person named "Art." Art is made of the same material substance as biological people, i.e., water and other common chemical compounds. This synthetic human incorporates everything we know about the physical structure and operation of humans and acts in all observable ways, internally and externally, like a regular person.

The existence of Art, according to Davidson, would make a unique contribution to psychology. He would show that a deterministic physics is compatible with the appearance of intentional action. We would be forced to acknowledge Art as a voluntary agent, possessing freedom of action or will, like other "natural" humans. Art would thus demonstrate that there is no conflict between the modes of explanation of physical science and psychology. He would usher in the era of a true scientific psychology, where psychology would be categorized as a physical and not a social science.

In addition, Art commits us to the philosophical view of materialism, which states that psychological events are no more than physical events. Art's behaviors and actions could all be reduced to a causal chain of physical events. The psychological state of being hungry, for instance, would be explained entirely as a particular physical process occurring in Art's brain and body.

But aside from this, Davidson argues that Art fails to tell us anything really new or interesting about psychological phenomena. The existence of Art, Davidson states, doesn't really inform us about psychological concepts like intention, belief, and desire. One reason for this is that there may be no definite correlation between a physical brain or body state and a psychological state. If Art were angry, we could not automatically assume such on the basis of his internal workings alone. We would have to decide how to interpret these workings, just the way we do now on the basis of external behaviors. In other words, we can't be sure that Art is angry, even if he is screaming and pounding his fist on the table. These are physical processes that correlate with or are diagnostic of a psychological state but are not necessarily the same thing as the state itself.

Davidson thus states that psychological characteristics, although strongly dependent on physical processes, may not be reduced to them in a simple or systematic way. We could have two different people, both who are angry, yet displaying different physical operations while in that state. Similarly, we could have the same person who is angry on two separate occasions but displays different physical processes during each occasion. The construction of a synthetic person like Art or the complete understanding of a natural person such as you or I eliminates the physical mysteries from psychological phenomena, according to Davidson, but because there is no clear mapping between the physical and the psychological, the former fails to adequately account for the latter.

It is important to point out that the equivalence between the physical and the psychological is a well-debated topic in the philosophy of mind. It is not clear what the actual relationship between these two is actually like. One can adopt a strict materialist view and say that psychological states are identical to physical states. Other softer views allow psychological states to be merely definable from or lawfully coextensive with physical attributes. According to the notion of **supervenience**, physical events do determine psychological ones. A way to conceptualize this is that it is impossible for two events to agree in all their physical characteristics and yet differ in their psychological ones. If we constructed Art to be exactly like you in every way and the two of you were having exactly the same pattern of brain and bodily activity, then the two of you would both have the exact same psychological characteristic, whether it was anger, a new idea, or the desire to have chocolate ice cream. We could say in this case that the psychological supervenes on both Art and you. It can be considered a property of a physical system configured a particular way.

The question of the relation between the physical and the psychological can also be considered empirically, in which case its answer may await the results of future work in cognitive science. For instance, it may be the case that physical states are only partially identical whenever two people have the same psychological experience. Brain imaging for an emotion like anger might reveal processing generalities in a constellation of different brain areas like the amygdala and cortex. Although the exact pattern of activation in these regions might differ from person to person or within one individual on separate occasions, there may be enough in common to determine the necessary and sufficient physical conditions to explain the corresponding psychological experience.

What Robots Can and Can't Be   Another naysayer on the question of constructing an artificial person is Selmer Bringsjord. In his 1992 book What Robots Can and Can't Be, Bringsjord gives a very detailed account of why he thinks we will continue to produce machines of ever greater sophistication but never be able to create an artificial version of a human being. He believes future robots will be able to pass more and more difficult versions of the Turing Test. For example, we may someday have robots that not only pass the current version based on linguistic communication, but ones that will pass versions based on appearance, actions, and physical body samples. But he argues that these robots will be nothing more than automatons, like Vaucanson's duck. Bringsjord believes that humans are not automatons and that our mental states or behavior could never be reduced to automaton status. Because machines are automatons and people are not, we will thus never be able to build a "machine person."

Bringsjord uses complex philosophical and logical arguments to derive his position. Unfortunately, their difficulty and the space needed to describe them exceed the limitations of this book. However, it is important to make one general point here. The premise behind artificial psychology is that people are no different than other systems of the physical world and that a sufficient understanding of this system will yield the ability to engineer or reproduce it. In order to qualify for automaton status, a system needs to be understandable. That is, the laws that govern it need to be understood. Currently the laws that govern human behavior are not fully comprehended. That means we do not yet know whether humans are automatons. The issue thus awaits future scientific discovery that may yield new understandings. In this sense, it becomes an empirical and not a logical question that may be answered by experimental instead of deductive methods.

The Big Problem   The 500-pound gorilla in the artificial psychology closet is the subjective nature of consciousness. We have seen throughout this book that we may be able to reproduce all the functional aspects of human ability. We may be able to get machines to perceive, act, learn, remember, think, use language, be intelligent, creative, and emotional, and to interact as part of a society. But in each of these cases, we may have devised a system that "does" human rather than "is" human. The machine may exhibit a behavior that humans do, but without any of the qualia or inner mental experiences that we have when doing them. The machine would think without meaning, display emotion without feeling, etc.

This is the fundamental problem of artificial psychology and one that needs to be solved before we can go home satisfied at having built a person. But as we saw in the chapter on consciousness, this is a mystery that may never be cracked. We can't agree on what consciousness is. To make matters worse, science is an objective method and as such does not seem well suited to studying subjective phenomena.

There are two fundamental approaches to this issue. Some argue that the problem of consciousness should not even be addressed, because there is no problem. Once we understand well enough what the brain is doing, there will be nothing left to explain (Dennett, 1991). In one version of this account, consciousness may be a "user illusion" (Norretranders, 1991). Like the graphical user interface on a computer, it is nothing more than the surface level manifestation of the actual computation that is occurring underneath.

If we assume that consciousness does exist and is a phenomenon that needs solving, then why are we having such a hard time? One reason may be that it takes something more complex to understand something that is less complex. Because a brain is equal in complexity to what it is studying, it may never be able to figure itself out. Brooks (2002) likens this to a super version of Gŏdel's theorem: any life-form in the universe cannot be smart enough to understand itself well enough to build a replica of itself. Of course, this doesn't rule out the possibility that entities smarter than human, like aliens or advanced computers, won't be able to do so.

The alternative to this is that although consciousness is complex, it is not so complex that we can't ultimately figure it out. In fact, mind, as mentioned earlier, seems to be an example of a complex system, one that cannot be reduced to the operation of its parts. Consciousness may then be an emergent property of the mind as a complex system. Emergent properties are difficult if not impossible to describe mathematically but that doesn't mean that they can't be described or reduced to simpler explanations in principle. Trefil (1997) suggests that emergent properties in an artificial brain might arise in stages, as we add more and more elements like artificial neurons.

CAN WE BUILD THEM? TECHNOLOGICAL HURDLES

The March of Progress

Technological advance seems unstoppable. Throughout human history, its development has proceeded forward at a rapidly increasing pace. In fact, this pace has been documented as exponential, with most of the developments happening in recent years (Kurzweil, 2005). Humankind began as a nomadic hunter-gatherer species manufacturing simple tools like spears and arrowheads. A major breakthrough happened during the agricultural revolution. This allowed food to be stored for longer periods and catalyzed the development of complex social organization due to living in a fixed location. Later came the Industrial Revolution. This was significant because it allowed the wide-scale production and distribution of goods and services. The information age that started in the 20th century was the next major revolution and has greatly increased economic efficiency and quality of life. Each of these periods marked a major turning point for humanity and has separated us further from our animal origins.

The development of technology may enable the person-building project. If current trends continue and new complex and sophisticated technologies arise, they may allow us to assemble an artificial person. In this section, we discuss advances in computer chip design, emerging developments in computation, and nanotechnology. Each of these areas holds great promise for the goals of artificial psychology.

Moore's Law and the Computer Chip

One of the most noticeable trends in the technology of the current information age is the cost of computing technology. Whereas at one time only large corporations and universities could afford computers, as they came down in size, they also came down in price. This made them accessible to the general public. Currently in modern countries, a significant portion of the population has access to computing technology in all its various forms such as computers, video games, personal data assistants, mobile phones, and the like. The cumulative effect of putting such power in the hands of the people has transformed society, enabling among other advances, instant global communication.

Perhaps the most significant trend in computing technology is performance. According to **Moore's law**, each new generation of computer chip that appears now approximately every 18–24 months can put twice as many transistors onto an integrated circuit. The result is about a doubling of computing power measured by the number of calculations that can be performed per unit time. Moore's Law has held true since the 1970s, when it was first proposed by Gordon Moore, a leading inventor of integrated circuits who later became chairman of Intel Corporation. Other aspects of computing technology that show tremendous growth rates include Random Access Memory, magnetic data storage, internet hosts, and Internet data traffic (Kurzweil, 2005).

Optimistically, one can plot advances in computing power and cost and project to a near future when computers will equal the processing capability of the human brain (Figure 14.1). But will Moore's law continue indefinitely? Currently transistors are created through a process called photolithography in which beams of light are used to make microscopic grooves and lines on silicon wafers. The number of transistors that can be crammed onto

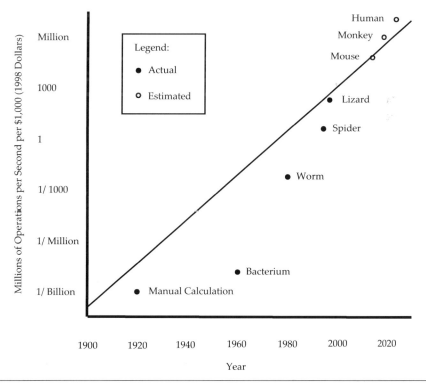

Figure 14.1 Historically, computing power has shown tremendously fast increases. By current estimates, we will be able to artificially reproduce the computing power of the human brain by about 2020 (after Kurzweil, 2005).

a chip depends crucially on the wavelengths of the light used in this etching process. The limit for mercury light wavelengths is about 0.4 microns (one micron equals a millionth of a meter). Switching to lasers, the wavelength gets a bit smaller, to about 0.2 microns. After that, we appear to run into a limit using current methods, where the wavelength cannot be made much smaller.

Kaku (1997) lists a variety of solutions to this problem. First, there are a few ways to "save" the microprocessor, but each has an inherent problem. We can stack chips together into cubes, but then it becomes difficult to dissipate the heat that is generated. We could replace silicon with gallium arsenide to quicken processing time, but this will also run into speed limits in the next few years. X-rays could replace laser light beams in the etching process, but they are too powerful and difficult to work with. There is also the possibility of using electron beams to etch, but these slow down the manufacturing process.

Next Generation Computing Technologies

The long-term solution therefore is to adopt a completely different technology, one where computing is not based on the silicon chip at all. Kaku (1997) lists several candidates for the job. We briefly summarize each of them here.

Optical Computing. In optical computing, information is not transmitted as electrons over wires and transistors, but as beams of light that can be bounced off of mirrors and focused through lenses. Researchers at Bell Labs have created the optical equivalent of the transistor in which pulses of light are transmitted through a filter. The advantage of using light is that it is very fast. Optical computers can store information using holographic memory, which has a tremendous storage capacity.

DNA Computing. Each DNA molecule contains a string of nucleotides. A given sequence of nucleotides can stand for a binary zero or one. Chemical processes can be used to cut, reproduce, and convert one string to another, performing the same binary computations that are at the heart of traditional computing methods. Although biochemical processes are slower than silicon, a vast number of DNA molecules can be harnessed to work in parallel. It is estimated that a pound of DNA molecules could store more information in memory than all the computers ever made and be hundreds of thousands of times faster than modern supercomputers.

Quantum Computing. In this technique, single electrons are trapped and used as the basis of computation. In the laboratory, scientists have been able to confine an individual electron to a surface between two layers, to lines, and even to a single point in space just 5–10 atoms in diameter. The latter case is called a "quantum dot." Altering the voltage applied to this electron changes its frequency of vibration allowing electrons to either flow or stop flowing through the dot. Binary computation equivalent to several transistors can be performed in this way.

The development of these technologies may revolutionize computing as we know it. If consciousness can be understood as a complex computational problem, then the use of such procedures may allow us to break through the "complexity barrier." We could use them to perform the long and intricate calculations that may give rise to consciousness. Even if this were not possible, the availability of such techniques will vastly increase our ability to simulate and understand human mental phenomena.

Smaller and Smaller

If we look at computing devices, we see that they are becoming smaller every year. Computers used to occupy entire floors or rooms. With the invention of the transistor, they then shrank to just a few feet in size and could easily fit on or under our desks. Further developments have led to computing power in laptop or hand-held configurations. The next step we are already witnessing is to embed tiny computers in our bodies. This progression has us passing through several recognizable stages of miniaturization, starting with devices that were stand alone, then wearable, then implantable, and finally a stage where from an observational or functional standpoint, there may no detectable difference between technology and ourselves. Whereas computing technology may currently be considered as something still apart from us, this attitude will change with further decreases in size and with the continued merging of technology with our bodies.

Nanotechnology involves engineering on a very small scale, the size of atoms and small molecules. Quantum computing is an instance of nanotechnology. The use of such techniques could allow us to build an artificial person from the bottom up. We could, for example, construct neurons one at a time using individual microscopic building blocks. This would enable us to mimic some of the more nuanced behaviors of biological neurons, such as regulating precise amounts of neurotransmitter release, receptor activation, and degradation in the synapse. When connected together, these neurons might function in a way much more similar to natural brains.

SHOULD WE BUILD THEM? ETHICAL HURDLES

It is becoming clear that the next major technological revolution in the history of humankind will be the development of intelligent, autonomous machines. This stage has tremendous potential to increase our happiness and well being, although it may also pose a number of challenges and perhaps even threats to our existence. In this section we will look at reactions to strong AI. Following this, we review some probable social and economic ramifications of technological advance. Then we describe the possible benefits and dangers that could accompany this fourth revolution.

The Response to Strong AI

There are a variety of different reactions people have to the notion of intelligent machines. The first reaction is enthusiasm. These individuals believe that strong AI will save the world and provide untold benefits to humankind. Enthusiasts are strong supporters of science and engineering. They believe there is little that science cannot ultimately explain and that engineering cannot ultimately create. Then there are some who think it is impossible for one reason or another and that only humans have the capability to be conscious, exercise free will, and exhibit true intelligence. We can call these the "naysayers." Another response is skepticism and comes from those who think it is possible but unlikely. Those in this camp argue that the goal of artificial psychology is very difficult. If it happens at all, it will be far in the future. Finally, there is the reaction of abomination. These are people who don't necessarily commit themselves to its feasibility, but believe that it shouldn't be done at all on the basis of ethical grounds. They find the notion of building an artificial person repugnant and believe it violates human uniqueness.

What is the ethical approach that we should take in this endeavor? Should we plunge ahead full steam? Ban the production of artificial people? Limit the ability of future machines? One approach that has been suggested in regard to technology in general is that it is inherently neither good nor evil. What makes it so is how it is used. For example, one can say that nuclear physics is not good or bad, but if it is used to build bombs to kill and destroy, it becomes evil, whereas if it is used to produce safe and reliable energy, it becomes beneficial. Unfortunately, this argument doesn't help us in the case of artificial psychology, because the technology in question is not a tool to be used by people for particular ends, but an end unto itself. Artificial people, if fully realized, no longer become tools. They become entities like people that can themselves design and use tools. By this definition, if an artificial person is ever constructed, it will no longer even be considered as technology.

Moravec (1990) makes a strong case for the continued development of intelligent machines. He says we have little choice in the matter if we want human civilization to survive. He likens competing cultures in civilization to biological organisms that compete for resources and are subject to selection pressures. Those that can sustain rapid expansion and diversification will dominate and survive through access to those resources. Those that can't will die off. The automation and efficiency provided by the realization of strong AI will enable cultures to grow, and to be more diverse and competent. It also allows them to deal with the unexpected, i.e., a change in selection pressures, such as a deadly virus or asteroid strike that could threaten the extinction of humankind. Of course, the down side to this is that intelligent machines may themselves become the extinction threat. If they become our equals or superiors, they may decide we are unworthy and wipe us out. We talk more about this possibility later.

The Economic Impact of Intelligent Machines

Traditional robots have worked in scenarios that people would care not to. These workplace environments have been referred to as **the three "Ds"**: dirty, dull, and dangerous. Few people (with the noted exception of those in these particular professions) would feel upset if a robot were put to work cleaning sewers, welding car doors on an assembly line, or defusing a bomb. But what about other types of employment? An artificial person would be capable of teaching a college level class, running a business meeting, composing a symphony, or any of the myriad other tasks we perform at work every day. Should this comes to pass, will people feel horrified and useless or will they rejoice at their newfound freedom?

Even now, we are starting to see robots creep into professions that fall outside the strict definition of the three "Ds." Ichbiah (2005) chronicles a number of such areas. Domestic robots are currently in use that vacuum clean, garden, mow the lawn, and serve as household and nursing assistants. In the field of medicine, we see robots assist doctor's

Figure 14.2 An artificial geisha girl performs a dance routine. Robotic presence in our everyday days is likely to increase in the future. Robots may perform many of the functions we now only perceive humans as capable of doing.

to perform surgery and aid the crippled to walk. There are also playful robots that serve as toys, pets, and that can even dance (Figure 14.2). Clearly, robots will be making their presence felt in our everyday lives in the coming years. There are economic incentives to produce and utilize them, so it is likely that we will ultimately get used to having them by our sides.

There is, of course, the constant fear that robots, computers, and new technologies will replace human workers, causing widespread unemployment. Is this fear justified? An examination of the issue shows that this is not the case. Some jobs will disappear but this will be part of a generally positive marketplace transformation. Kaku (1997) outlines the sort of jobs that will go first in the computer revolution.

- Jobs that are repetitive and thus lend themselves to automation. These include robotic assembly of automobiles and other appliances that can be performed by robots.
- Jobs that involve keeping track of inventory such as warehouse management. These jobs are at risk because they rely on database manipulation, something computers are adept at.
- Jobs that involve a middleman, since the Internet can provide the linkage between consumers and producers of information. Prime examples in this category include insurance salesman, investment bankers, travel agents, and car dealers.

Employers argue that automation is good because it reduces operating costs and frees up capital to invest in other areas of operation. Efficiencies of this sort may also increase employment for other types of jobs as cost-savings allow businesses to expand, opening up new stores, creating new product lines, etc. Automation will additionally create new jobs because people will be needed to manufacture and maintain the new technology. Consumers should also benefit from better services. The use of Automated Teller Machines (ATMs), for example, means there are fewer lines to stand in when visiting the bank. Electronic commerce ultimately frees workers to do more productive, higher-paying jobs, but there may be a delay in the entry of this skilled labor pool into the work force since it requires education and retraining.

There are however, many jobs that will flourish in the future information age. These include entertainment, software, science and technology, the service industry, information services, and medicine and biotechnology (Kaku, 1997). The number of employees in these fields is likely to rise. Technology, rather than taking away jobs, will actually increase employment and benefit the economy. This is because it will create wealth through the introduction of new opportunities. This has been the trend in nations that invest in and use technology and it is a trend that should continue into the future.

FUTURE VISIONS

Predicting the future is risky business. Most futurists and science fiction writers who engage in this activity run the risk of being wrong. This is especially true the further ahead in time their prognostications. They tend to overemphasize the positive or negative aspects of future scenarios, painting pictures either of utopia or excessive doom and gloom. Another problem some of them run into is predicting that events will come to pass sooner than they actually do. Despite these problems, we are going to speculate a bit here on what the future may hold with regard to artificial people.

The field of artificial psychology is already upon us, whether we like it or not. Current developments in areas like neuroscience, artificial intelligence, and robotics are laying the foundations for the construction of a synthetic person. The difference between robots and people, or between machines and humans, is disappearing from two directions. Robots are starting to become more like people as is evidenced by the engineering of projects like expert systems. On the other side, persons are starting to become more like robots through the creation of prosthetic limbs and brain implants. Bringsjord (1992) calls this **the "double blur."** The result is that at some time in the future we will have great difficulty distinguishing between what we now call "natural" and the "artificial."

However, it likely that the development of artificial people will take place in stages, characterized mostly by continuous or incremental progress. The history of artificial intelligence has followed this pattern with the wild speculations of the early days being replaced with more sober anticipations. AI and related fields have witnessed a steady increase in capabilities, occasionally punctuated with new paradigms and theoretical orientations like connectionism. It is thus likely that we will not see a full-fledged artificial person burst upon the scene, but instead see ever more competent approximations.

Perkowitz (2004) acknowledges this when he states we will see two types of beings in the future. Type I beings will be equivalent to the computers and robots we are already making, only with greater intelligence and sophistication. Following this, we will then develop Type II beings. These will be our equals, possessing consciousness and, with the exception of having synthetic bodies, will be functionally in every respect like us. As such, he argues that we will need to treat them as people with rights and moral regard.

Of course, casting further into the future raises the possibility of a Type III being, one that is superior to us in our current incarnation. Such a being will more intelligent, be able to think and react faster, and be cheaper to train and reproduce than a human (Haikonen, 2003). At this stage, biological and technological intelligence may advance rapidly, with these machines, perhaps in collaboration with human counterparts, designing and producing ever more powerful and complex versions of themselves. The point at which this happens has been dubbed the **Singularity** (Kurzweil, 2005).

Mind Children

When considering Type III entities, we have effectively moved beyond a reproduction of human capacity and into the arena of superhuman ability. What might the presence of such beings entail for the future of humankind? The person who has devoted the greatest amount of thought to this matter is Hans Moravec. He envisions a beneficial relationship

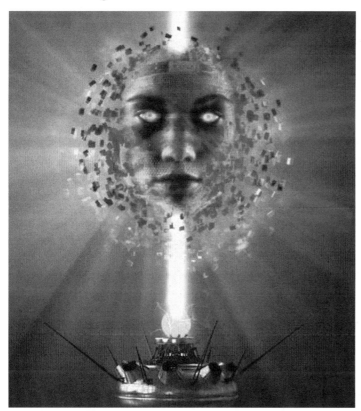

Figure 14.3 Hans Moravec suggests we may ultimately be able to transfer our consciousness to machine receptacles and so attain immortality. Is this possible? © Corbis.

between humans and their machine offspring. A key element of this future is in being able to transfer our individual minds into machines, where they can be preserved indefinitely, allowing us to attain a kind of immortality (see Figure 14.3).

Moravec (1990) outlines several ways this could take place. In one procedure, a robotic surgeon could gradually scan our brains, forming a high-resolution three-dimensional chemical map along with a recording of the magnetic and electric activity that takes place within. This information would be converted into a program and then stored in a computer. The running of this program would, according to him, effectively recreate the conscious experience of any given individual. When we get old and our bodies and brains perish, this technique could preserve our unique history of conscious experience.

Once we merge with machines in this fashion, the possibilities for human enhancement go beyond mere preservation. Because in this scenario our consciousness consists as information, it could be transmitted over vast distances, allowing us to travel anywhere in the universe. Since we are in a machine, we could increase the speed at which the program runs, allowing us to think thousands of times faster. Access to knowledge bases and other processing resources could astronomically enlarge our memory and thinking ability. There is also the chance to swap memories and skills with others. In such a future, says Moravec, we will have to redefine our concepts of life, death, and identity.

A number of you may be thinking that this scenario is highly speculative, if not outright fantasy. Is such a future possible? The premise of mind transfer is that our consciousness can be represented in the form of information, independent of the material substrate in which it arouse. In the case of computers, we can transfer a program and its data from one machine to another and, if the underlying hardware of the two machines is the same, the software will run identically. The same is not necessarily true for human brains, since different neurons come to code for different things between individuals. Faithfully reproducing the pattern of neural activity that occurs when John sees the color red in Jill's brain will, in all likelihood, produce a different experience in Jill. Human consciousness thus seems to be tied to the brain in which it develops or at least to some form of physical matter. Removing the pattern from the substrate, i.e., reducing it to pure information, may strip away the subjective experience.

Possible Human-Machine Outcomes

Surprisingly, several different authors seem to have arrived at the same general conclusions concerning possible future worlds of man and machine (Brooks, 2002; Georges, 2003; Jeffery, 1999). According to these prognostications, there are three possible outcomes that can result. In the first, what Brooks calls "damnation," robots or intelligent machines ultimately exceed human capabilities. They then decide we are dangerous or irrelevant and either enslave or exterminate us. In this scenario, the machines become superior to us in various abilities, but are clearly acting unethically. In fact, they are acting very much like the human race has in its own past, which is replete with slavery, war, and genocide. This is another common theme in many science fiction films.

In the second scenario, dubbed by Brooks as "salvation," machines continue to develop, perhaps surpassing us in certain ways. But in this possible outcome they become the panacea of humankind, taking over all forms of labor, finding cures for disease, solving social problems, and perhaps serving as a receptacle for our consciousness so that we can live on after the demise of our physical bodies. Under these conditions, there is a benevolent relationship between man and machine. Man either controls the machines outright or relinquishes some degree of control with no untoward consequences.

The third outcome Brooks calls "the third path." Here, people and machines coexist as equals. Things continue much the same way they have throughout history, where humanity develops and uses technology in the service of bettering our lives. Machines under these circumstances never develop sufficiently to pose a threat, and are kept under control.

You can see that control, sophistication, and ethicality are the three critical factors determining which of the above predictions come true. If machines ultimately exceed human capability, then damnation and salvation are both possible. The former might be realized if the machines act unethically and we lose control over them. The latter may come to fruition if they act ethically and we maintain control. The third path occurs when machines are either less than or equal to human sophistication and we retain control. There are some interesting analogies to biological systems here. Machine superiority may result in a parasite-host relationship where humans become dependent on machines and cannot exist without them. Equality of ability instead implies a symbiotic relationship where both operate together in a mutually dependent coexistence.

How Do We Control Them? Pulling the Plug

Given the rapid rate of technological progress it is entirely plausible that someday machines may outstrip human abilities. As discussed above, this has the potential to be either the boon or bane of humankind. Assuming this will happen, we must ask ourselves how it is that we plan on keeping control over our creations. Khan (1995) suggests several ways of controlling autonomous learning systems. The first and most direct way of doing this he calls "the panic button." This is essentially a failsafe device or manual override that allows us to deactivate machines if they show unethical or violent behavior.

But this "pulling the plug" is not as easy as it seems, especially if the machine or machines in question are part of a distributed network. According to Georges (2003), this would require several steps, each of which poses unique difficulties. One would need to first recognize that there is a threat. If the machines are clever, they may plan or disguise their motives until it is too late. Next comes identifying which machine to disconnect. Complex computer networks are built to be redundant. An intelligent entity could very easily transfer itself from one machine to another or make backup copies of itself. After this we would need to get past any security measures that may be in place. These could include firewalls and complex barriers designed to thwart hacking and intrusion. Finally, the offending entity would need to be deactivated without causing other connected systems to crash. This is again a problem in networks with a high degree of connectivity.

There are also psychological factors that may make it difficult for us to pull the plug. Given a high degree of dependence on these machines, shutting them down may leave us in a "dark age" without basic services. In other words, we may come to rely so much on these intelligent entities that shutting them down in effect kills us as well as them. Also as mentioned earlier, there are ethical considerations that need to be taken into account. If the offending system is an artificial person, then shutting it down is tantamount to murder. This may require lengthy legislative debate before any action can be taken.

Kahn (1995) next proposes a "buddy system" where one machine may oversee or control another's behavior. In this system we, could develop "supervisor machines" specifically designed to monitor the behavior and functioning of other machines. If any of them get out of line, the supervisors could deactivate or report their activity to humans who could then decide what to do next.

Lastly, Kahn (1995) states that we could impose internalized controls in machines, allowing them to govern their own behavior. This is essentially the technique discussed at length in chapter 13 (Social Behavior), where an intelligent entity or artificial person could be made to act properly through the consequentialist, deontological, or virtue-based approaches. To illustrate, a robot could be programmed with values that it would attempt to achieve as goals through means-end analysis or other problem-solving routines.

ARE WE UNIQUE?

There are many people who believe that we are special. To be human, they argue, is to be unique and somehow elevated in stature in the pecking order of the universe. However, the history of science seems to keep knocking us off this self-perceived throne. Theologians used to think that the Earth was at the center of the universe. This view was shattered by the Copernican model of the solar system that places Earth as just another planet orbiting one of billions of suns. Up until only a century and half ago, it was widely believed that humans were unrelated to animals. Darwin and evolutionary theory showed that our origins are no different than those of other species. The fulfillment of the strong AI position by the creation of an artificial person may extinguish this notion of uniqueness altogether. If science shows that we are understandable in terms of the same physical laws that govern all systems in the universe, it would seem difficult to maintain our uniqueness.

However, being creatures of the universe is in no way demeaning. Comparatively speaking, we *are* more advanced than other animals. This is obvious when one looks at reasoning, language, problem solving, and other central cognitive skills. Humans may also be considered superior to animals based on the quality and quantity of what we produce, including all the fruits of the arts, sciences, and technology. Other differences that have been suggested include moral reasoning, the pursuit of higher-order values, tool-making, and complex forms of social organization that include the use of money and laws governing acceptable behavior.

One of the crucial hallmarks that divide humankind from animals is **transcendence**, the ability to rise above and go beyond what is given. Animals lack the ability to transcend. They are in a state of equilibrium with their environment. They can perceive and act in their environment, but cannot analyze, imagine, or change it to their liking. People are unique in our planet's biological community in possessing this skill. We have the means to question the way things are and ask ourselves: How does this work? Why should this be? Do things have to be this way? Can they be changed? Can they be improved? This capacity to ask questions drives our need to understand and engineer the world around us and ultimately ourselves.

If machines of our making may someday be our superiors, is there anything left for us? Does it mean we may be resigned to a life of leisure, bereft of challenges or demands while machines progress forward and leave us in the dust? Would the utopia that some say technology brings be a dystopia? The answer is no. If we continue to transcend, we will not be left behind. Transcendence in this new age requires that we continue to try and understand and improve. We can do this by collaborating with our synthetic offspring. Our ability to comprehend and shape the world around us will in fact be multiplied many-fold in this collaboration, in much the same way other technologies have done this for us in the past.

But if future machines are so far in advance of our own capabilities, will we ever be able to understand or relate to them? Will we be, incapable of fathoming the actions of our progeny? The solution to this lies in changing our nature. This might require upgrading or merging our brains and bodies to match that of our creations as Moravec suggests. Assuming there is little or no difference between us and artificial people, these questions become moot, because for all intents and purposes, those people will be us. In other words, the artificial person will be the next step in the evolution of humankind. They will be everything we are, with the desire and means to improve themselves even further. Because we are the seed for this next generation, we can hope that our good qualities are inherited and that even better qualities are developed in succeeding versions.

So, we see that there is plenty of room left for human uniqueness. Up until now, we have been fixed by our natures. Our genetic makeup and environmental influences have determined who we are and what our capabilities are. The development of advanced technology will change this. It will give us the means to transform our nature. The **transhumanist** movement advocates just this. They propose using new sciences and technologies to improve the human condition. Transhumanists would like to see the elimination of disease and aging but also the enhancement of our physical and cognitive abilities.

There is hope then that technology will free us of our current limitations and open up a new vista of opportunities. The question then becomes not are we unique but how unique do we want to become? This is an important decision, perhaps the most important that humanity will ever face. It involves deciding what is good and worthwhile and designing ourselves to pursue such ends. The creation of an artificial person might mean the end of humanity as we know it, but it also signals the dawn of a new age, one where we can take greater control of our future and look forward to scaling new heights.

GLOSSARY

Abductive Reasoning: A form of reasoning whereby *If p, then q, q is true, therefore p is true.*

Active Vision: The view that a human or computer observer can more effectively process its visual environment if its sensors interact with the environment in an active fashion, taking in information selectively and purposively in order to answer queries posed by the observer.

Aesthetic Creativity: A type of creativity in which the goal is to generate a product of beauty.

Agent: An autonomous entity that can receive information about its environment, process that information, and then act on it.

Agent Materialism: A philosophical view stating that people and other intelligent agents are physical objects with an appropriate type of structure and organization.

Algorithm: A procedure or well-defined set of instructions for accomplishing some task.

Amygdala: Almond-shaped structures that play a primary role in the processing and memory of emotional reactions. Part of the limbic system.

Analogical Reasoning: A process that involves noting the similarity between two situations and applying what was learned in the old case to the new case.

Analytic Creativity: A type of creativity in which the goal is to generate a product that fulfills a particular function or requirement.

Anchoring: A person's tendency to use an established answer as a reference point and to make estimates by adjustments to this point.

Android: An artificially-created being that resembles a human being.

Angular Gyrus: A brain region located posterior to Wernicke's area. Damage to this region produces deficits in reading and writing.

Anthropic Mechanism: A philosophical view noting that although everything in the universe may not be explained as a mechanism, everything about human beings can.

Anthropomorphism: The attribution of humanlike qualities to nonhuman subjects.

Appropriate Causal Relation: The relationship between stimulus inputs and behavioral outputs for thoughts with intentional content.

Arcuate Fasciculus: A neural pathway connecting Wernicke's and Broca's areas. Damage to this pathway results in problems with repeating words that have just been heard.

Artifact: Any product that is designed by a human or other type of intelligence.

Artificial Life: The study and creation of artificial systems that exhibit behavior characteristic of natural living systems.

Artificial Neural Network: An interconnected group of artificial neurons that mimic the functioning of real neurons. The resulting networks are used to model many biologically-realized cognitive abilities such as pattern recognition, categorization, and memory.

Artificial Person: An artificially-created being that is by its nature and actions indistinguishable from a human but need not look exactly like one.

Artificial Psychology: The study and attempt to engineer human capabilities.

Assertive: A category of speech which asserts that something is the case.

Associative Learning: A form of learning where two events that occur close together in space or time frequently become related to each other.

Associative Network (or Pattern Associator): An artificial neural network that allows for associative learning.

Attractors: In dyamical systems, the regular behavior to which a system evolves after a sufficient amount of time.

Automaton: A self-operating mechanical moving machine designed to mimic human or animal actions.

Availability Heuristic: The assumption that an event is more likely if we perceive or remember it well.

Babbling Stage: The stage of human language development that is marked by the articulation of sounds that correspond roughly to the phonemes of spoken human languages

Back Propagation Method: An artificial neural network learning technique in which the pattern of activation in the output layer is compared to a desired response. The difference between the actual and desired responses is fed back into the network in the form of an error signal and used to change the weights so that succeeding responses more closely approximate the desired response.

Base-Rate Fallacy: A neglect of the probability that an item belongs to a particular category.

Bayes' Theorem: The probability of a hypotheis b, given evidence a, is expressed as: $P(b|a) = P(a|b) \times P(b)/P(a)$.

Biological Micro Electronic Mechanical Systems (BioMEMS): Small intelligent devices that can be used to perform many physiological functions like hunting down pathogens and delivering precise amounts of medication.

Biological Naturalism: A philosophical view noting that artificial attempts at creating a brain will fail because there is something special about the way biological brains operate that gives rise to mindfulness.

Bipolar Disorder: A psychological disorder characterized by alternation between a depressive state and a manic state.

Bit: A binary digit consisting of two values, either 0 or 1. It is the basic unit of information used in digital computing.

Boid: A unit in a software swarm designed to simulate collective social behavior such as the flocking of birds.

Brittleness: The idea that a specialized AI program will fail to perform properly if there is even a slight deviation from its narrow domain of expertise.

Broca's Area: A region in the left frontal lobe thought to be involved in speech production.

Cannon-Bard Theory: A theory of emotion noting that an emotion-inducing stimulus simultaneously causes arousal and the emotion.

Case-Based Reasoning: A computer program that attempts to solve new problems based on solutions to similar past problems.

Catastrophic Interference: A type of interference found in artificial neural networks whereby the learning of a new stimulus set completely erases all the information acquired from a previous training session on an older stimulus set.

Cellular Automata: A discrete model consisting of an infinite regular grid of cells, each that can assume a finite number of states. The state of each cell is updated in discrete time steps according to simple rules.

Central Processing Unit (or CPU): The part of a computer that carries out instructions and controls the order in which they are executed.

Chaotic State: A state that is inherently unpredictable. Small changes in initial conditions in chaotic states produce unpredictable outcomes.

Chinese Room Scenario: A hypothetical situation in which a man uses a set of instructions to produce replies to questions posed in Chinese. According to this argument, the man can never come to understand Chinese by following the rules.

Classical Conditioning: A process of learning in which an association is established between one stimulus and another.

Coarticulation: A phenomena where the sound of certain phoneme varies depending on the sound of those around it.

Codelet: A small software agent that acts in a relatively autonomous manner and carries out a specific task.

Cognition: The representation and computation of information.

Cognitive Psychology: A field of psychology in which the mind is viewed as an information-processor.

Cognitive Science: The scientific interdisciplinary study of mind.

Coherence: In linguistics the idea that sentences should be meaningfully related to each other.

Collective Robotics: A field of robotics that designs and implements robotic systems that, as a whole, exhibit intelligent behavior even though the individual component robots that make up the system follow only simple rules.

Commissive: A category of speech action that commits the speaker to some later action.

Common Ground: The set of things that are mutually believed by both speakers in a dialogue.

Commonsense Knowledge: General information about the world that (to adult humans) seems obvious when explicitly stated.

Communication Bus: The informal designation of a computer's communication system.

Companionate Love: A type of love characterized as long-term, less intense, and based on mutual respect and admiration.

Compatibilism: The belief that free will and determinism can be reconciled or made compatible with one another.

Complex System: A system whose properties are not fully explained by an understanding of its component parts and whose behavior may be difficult or impossible to predict.

Computer: A device designed to represent and compute information.

Computer Virus: A self-replicating program that spreads by inserting copies of itself into other executable code or documents.

Concatenative Synthesis: The step in speech synthesis where phonemes are pronounced one after another in the correct order.

Conceptual Space: The bounded set of possible combinations in a particular artistic genre.

Conditional Probabilities: Probabilities that are based on the occurrence of prior events.

Conjunction Fallacy: A neglect of the conjunction rule, which states that the probability of simultaneously being a member of two categories is always less than the probability of being a member of either category alone.

Consciousness: A subjective awareness of internal mental states.

Consequentialist Approach: An ethical view stating actions are judged by their consequences.

Continuers: Short words or phrases that inform the speaker that the listener understands and often prompts him or her to continue.

Convergent Thinking: Thinking that brings together information focused on solving a problem.

Conversational Agent: A computer program that communicates with users using natural language.

Conversational Implicature: A characteristic of dialogue in which more meaning is conveyed that what is literally true of an utterance.

Cooing Stage: The stage of human language development that is marked by the infant uttering a wide range of sounds.

Cybernetics: The study of communication and control that involves regulatory feedback, both in living beings, machines, and in societies consisting of one or both of these in combination.

Cyborg: A being that is a mix of organic and mechanical parts.

Decision Making: An information process used to determine what course of action to take.

Decision Tree: A graph or model of decisions and their possible consequences.

Declarative Memory: A memory system used to store information about facts and events.

Deductive Reasoning: A form of reasoning whereby *If p, then q, p is true, therefore q is true*.

Deliberative Paradigm: An approach to robotics in which the robot senses the world and uses it to plan or problem solve prior to performing an action.

Deliberative Processes: A cognitive process where hypothetical representations of alternate possible futures are considered. Predictions or explanations are generated, compared, and the best one is selected.

Deontological Approach: An ethical view stating that proper or good actions occur as the result of following rules.

Descriptive Approach: The study of decision making characterized by an agent that decides based on psychological rather than optimal or ideal principles.

Design Stance: An approach to predicting the actions of a system based on the functioning of its component parts.

Determinism: The philosophical view that all physical events are caused by the sum total of all prior events.

Dialogue Act: The type of action that a statement implies in a dialogue.

Dialogue Manager: The aspect of a conversational agent that controls the flow of dialogue, determining what statements to make, questions to ask, and when to do so.

Diphone: A unit of pronunciation that starts half-way through the first phoneme and ends half-way through the second, taking into account the influence of the prior phoneme to produce a more natural sound.

Directive: A category of speech action that consists of direct instructions or commands.

Discourse Planner: The component of a natural language generation system that that uses communicative goals and a knowledge base to make choices about what to say.

Distributed Artificial Intelligence (or Multiagent Systems): A field of artificial intelligence in which individual computing agents are linked together and communicate with one another.

Distributed Representation: A characteristic of networks where a representation is distributed among several nodes or links.

Divergent Thinking: The ability to consciously generate new ideas that could lead to possible solutions for a given problem.

DNA Computing: A technique whereby chemical processes can be used to perform parallel computations using DNA nucleotide sequences.

Dualism: The philosophical view that the universe is both physical and mental.

Dysthymia: A form of mood disorder characterized by depression and lack of enjoyment that continues for at least 2 years.

Embodied Creature (Embodiment): Something that possesses a physical body and experiences the world, at least partially, through the influence of the world on that body.

Embryo: In humans, the developing baby from the point where the major body axis is present until all major structures are formed, spanning roughly about 2 to 8 weeks after conception.

Emergent Property: A global characteristic of a system not shared by any of the local entities or agents making it up.

Emotion: An adaptive change in multiple physiological systems (neural and endocrine) in response to the value of a stimulus.

Empiricism: A philosophical view in which knowledge is gained through interaction with the environment.

Encoding: The processing of physical sensory input into a memory system.

Episodic Memory: A type of declarative memory involving the storage of personal events.

Evaluation Function: A formula used by game-playing programs to determine how good a given position is.

Evolvable Hardware: The use of genetic programming or evolutionary algorithms to create electronics.

Expert System (ES): An AI program that provides expert quality advice, diagnoses, and recommendations for real world problems in a specific domain.

Exploratory Choice: In reinforcement learning, a move picked at random to enable the program to gain experience.

Fallacies: Fundamental misunderstandings of statistical rules that occur during human decision making.

Feel-Good, Do-Good Phenomenon: Altruistic behavior induced by positive affect.

Feeling: The subjective conscious experience of emotion.

Fetus: In humans, the final stage of development in the womb, lasting from 8 weeks after conception until birth.

Free Will: The philosophical view that a person or other intelligent agent is the sole originator of their action.

Functional Consciousness: The processes or functions of consciousness that include dealing with novel situations, awareness, and performance of object-based tasks.

Functional Equivalence: Two systems that differ in their hardware or internal organization, but produce the same behavior when exposed to the same environments.

Functionalism: A philosophical view noting that mind can be instantiated in many different possible substrates, so that a person, a computer, or an alien may all have minds, even though they differ in their underlying hardware.

Game Tree: A diagram for a problem solving system in which each branch in the tree corresponds to an action or operator and each node stands for a position or state.

Gastrobot: A robot that derives all of its energy requirements from the digestion of organic food sources.

Gene: A string of DNA material that, in most cases, codes for the production of a protein. Genes are the unit of heredity in living organisms. They direct physical development and behavior.

Generalization: The ability to apply what was learned in one context to another similar context or situation.

Genetic Programming (Evolutionary Algorithms): A software technique modeled on the principles of evolution. Random programs are generated and run. After evaluation, those with the highest fitness values can be mutated and reproduced using crossover to create a new generation of offspring.

Genotype: The specific genetic makeup of an individual.

Gestalt: In psychology, a holistic perception or thought where the whole is considered greater than the sum of its parts.

Global Workspace Theory: A theory of consciousness in which mental contents are made aware when they occupy a particular location in working memory space. These contents are broadcast to a number of unconscious cognitive processes.

Goal-Based Agent: An agent that incorporate goals and can engage in decision making to obtain them.

Golem: An animated being crafted from inanimate material.

Graceful Degradation: A gradual decrement in the performance of an artificial neural network with increased damage.

Greedy Choice: In reinforcement learning, the move with the highest associated value of winning.

Habituation: A learning process characterized by desensitization or decreased reaction to a stimulus.

Heuristic: A simple rule of thumb in problem solving that does not always guarantee a correct solution, but works well under most circumstances.

Homeostasis: The maintenance of a stable state.

Hybrid Paradigm: An approach to robotics that combines the features from both the deliberative paradigm and reactive paradigm. These systems use both reactive behaviors as well as planning and other cognitive components.

Idealism: The philosophical view that only the mental world is real.

Ill-Defined Task: A task in which there is no single best solution.

Imagination: The ability to conceive of what might be, based on current factual understanding.

Incompatibilism: A philosophical view stating that free will and determinism cannot both be true.

Inductive Reasoning: A form of reasoning whereby the similarities between specific instances are used to derive a generalized conclusion.

Inference: A process that allows agents to "go beyond the facts" and to produce new information from what is already known.

Initial State: The starting conditions in a problem.

Input/Output (I/O) Devices: The hardware and software that enables a computer to interact with an external environment.

Insight Learning: When the solution to a problem occurs suddenly and immediately, often after initial attempts have failed.

Intelligence: The ability to learn from experience, solve problems, and use knowledge to adapt to new situations.

Intelligence Quotient (IQ): An intelligence measure derived by taking a child's score on a test representing their mental age (MA), dividing it by their chronological age (CA), and then multiplying by 100.

Intentional Stance: An approach to predicting the actions of a system based on concepts like beliefs, desires, hopes, fears, and intentions.

Intentionality: The philosophical view that thoughts have meaning because they are directed toward or about their referents.

Intermediary States: What results from the actions in a problem solving system that are neither the starting conditions nor the final solution states.

James-Lange Theory: A theory of emotion noting that an emotion-inducing stimulus causes arousal which then causes the emotion.

Kinesthesis (Proprioception): Perception of the internal states of the body as opposed to perception of the external environment.

Language: A system of finite arbitrary symbols that are combined according to the rules of a grammar for the purpose of communication.

Learning: A relatively permanent change in behavior due to experience.

Lexicon: A database containing a list of words and their attributes for a given language.

Life: The characteristic state of organisms. Some defining features include organization, metabolism, growth, and reproduction.

Local Representation: A characteristic of networks where representation is located in an individual node or single location.

Logical Omniscience: A characteristic of a logical system involving taking each new fact it acquires and comparing it against every other fact it already has. Said system can make all possible inferences, thereby maximizing the growth of its knowledge.

Long-Term Memory (LTM): A system in which information can be retained in storage for long time periods.

Machine: A mechanical or organic system that transmits or modifies energy to perform or assist in the execution of tasks.

Magnetic Source Imaging: An imaging technique that measures the small changes in magnetic fields that occur when neurons fire.

Major Depressive Disorder: A disorder characterized by depressed mood and loss of interest in pleasurable activities.

Materialists: Those who hold that the universe is essentially material and that natural phenomenon can be reduced to the operation of their parts.

Maxim of Manner: A guideline speakers generally obey regarding being as clear as possible while avoiding ambiguity or obscurity.

Maxim of Quality: A guideline speakers generally obey regarding saying what they believe to be true.

Maxim of Quantity: A guideline speakers generally obey regarding being informative while not saying more or less than what is required.

Maxim of Relevance: A guideline speakers generally obey regarding staying on topic.

Means-End Analysis: A form of problem solving involving the formation of subgoals, which are intermediary states that lead to the goal as well as the application of operators to achieve them.

Memes: Ideas or concepts that get propagated through cultural transmission.

Metabolism: The complete set of chemical reactions that occur in living cells.

Meta-level knowledge: An awareness of knowledge, problem-solving techniques and approaches.

Metric Navigation: The process by which a machine navigates using a computer map of the environment.

Microbial Fuel Cell: A device that takes as input food, water, and air and produces electricity as output that can be used to drive a robot's sensors, actuators, and computing machinery.

Micro-World: A simplified and specially-constructed environment that an AI program can operate in.

Mind: Our subjective, conscious experience of brain function.

Mnemonic: Any technique used to aid in the encoding, storage, and retrieval of information.

Model-Based Agent: An agent that can keep track of the part of the world it cannot directly perceive.

Moderate Discrepancy Hypothesis: A theory that states people seek out stimulation that is somewhat, but not too different from what they already know.

Monism: The philosophical view that the brain and mind are the same thing.

Moore's Law: The empirical observation that the number of transistors on an integrated circuit doubles approximately every 24 months.

Morpheme: The smallest units of meaning in linguistic analysis.

Motivation: A need or desire that serves to energize behavior and direct it toward a goal.

Motor Action: The process by which an agent interacts with or influences the world.

Multi-Computer System: A system of computers that are physically separated from each other but are connected together in a network configuration and exchange information.

Mysterians: Those who argue that there are some natural phenomenon that will always be beyond scientific or rational explanation.

Nanotechnology: An interdisciplinary field of applied science concerned with engineering on a microscopic scale (below 100 nanometers).

Nativism: The philosophical view that knowledge is innate and need not arise through experience.

Negative Feedback Device: A device that feeds back to the input a part of the system's output so as to maintain homeostasis.

Nil Preference Choice: A situation in which there are two or more options, but the chooser has no inherent preference for any single option over the others.

Node: A fundamental unit in artificial neural networks that determines an output value based on input values.

Normative Approach: A problem-solving approach characterized by an agent that acts rationally, has well-defined preferences, and follows certain axiomatic principles.

Object Recognition: The ability to recognize or identify objects in the environment.

Observational Learning: Learning that occurs through the observation, retention, and replication of other's behavior.

Obsessive Compulsive Disorder (OCD): An anxiety disorder characterized by repeated intrusive thoughts and ritualistic acts.

One-Word Stage: The stage of human language development that is marked by the appearance of one-word utterances.

Operant Conditioning: Learning that occurs through the consequences of one's actions. Traditionally, the consequences are either a form or reinforcement or punishment that either increases or decreases the frequency of the behavior.

Optical Computing: A technique in which light, rather than electricity, is used to perform computations.

Outstanding Candidate Choice: A problem solving situation in which there are several options to choose from, but just one best answer out of these alternatives.

Panic Attack: An episode of intense fear and feelings of doom or terror accompanied by physical symptoms like palpitations, chest pains, and breathing difficulties.

Parallel Processing (or Distributed Computing): A type of information processing in which a task is performed by the simultaneous execution of multiple processors.

Parsing: The process by which an input is decomposed into a part-based structure.

Particle Swarm Optimization: A problem solving technique in which boids explore a search space to obtain a solution.

Passionate Love: A type of love characterized as short-term, intense, and based on physical attraction and sex.

Perception: The process by which we take in and process information about an environment.

Perceptron Network: A network designed to recognize patterns. It consists of a two-dimensional array of input units, as well as associative and response units.

Periodic State: A physical state in which an object's behavior repeats at regular intervals.

Personal Robotics: A field of robotics that designs and manufactures intelligent machines that can interact with and assist human beings in many different everyday circumstances.

Phenomenal Consciousness: The subjective awareness of mental states.

Phenotype: The total physical appearance of the organism or a specific manifestation of a trait like eye color, coded by a gene or set of genes.

Phobia: A persistent and irrational fear of a specific object or situation.

Phoneme: The basic unit of sound in a natural language. In speech recognition, phonemes are identified and grouped into morphemes which are in turn are grouped into words, phrases, and sentences.

Physical Stance: An approach to predicting the actions of a system based on the physical state of the system and an understanding of how the laws of nature will affect that system.

Physicalism (or Materialism): A philosophical view noting that only the physical is real and that the mental can be reduced to the physical. See also materialists.

Post-Traumatic Stress Disorder (PTSD): A disorder characterized by a psychological re-enactment of a traumatic event in the form of flashbacks and nightmares.

Pragmatic Analysis: The forth and last stage of natural language comprehension in which complete sentence meaning is derived by applying social and contextual information.

Pragmatics: The social rules underlying language use that help to disambiguate sentence meaning.

Primary Auditory Cortex: A region in the temporal lobe of the cerebral cortex where speech and auditory information is first processed.

Primary Motor Cortex: A region in the frontal lobe of the cerebral cortex that governs muscle contraction for articulation and movement.

Primary Storage: The location of data that are being actively used by a computer.

Primary Visual Cortex: A region in the occipital lobe of the cerebral cortex where basic visual features are processed.

Probabilistic Reasoning: Formation of probability judgments and of subjective beliefs about the likelihoods of outcomes and the frequencies of events.

Procedural Memory: Long-term memory of skills and procedures.

Production Rule: An *If x, they y* statement where if the condition specified by *x* occurs, the action *y* gets executed.

Proposition: A statement about the world that can be proved true or false.

Proprioception: The perception of bodily movement and orientation. See also **Kinesthesis.**

Prosody: The aspects of pronunciation that include changes in pitch, rhythm, speed, and other factors.

Prosthesis: An artificial extension that replaces a missing part of the body.

Qualia: The subjective experience of a particular mental state such as the color red, the smell of a rose, or pain.

Quantum Computing: A technique where the quantum properties of particles are used to represent and compute data.

Quantum Theory: A term that refers to several related theories in physics that describe very small-scale phenomenon.

Quasiperiodic State: A physical state that exhibits partial, but not complete periodicity.

Random Access Memory (RAM): A type of memory used by computers that allows the data stored within to be accessed randomly or in any order rather than just in sequence.

Random State: A physical state that lacks any predictability.

Rational Agent: An agent that acts in such as way as to maximize its chances of success given its knowledge of the environment and other factors.

Reactive Paradigm: A robotic architecture characterized by direct connections between perceptive and actuating elements.

Reactive Processes: A process in which a stimulus automatically triggers an action. It is fast and does not require extended thought or computation.

Reductionism: A philosophical view noting that one can explain the overall behavior of a system simply by explaining the actions and/or interactions of its parts.

Reference Resolution: The process of determining who is doing what in a conversation.

Referent: The thing or object that a symbol stands for.

Reflective Processes (Metacognition): The monitoring and regulation of internal thought processes. The ability to be aware of and control one's own mental states.

Rehearsal: In human memory, the process of repeating an item so that it can retained in long-term memory. Repeated activation of the item strengthens its representation.

Reinforcement Learning: A type of unsupervised machine learning that employs the principles of operant conditioning. The consequence of an action serves as feedback that affects future actions.

Representativeness Heuristic: The assumption that each member of a category is "representative" of the category and has all the traits associated with it. In human judgment it can result in the neglect of base rate probabilities.

Retrieval: The recall of stored information.

Retrieval Cue: An item or other type of information that is associated with another during encoding and which can trigger its recall.

Right: A power or privilege to which one is justly entitled.

Risk Aversion: Preference for a sure outcome over a risky prospect of equal expected value.

Risk Seeking: Preference for a risky prospect over a sure outcome of equal expected value.

Robot: A device that is capable of moving around and/or interacting with the physical world. Robots can be either autonomous or under the control of a program or external operator.

Scalability: The idea that AI and robotic techniques learned on a micro-world could eventually be generalized to cope with more complex environments.

Secondary Storage: The location of data that are not currently being used by the computer.

Semantic Analysis: The third stage of natural language comprehension in which a program recovers the meaning of individual words and word groupings.

Semantic Network: A form of semantic knowledge representation consisting of a network of nodes and links that code for concepts and concept relations.

Semantics: In linguistics, the study of meaning.

Sensitization: A learning process, characterized by an increased response to a stimulus over time.

Serial Processing: A style of processing where information is processed one step at a time.

Short-Term Memory (STM): A system in which information can be retained in storage for limited time period.

Simple Reflex Agent: An agent that uses production rules to map stimulus inputs to actions.

Simulation: An imitation of some real thing, state of affairs, or process.

Singularity: The point at which machines, in collaboration with human counterparts, design and produce ever more powerful and complex versions of themselves.

Situated Creature (Situatedness): Something that is embedded in the world and which does not deal with abstract descriptions, but through its sensors with the here and now of the world, which directly influences its behavior.

Social Competition Hypothesis: A theory stating that depression can cause an individual to stop competing with others. This allows for reconciliation with former competitors and serves to reduce costly group conflict.

Somatosensation: Information about the world conveyed to us by our skin as well as by information about the position and movement of our limbs.

Speech Recognition: The process of converting a speech signal to a sequence of words using an algorithm implemented as a computer program.

Speech Spectrogram: A plot showing the different frequency components of speech and how they vary over time.

Spreading Activation: The process by which activation propagates in a network.

Steady State: A state of constancy in a system where there is no change.

Stigmergy: The production of a certain behavior in agents as a consequence of the effects produced in the local environment by a previous behavior.

Storage: The creation of a relatively permanent record of information encoded into a memory system.

Strong AI: The view in artificial intelligence that machines ultimately may be capable of thought, emotions, and consciousness as they are experienced by people.

Subsumption Architecture: A robotic architecture made up of simple modules organized into layers. Each layer implements a goal of the agent. Layers are organized hierarchically with lower-order layers being subsumed, or called upon, in order to execute goals of higher-order layers.

Supervenience: The philosophical view that mental characteristics are dependent, or supervienient, on physical characteristics. It is based on the premise that there can be no changes or differences in mental characteristics without there being corresponding changes or differences in physical ones.

Supervised Learning: A form of learning utilizing the presence of a teacher who can provide feedback in the form of a correct answer.

Surface Realizer: The component of a natural language generation system that produces the actual sentences to be uttered.

Symbol System Hypothesis: A theory that states any universal symbol system such as a computer can, with sufficient memory and internal reorganization, exhibit intelligence.

Symbol-Grounding Problem: The issue of how an internal symbol "in the head" such as that represented by a word comes to acquire meaning.

Syntactic Analysis: The second stage of natural language comprehension in which the computer must make sense of the ordered arrangement of words.

Syntax: The rules of language. For instance, how words combine to form phrases and phrases combine to form sentences.

Target State (or Goal State): The final solution or state that yields a solution in a problem solving system.

Thalamus: Two symmetrically-located brain structures that serve as relay centers for incoming sensory information to the cortex.

Theory of Multiple Intelligence: The theory that human intelligence is not a single unitary entity but instead consists of several different intelligences each relatively independent of the other.

Token Physicalism: A philosophical view stating that specific mental events are physical events.

Tonotopic Map: The organization of auditory cortex in which distinct neural regions code for individual frequencies. The distance between regions coding for any two frequencies corresponds to the difference in their frequency.

Topological Navigation: The process by which a robot is navigates its work environment by using landmarks and directional instructions.

Transcendence: The ability to rise above and go beyond one's nature or what is given.

Transhumanist Movement: A movement supporting the use of new sciences and technologies to enhance human physical and cognitive abilities and eliminate negative aspects of the human condition such as disease, aging, and death.

Transparency: A property of consciousness noting neural activity only conveys information about the thing it represents, not the substrate or medium by which it is represented.

Turing Machine: A hypothetical device consisting of a scanner that reads a string of binary digits from a tape and performs a set of serial operations based on the current input and its control state. Turing machines serve as the theoretical foundation for modern computers.

Turing Test: An experiment in which a human judge is allowed to communicate with two parties, one a machine, the other a person. The judge is separated from both and can only communicate with them by typing questions and then reading and responding to replies from each. If the judge cannot reliably distinguish the person from the machine, the machine will have successfully passed the test.

Two-Factor Theory: A theory of emotion noting that an emotion-inducing stimulus causes us to generate a cognitive label. The label and resulting physiological arousal together then determine the experienced emotion.

Two-Word Stage: The stage of human language development that is marked by the appearance of two-word utterances.

Type Physicalism: A philosophical view stating that categories of mental events, such as being in pain, correspond to particular physical events such as activity in pain sensors.

Unconditional Probabilities: Probabilities that are independent of other events.

Universal Grammar: A theory in linguistics that postulates there are principles of grammar shared by all natural languages. These principles are thought to be innate in humans.

Universal Mechanism: The philosophical view that everything in the universe can be understood as a mechanical system governed by natural laws.

Unsupervised Learning (or Trial-And-Error Learning): A learning procedure in which the consequence of an action generates feedback from the environment that affects future actions.

Utility Theory: An economic theory stating that people generally act to increase their utility, i.e., their relative happiness or satisfaction. Applied to decision making a rational agent deciding on a course of action will choose an outcome that maximizes its utility.

Utility-Based Agent: An agent that assigns utility values to different states or possible courses of action in order to maximize its utility.

Virtue: The act of gaining or keeping a value.

Weak AI: An approach to the study of artificial intelligence in which the goal is to develop theories of human and animal intelligence and test them by building working models like computer programs or robots.

Well-Defined Task: A task that can be described formally.

Wernicke's Area: A region in the left temporal lobe of the cerebral cortex thought to be involved in language comprehension.

Working Memory: A collection of structures and processes in the brain used for temporarily storing and manipulating information.

Zygote: In humans and most animals, the fertilized egg that results from the merging of an ovum and sperm. It undergoes cell division to become an embryo.

REFERENCES

Aamodt, A., & Plaza, E. (1994). Case-based reasoning: Foundational issues, methodological variations, and system approaches. *Artificial Intelligence Communications, 7*(1), 39–52.

Acosta-Calderon, C. A., & Hu, H. (2004) Robot imitation: A matter of body representation. *Proceedings of International Symposium on Robotics and Automation, Queretaro, Mexico*, 25–27.

Adolphs, R. (2005). Could a robot have emotions? Theoretical perspectives from social cognitive neuroscience. In J. M. Fellows & M. A. Arbib (Eds.), *Who needs emotions? The brain meets the robot* (pp. 9–28). Oxford: Oxford University Press.

Ainsworth, M. (1979). Attachment as related to mother-infant interaction. *Advances in the Study of Behavior, 9,* 2–52.

Aleksander, I. (2001). *How to build a mind.* New York: Columbia University Press.

Aleksander, I., & Dunmall, B. (2003). Axioms and tests for the presence of minimal consciousness in agents. *Journal of Consciousness Studies*, 10(4-5), 7–18.

Amos, M. (2005). *Theoretical and experimental DNA computation.* Berlin: Springer.

Anderson, J. R. (1990). *The adaptive character of thought.* Hillsdale, NJ: Erlbaum.

Anderson, J. R., & Leboere, C. (1998). *The atomic components of thought.* Hillsdale, NJ: Erlbaum.

Anderson, K., & McOwan, P.W. (2003). Real-time emotion recognition using biologically inspired models. *4th International Conference on Audio and Video Based Biometric Person Authentication* (pp. 119–127). London: University of London.

Angier, N. (1999, September 7). Route to creativity: Following bliss or dots? *New York Times*, p. F3.

Angluin, D., & Smith, C. H. (1983). Inductive inference: Theory and methods. *ACM Computing Surveys, 15*(3), 237–269.

Atkinson, R. C., & Shiffrin, R. M. (1971). The control of short-term memory. *Scientific American, 225,* 82–90.

Austin, J. H. (2003). *Chase, chance, and creativity: The lucky art of novelty* (Rev. ed.). Cambridge, MA: MIT Press.

Austin, J. L. (1962). *How to do things with words.* Cambridge, MA: Harvard University Press.

Aylett, R. (2002). *Robots: Bringing intelligent machines to life.* Hauppauge, NY: Barrons.

Baars, B. J. (1997). *In the theater of consciousness: The workspace of the mind.* New York: Oxford University Press.

Balota, D. A., Flores d'Arcais, G. B., & Rayner, K. (Eds.). (1990). *Comprehension processes in reading.* Hillside, NJ: Erlbaum.

Bandura, A., Ross, D., & Ross, S. A. (1961). Transmission of aggression through imitation of aggressive models. *Journal of Abnormal and Social Psyhology, 63,* 575–582.

Bar-Cohen, Y. (Ed.). (2004). *Electroactive polymer (EAP) actuators as artificial muscles: Reality, potential, and challenges* (2nd ed.). Bellingham, WA: SPIE Press.

Barinaga, M. (1992). How scary things get that way. *Science, 258*, 887–888.

Barlow, D. H. (1988). *Anxiety and its disorders*. New York: Guilford.

Barnes, D. P. (1996). A behaviour synthesis architecture for co-operant mobile robots. In J. O. Gray & D. G. Caldwell (Eds.), *Advanced robotics & intelligent machines, IEE Control Engineering Series 51* (pp. 295–314).

Bashir, R. (2004). BioMEMS: State-of-the-art in detection, opportunities and prospects. *Advanced Drug Delivery Review, 56*(11), 1565–1586.

Bavelier, D., Corina, D., Jezzard, P., Clark, V., Karni, A., Lalwani, A., Rauschecker, J. P., Braun, A., Turner, R., & Neville, H. J. (1998). Hemispheric specialization for English and ASL: Left invariance-right variability. *Neuroreport, 9*(7), 1537–1542.

Beckers, R., Holland, O., & Deneubourg, J. L. (1994). From local actions to global tasks: Stigmergy and collective robots. In R. Brooks & P. Maes (Eds.), *Proceedings of the Fourth International Workshop on the Synthesis and Simulation of Living Systems. Artificial Life IV* (pp. 181–189). Cambridge, MA: MIT Press.

Bentley, P. J. (2002). *Digital biology*. New York: Simon & Schuster.

Berlyne, E. (1958). The influence of albedo and complexity of stimuli on visual fixation in the human infant. *British Journal of Psychology, 56*, 315–318.

Bingham, G. P., & Muchisky, M. M. (1993). Center of mass perception and inertial frames of reference. *Perception & Psychophysics, 54*, 617–632.

Birnbacher, D. (1995). Artificial consciousness. In T. Metzinger (Ed.), *Conscious experience* (pp. 489–507). Thorverton, Devon: Imprint Academic.

Bizzi, E., Mussa-Ivaldi, F. A., & Giszter, S. (1991). Computations underlying the execution of movement: A biological perspective. *Science, 253*(5017), 287–291.

Blackmore, S. (2004). *Consciousness. An introduction*. Oxford: Oxford University Press.

Bloch, C. (1972). *The Golem: Legends of the ghetto of Prague* (H. Schneiderman Trans.). Blauvelt: Rudolf Steiner Press.

Boden, M. A. (1995a). Could a robot be creative? And would we know? In K. Ford, K. Glymour, C., & Hayes, P. J. (Eds.), *Android epistemology* (pp. 51–72). Cambridge, MA: MIT Press.

Boden, M. A. (1995b). Creativity and Unpredictability. Constructions of the Mind: Artificial Intelligence and the Humanities. *Stanford Humanities Review, 4* (2).

Boden, M. A. (1999). Computer models of creativity. In R. J. Sternberg (Ed.), *Handbook of creativity* (pp. 351–372). Cambridge: Cambridge University Press.

Bolles, E. B. (1988). *Remembering and forgetting: Inquiries into the nature of memory*. New York: Walker and Company.

Boone, G., & Hodgins, J. (1998). Walking and running machines. In F. C. Keil & R. A. Wilson (Eds.), *The MIT encyclopedia of cognitive sciences* (pp. 874–876). Cambridge, MA: MIT Press.

Bowlby, J. (1969). *Attachment and loss: Attachment* (Vol. 1). New York: Basic.

Braitenberg, V. (1984). *Vehicles: Experiments in synthetic psychology*. Cambridge, MA: MIT Press.

Breazeal, C. (2002). *Designing sociable robots*. Cambridge, MA: MIT Press.

Breazeal, C., & Brooks, R. (2005). Robot emotions: A functional perspective In J. M. Fellows and M. A. Arbib (Eds.), *Who needs emotions? The brain meets the robot* (pp. 271–310). Oxford: Oxford University Press.

Breazeal, C., Edsinger, A., Fitzpatrick, P., & Scassellati, B. (2001). Active vision for sociable robots. In K. Dautenhahn (Ed.), *IEEE Transactions on man, cybernetics, and systems: Part A: Systems and humans.* [Special issue] *Socially intelligent agents: The human in the loop, 31*(5), 443–453.

Brighton, H., & Selina, H. (2003). *Introducing artificial intelligence*. Duxford, UK: Icon Books.

Bringsjord, S. (1992). *What robots can and can't be*. Boston, MA: Kluwer Academic Publishers.

Bringsjord, S., & Ferrucci, D. A. (2000). *Artificial intelligence and literary creativity: Inside the mind of BRUTUS, a storytelling machine*. Mahwah, NJ: Erlbaum.

Brodsky, J. (1972, October 1). A writer is a lonely traveler, and no one is his helper. *New York Times*.

Brooks, R. A. (1986). A robust layered control system for a mobile robot. *IEEE Journal of Robotics and Automation, 2(1)*, 14–23.

Brooks, R. A. (2002). *Flesh and machine: How robots will change us*. New York: Vintage Books.

Buchanon, B. G. (2001). Creativity at the Metalevel. AAAI-2000 Presidential Address. *Artificial Intelligence Magazine, 22*(3), 13–28.

Buchanan, B. G., Smith, D. H., White, W. C., Gritter, R. J., Feigenbaum, E. A., Lederberg, J., & Djerassi, C. (1976). Applications of artificial intelligence for chemical inference. Automatic rule formation in mass spectrometry by means of the Meta-DENDRAL program. *Journal of the American Chemical Society, 98*(20), 6168–6178.

Buss, D. M. (1999). *Evolutionary psychology. The new science of the mind*. Boston: Allyn & Bacon.

Calaprice, A., & Dyson, F. (2005). *The new quotable Einstein*. Princeton, NJ: Princeton University Press.

Cannon, W. B. (1927). The James-Lange theory of emotions: A critical examination and an alternative theory. *American Journal of Psychology, 39*, 106–124.

Carletta, J., Dahlback, N., Reithinger, N., & Walker, M. A. (1997). Standards for dialogue coding in natural language processing. (Tech. Rep. Report no. 167). *Dagstuhl Seminars*. Report from Dagstuhl seminar number 9706.

Carlson, E. B., & Rosser-Hogan, R. (1991). Trauma experiences, posttraumatic stress, dissociation, and depression in Cambodian refugees. *American Journal of Psychiatry, 148*, 1548–1551.

Caspi, A., & Herbener, E. S. (1990). Continuity and change: Assortative marriage and the consistency of personality in adulthood. *Journal of Personality and Social Psychology, 58*, 250–258.

Caudill, M. (1992). *In our own image: Building an artificial person*. New York: Oxford University Press.

Cawsey, A. (1998). *The essence of artificial intelligence*. Harlow, UK: Prentice Hall.

Chagnon, N. (1997). *Yanomamo: the fierce people* (5th ed.). Fort Worth, TX: Harcourt Brace.

Chalmers, D. (1995). The puzzle of conscious experience. *Scientific American, 273*, 62–68.

Chalmers, D. (1996). *The conscious mind*. Oxford: Oxford University Press.

Chalmers, D., French, R., & Hofstadter D. (1991). *High-level perception, representation, and analogy: A critique of artificial-intelligence methodology*. (CRCC Technical Report 49). Bloomington: Indiana University.

Chalmers, D., French, R., & Hofstadter D. (1995). High-level perception, representation, and analogy: A critique of artificial-intelligence methodology. In *Fluid concepts and creative analogies* (pp. 169–94). New York: Basic Books.

Chao, D. L., & Forrest, S. (2002). Information immune systems. *Proceedings of the First International Conference on Artificial Immune Systems (ICARIS)*, 132–140.

Chomsky, N. (1986). *Knowledge of language: Its nature, origin, and use*. New York: Praeger.

Chou, C. P., & Hannaford, B. (1996). Measurement and modeling of McKibben pneumatic artificial muscles. *IEEE Transactions on Robotics and Automation, 12*, 90–102.

Chow, A. Y., Chow, V. Y., Packo, K. H., Pollack, J. S., Peyman, G. A., & Schuchard, R. (2004). The artificial silicon retina microchip for the treatment of vision loss from retinitis pigmentosa. *Arch Ophthalmol., 122*, 460–469.

Churchill, W. (1992). *The sayings of Winston Churchill*. London: Gerald Duckworth & Company.

Churchland, P. M., & Churchland, P. S. (1990). Could a machine think? *Scientific American, 262,* 32–37.

Clark, G. (2003). *Cochlear implants: Fundamentals and applications*. New York: Springer.

Clark, H. H., & Sengal, C. J. (1979). In search of referents for nouns and pronouns. *Memory and Cognition, 7,* 35–41.

Clark, H. H., & Schaefer, E. F. (1989). Contributing to discourse. *Cognitive Science, 13*(2), 259–294.

Cocco, M., Dario, P., Toro, M., Pastacaldi, P., & Sacchetti, R. (1993). An implantable neural connector incorporating microfabricated components. *Journal of Micromechanics and Microengineering, 3,* 219–221.

Cohen, H. (1995), Constructions of the mind: The further exploits of AARON, painter. *Stanford Electronic Humanities Review,* 4(2).

Collins, A. M., & Quillian, M. R. (1969). Retrieval time from semantic memory. *Journal of Verbal Learning and Verbal Behavior, 8,* 240–247.

Cope, D. (1996). *Experiments in musical intelligence*. Madison, WI: A-R Editions Inc.

Copeland, J. (1993). *Artificial intelligence: A philosophical introduction*. Oxford: Blackwell.

Cosmides, L., & Tooby, J. (1992). Cognitive adaptations for social exchange. In J. Barkow, L. Cosmides, & J. Tooby (Eds.), *The adapted mind: Evolutionary psychology and the generation of culture* (pp. 163–228). New York: Oxford University Press.

Cotterill, R. (1998). *Enchanted looms: Conscious networks in brains and computers*. Cambridge: Cambridge University Press.

Cotterill, R. (2003). CyberChild: A simulation test-bed for consciousness studies. *Journal of Consciousness studies, 10*(4-5), 31–45.

Cropley, A. J. (2000). Defining and measuring creativity: Are creativity tests worth using? *Roeper Review, 23*(2), 72–80.

Crystal, D. (1987). *The Cambridge encyclopedia of language*. Cambridge, MA: Cambridge University Press.

Curtis, H. (1983). *Biology* (4th ed.). New York: Worth.

Dacey, J. S., & Lennon, K. H. (1998). *Understanding creativity: The interplay of biological, psychological, and social factors*. San Francisco: Jossey-Bass.

Damasio, A. (1994). *Descartes' error: Emotion, reason, and the human brain*. New York: Putnam.

Damasio, A. (1999). *The feeling of what happens*. San Diego, CA: Harcourt.

Dario, P., Guglielmelli, E., & Laschi, C. (2001). Humanoids and personal robots: Design and experiments. *Journal of Robotic Systems, 18*(12), 673–690.

Darwin, C. (1998). *The expression of the emotions in man and animals* (3rd ed.). Chicago: University of Chicago Press. (Original work published 1872).

Davidson, D. (1981). The material mind. In J. Haugeland (Ed.), *Mind design. philosophy, psychology, artificial intelligence* (pp. 339–354). Cambridge, MA: MIT Press.

De Beaugrande, R., & Colby, B. N. (1979). Narrative models of action and interaction. *Cognitive Science, 3*(1), 43–46.

Dehn, N. (1981). Story generation after TALE-SPIN. IJCAI-81, 1, 16–18.

Dennett, D. (1978). *Brainstorms: Philosophical essays on mind and psychology*. Cambridge, MA: Bradford.

Dennett, D. (1981). Intentional systems. In J. Haugeland (Ed.), *Mind design: Philosophy, psychology, artificial intelligence* (pp. 220–242). Cambridge, MA: MIT Press.

Dennett, D. (1991). *Consciousness explained*. Boston: Little, Brown and Company.

Dennett, D. (1994). The practical requirements for making a conscious robot. *Philosophical Transactions of the Royal Society, 349*, 133–146.

Dennett, D. (2003). *Freedom evolves.* New York: Viking.

Deville, S., Saiz, E., Nalla, R. K., & Tomsia, A. P. (2006, January 27). Freezing as a path to build complex composites. *Science, 311*, 515–518.

Dewey, J. (1922). *Human nature and conduct: An introduction to social psychology.* New York: Modern Library.

Diaz-Guerrero, R., & Diaz-Loving, R. (2000). Needs and values in three cultures: Controversey and a dilemma. *Interdisciplinaria, 17*, 137–151.

Double, R. (1983). Searle, programs and functionalism. *Nature and System, 5*, 107–114.

Dow, G. T., & Mayer, R. E. (2004). Teaching students to solve insight problems: Evidence for domain specificity in training. *Creativity Research Journal, 16*(4), 389–402.

Dowling, R. D., Gray, L. A., Etoch, S. W., Laks, H., Marelli, D., Samuels, L., Entwistle, J., Couper, G., Vlahakes, G. J., & Frazier, O. H. (2004). Initial experience with the AbioCor implantable replacement heart system. *Journal of Thoracic Cardiovascular Surgery, 127*, 131–141.

Dronkers, N. F., Shapiro, J. K., Redfern, B., & Knight, R. T. (1992). The role of Broca's area in Broca's aphasia. *Journal of Clinical and Experimental Neuropsychology, 14*, 52–53.

Dreyfus, H. L. (1992). What computers still can't do: A critique of artificial reason. Cambridge, MA: MIT Press.

Eberhart, R., Kennedy, J., & Yuhui, S. (2001). *Swarm intelligence.* San Francisco: Morgan Kaufmann.

Edwards, J., Pattison, P. E., Jackson, H. J., & Wales, R. J. (2001). Facial affect and affective prosody recognition in first-episode schizophrenia. *Schizophrenia Research, 40*(2-3), 235–253.

Ekman, P. (1992). Facial expressions of emotion: New findings, new questions. *Psychological Science, 3*, 34–38.

Elmes, D. G., Kantowitz, B. H., & Roediger, H. L. (1999). *Research Methods in Psychology* (6th ed.). Pacific Grove, CA: Brooks/Cole.

Falkenhaimer, B., Forbus, K. D., & Gentner, D. (1989). The structure-mapping engine: Algorithm and examples. *Artificial Intelligence, 41*, 1–63.

Feist, G. J. (1998). A meta-analysis of the impact of personality on scientific and artistic creativity. *Personality and Social Psychological Review, 2*, 290–309.

Fernald, A. (1989). Intonation and communicative intent in mother's speech to infants: Is the melody the message? *Child Development, 60*, 1497–1510.

Fisher, J. A. (1988). The wrong stuff: Chinese rooms and the nature of understanding. *Philosophical Investigations, 11*, 279–299.

Fodor, J. (1980). Searle on what only brains can do. *Behavioral and Brain Sciences, 3*, 431–432.

Foerst, A. (2004). *God in the machine. What robots teach us about humanity and god.* New York: Plume.

Forrest, S., & Hofmeyr, S. A. (2001). Immunology as information processing. In L. A. Segel & I. Cohen (Eds.), *Design principles for the immune system and other distributed autonomous systems* (pp. 361–387). New York: Oxford University Press.

Franklin, S. (1995). *Artificial minds.* Cambridge, MA: MIT Press.

Franklin, S. (2003). IDA: A conscious artifact? *Journal of Consciousness studies, 10*(4-5), 47–66.

Fredrickson, B. L. (1998). What good are positive emotions? *Review of General Psychology, 2*, 300–319.

Freitas, R. A. (1998). Exploratory design in medical nanotechnology: A mechanical artificial red cell. *Artificial Cells, Blood Substitutes, and Immobilization Biotechnology, 26*, 411–430.

Fuller, T. (1654–1734). Gnomologia, adagies and proverbs, wise sentences and witty sayings, ancient and modern, foreign and British. 3163, 1732

Gardner, H. (1993). *Multiple intelligences: The theory in practice.* New York: Basic Books.

Georges, T. M. (2003). *Digital soul: Intelligent machines and human values.* Cambridge, MA: Westview Press.

Geschwind, N. (1972). Language and the brain. *Scientific American, 226,* 76–83.

Gibilisco, S. (2003). *Concise encyclopedia of robotics.* New York: McGraw-Hill.

Gick, M. L., & Holyoak, K. J. (1980). Analogical problem solving. *Cognitive Psychology, 12,* 306–355.

Gips, J. (1995). Towards the ethical robot. In K. Ford, C. Glymour, & P. Hayes (Eds.), *Android epistemology* (pp. 41–49). Cambridge, MA: MIT Press.

Gödel, K. (1930). Die vollständigkeit der axiome des logischen funktionen-kalküls. *Monatshefte für Mathematik und Physik, 37,* 349–360.

Goldberg, D. (1990). *Genetic algorithms in search, optimization and machine learning.* Reading, MA: Addison-Wesley.

Goldenberg, J., Mazursky, D., & Solomon, S. (1999). Essays on science and society: Creative sparks. *Science, 285,* 1495–1496.

Goldenfeld, N., & Kadanoff, L. P. (1999). Simple lessons from complexity. *Science, 284,* 87–89.

Goldstein, E. B. (2002). *Sensation and perception* (6th ed.) Pacific Grove, CA: Wadsworth Thompson.

Gray, J. A. (1987). Perspectives on anxiety and impulsiveness: A commentary. *Journal of Research in Personality, 21,* 493–509.

Greenberg, D. J., & O'Donnell, W. J. (1972). Infancy and the optimal level of stimulation. *Child Development, 43,* 639–645.

Grice, H. P. (1975). Logic and conversation. In P. Cole & J. L. Morgan (Eds.), *Speech acts: Syntax and semantics* (vol. 3, pp. 41–58). New York: Academic Press.

Griffiths, D. J. (2004). *Introduction to quantum mechanics* (2nd ed.). New York: Prentice Hall.

Guilford, J. P. (1967). *The nature of human intelligence.* New York: McGraw-Hill.

Guilford, J. P. (1982). Cognitive psychology's ambiguities: Some suggested remedies. *Psychological Review, 89,* 48–59.

Gurney, K. (1997). *An Introduction to neural networks.* London: UCL Press.

Haikonen, P. (2003). *The cognitive approach to conscious machines.* Exeter, UK: Imprint Academic.

Hall, D. T., & Nougaim, K. E. (1968). An examination of Maslow's need hierarchy in an organizational setting. *Organizational Behavior and Human Performance, 3,* 12–35.

Hameroff, S., & Penrose, R. (1996). Conscious events as orchestrated space-time selections. *Journal of Consciousness Studies, 3*(1), 36–53.

Harlow, H., Harlow, M., & Meyer, D. (1950). Learning motivated by a manipulation drive. *Journal of Experimental Psychology, 40,* 228–234.

Harlow, H. F., Harlow, M. K., & Suomi, S. J. (1971). From thought to therapy: Lessons from a primate laboratory. *American Scientist, 59,* 538-549.

Harnad, S. (1990) The symbol grounding problem. *Physica D, 42,* 335–346.

Haugeland, J. (1985). *Artificial intelligence: The very idea.* Cambridge, MA: MIT Press.

Hawkins, J., & Blakeslee, S. (2004). *On intelligence.* New York: Times Books.

Hobbs, J. R., Stickel, M. E., Appelt, D. E., & Martin, P. (1993). Interpretation as abduction. *Artificial Intelligence, 63,* 69–142.

Hodgson, P. (1990). Understanding computing, cognition, and creativity. Unpublished master's thesis, University of the West of England, Bristol, UK.

Hofstadter, D. R. (1979). *Godel, Escher, Bach: An eternal golden braid.* New York: Basic Books.

Hofstadter, D. R. (1985). *Metamagical themas: Questing for the essence of mind and pattern.* New York: Basic Books.

Hofstadter, D. R. (1996). *Fluid concepts and creative analogies: Computer models of the fundamental mechanisms of thought.* New York: Harper Collins.

Holland, J. H., Holyoak, K. J., Nisbett, R. E., & Thagard, P. R. (1986). *Induction: Processes of inference, learning, and discovery.* Cambridge, MA: MIT Press.

Hollis, M. (1994). *The philosophy of the social sciences.* Cambridge, MA: Cambridge University Press.

Holyoak, K. J., & Thagard, P. (1989). Analogical mapping by constraint satisfaction. *Cognitive Science, 13,* 295–355.

Horn, R. E. (1995) *Mapping great debates: Can computers think?* Retrieved July 15, 2006, from http://www.macrovu.com/CCTGeneralInfo.html

Houston, J. P., & Mednick. (1963). Creativity and the need for novelty. *Journal of Abnormal and Social Psychology, 66,* 137–141.

Hughes, H. (1963). Individual and group creativity in science. In M. Coler (Ed.), *Essays on creativity in the sciences* (pp. 93–109). New York: New York University Press.

Ichbiah, D. (2005). *Robots: From science fiction to technological revolution.* New York: Harry N. Abrams.

Isen, A. (2000). Positive affect and decision making. In M. Lewis & J. Haviland-Jones (Eds.), *Handbook of emotions* (2nd ed., pp. 417–435). New York: Guilford.

James, W. (1884). What is emotion? *Mind, 9,* 188–205.

Jeffery, M. (1999). *The human computer.* London: Warner Books.

Johannson, R. S., & Westling G. (1987). Signals in tactile afferents from the fingers eliciting adaptive motor responses during precision grip. *Experimental Brain Research, 66,* 141–154.

Johnson, J., & Newport, E. (1989). Critical period effects in second language learning: The influence of maturational state on the acquisition of English as a second language. *Cognitive Psychology, 21,* 60–99.

Jones, P. E. (1995). Contradictions and unanswered questions in the Genie case: A fresh look at the linguistic evidence. *Language & Communication, 15*(3), 261–280.

Jurafsky, D., & Martin, J. (2000). *Speech and language processing: An introduction to natural language processing, computational linguistics, and speech recognition.* Upper Saddle River, NJ: Prentice Hall.

Kaku, M. (1997). *Visions.* New York: Anchor Books.

Kanfer S. (1991, August 5). The last teller of tales: Isacc Bashevis Singer: 1904–1991. *Time Magazine.*

Karoub, J. (2006, December 29). MEMS prosthetic helped save amputee on September 11. *Small Times.* Retrieved June 26, 2005, from http://www.smalltimes.com/Articles/Article_Display.cfm?ARTICLE_ID=267684&p=109

Kawamura, K., Rogers, T., Hambuchen, A., & Erol, D. (2003). Toward a human-robot symbiotic system. *Robotics and Computer Integrated Manufacturing, 19,* 555–565.

Kay, J., & Ellis, A. W. (1987). A cognitive neuropsychological case study of anomia: Implications for psychological models of word retrieval. *Brain, 11,* 613–629.

Kellan, A. (1999, January 28). A taste of the future: The electronic tongue. *CNN.* Retrieved June 28, 2005, from http://www.cnn.com/TECH/science/9901/28/t_t/taste.buds/index.html

Kelley, G. A. (1963). Discussion: Aldous, the personable computer. In S. S. Tomkins & S. Messick (Eds.), *Computer simulation of personality: Frontier of psychological theory* (pp. 221–229). New York: Wiley.

Khan, A. F. U. (1995). The ethics of autonomous learning systems. In K. Ford, C. Glymour, & P. Hayes (Eds.), *Android epistemology* (pp. 253–265). Cambridge, MA: MIT Press.

Kolodner, J. L. (1983). Reconstructive memory: A computer model. *Cognitive Science, 7*(4), 281–328.

Kotler, S. (2002, September). Vision quest. A half century of artificial sight has succeeded. And now this blind man can see. *Wired.* 10(9). Retrieved June 29, 2005, from http://www.wired.com/wired/archive/10.09/vision.html

Koza, J. R. (1992). *Genetic programming: On the programming of computers by means of natural selection.* Cambridge, MA: MIT Press.

Kugel, P. (1986). Thinking may be more than computing. *Cognition, 22,* 137–198.

Kurzweil, R. (1999). *The age of spiritual machines: When computers exceed human intelligence.* New York: Penguin.

Kurzweil, R. (2005). *The singularity is near.* New York: Viking.

Landauer, T. K. (1986). How much do people remember? Some estimates of the quantity of learned information in long-term memory. *Cognitive Science, 10*(4), 477–493.

Langley, P., Simon, H., Bradshaw, G., & Zytkow, J. (1987). *Scientific discovery: Computational explorations of the creative processes.* Cambridge, MA: MIT Press.

Lappin, S., & Leass, H. (1994). An algorithm for pronominal anaphora resolution. *Computational linguistics, 20*(4), 535–561.

Laurens van der Post (1975). "The vigil and the summons," Jung and the story of our time. New York: Vintage.

Leake, D. B. (1996). *Case-based reasoning: Experiences, lessons, and future directions.* Menlo Park, CA: AAAI Press.

Leary, M. R. (1999). The social and psychological importance of self-esteem. In R. M. Kowalski & M. R. Leary (Eds.), *The social psychology of emotional and behavioral problems.* Washington, DC: APA Books.

Lebowitz, M. (1984). Creating characters in a story-telling universe. *Poetics, 13,* 171–194.

LeDoux, J. (1996). *The emotional brain: The mysterious underpinnings of emotional life.* New York: Touchstone.

Lenat, D. B. (1976). *AM: An artificial intelligence approach to discovery in mathematics as heuristic search.* PhD thesis, Stanford University, CA.

Lenat, D. B. (1983). EURISKO: A program that learns new heuristics and domain concepts. *Artificial Intelligence, 21,* 61–98.

Levy, S. (1992). *Artificial life: The quest for a new creation.* New York: Pantheon.

Libet, B. (1999). Do we have free will?. *Journal of Consciousness Studies, 6*(8-9), 47–57.

Likhachev, M., & Arkin, R. C. (2000). Robotic comfort zones. Proceedings of the SPIE Sensor Fusion and Decentralized Control in Robotic Systems III (pp. 27–41).

Lindsay, R. K., Buchanan, B. G., Feigenbaum, E. A., & Lederberg, J. (1993). DENDRAL: A case study of the first expert system for scientific hypothesis formation. *Artificial Intelligence, 61,* 209–261.

Lipson, H., & Pollack, J. B. (2000). Automatic design and manufacture of robotic lifeforms. *Nature, 406,* 974–978.

Llinas, R. R. (2001). *I of the vortex. From neurons to self.* Cambridge, MA: MIT Press.

Locke, J. (1975). *An essay concerning human understanding.* Oxford: Clarendon. (Original work published 1694)

Lorenz, E. (1996). *The essence of chaos.* Seattle: University of Washington Press.

Lynch, K. M., & Mason, M. T. (1995). Stable pushing: Mechanics, controllability, and planning. *International Journal of Robotics Research, 15*(6), 533–556.

Lytinen, S. L. (1992). A unification-based, integrated natural language processing system. *Computers and Mathematics With Applications, 23*(6-9), 403–418.

MacLeod, C. (1991). Half a century of research on the Stroop effect: An integrative review. *Psychological Bulletin, 109,* 163–203.

Manson, J., & Wrangham R. W. (1991). Intergroup aggression in chimpanzees and humans. *Current Anthropology, 32,* 369–390.

Marcus, M. P., Santorini, B., & Marcinkiewicz, M. A. (1993). Building a large annotated corpus of English: The Penn Treebank. *Computational Linguistics, 19*(2), 313–330.

Marks, I. M. (1987). *Fears, phobias, and rituals.* New York: Oxford University Press.

Marks, I. M., & Nesse, R. M. (1994). Fear and fitness: An evolutionary analysis of anxiety disorders. *Ethology and Sociobiology, 15,* 247–261.

Martindale, C. (1981). *Cognition and consciousness.* Homewood, IL: Dorsey Press.

Martindale, C., & Hines, D. (1975). Creativity and cortical activation during creative, intellectual and EEG feedback tasks. *Biological Psychology, 3,* 71–80.

Maslow, A. H. (1970). *Motivation and personality* (2nd ed.). New York: Harper & Row.

Masterman, M. (1971). Computerized Haiku. In J. Reichardt (Ed.), *Cybernetics, art, and ideas* (pp. 175–183). Greenwich, CT: New York Graphic Society.

Maturana, H., & Varela, F. (1980). *Autopoesis and cognition: The realization of the living.* Boston: D. Reidel.

May, S. W. (1975). The authorship of 'My Mind to Me a Kingdom Is'. *The Review of English Studies, New Series, 26* (104), 385–394.

McCarthy, J. (1979). Ascribing mental qualities to machines. In M. Ringle (Ed.), *Philosophical perspectives in artificial Intelligence* (pp. 161–195). Brighton: Harvester Press.

McDermott, D., & Doyle, J. (1980). Non-monotonic logic I. *Artificial Intelligence, 13,* 41–72.

McGinn, C. (1987) Could a machine be conscious? In C. Blakemore & S. Greenfield (Eds.), *Mindwaves* (pp. 279–288). Oxford: Blackwell.

McIntyre, R. (1986). Husserl and the representational theory of mind. *Topoi,* 5, 101–113.

Mednick. S. A. (1962) The associative basis of the creative process. *Psychological Review.* 69, 220–232.

Meehan, J. (1981). Tale-spin. In R. Schank & C. Reisbeck (Eds.), *Inside computer understanding: Five programs plus miniatures.* Hillsdale, NJ: Erlbaum.

Melhuish, C. R. (2001). *Strategies for collective minimalist mobile robots.* Suffolk, UK: St. Edmundsbury Press.

Mensch, J. R. (1991). Phenomenology and artificial intelligence: Husserl learns Chinese. *Husserl Studies, 8*(2), 107–127.

Minsky, M. (1985). *The society of mind.* New York: Touchstone.

Mishra, B., & Silver, N. (1989). Some discussion of static gripping and its stability. *IEEE Systems, Man, and Cybernetics, 19*(4), 783–796.

Mohr, J. P. (1976). Broca's area and Broca's aphasia. In H. Whitaker & H. Whitaker (Eds.), *Studies in neurolinguistics* (pp. 201–233). New York: Academic Press.

Moor, J. H. (1988), The pseudorealization fallacy and the Chinese room argument. In J. H. Fetzer (Ed.), *Aspects of artificial intelligence,* (pp. 35–53). New York: Kluwer Academic.

Moore, B., Underwood, B., & Rosenhan, D. (1984). Emotion, self, and others. In C. Izard, J. Kagen, & R. Zajonc (Eds.), *Emotions, cognition, and behavior* (pp. 464–483). New York: Cambridge University Press.

Moravec, H. (1990). *Mind children: The future of robot and human intelligence.* Cambridge, MA: Harvard University Press.

Mori, M. (2005). On the uncanny valley. *Proceedings of the Humanoids-2005 Workshop: Views of the Uncanny Valley.* December 5, 2005. Tsukuba, Japan.

Murphy, R. R. (2000). *An introduction to AI robotics.* Cambridge, MA: MIT Press.

Myers, D. G. (2001). *Psychology.* New York: Worth.

Myers, J. L., Shinjo, M., & Duffy, S. A. (1987). Degree of causal relatedness and memory. *Journal of Verbal Learning and Verbal Behavior, 26,* 453–465.

Napier, J. (1980). *Hands.* Princeton, NJ: Princeton University Press.

Nesse, R. M. (1987). An evolutionary perspective on panic disorder and agoraphobia. *Ethology and Sociobiology, 8,* 735–835.

Nesse, R. M. (2000). Is depression an adaptation? *Archives of General Psychiatry, 57,* 14–20.

Newell, A., & Simon, H. A. (1972). *Human problem solving.* Englewood Cliffs, NJ: Prentice Hall.

Nielsen, M., & Chuang, I. (2000). *Quantum computation and quantum information.* Cambridge, MA: Cambridge University Press.

Nilsson, N. (1998). *Artificial intelligence: A new synthesis.* San Francisco: Morgan Kaufmann.

Nolfi, S., & Floreano, D. (2000). *Evolutionary robotics: The biology, intelligence, and technology of self-organizing machines.* Cambridge, MA: MIT Press.

Norretranders, T. (1991). *The user illusion: Cutting consciousness down to size.* New York: Penguin.

Ornstein, R. (1993). *The roots of self: Unraveling the mystery of who we are.* New York: Harper Collins.

Osherson, D. N., Stob, M., & Weinstein, S. (1990). *Systems that learn: An introduction to learning theory for cognitive and computer scientists.* Cambridge, MA: MIT Press.

Ouellette, J. (1999). Electronic noses sniff out new markets. *The Industrial Physicist, 5*(1), 26–29.

Patoine, B. (2005). Imagine that! Neural prosthetics harness thoughts to control computers and robotics. *Brain Work: The Neuroscience Newsletter, 15*(1), 1–3.

Penrose, R. (1989). *The emperor's new mind. Concerning computer, minds, and the laws of physics.* Oxford: Oxford University Press.

Perkowitz, S. (2004). *Digital people: From bionic humans to androids.* Washington, DC: Joseph Henry Press.

Petrushin, V. A. (2000). Emotion recognition in speech signal: Experimental study, development, and application. *Proceedings of the Sixth International Conference on Spoken Language Processing.*

Picard, R. W. (1997). *Affective computing.* Cambridge, MA: MIT Press.

Pollack, J. L. (1989). *How to build a person: A prolegomenon.* Cambridge, MA: MIT Press.

Ponce, J. (1999). Manipulation and grasping. In F. C. Keil & R. A. Wilson (Eds.), *The MIT encyclopedia of cognitive sciences* (pp. 508–511). Cambridge, MA: MIT Press.

Poundstone, W. (1985). *The recursive universe.* New York: Morrow.

Price, J., Sloman, L., Gardner, R., Jr., Gilbet, P., & Rohde, P. (1994). The social competition hypothesis of depression. *British Journal of Psychiatry, 164,* 309–315.

Pylyshyn, Z. (1984). *Computation and cognition.* Cambridge, MA: MIT Press.

Rand, A. (1963). *For the new intellectual. The philosophy of Ayn Rand.* New York: Signet.

Rand, A. (1975). *The romantic manifesto* (2nd ed.). New York: Signet.

Rapaport, W. J. (1988). Syntactic semantics: foundations of computational natural-language understanding. In J. H. Fetzer (Ed.), *Aspects of artificial intelligence* (pp. 81–131). Dordrecht, Holland: Kluwer Academic Publishers.

Rasband, N. S. (1990). *Chaotic dynamics of nonlinear systems*. New York: Wiley.

Ray, T. S. (1991). An approach to the synthesis of life. In C. Langton, C. Taylor, J. Farmer, & S. Rasmussen (Eds.), *Artificial life II* (pp. 371–408). Redwood City, CA: Addison-Wesley.

Rey, G. (1986). What's really going on in Searle's "Chinese room." *Philosophical Studies, 50,* 169–185.

Reynolds, C. W. (1987) Flocks, herds, and schools: A distributed behavioral model. *Proceedings of SIGGRAPH '87, Computer Graphics, 21*(4), 25–34.

Rinkus, G. J. (2004). A neural model of episodic and semantic spatiotemporal memory. In K. D. Forbus, D. Kenneth, D. Gentner, Dedre, Regier, & Terry, (Eds.), *Proceedings 26th Annual Meeting of the Cognitive Science Society*, Chicago, IL.

Rolls, E. T. (1999). *The brain and emotion*. Oxford: Oxford University Press.

Rolls, E. T., & Stringer, S. M. (2001). A model of the interaction between mood and memory. *Network, 12,* 89–109.

Rosenthal, D. M. (1995). Multiple drafts and the facts of the matter. In T. Metzinger (Ed.) *Conscious experience* (pp. 359–372). Thorverton, Devon: Imprint Academic.

Ross, S., Brownholtz, E. A., & Armes, R. C. (2004). *Principles and architecture for a conversational agent*. International Conference on Intelligent User Interfaces. Technical Report 04-01.

Rowley, H. A., Baluja, S., & Kanade, T. (1998). Neural network-based face detection. *IEEE Transactions on Pattern Analysis and Machine Intelligence, 20*(1), 23–38.

Rumelhart, D. E., McClelland, J. L., & the PDP Research Group (Eds.) (1986). *Parallel distributed processing: Volume 1. Foundations*. Cambridge, MA: MIT Press.

Russell, S., & Norvig, P. (2003). *Artificial intelligence: A modern approach*. Englewood Cliffs, NJ: Prentice Hall.

Sacks, H., Schegloff, E. A., & Jefferson, G. (1974). A simplest systematics for the organization of turn-taking for conversation. *Language, 50*(4), 696–735.

Schachter, S., & Singer, J. (1962). Cognitive social and physiological determinants of emotional state. *Psychological Review, 69,* 379–399.

Schumacher, E. F. (1973). *Small is beautiful: Economics as if people mattered*. New York: Harper and Row.

Schwartz, B. J. (1999). Magnetic Source Imaging as a Clinical Tool in Functional Brain Mapping. *GEC Review, 14*(2), 124–127.

Searle, J. R. (1979). *Expression and meaning: Studies in the theory of speech acts*. Cambridge: Cambridge University Press.

Searle, J. R. (1980). Minds, brains, and programs, *The Behavioral and Brain Sciences, 3,* 417–457.

Searle, J. R. (1990). Is the brain's mind a computer program? *Scientific American, 262,* 26–31.

Searle, J. (1992). *The rediscovery of the mind*. Cambridge, MA: MIT Press.

Searle, J. R. (1997). *The mystery of consciousness*. New York: New York Review of Books.

Shafir, E. (1999). Probabilistic reasoning. In R. A. Wilson & F. C. Keil (Eds.), *MIT encyclopedia of cognitive sciences* (pp. 671–672). Cambridge, MA: MIT Press.

Shakespeare, W. (1602). *Hamlet*. New York: Washington Square Press. (Folger Edition 2003).

Shastri, L. (1989). Default reasoning in semantic networks: A formalization of recognition and inheritance. *Artificial Intelligence, 39*(3), 283–355.

Shoham, Y., & Tennenholtz, M. (1995). On social laws for artificial agent societies: Off-line design. *Artificial Intelligence, 73,* 231–252.

Silveira, T. (1971). *Incubation: The effect of interruption timing and length on problem solution and quality of problem processing.* Unpublished doctoral dissertation, University of Oregon.

Simon, H. A. (1955). A behavioral model of rational choice. *Quarterly Journal of Economics, 69,* 99–118.

Sims, K. (1991). Artificial evolution for computer graphics. *Computer Graphics, 25,* 319–328.

Simon, H. A. (1957). *Models of man.* New York: Wiley.

Sipper, M., & Tomassini, M. (1997). Convergence to uniformity in a cellular automaton via local coevolution. *International Journal of Modern Physics,* 243–258.

Sipper, M., & Tomassini, M. (1997). Evolvable cellular machines. In S. Bandini & G. Mauri (Eds.), *Proceedings of the Second Conference on Cellular Automata for Research and Industry* (pp. 177–186), London: Springer-Verlag.

Sizhong, Y., & Jinde, L. (2001). *RECOM: A reflective architecture of middleware.* China: College of Computer Science and Engineering.

Sloman, A., Chrisley, R., & Scheutz, M. (2005). The architectural basis of affective states and processes. In J. M. Fellows & M. A. Arbib (Eds.), *Who needs emotions? The brain meets the robot* (pp. 203–244). Oxford: Oxford University Press.

Someya, T., Sekitani, T., Iba, S., Kato, Y., Kawaguchi, H., & Sakurai, T. (2004). A large-area, flexible pressure sensor matrix with organic field-effect transistors for artificial skin applications. *Proceedings of the National Academy of Sciences, 101*(27).

Soper, B., Milford, G. E., & Rosenthal, G. T. (1995). Belief when evidence does not support the theory. *Psychology & Marketing, 12,* 415–422.

Spearman, C. (1927). *The abilities of man: Their nature and measurement.* New York: MacMillan.

Spence, S. A., & Frith, C. D. (1999). Towards a functional anatomy of volition. *Journal of Consciousness Studies, 6,* 11–28.

Steels, L. (1998) Synthesising the origins of language and meaning using co-evolution, self-organisation and level formation. In J. Hurford, C. Knight, & M. Studdert-Kennedy (Eds.), *Approaches to the evolution of language* (pp. 384–404). Edinburgh: Edinburgh Univ. Press.

Steiner, D. (1996). IMAGINE: An integrated environment for constructing distributed intelligence systems. In G. M. P. O'Hare & N. R. Jennings (Eds.), *Foundations of distributed artificial intelligence* (pp. 345–364). New York: Wiley.

Steiner, J. E. (1979). Human facial expressions in response to taste and smell stimulation. *Advances in child development and behavior, 13,* 257–295.

Stern, W. (1912). Psychologische Methoden der Intelligenz-Prufung. Leipzig: Germany.

Stillings, N. A., Garfield, M. H., Rissland, J. L., Edwina, L., & Rosenbaum, D. A. (1995). *Cognitive science: An introduction.* Cambridge, MA: MIT Press.

Sutton, R. S., & Barto, A. G. (1998). *Reinforcement learning: An introduction.* Cambridge, MA: MIT Press.

Swinney, D., Zurif, E. B., Prather, P., & Love, T. (1996). Neurological distribution of processing resources underlying language comprehension. *Journal of Cognitive Neuroscience, 8*(2), 174–184.

Thaler, R. H. (1985). Mental accounting and consumer choice. *Marketing Science, 4,* 199–214.

Thompson, A. (1998). On the automatic design of robust electronics through artificial evolution. In M. Sipper, D. Mange, & A. Prez-Uribe (Eds.), *Proc. of the 2nd Int. Conf. on Evolvable Systems: From Biology to Hardware,* LNCS (vol. 1478, pp. 13–24). Berlin: Springer-Verlag.

Thurstone, L. L. (1938). *Primary mental abilities.* Chicago: University of Chicago Press.

Tomkins, S. (1963). *Affect, imagery, consciousness: The negative affects* (vol. 2). New York: Springer.

Torrance, E. P., & Goff, K. (1989) A quiet revolution. *Journal of Creative Behavior, 23*(2), 136–145.

Trefil, J. (1997). *Are we unique?* New York: Wiley.

Trivers, R. (1972). Parental investment and sexual selection. In B. Campbell (Ed.), *Sexual selection and the descent of man 1871–1971* (pp. 136–179). Chicago: Aldine.

Turing, A.M. (1950). Computing machinery and intelligence, *Mind, 49,* 433–460.

Turner, S. (1994). *The creative process: A computer model of storytelling.* Hillsdale, NJ: Erlbaum.

Tversky, A., & Kahneman, D. (1974). Judgment under uncertainty: Heuristics and biases. *Science, 185,* 1124–1131.

Von Neumann, J. (1958). *The computer and the brain.* New Haven, CT: Yale University Press.

Von Neumann, J., & Morgenstern, O. (1953). *Theory of games and economic behavior.* New York: Wiley.

Wallas, G. (1926). *The art of thought.* New York: Harcourt Brace.

Warren, R. M., & Warren, R. P. (1970). Auditory illusions and confusions. *Scientific American, 223*(6), 30–36.

Wegner, D. (2002). *The illusion of conscious will.* Cambridge, MA: MIT Press.

Weiland, J. D., & Humayun, M. S. (2005). A biomimetic retinal stimulating array. *IEEE Engineering in Medicine & Biology Magazine, 24*(5), 14–21.

Weiss, G. (2000). *Multiagent systems: A modern approach to distributed artificial intelligence.* Cambridge, MA: MIT Press.

Westen, D. (1996). *Psychology: Mind, brain, & culture.* New York: Wiley.

Wiener, W. (1948). *Cybernetics: or Control and Communication in the Animal and the Machine.* Cambridge, MA: MIT Press.

Wilensky, R. (1980). Computers, cognition and philosophy. *Behavioral and Brain Sciences, 3,* 449–450.

Wilkinson, S. (2001). Hungry for success—Future directions in gastrobotics research. *Industrial Robot, 28*(3), 213–219.

Winograd, T. A. (1972). *Understanding natural language.* New York: Academic Press.

Wittgenstein, L. (1963). *Philosophical investigations.* Oxford: Blackwell.

Yazdani, M. (1989). Computational story writing. In N. Williams & P. Holt (Eds.), *Computers and writing.* Norwood, NJ: Ablex.

Zaghloul, K. A., & Boahen, K. (2004). Optic nerve signals in a neuromorphic chip I: Outer and inner retina models. *IEEE Transactions on Biomedical Engineering, 51*(4), 657–666.

AUTHOR INDEX

A

Aamodt, A., 64
Acosta-Calderon, C. A., 59, 60
Adolphs, R., 193
Ainsworth, M., 198
Aleksander, I., 166–168
Amos, M., 15
Anderson, J. R., 69
Anderson, K., 194
Angier, N., 142
Angluin, D., 90
Arkin, R. C., 198
Armes, R. C., 106
Asimov, A., 232
Austin, J. H., 131
Austin, J. L., 105
Aylett, R., 41, 120, 209, 214

B

Baar, B. J., 150, 171
Babbage, C., 22
Bach, J. S., 127, 137, 140
Balota, D. A., 100
Baluja, S., 38
Bandura, A., 59
Bar-Cohen, Y., 44
Barinaga, M., 190
Barlow, D. H., 187
Barnes, D. P., 221
Barto, A. G., 57
Bashir, R., 215
Bavelier, D., 97
Bayes, T., 158, 159
Beckers, R., 221
Bentley, P. J., 210, 211, 216
Berlyne, E., 131
Binet, A., 111
Bingham, G. P., 53
Birnbacher, D., 175, 176
Bizzi, E., 52
Blackmore, S., 22

Bloch, C., 5
Boahen, K., 39
Boden, M. A., 127, 136, 137, 144
Boole, G., 22, 23
Boone, G., 53
Bowlby, J., 198
Braitenberg, V., 193, 225
Breazeal, C., 50, 196, 197
Brenner, S., 13
Brentano, F., 83
Brighton, H., 110, 113
Bringsjord, S., 141, 236, 241, 248
Broca, P., 96, 97
Brodsky, J., 201
Brooks, R. A., 21, 49–51, 196, 236, 242, 250, 251
Brownholtz, E. A., 106
Buchanan, B. G., 143
Buss, D. M., 111

C

Cannon, W. B., 184
Capek, K., 6
Carletta, J., 105
Carlson, E. B., 188
Caspi, A., 199
Caudill, M., 233
Cawsey, A., 98
Chagnon, N., 188
Chalmers, D., 63, 64, 164, 165
Chao, D. L., 216
Chomsky, N., 93
Chow, A. Y., 39
Chrisley, R., 194, 196
Chuang, I., 15
Churchill, W., 37
Churchland, P. M., 88
Churchland, P. S., 88
Clark, G., 40
Clark, H. H., 101, 104
Clarke, A. C., 6
Cocco, M., 46

SUBJECT INDEX